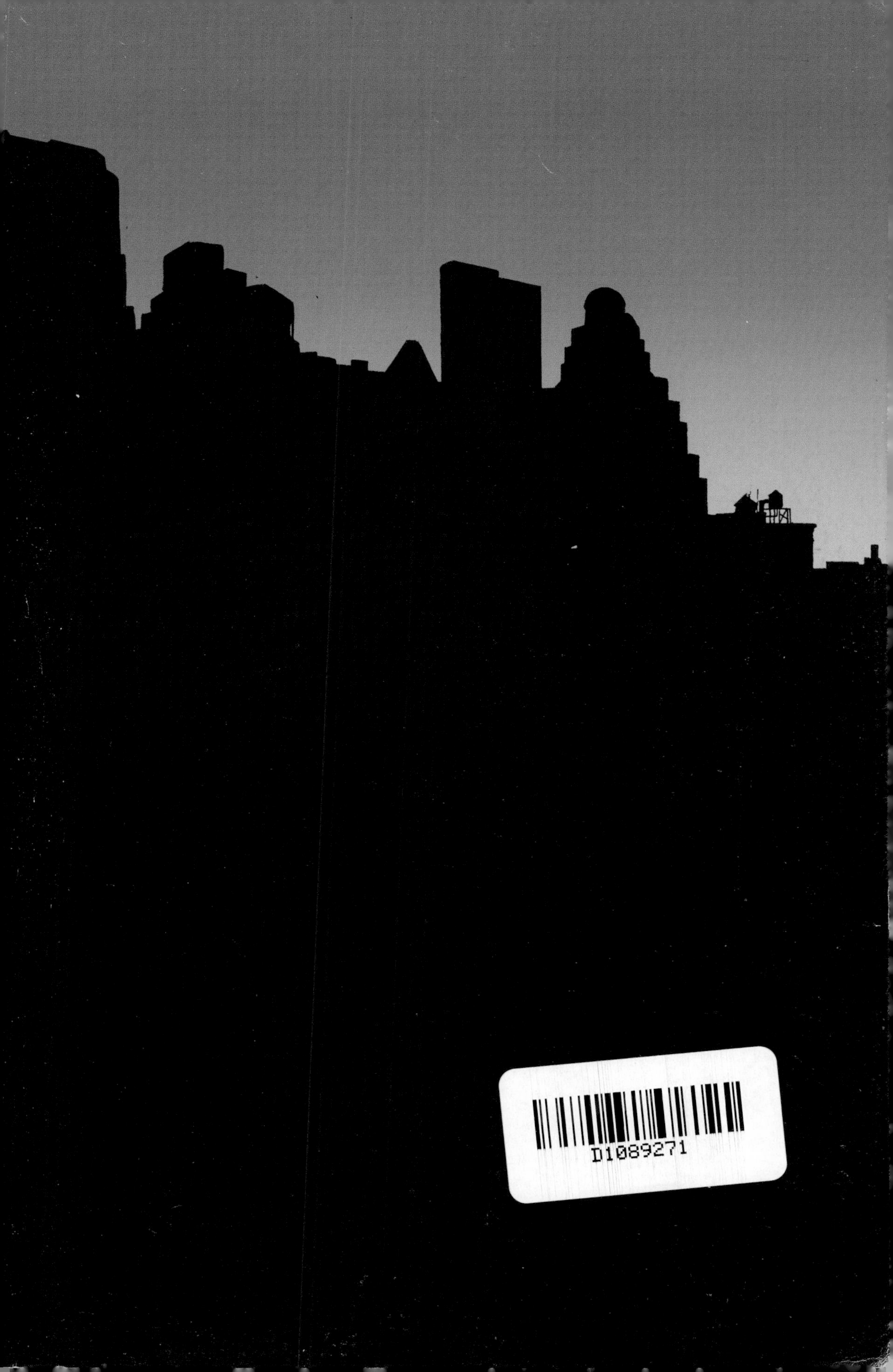

POW

BUR

★ ★ ★

CREATED AND PRODUCED
BY
BRIAN MICHAEL BENDIS
AND
MICHAEL AVON OEMING

ERS
AU ★★★

COLORING
NICK FILARDI

LETTERS
CHRIS ELIOPOULOS
WITH **CLAYTON COWLES** (#2)

EDITING AND PRODUCTION
JENNIFER GRÜNWALD

BUSINESS AFFAIRS
ALISA BENDIS

COLLECTION DESIGNER
PATRICK McGRATH

Previously in Powers:

Homicide Detectives Christian Walker, Deena Pilgrim and Enki Sunrise used to investigate murders specific to superhero cases...but after a powers-related disaster, the government declares all powers cases are federal cases.

After Walker is forced to reveal that he has regained his once-lost powers...he disappears.

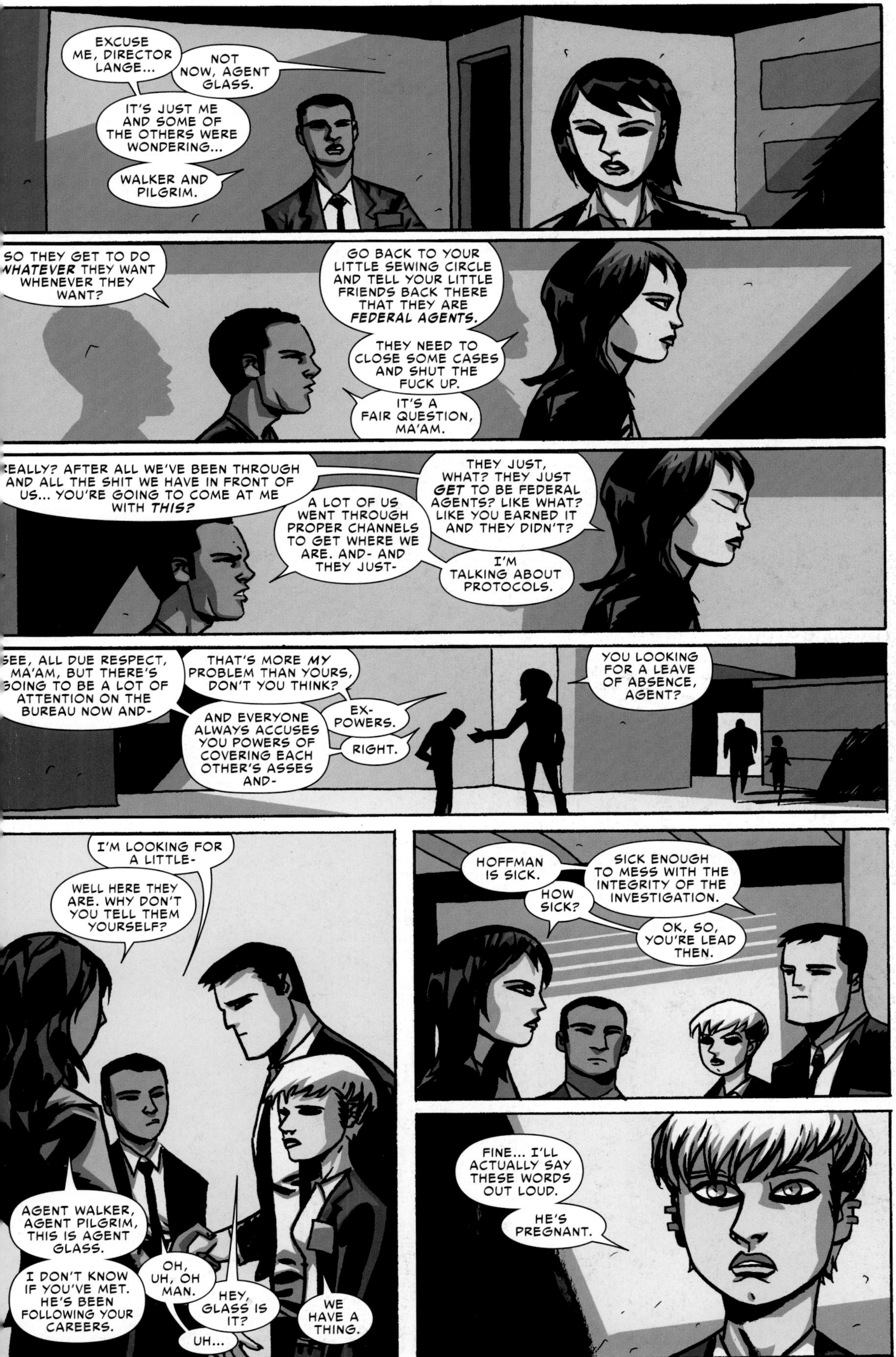
EXCUSE ME, DIRECTOR LANGE...
NOT NOW, AGENT GLASS.
IT'S JUST ME AND SOME OF THE OTHERS WERE WONDERING...
WALKER AND PILGRIM.
SO THEY GET TO DO WHATEVER THEY WANT WHENEVER THEY WANT?
GO BACK TO YOUR LITTLE SEWING CIRCLE AND TELL YOUR LITTLE FRIENDS BACK THERE THAT THEY ARE FEDERAL AGENTS.
THEY NEED TO CLOSE SOME CASES AND SHUT THE FUCK UP.
IT'S A FAIR QUESTION, MA'AM.
REALLY? AFTER ALL WE'VE BEEN THROUGH AND ALL THE SHIT WE HAVE IN FRONT OF US... YOU'RE GOING TO COME AT ME WITH THIS?
A LOT OF US WENT THROUGH PROPER CHANNELS TO GET WHERE WE ARE. AND- AND THEY JUST-
THEY JUST, WHAT? THEY JUST GET TO BE FEDERAL AGENTS? LIKE WHAT? LIKE YOU EARNED IT AND THEY DIDN'T?
I'M TALKING ABOUT PROTOCOLS.
SEE, ALL DUE RESPECT, MA'AM, BUT THERE'S GOING TO BE A LOT OF ATTENTION ON THE BUREAU NOW AND-
THAT'S MORE MY PROBLEM THAN YOURS, DON'T YOU THINK?
AND EVERYONE ALWAYS ACCUSES YOU POWERS OF COVERING EACH OTHER'S ASSES AND-
EX-POWERS.
RIGHT.
YOU LOOKING FOR A LEAVE OF ABSENCE, AGENT?
I'M LOOKING FOR A LITTLE-
WELL HERE THEY ARE. WHY DON'T YOU TELL THEM YOURSELF?
AGENT WALKER, AGENT PILGRIM, THIS IS AGENT GLASS.
I DON'T KNOW IF YOU'VE MET. HE'S BEEN FOLLOWING YOUR CAREERS.
OH, UH, OH MAN.
UH...
HEY, GLASS IS IT?
WE HAVE A THING.
HOFFMAN IS SICK.
HOW SICK?
SICK ENOUGH TO MESS WITH THE INTEGRITY OF THE INVESTIGATION.
OK, SO, YOU'RE LEAD THEN.
FINE... I'LL ACTUALLY SAY THESE WORDS OUT LOUD.
HE'S PREGNANT.

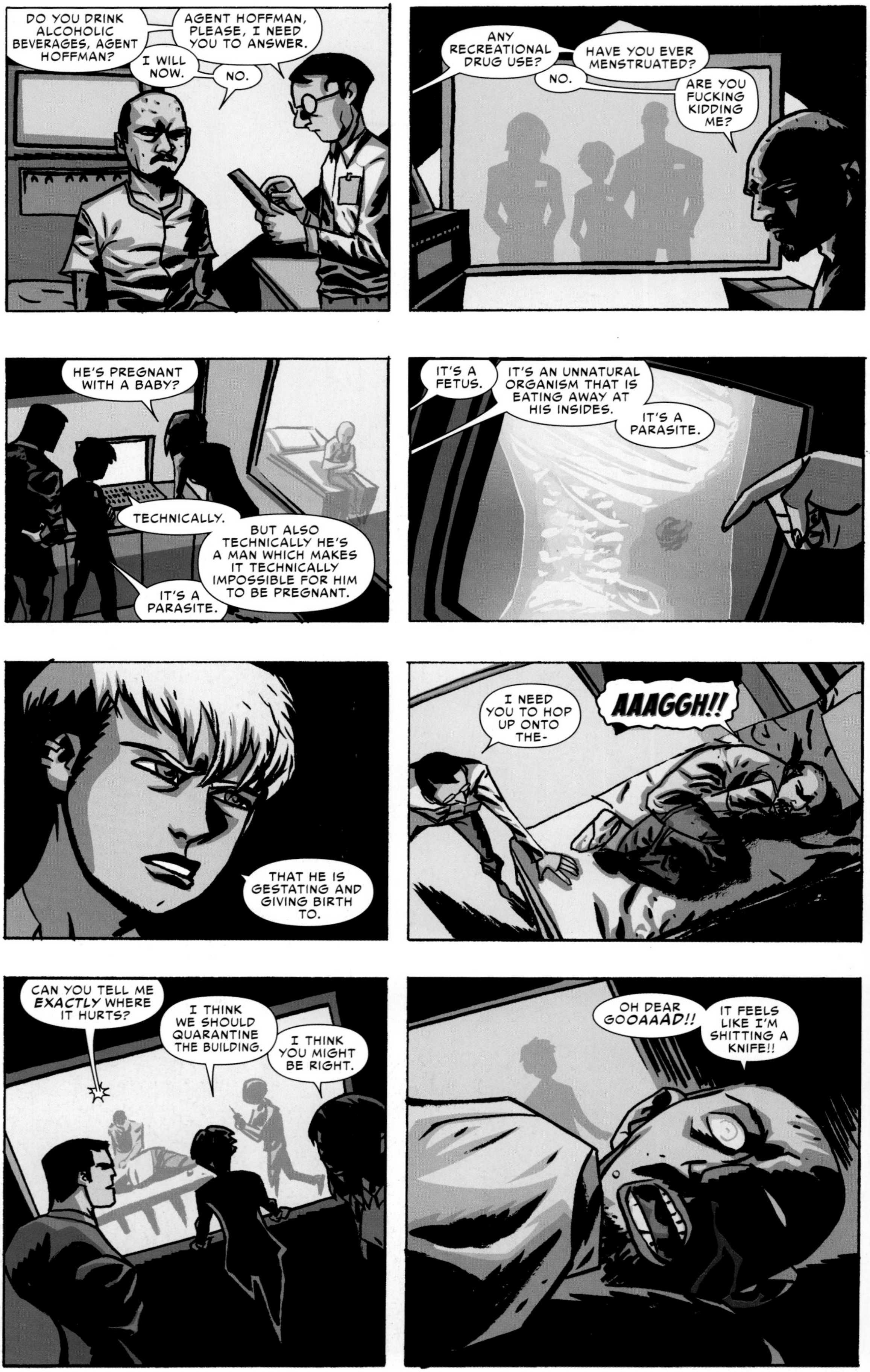
DO YOU DRINK ALCOHOLIC BEVERAGES, AGENT HOFFMAN?
AGENT HOFFMAN, PLEASE, I NEED YOU TO ANSWER.
I WILL NOW.
NO.
ANY RECREATIONAL DRUG USE?
HAVE YOU EVER MENSTRUATED?
NO.
ARE YOU FUCKING KIDDING ME?
HE'S PREGNANT WITH A BABY?
TECHNICALLY.
BUT ALSO TECHNICALLY HE'S A MAN WHICH MAKES IT TECHNICALLY IMPOSSIBLE FOR HIM TO BE PREGNANT.
IT'S A PARASITE.
IT'S A FETUS.
IT'S AN UNNATURAL ORGANISM THAT IS EATING AWAY AT HIS INSIDES.
IT'S A PARASITE.
THAT HE IS GESTATING AND GIVING BIRTH TO.
I NEED YOU TO HOP UP ONTO THE-
AAAGGH!!
CAN YOU TELL ME *EXACTLY* WHERE IT HURTS?
I THINK WE SHOULD QUARANTINE THE BUILDING.
I THINK YOU MIGHT BE RIGHT.
OH DEAR GOOAAAD!!
IT FEELS LIKE I'M SHITTING A KNIFE!!

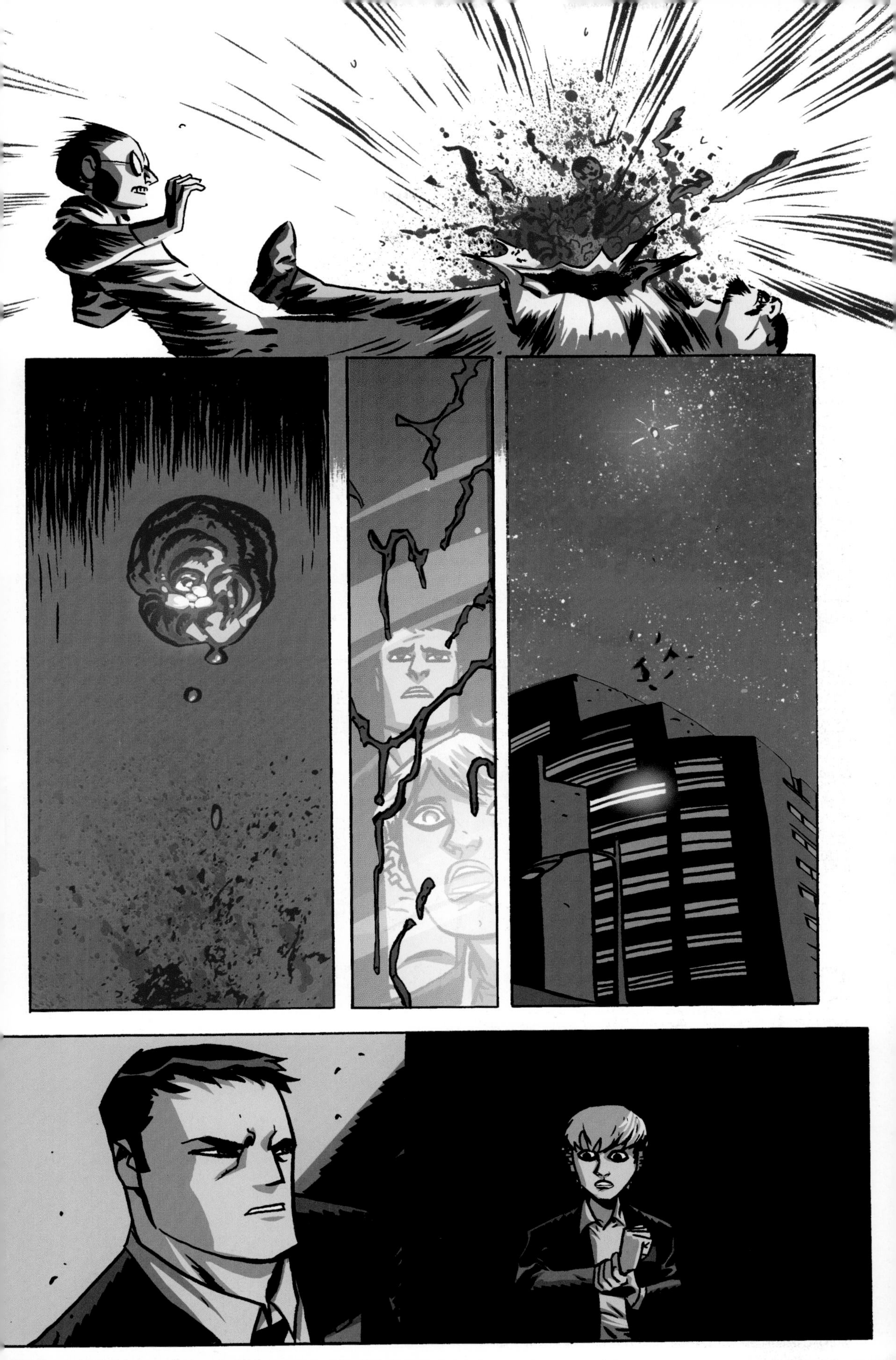

POW

BUR

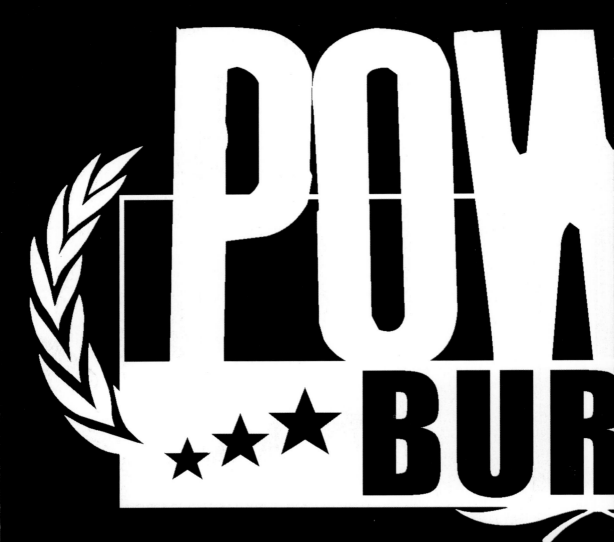

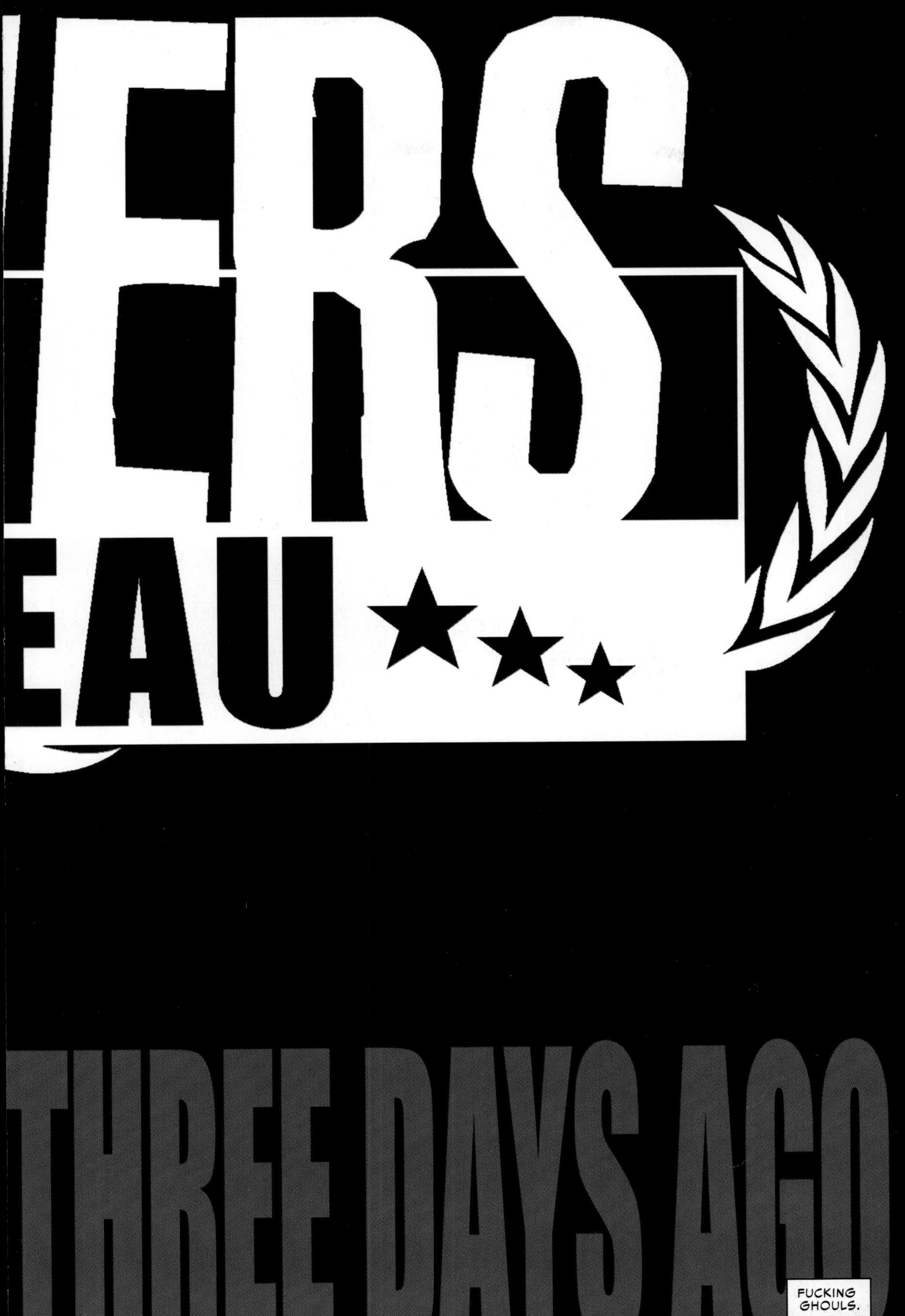
ERS
EAU
THREE DAYS AGO
FUCKING GHOULS.

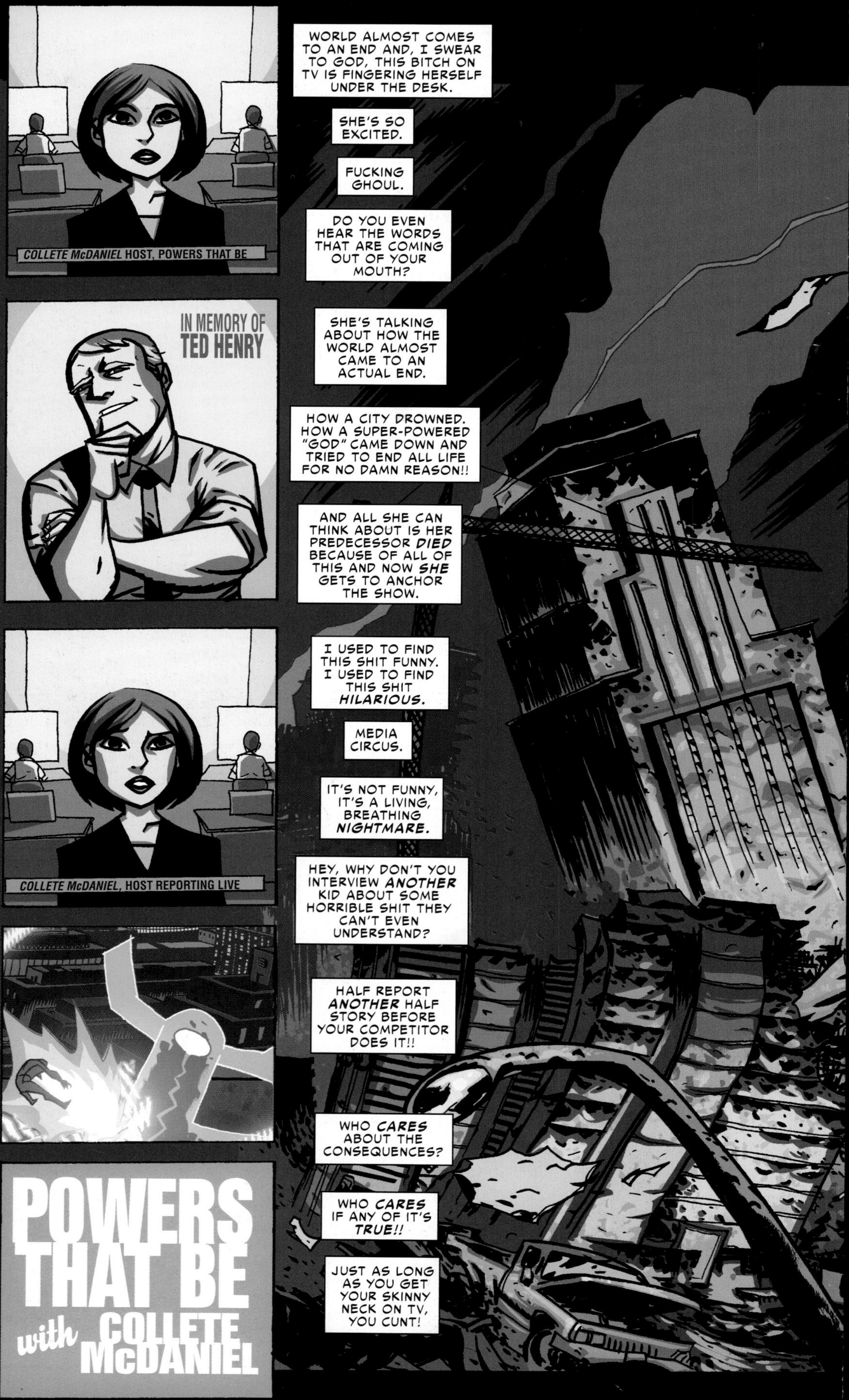

COLLETE McDANIEL HOST, POWERS THAT BE
WORLD ALMOST COMES TO AN END AND, I SWEAR TO GOD, THIS BITCH ON TV IS FINGERING HERSELF UNDER THE DESK.
SHE'S SO EXCITED.
FUCKING GHOUL.
DO YOU EVEN HEAR THE WORDS THAT ARE COMING OUT OF YOUR MOUTH?
IN MEMORY OF TED HENRY
SHE'S TALKING ABOUT HOW THE WORLD ALMOST CAME TO AN ACTUAL END.
HOW A CITY DROWNED. HOW A SUPER-POWERED "GOD" CAME DOWN AND TRIED TO END ALL LIFE FOR NO DAMN REASON!!
AND ALL SHE CAN THINK ABOUT IS HER PREDECESSOR DIED BECAUSE OF ALL OF THIS AND NOW SHE GETS TO ANCHOR THE SHOW.
COLLETE McDANIEL, HOST REPORTING LIVE
I USED TO FIND THIS SHIT FUNNY. I USED TO FIND THIS SHIT HILARIOUS.
MEDIA CIRCUS.
IT'S NOT FUNNY, IT'S A LIVING, BREATHING NIGHTMARE.
HEY, WHY DON'T YOU INTERVIEW ANOTHER KID ABOUT SOME HORRIBLE SHIT THEY CAN'T EVEN UNDERSTAND?
HALF REPORT ANOTHER HALF STORY BEFORE YOUR COMPETITOR DOES IT!!
WHO CARES ABOUT THE CONSEQUENCES?
WHO CARES IF ANY OF IT'S TRUE!!
JUST AS LONG AS YOU GET YOUR SKINNY NECK ON TV, YOU CUNT!
POWERS THAT BE with COLLETE McDANIEL

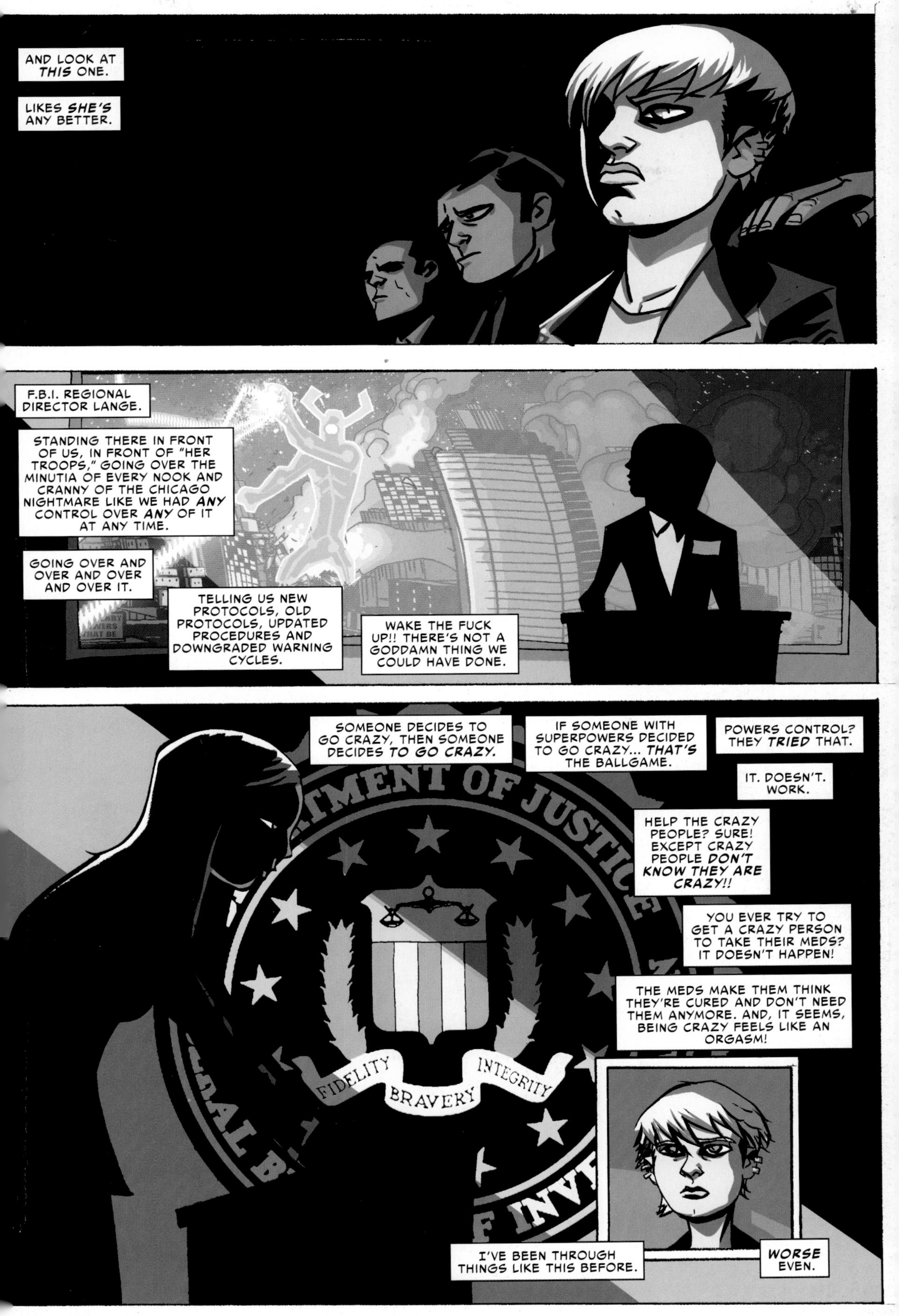
AND LOOK AT *THIS* ONE.
LIKES *SHE'S* ANY BETTER.
F.B.I. REGIONAL DIRECTOR LANGE.
STANDING THERE IN FRONT OF US, IN FRONT OF "HER TROOPS," GOING OVER THE MINUTIA OF EVERY NOOK AND CRANNY OF THE CHICAGO NIGHTMARE LIKE WE HAD *ANY* CONTROL OVER *ANY* OF IT AT ANY TIME.
GOING OVER AND OVER AND OVER AND OVER IT.
TELLING US NEW PROTOCOLS, OLD PROTOCOLS, UPDATED PROCEDURES AND DOWNGRADED WARNING CYCLES.
WAKE THE FUCK UP!! THERE'S NOT A GODDAMN THING WE COULD HAVE DONE.
SOMEONE DECIDES TO GO CRAZY, THEN SOMEONE DECIDES *TO GO CRAZY.*
IF SOMEONE WITH SUPERPOWERS DECIDED TO GO CRAZY... *THAT'S* THE BALLGAME.
POWERS CONTROL? THEY *TRIED* THAT.
IT. DOESN'T. WORK.
HELP THE CRAZY PEOPLE? SURE! EXCEPT CRAZY PEOPLE *DON'T KNOW THEY ARE CRAZY!!*
YOU EVER TRY TO GET A CRAZY PERSON TO TAKE THEIR MEDS? IT DOESN'T HAPPEN!
THE MEDS MAKE THEM THINK THEY'RE CURED AND DON'T NEED THEM ANYMORE. AND, IT SEEMS, BEING CRAZY FEELS LIKE AN ORGASM!
FIDELITY
BRAVERY
INTEGRITY
I'VE BEEN THROUGH THINGS LIKE THIS BEFORE.
WORSE EVEN.

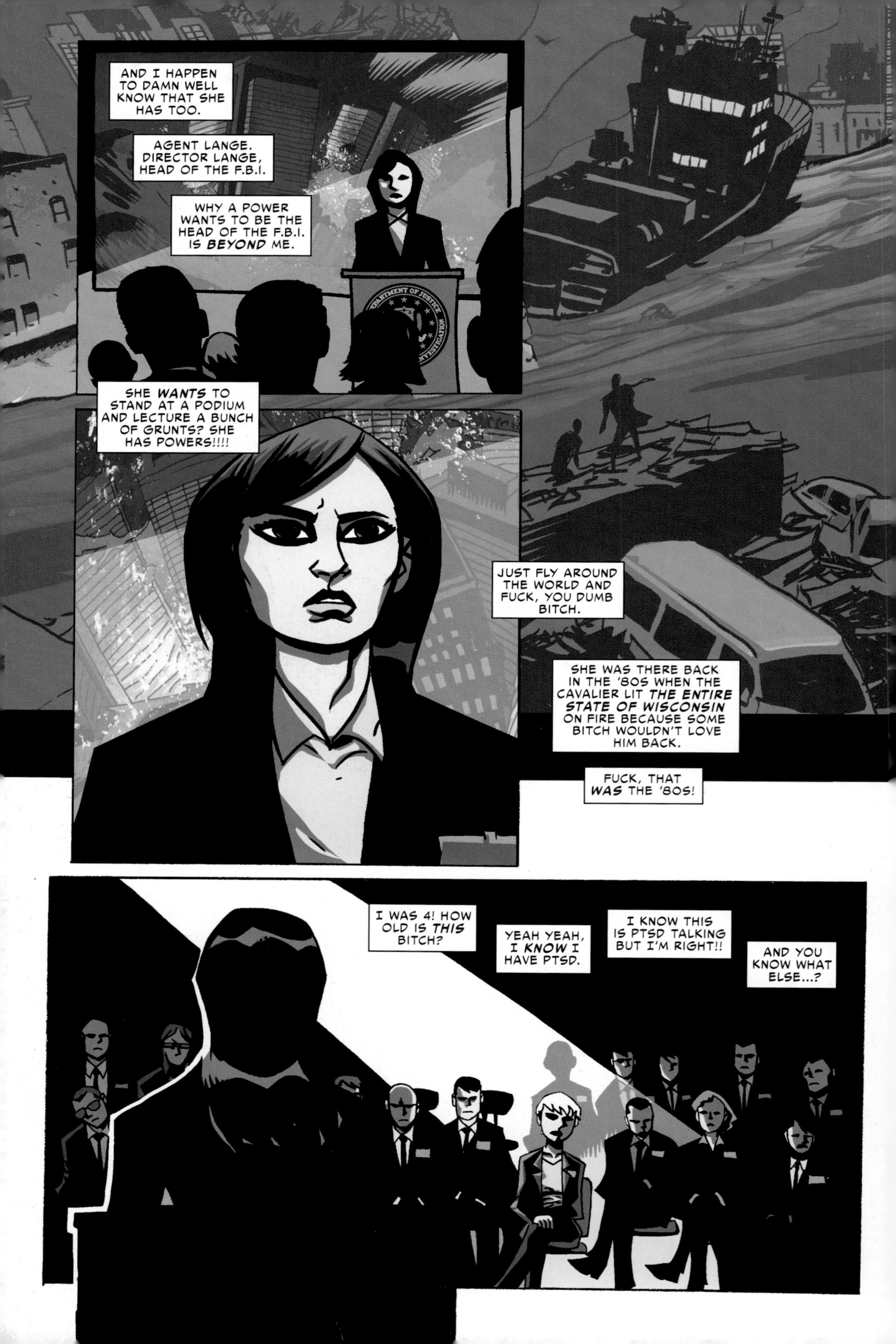
AND I HAPPEN TO DAMN WELL KNOW THAT SHE HAS TOO.
AGENT LANGE. DIRECTOR LANGE, HEAD OF THE F.B.I.
WHY A POWER WANTS TO BE THE HEAD OF THE F.B.I. IS *BEYOND* ME.
SHE *WANTS* TO STAND AT A PODIUM AND LECTURE A BUNCH OF GRUNTS? SHE HAS POWERS!!!!
JUST FLY AROUND THE WORLD AND FUCK, YOU DUMB BITCH.
SHE WAS THERE BACK IN THE '80S WHEN THE CAVALIER LIT *THE ENTIRE STATE OF WISCONSIN* ON FIRE BECAUSE SOME BITCH WOULDN'T LOVE HIM BACK.
FUCK, THAT *WAS* THE '80S!
I WAS 4! HOW OLD IS *THIS* BITCH?
YEAH YEAH, I *KNOW* I HAVE PTSD.
I KNOW THIS IS PTSD TALKING BUT I'M RIGHT!!
AND YOU KNOW WHAT ELSE...?

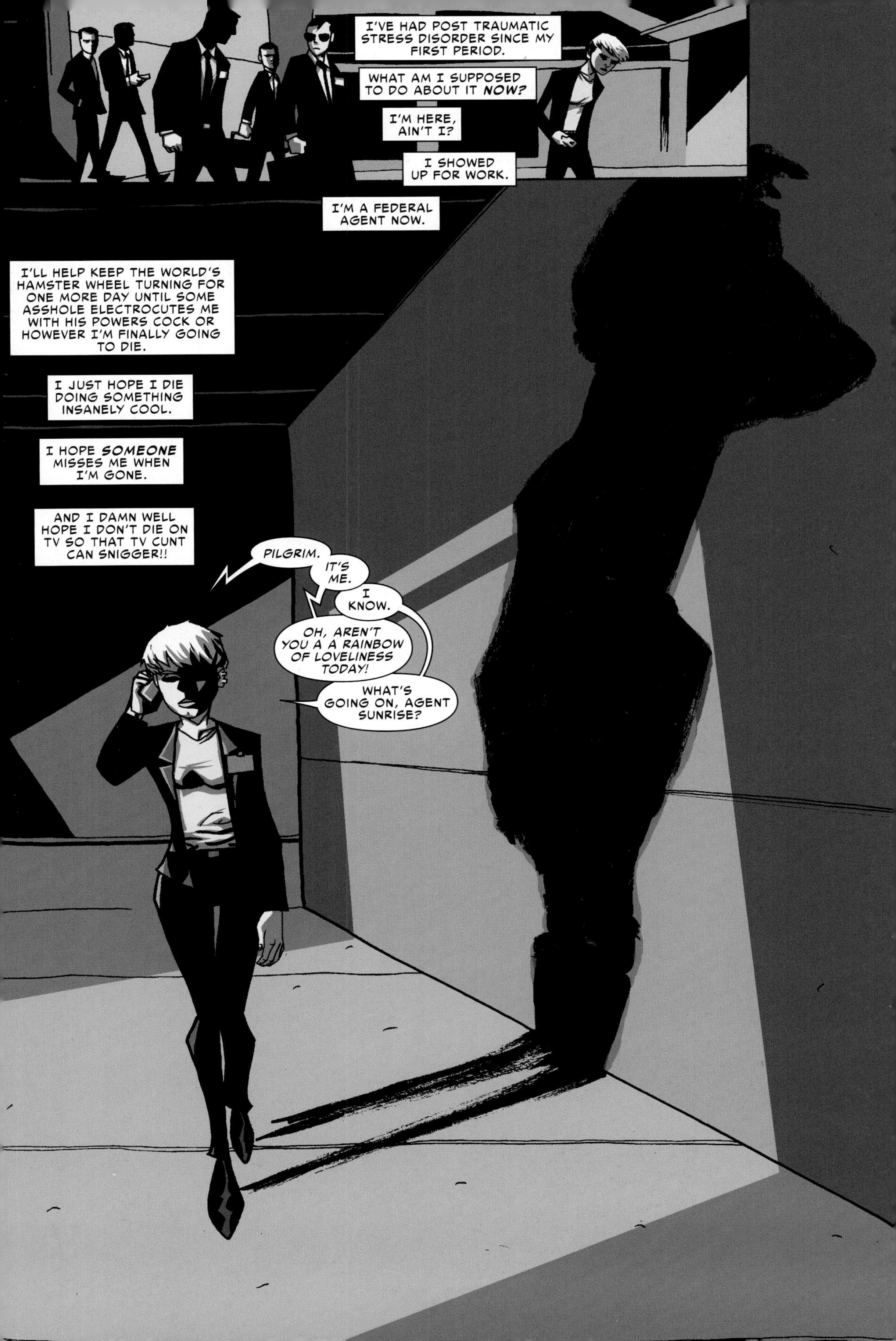
I'VE HAD POST TRAUMATIC STRESS DISORDER SINCE MY FIRST PERIOD.
WHAT AM I SUPPOSED TO DO ABOUT IT NOW?
I'M HERE, AIN'T I?
I SHOWED UP FOR WORK.
I'M A FEDERAL AGENT NOW.
I'LL HELP KEEP THE WORLD'S HAMSTER WHEEL TURNING FOR ONE MORE DAY UNTIL SOME ASSHOLE ELECTROCUTES ME WITH HIS POWERS COCK OR HOWEVER I'M FINALLY GOING TO DIE.
I JUST HOPE I DIE DOING SOMETHING INSANELY COOL.
I HOPE SOMEONE MISSES ME WHEN I'M GONE.
AND I DAMN WELL HOPE I DON'T DIE ON TV SO THAT TV CUNT CAN SNIGGER!!
PILGRIM.
IT'S ME.
I KNOW.
OH, AREN'T YOU A A RAINBOW OF LOVELINESS TODAY!
WHAT'S GOING ON, AGENT SUNRISE?

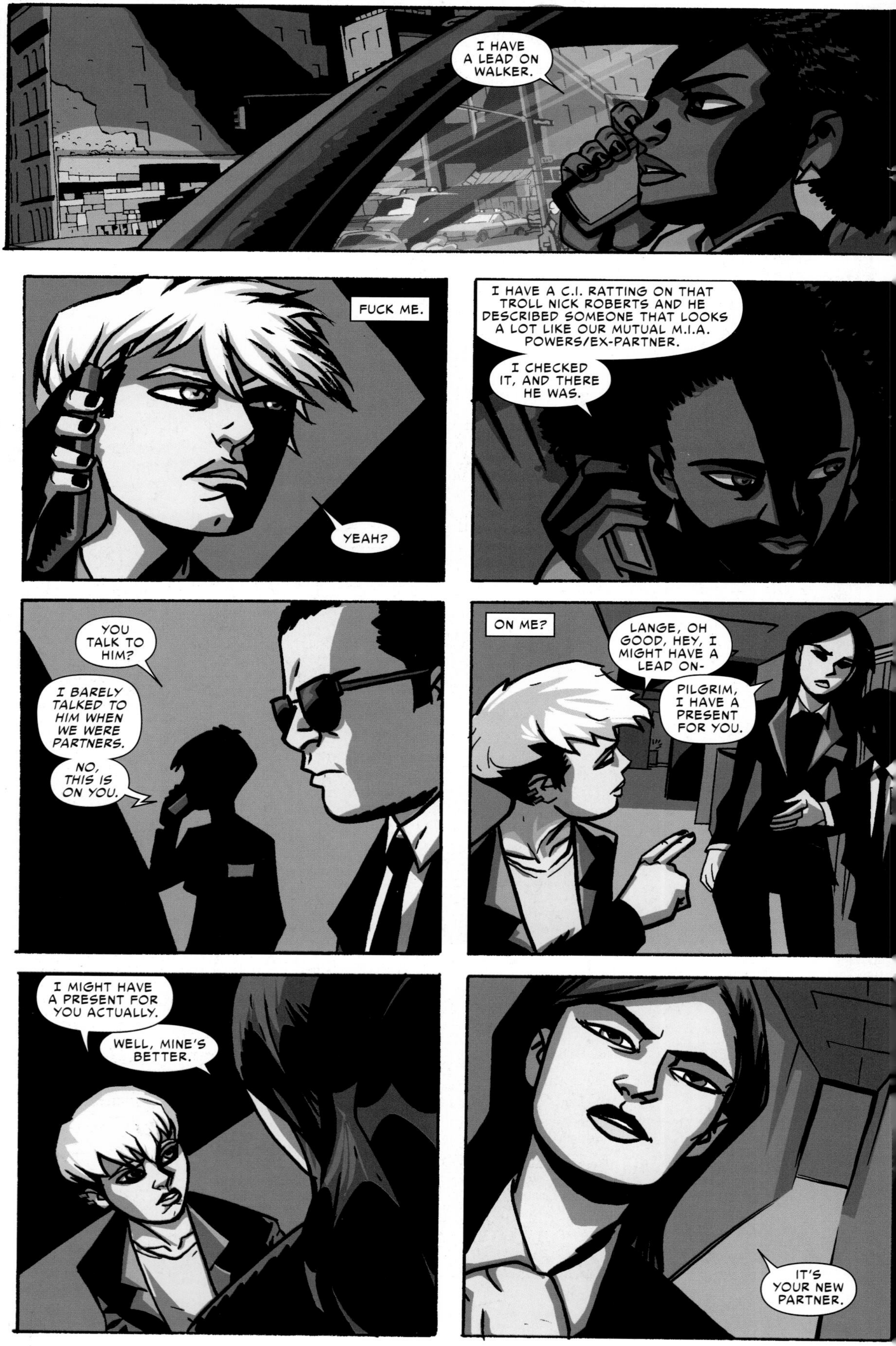

I HAVE A LEAD ON WALKER.
FUCK ME.
YEAH?
I HAVE A C.I. RATTING ON THAT TROLL NICK ROBERTS AND HE DESCRIBED SOMEONE THAT LOOKS A LOT LIKE OUR MUTUAL M.I.A. POWERS/EX-PARTNER.
I CHECKED IT, AND THERE HE WAS.
YOU TALK TO HIM?
I BARELY TALKED TO HIM WHEN WE WERE PARTNERS.
NO, THIS IS ON YOU.
ON ME?
LANGE, OH GOOD, HEY, I MIGHT HAVE A LEAD ON-
PILGRIM, I HAVE A PRESENT FOR YOU.
I MIGHT HAVE A PRESENT FOR YOU ACTUALLY.
WELL, MINE'S BETTER.
IT'S YOUR NEW PARTNER.

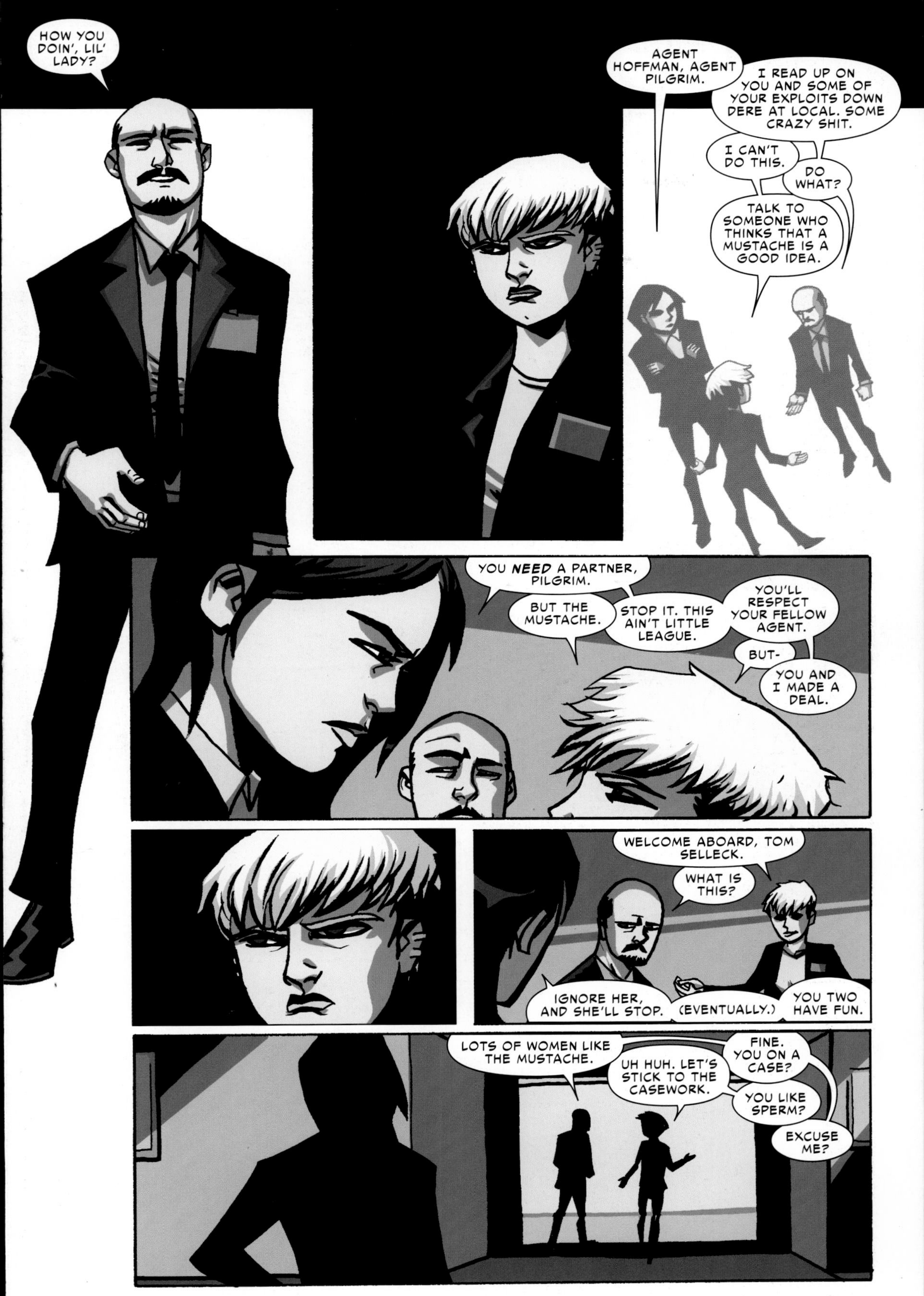
HOW YOU DOIN', LIL' LADY?
AGENT HOFFMAN, AGENT PILGRIM.
I READ UP ON YOU AND SOME OF YOUR EXPLOITS DOWN DERE AT LOCAL. SOME CRAZY SHIT.
I CAN'T DO THIS.
DO WHAT?
TALK TO SOMEONE WHO THINKS THAT A MUSTACHE IS A GOOD IDEA.
YOU NEED A PARTNER, PILGRIM.
BUT THE MUSTACHE.
STOP IT. THIS AIN'T LITTLE LEAGUE.
YOU'LL RESPECT YOUR FELLOW AGENT.
BUT-
YOU AND I MADE A DEAL.
WELCOME ABOARD, TOM SELLECK.
WHAT IS THIS?
IGNORE HER, AND SHE'LL STOP.
(EVENTUALLY.)
YOU TWO HAVE FUN.
LOTS OF WOMEN LIKE THE MUSTACHE.
UH HUH. LET'S STICK TO THE CASEWORK.
FINE. YOU ON A CASE?
YOU LIKE SPERM?
EXCUSE ME?

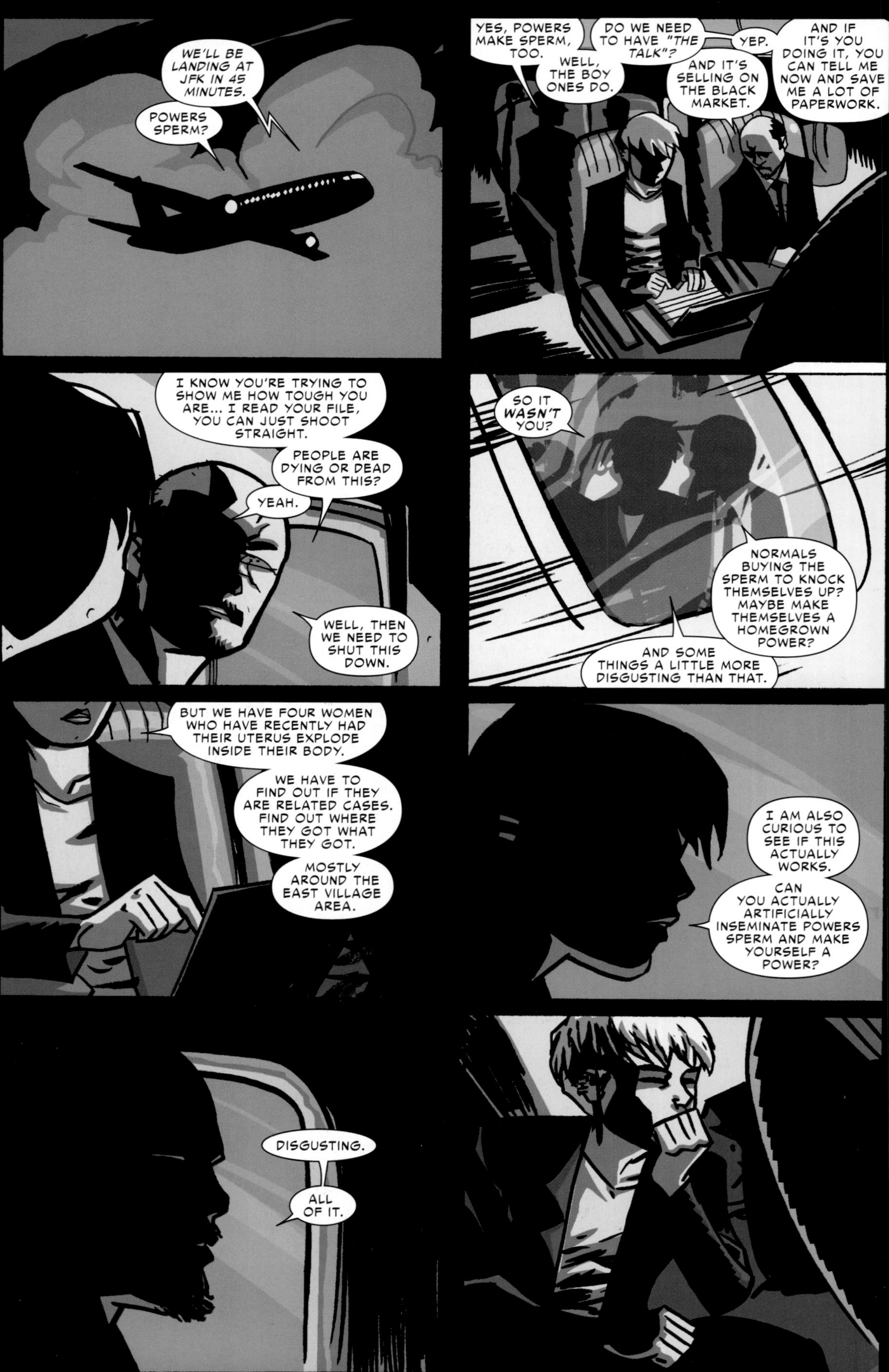
WE'LL BE LANDING AT JFK IN 45 MINUTES.
POWERS SPERM?
YES, POWERS MAKE SPERM, TOO.
DO WE NEED TO HAVE "THE TALK"?
WELL, THE BOY ONES DO.
YEP.
AND IT'S SELLING ON THE BLACK MARKET.
AND IF IT'S YOU DOING IT, YOU CAN TELL ME NOW AND SAVE ME A LOT OF PAPERWORK.
I KNOW YOU'RE TRYING TO SHOW ME HOW TOUGH YOU ARE... I READ YOUR FILE, YOU CAN JUST SHOOT STRAIGHT.
PEOPLE ARE DYING OR DEAD FROM THIS?
YEAH.
WELL, THEN WE NEED TO SHUT THIS DOWN.
SO IT *WASN'T* YOU?
NORMALS BUYING THE SPERM TO KNOCK THEMSELVES UP? MAYBE MAKE THEMSELVES A HOMEGROWN POWER?
AND SOME THINGS A LITTLE MORE DISGUSTING THAN THAT.
BUT WE HAVE FOUR WOMEN WHO HAVE RECENTLY HAD THEIR UTERUS EXPLODE INSIDE THEIR BODY.
WE HAVE TO FIND OUT IF THEY ARE RELATED CASES. FIND OUT WHERE THEY GOT WHAT THEY GOT.
MOSTLY AROUND THE EAST VILLAGE AREA.
I AM ALSO CURIOUS TO SEE IF THIS ACTUALLY WORKS.
CAN YOU ACTUALLY ARTIFICIALLY INSEMINATE POWERS SPERM AND MAKE YOURSELF A POWER?
DISGUSTING.
ALL OF IT.

THERE YOU GO. LEASE SIGNED.

IT IS ALL YOURS FOR A WHOLE YEAR.

ANYTHING YOU NEED, JUST ASK ME OR LIL' SHILOH HERE.

I KNOW EVERYTHING AND EVERYONE.

EVERYTHING?

EVEN THE GHOSTS.

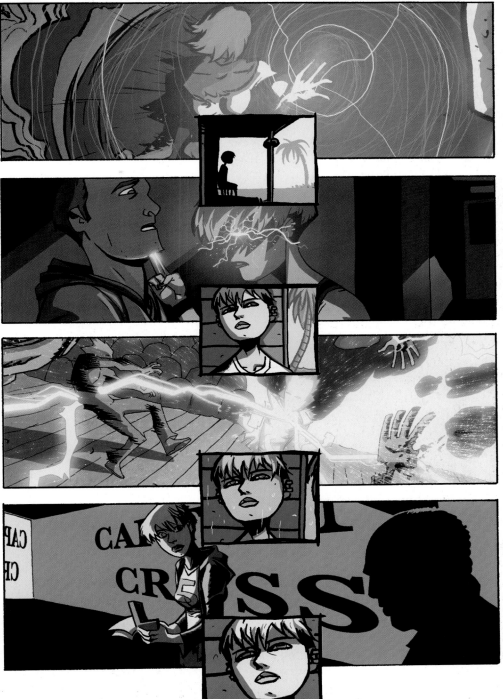

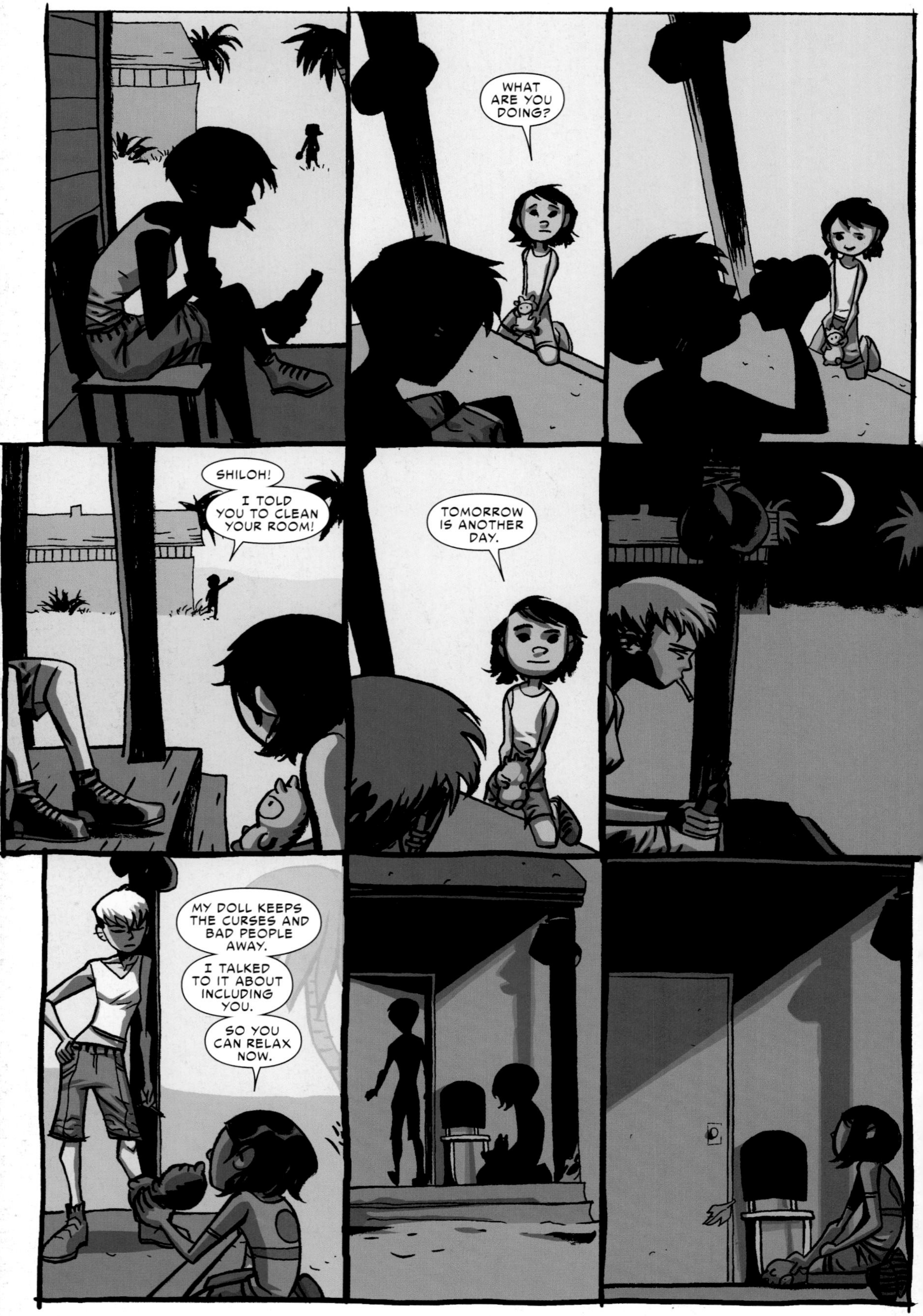

WHAT ARE YOU DOING?
SHILOH!
I TOLD YOU TO CLEAN YOUR ROOM!
TOMORROW IS ANOTHER DAY.
MY DOLL KEEPS THE CURSES AND BAD PEOPLE AWAY.
I TALKED TO IT ABOUT INCLUDING YOU.
SO YOU CAN RELAX NOW.

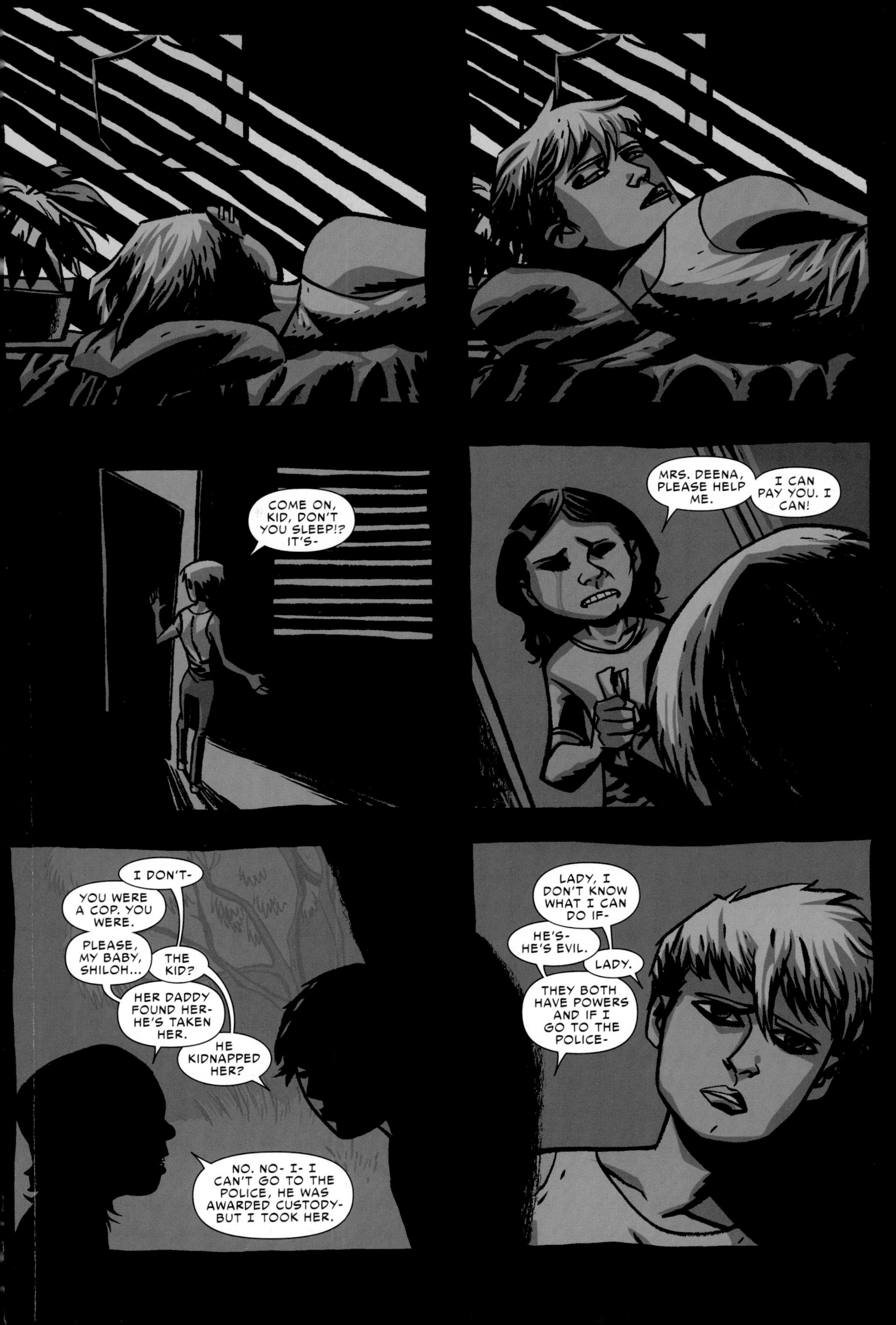
COME ON, KID, DON'T YOU SLEEP!? IT'S-
MRS. DEENA, PLEASE HELP ME.
I CAN PAY YOU. I CAN!
I DON'T-
YOU WERE A COP. YOU WERE.
PLEASE, MY BABY, SHILOH...
THE KID?
HER DADDY FOUND HER- HE'S TAKEN HER.
HE KIDNAPPED HER?
NO. NO- I- I CAN'T GO TO THE POLICE, HE WAS AWARDED CUSTODY- BUT I TOOK HER.
LADY, I DON'T KNOW WHAT I CAN DO IF-
HE'S- HE'S EVIL.
LADY.
THEY BOTH HAVE POWERS AND IF I GO TO THE POLICE-

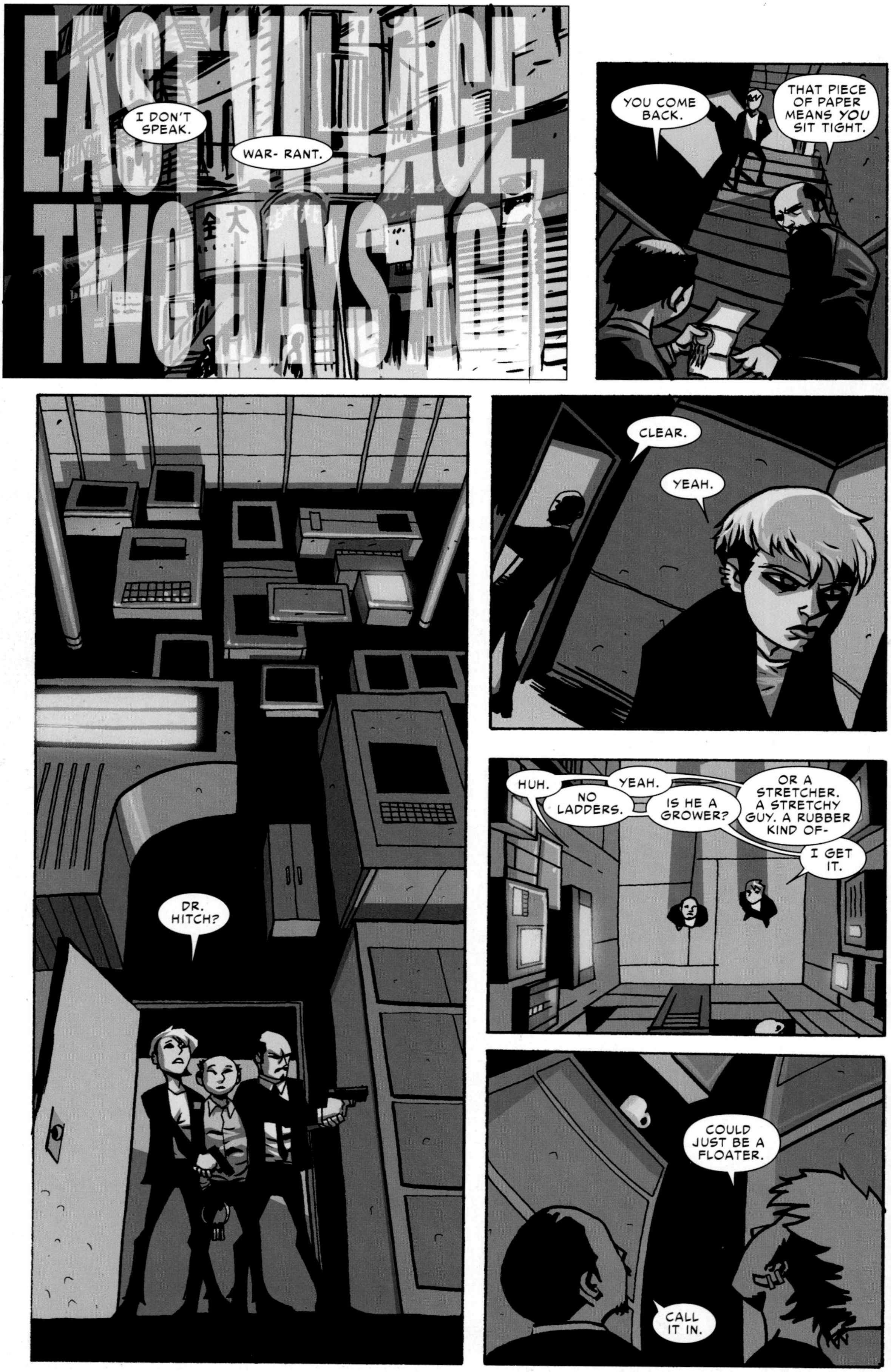
EAST VILLAGE, TWO DAYS AGO
I DON'T SPEAK.
WAR- RANT.
YOU COME BACK.
THAT PIECE OF PAPER MEANS YOU SIT TIGHT.
DR. HITCH?
CLEAR.
YEAH.
HUH.
YEAH.
NO LADDERS.
IS HE A GROWER?
OR A STRETCHER. A STRETCHY GUY. A RUBBER KIND OF-
I GET IT.
COULD JUST BE A FLOATER.
CALL IT IN.

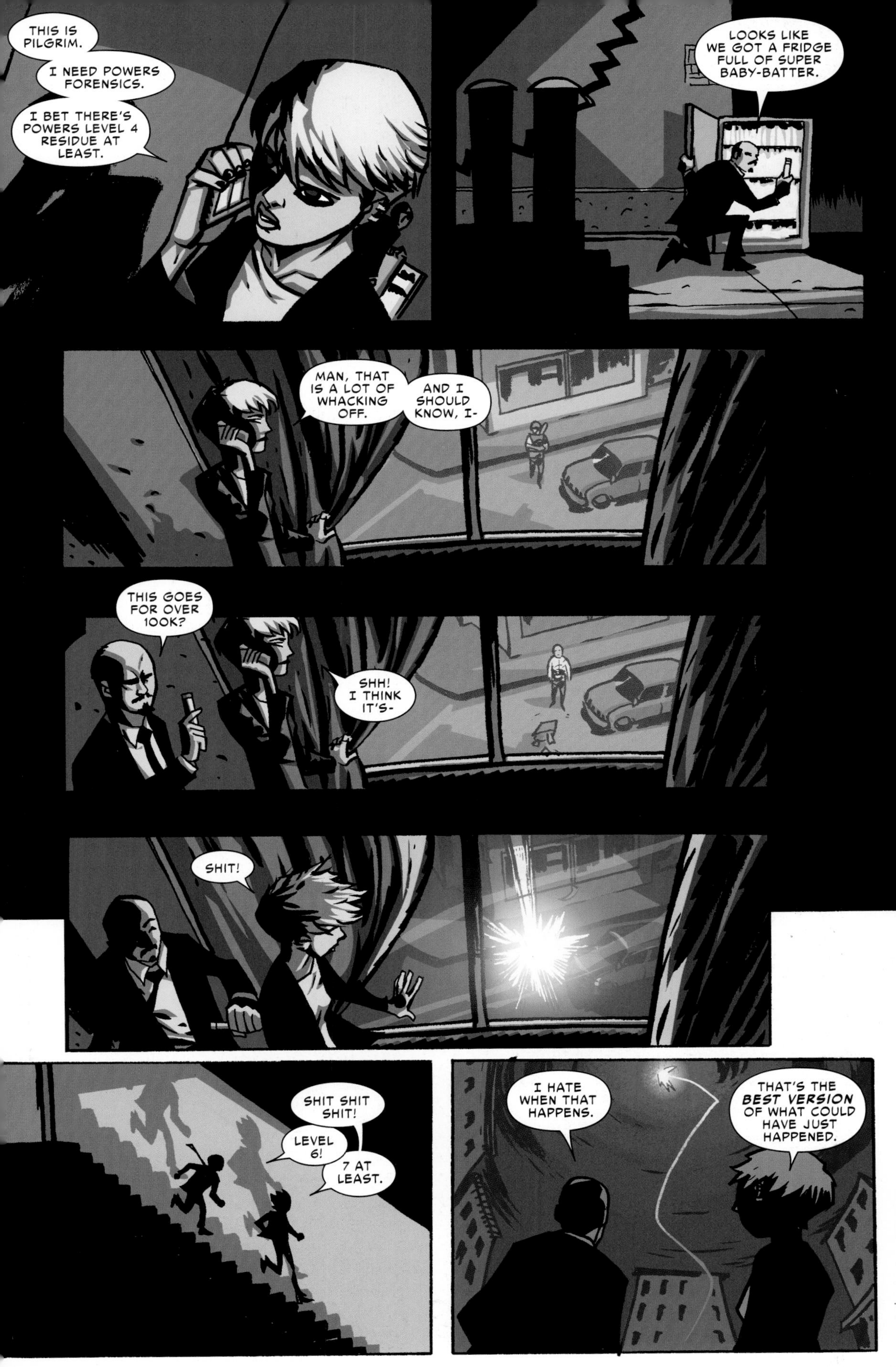
THIS IS PILGRIM.
I NEED POWERS FORENSICS.
I BET THERE'S POWERS LEVEL 4 RESIDUE AT LEAST.
LOOKS LIKE WE GOT A FRIDGE FULL OF SUPER BABY-BATTER.
MAN, THAT IS A LOT OF WHACKING OFF.
AND I SHOULD KNOW, I-
THIS GOES FOR OVER 100K?
SHH! I THINK IT'S-
SHIT!
SHIT SHIT SHIT!
LEVEL 6!
7 AT LEAST.
I HATE WHEN THAT HAPPENS.
THAT'S THE *BEST VERSION* OF WHAT COULD HAVE JUST HAPPENED.

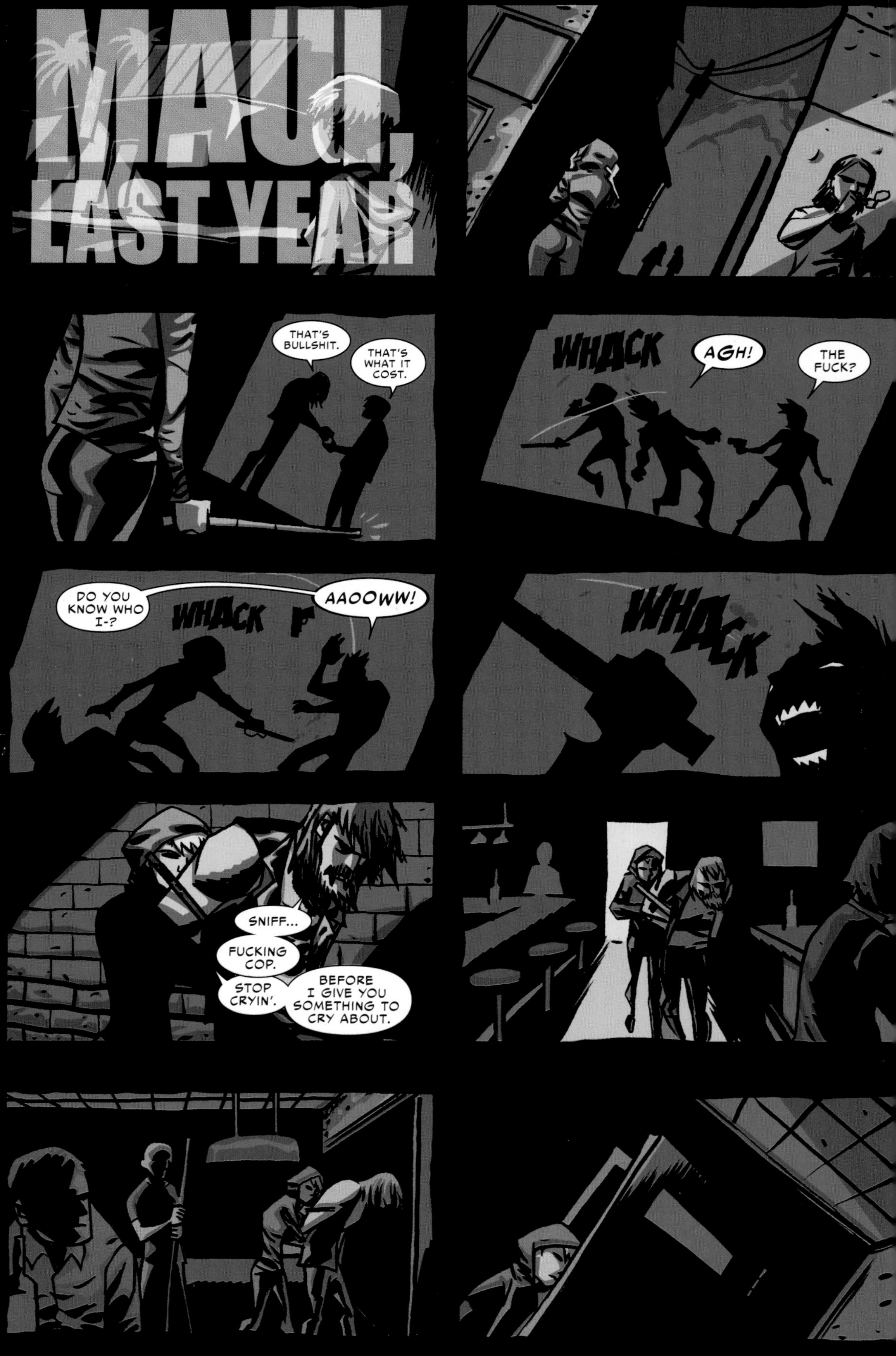
MAUI, LAST YEAR
THAT'S BULLSHIT.
THAT'S WHAT IT COST.
WHACK
AGH!
THE FUCK?
DO YOU KNOW WHO I-?
WHACK
AAOOWW!
WHACK
SNIFF...
FUCKING COP.
STOP CRYIN'.
BEFORE I GIVE YOU SOMETHING TO CRY ABOUT.

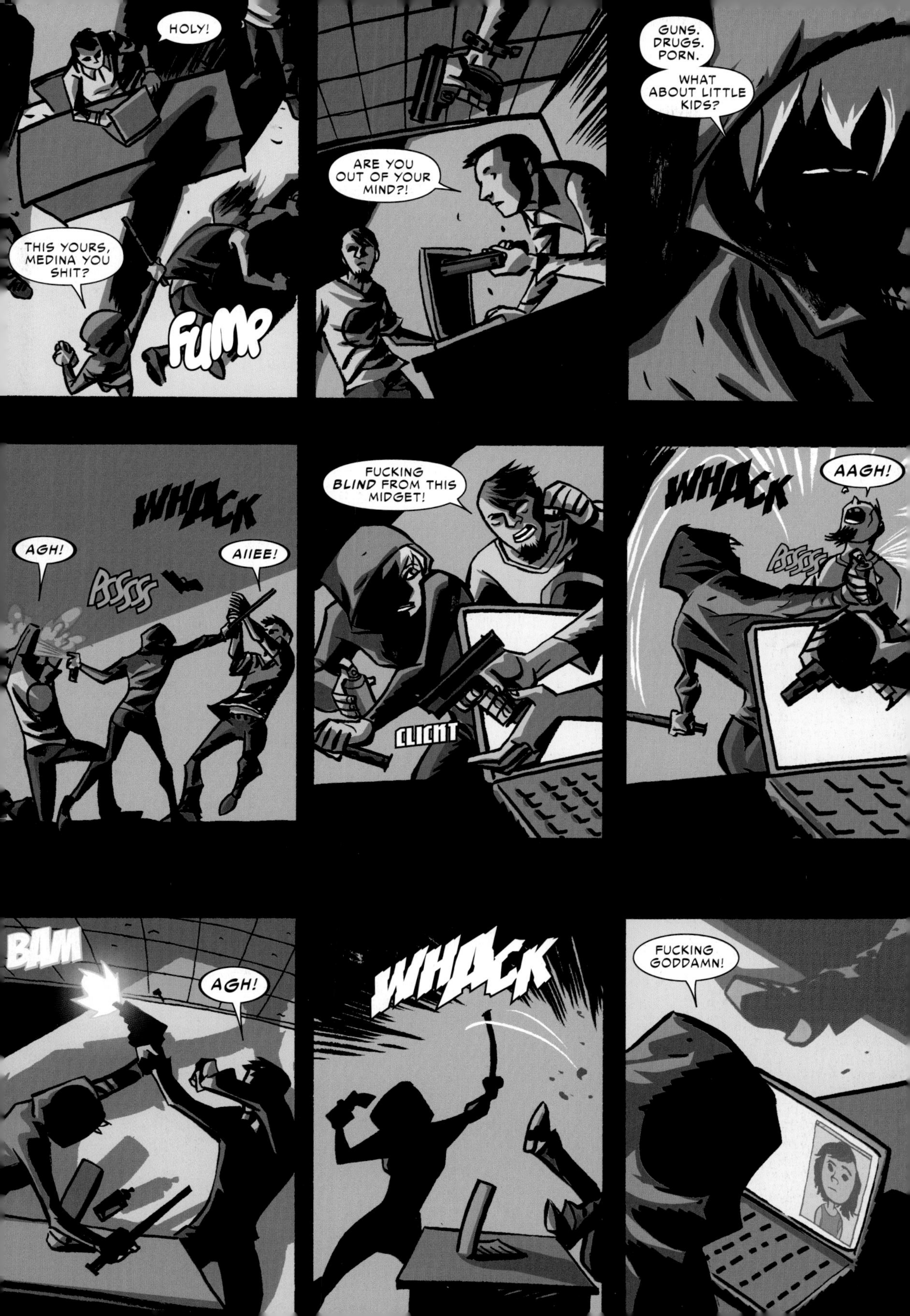
HOLY!
THIS YOURS, MEDINA YOU SHIT?
FUMP
ARE YOU OUT OF YOUR MIND?!
GUNS. DRUGS. PORN.
WHAT ABOUT LITTLE KIDS?
WHACK
AGH!
AIIEE!
BSSSS
FUCKING BLIND FROM THIS MIDGET!
CLICKT
WHACK
AAGH!
BSSSS
BAM
AGH!
WHACK
FUCKING GODDAMN!

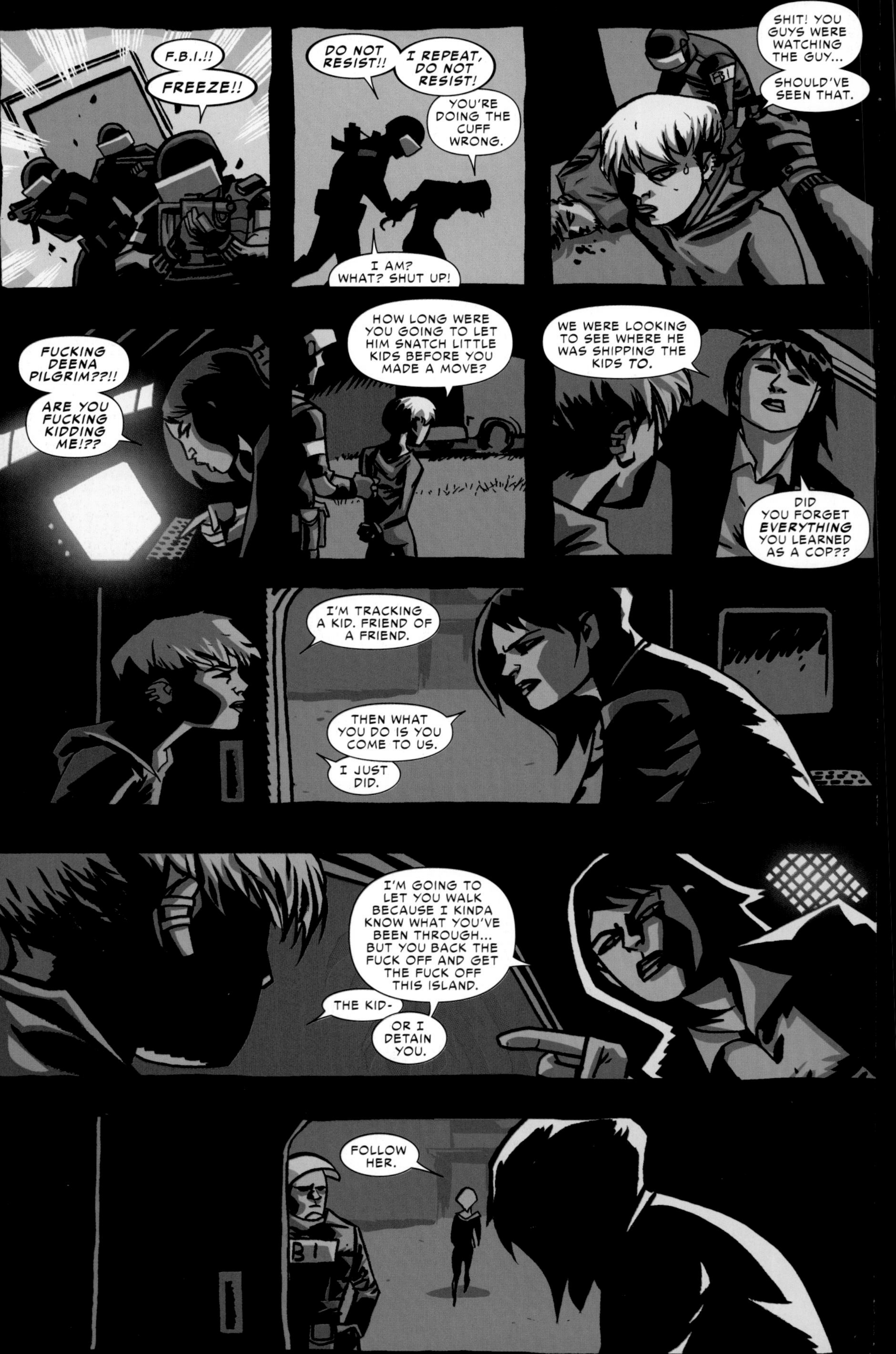
F.B.I.!!
FREEZE!!
DO NOT RESIST!!
I REPEAT, DO NOT RESIST!
YOU'RE DOING THE CUFF WRONG.
I AM? WHAT? SHUT UP!
SHIT! YOU GUYS WERE WATCHING THE GUY...
SHOULD'VE SEEN THAT.
FUCKING DEENA PILGRIM??!!
ARE YOU FUCKING KIDDING ME!??
HOW LONG WERE YOU GOING TO LET HIM SNATCH LITTLE KIDS BEFORE YOU MADE A MOVE?
WE WERE LOOKING TO SEE WHERE HE WAS SHIPPING THE KIDS TO.
DID YOU FORGET EVERYTHING YOU LEARNED AS A COP??
I'M TRACKING A KID. FRIEND OF A FRIEND.
THEN WHAT YOU DO IS YOU COME TO US.
I JUST DID.
I'M GOING TO LET YOU WALK BECAUSE I KINDA KNOW WHAT YOU'VE BEEN THROUGH... BUT YOU BACK THE FUCK OFF AND GET THE FUCK OFF THIS ISLAND.
THE KID-
OR I DETAIN YOU.
FOLLOW HER.

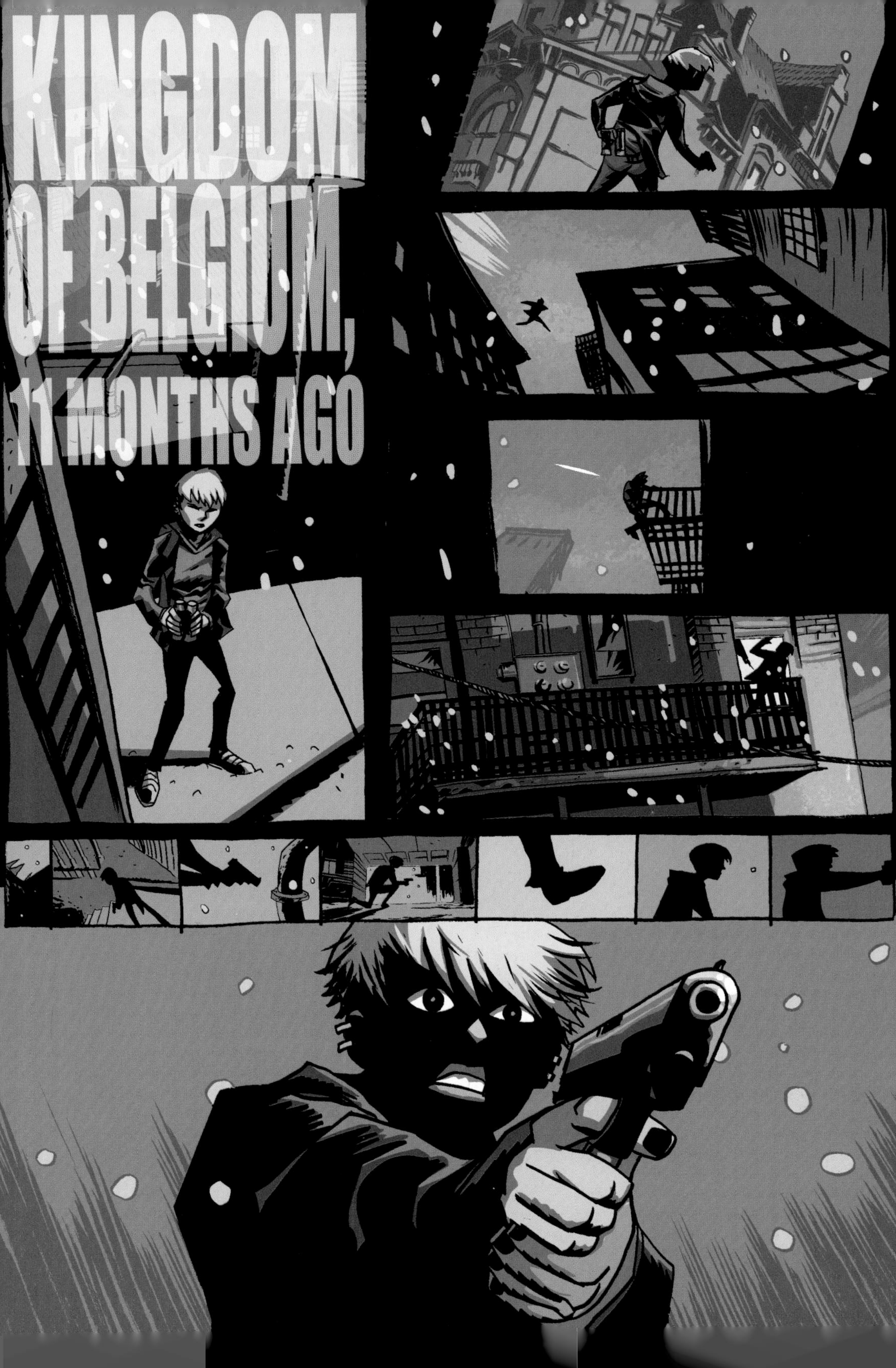
KINGDOM OF BELGIUM, 11 MONTHS AGO

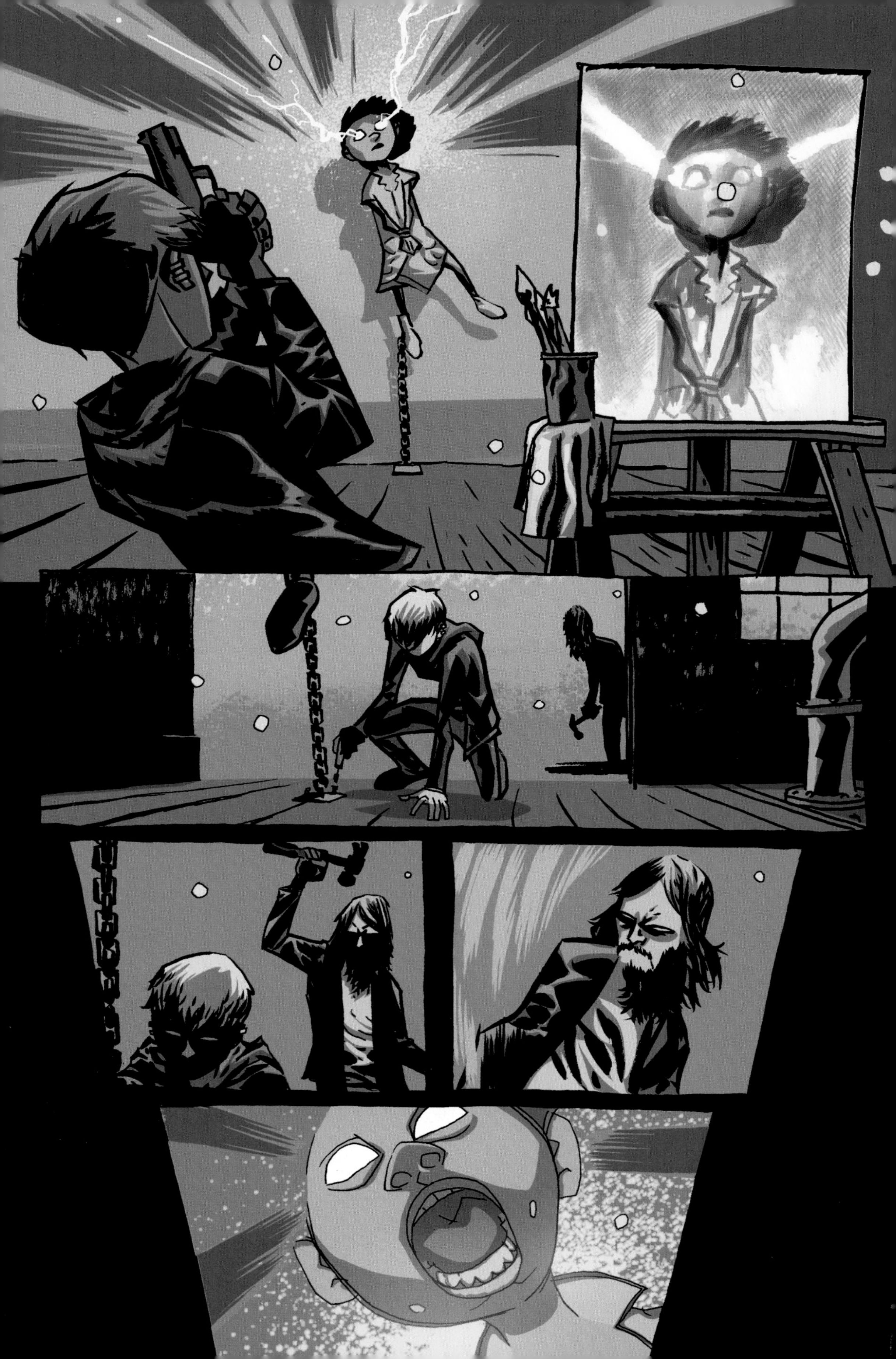

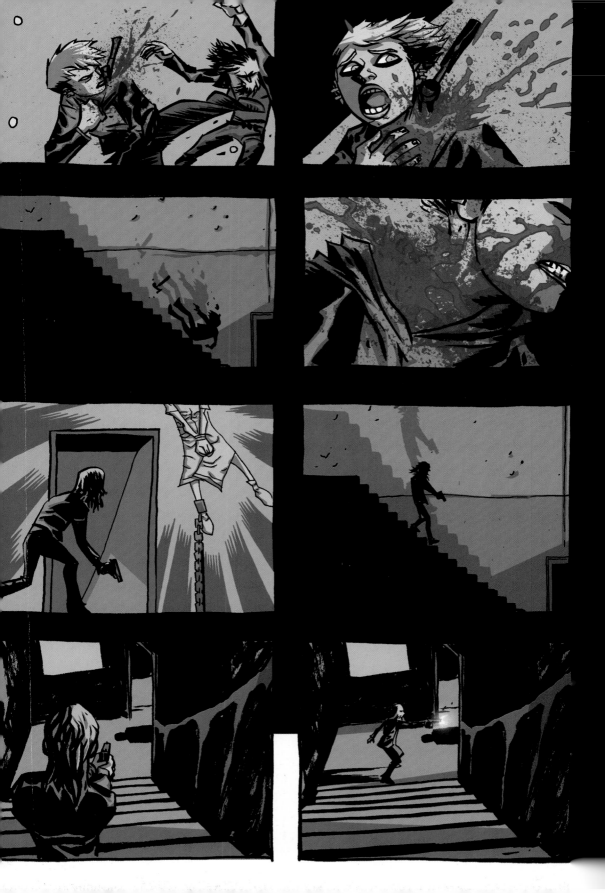

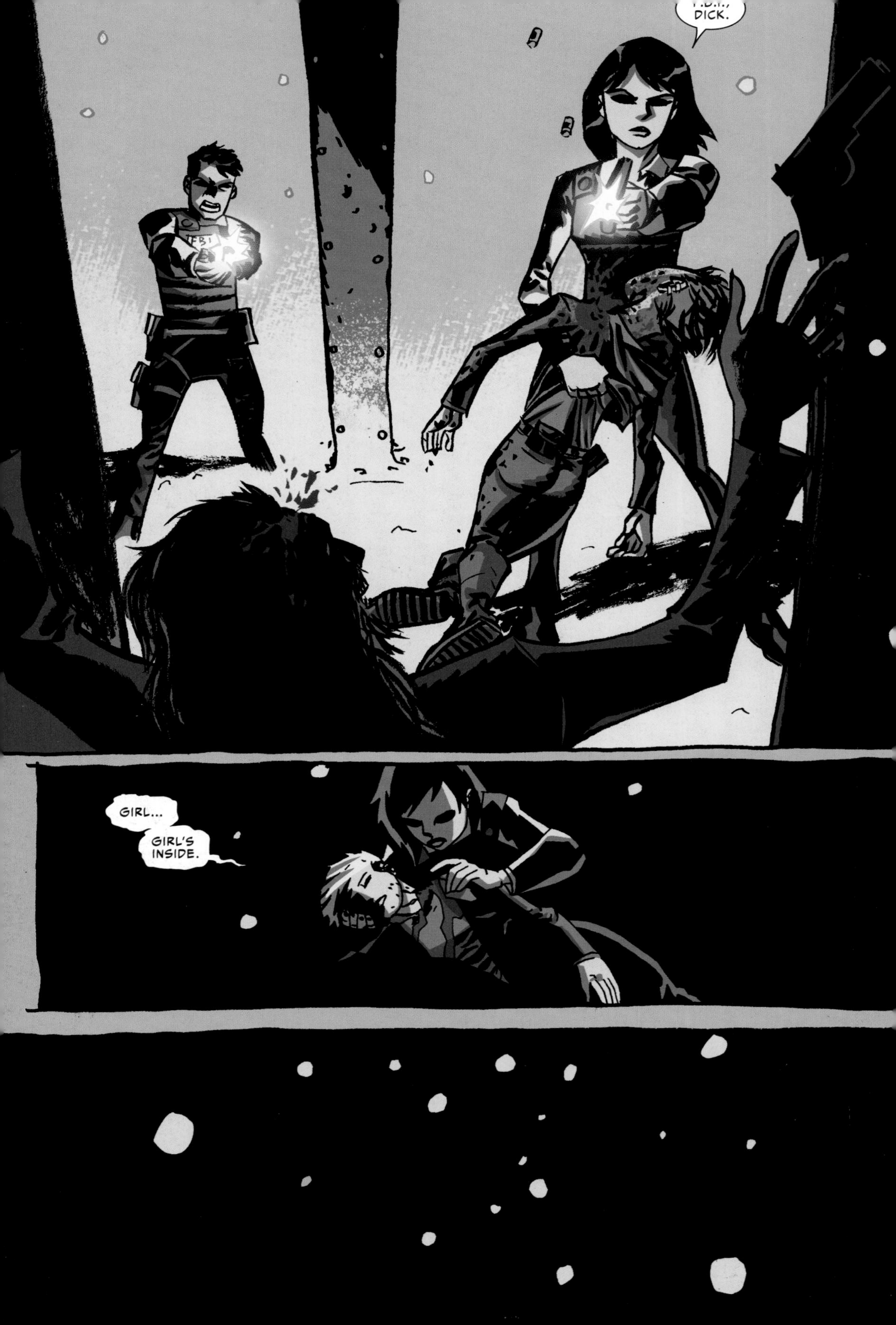
DICK.
GIRL...
GIRL'S INSIDE.

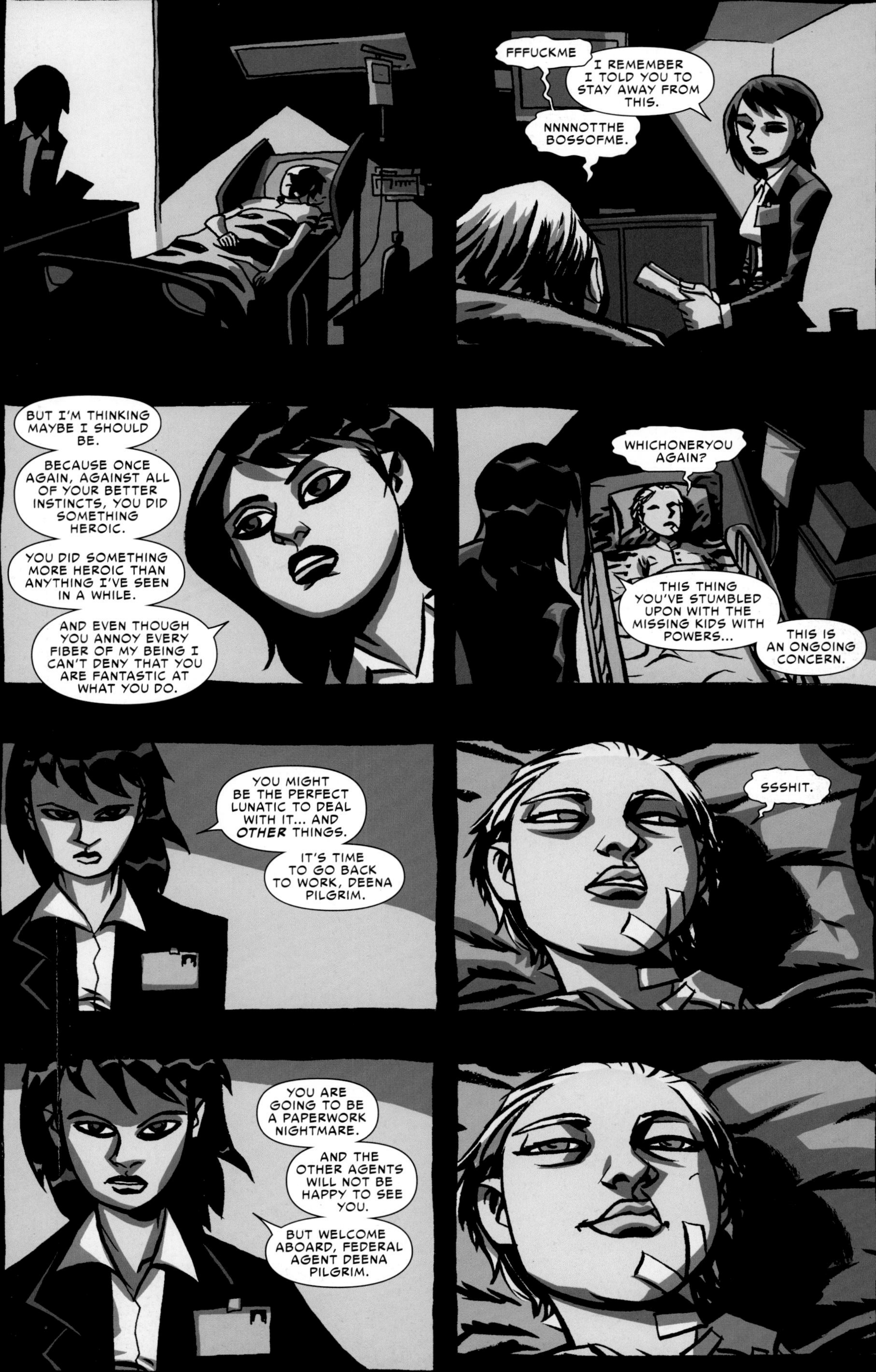
FFFUCKME
I REMEMBER I TOLD YOU TO STAY AWAY FROM THIS.
NNNNOTTHE BOSSOFME.
BUT I'M THINKING MAYBE I SHOULD BE.
BECAUSE ONCE AGAIN, AGAINST ALL OF YOUR BETTER INSTINCTS, YOU DID SOMETHING HEROIC.
YOU DID SOMETHING MORE HEROIC THAN ANYTHING I'VE SEEN IN A WHILE.
AND EVEN THOUGH YOU ANNOY EVERY FIBER OF MY BEING I CAN'T DENY THAT YOU ARE FANTASTIC AT WHAT YOU DO.
WHICHONERYOU AGAIN?
THIS THING YOU'VE STUMBLED UPON WITH THE MISSING KIDS WITH POWERS...
THIS IS AN ONGOING CONCERN.
YOU MIGHT BE THE PERFECT LUNATIC TO DEAL WITH IT... AND *OTHER* THINGS.
IT'S TIME TO GO BACK TO WORK, DEENA PILGRIM.
SSSHIT.
YOU ARE GOING TO BE A PAPERWORK NIGHTMARE.
AND THE OTHER AGENTS WILL NOT BE HAPPY TO SEE YOU.
BUT WELCOME ABOARD, FEDERAL AGENT DEENA PILGRIM.

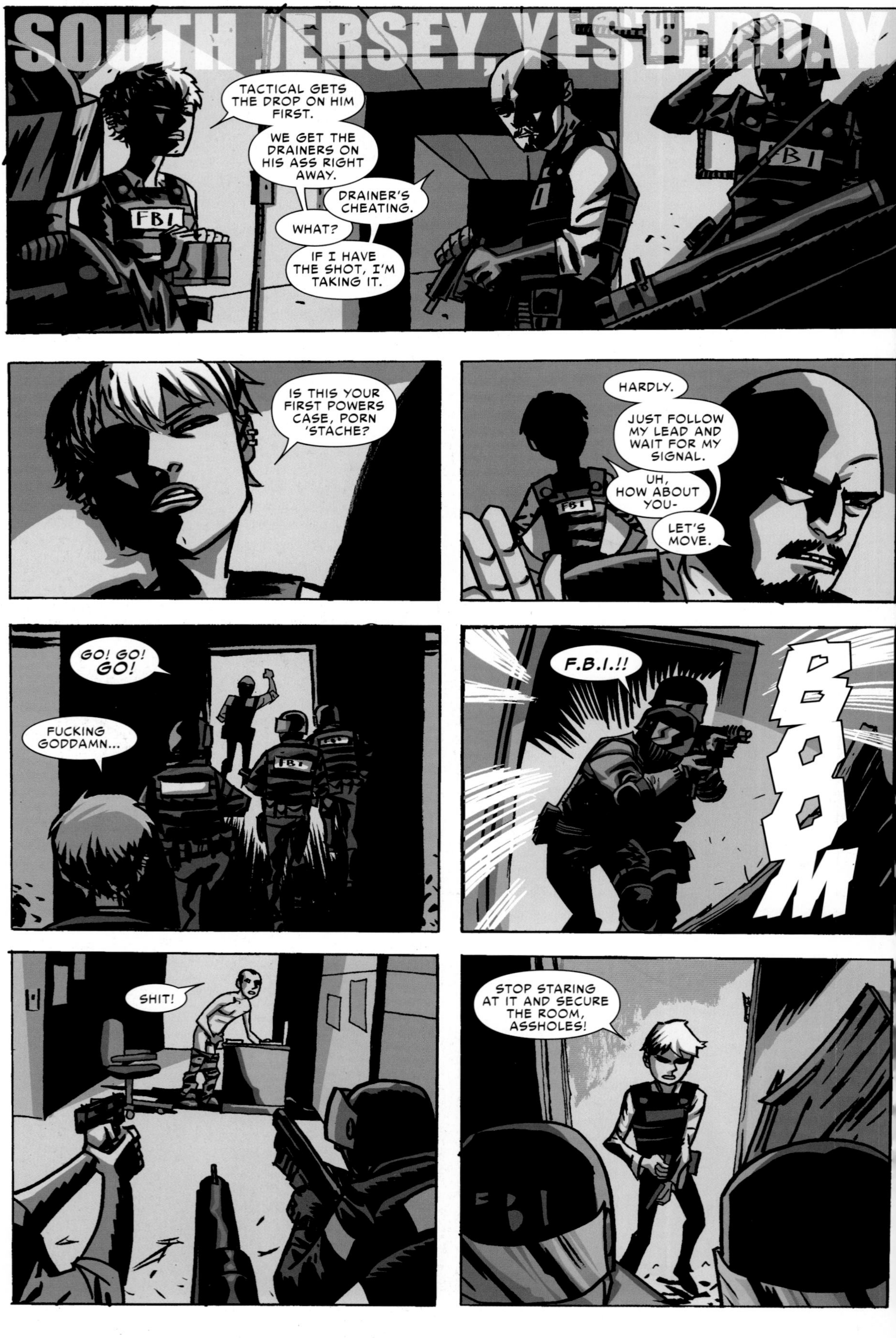
SOUTH JERSEY, YESTERDAY
TACTICAL GETS THE DROP ON HIM FIRST.
WE GET THE DRAINERS ON HIS ASS RIGHT AWAY.
DRAINER'S CHEATING.
WHAT?
IF I HAVE THE SHOT, I'M TAKING IT.
IS THIS YOUR FIRST POWERS CASE, PORN 'STACHE?
HARDLY.
JUST FOLLOW MY LEAD AND WAIT FOR MY SIGNAL.
UH, HOW ABOUT YOU-
LET'S MOVE.
GO! GO! GO!
FUCKING GODDAMN...
F.B.I.!!
BOOM
SHIT!
STOP STARING AT IT AND SECURE THE ROOM, ASSHOLES!

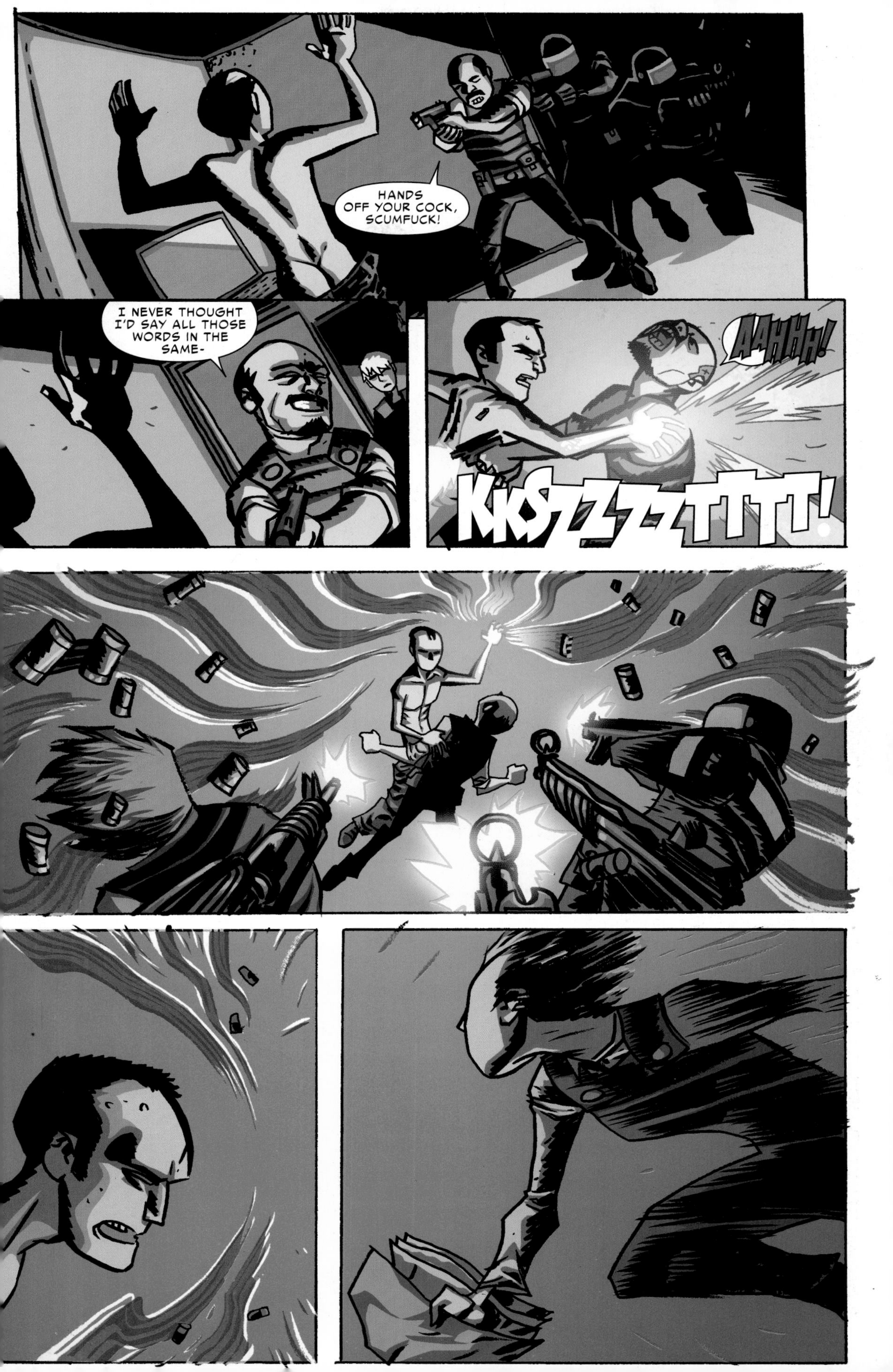
HANDS OFF YOUR COCK, SCUMFUCK!
I NEVER THOUGHT I'D SAY ALL THOSE WORDS IN THE SAME-
AAHHH!
KKSZZZZTTTT!

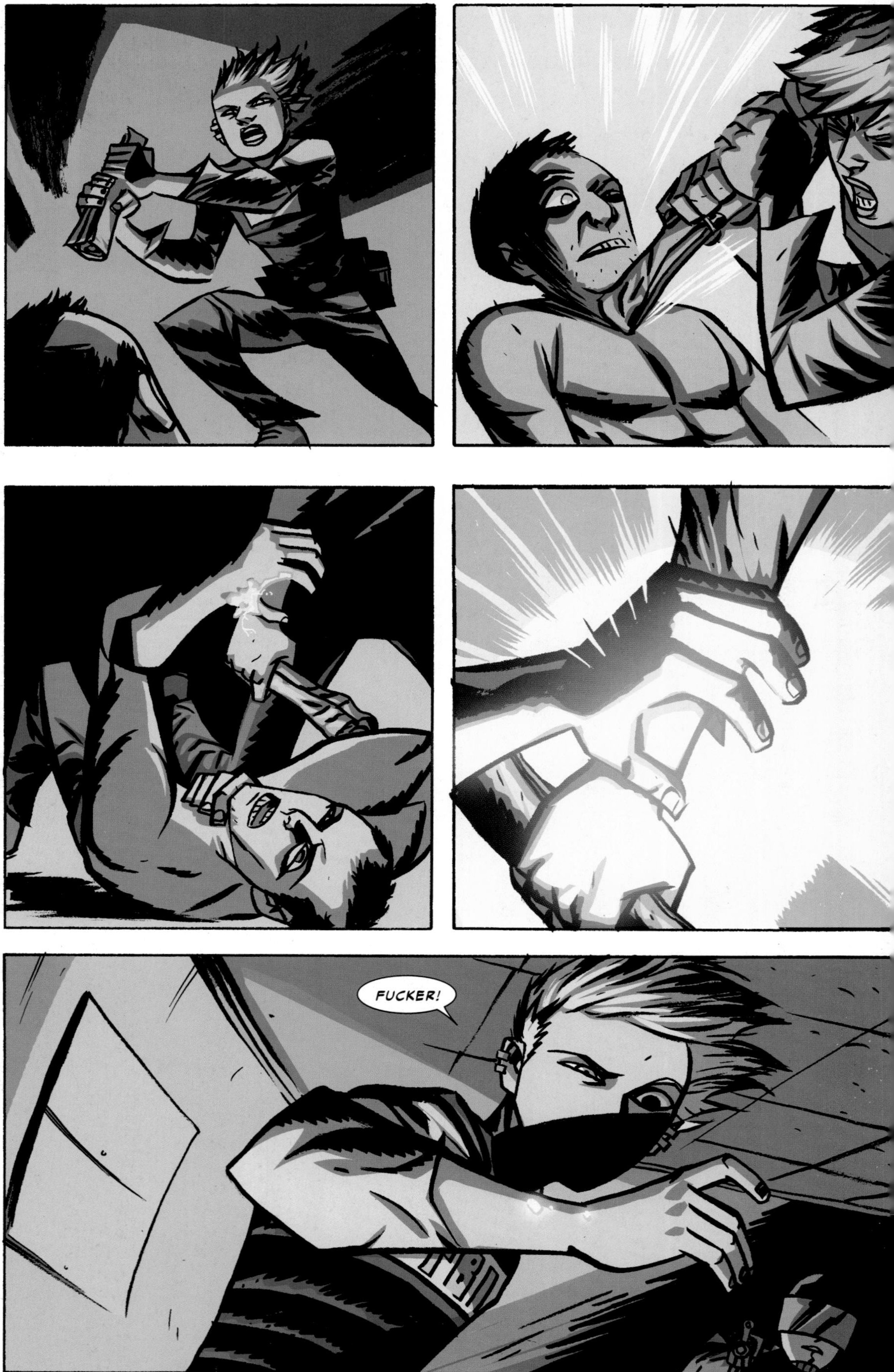
FUCKER!

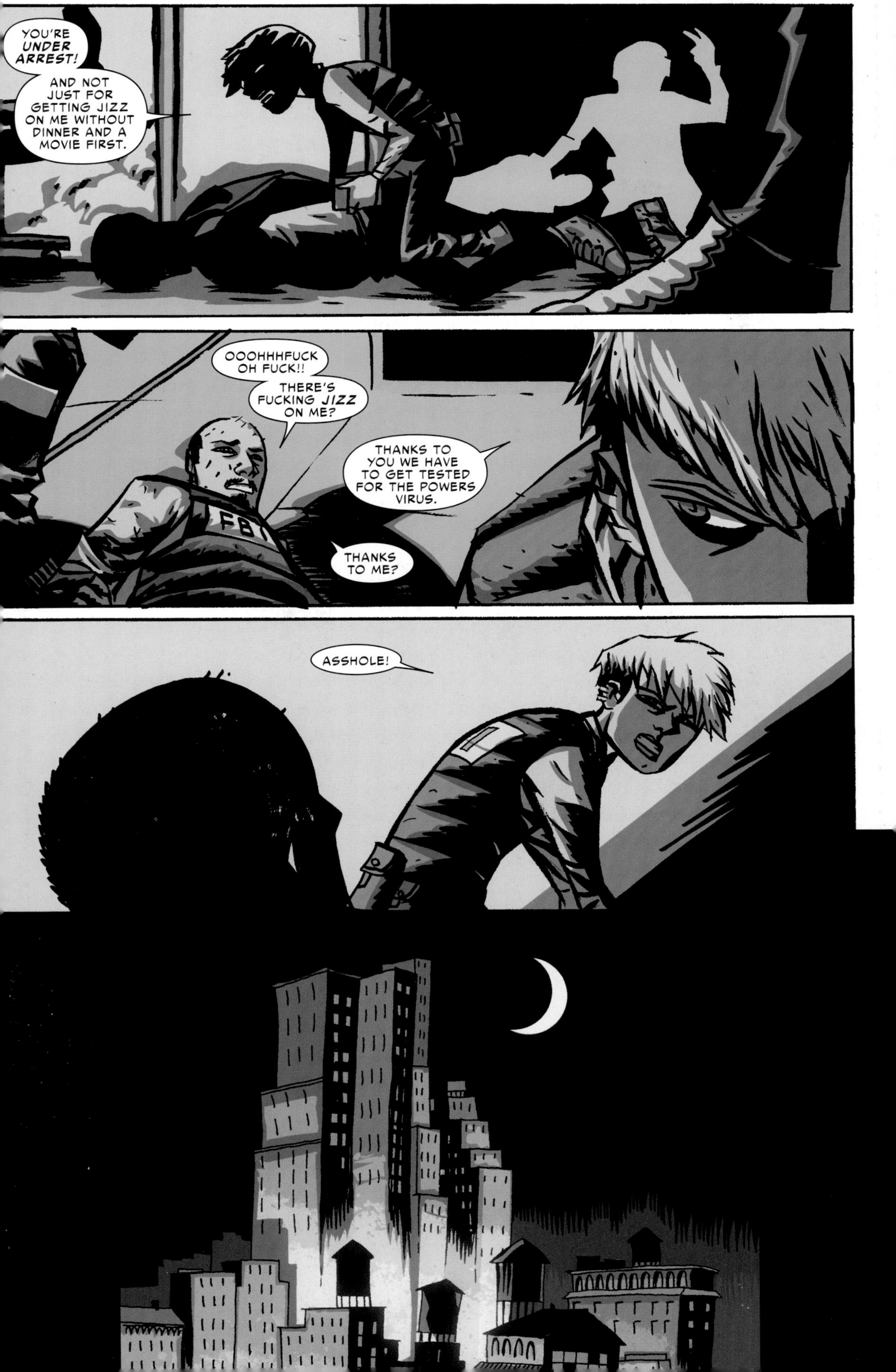
YOU'RE UNDER ARREST!
AND NOT JUST FOR GETTING JIZZ ON ME WITHOUT DINNER AND A MOVIE FIRST.
OOOHHHFUCK OH FUCK!!
THERE'S FUCKING JIZZ ON ME?
THANKS TO YOU WE HAVE TO GET TESTED FOR THE POWERS VIRUS.
THANKS TO ME?
ASSHOLE!

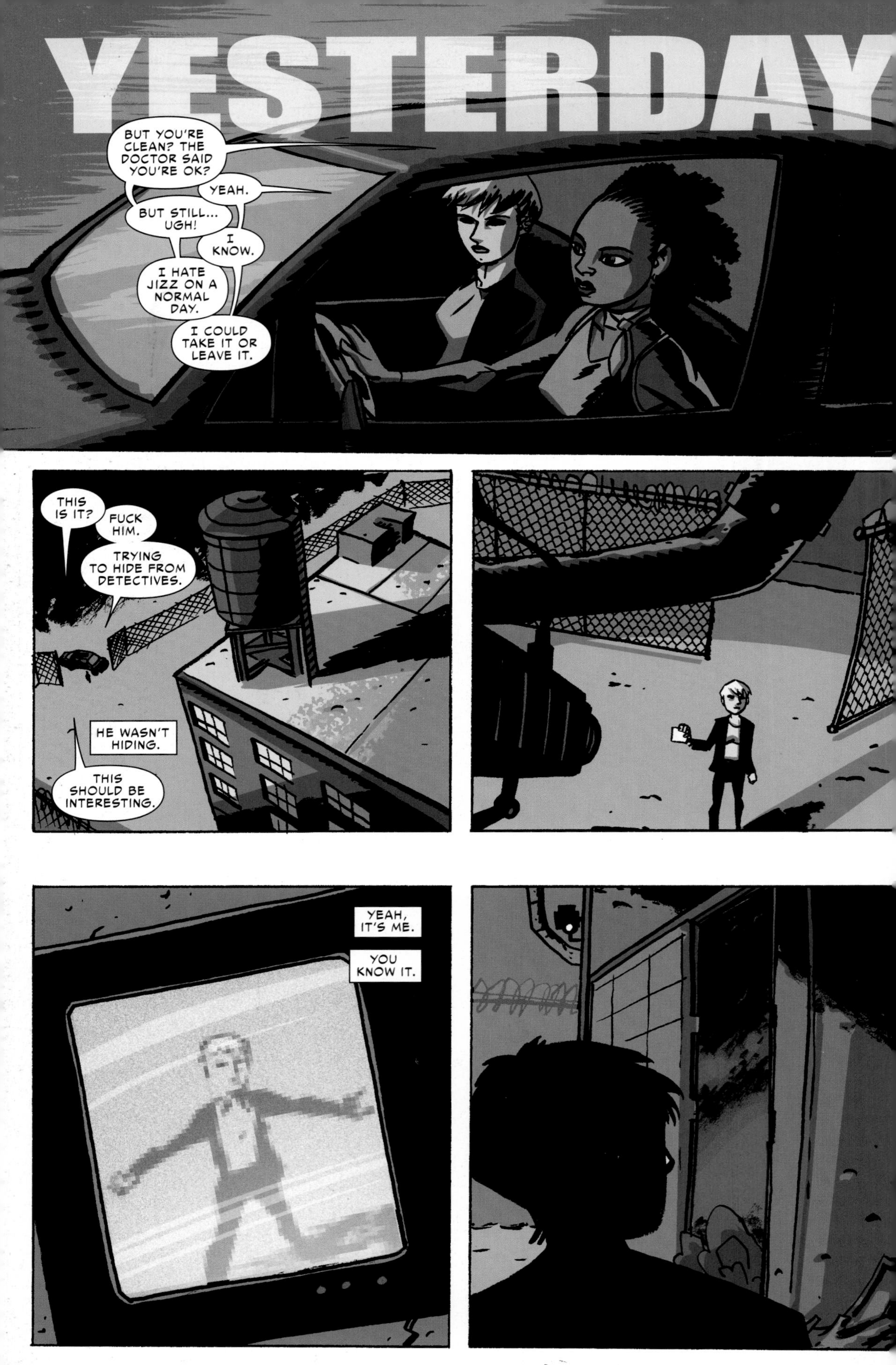
YESTERDAY
BUT YOU'RE CLEAN? THE DOCTOR SAID YOU'RE OK?
YEAH.
BUT STILL... UGH!
I KNOW.
I HATE JIZZ ON A NORMAL DAY.
I COULD TAKE IT OR LEAVE IT.
THIS IS IT?
FUCK HIM.
TRYING TO HIDE FROM DETECTIVES.
HE WASN'T HIDING.
THIS SHOULD BE INTERESTING.
YEAH, IT'S ME.
YOU KNOW IT.

AM I UNDER ARREST?

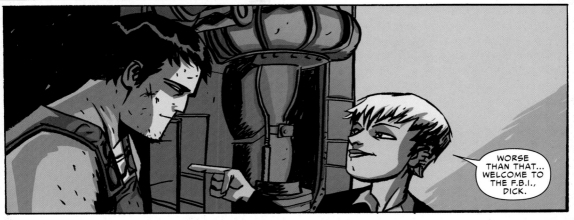

WORSE THAN THAT... WELCOME TO THE F.B.I., DICK.

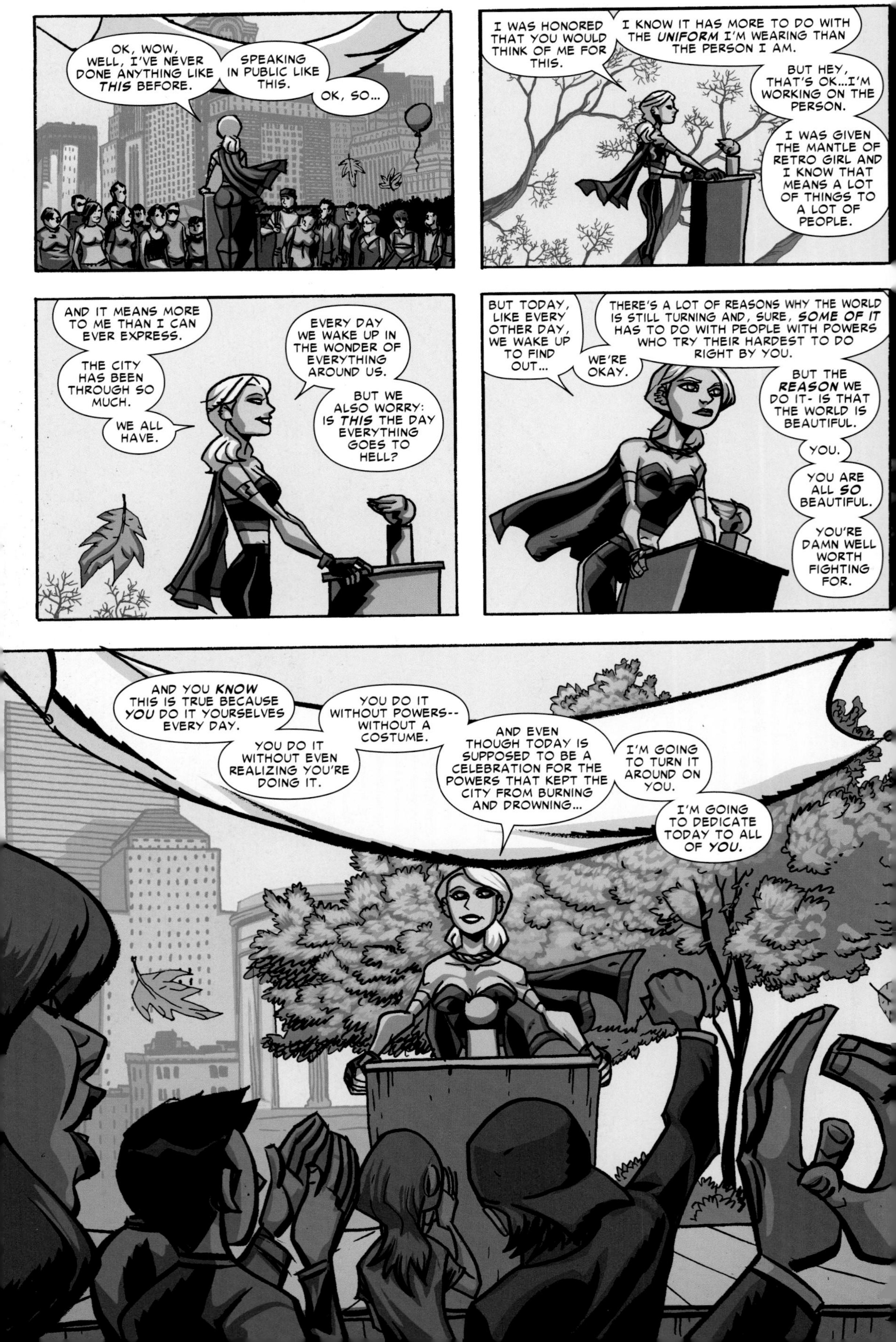
OK, WOW, WELL, I'VE NEVER DONE ANYTHING LIKE *THIS* BEFORE.
SPEAKING IN PUBLIC LIKE THIS.
OK, SO...
I WAS HONORED THAT YOU WOULD THINK OF ME FOR THIS.
I KNOW IT HAS MORE TO DO WITH THE *UNIFORM* I'M WEARING THAN THE PERSON I AM.
BUT HEY, THAT'S OK...I'M WORKING ON THE PERSON.
I WAS GIVEN THE MANTLE OF RETRO GIRL AND I KNOW THAT MEANS A LOT OF THINGS TO A LOT OF PEOPLE.
AND IT MEANS MORE TO ME THAN I CAN EVER EXPRESS.
THE CITY HAS BEEN THROUGH SO MUCH.
WE ALL HAVE.
EVERY DAY WE WAKE UP IN THE WONDER OF EVERYTHING AROUND US.
BUT WE ALSO WORRY: IS *THIS* THE DAY EVERYTHING GOES TO HELL?
BUT TODAY, LIKE EVERY OTHER DAY, WE WAKE UP TO FIND OUT...
WE'RE OKAY.
THERE'S A LOT OF REASONS WHY THE WORLD IS STILL TURNING AND, SURE, *SOME OF IT* HAS TO DO WITH PEOPLE WITH POWERS WHO TRY THEIR HARDEST TO DO RIGHT BY YOU.
BUT THE *REASON* WE DO IT- IS THAT THE WORLD IS BEAUTIFUL.
YOU.
YOU ARE ALL *SO* BEAUTIFUL.
YOU'RE DAMN WELL WORTH FIGHTING FOR.
AND YOU *KNOW* THIS IS TRUE BECAUSE *YOU* DO IT YOURSELVES EVERY DAY.
YOU DO IT WITHOUT EVEN REALIZING YOU'RE DOING IT.
YOU DO IT WITHOUT POWERS-- WITHOUT A COSTUME.
AND EVEN THOUGH TODAY IS SUPPOSED TO BE A CELEBRATION FOR THE POWERS THAT KEPT THE CITY FROM BURNING AND DROWNING...
I'M GOING TO TURN IT AROUND ON YOU.
I'M GOING TO DEDICATE TODAY TO ALL OF *YOU.*

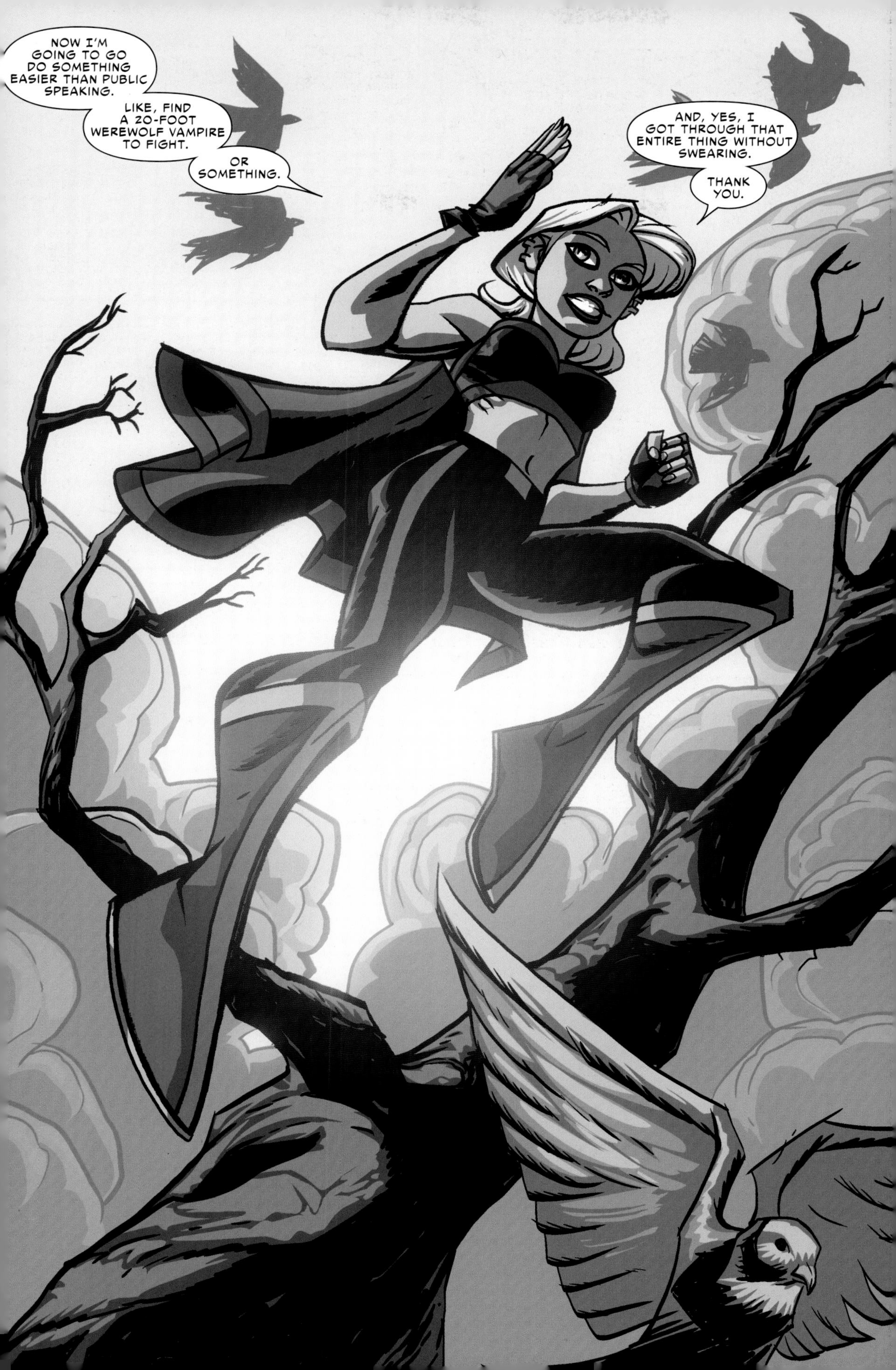
NOW I'M GOING TO GO DO SOMETHING EASIER THAN PUBLIC SPEAKING.
LIKE, FIND A 20-FOOT WEREWOLF VAMPIRE TO FIGHT.
OR SOMETHING.
AND, YES, I GOT THROUGH THAT ENTIRE THING WITHOUT SWEARING.
THANK YOU.

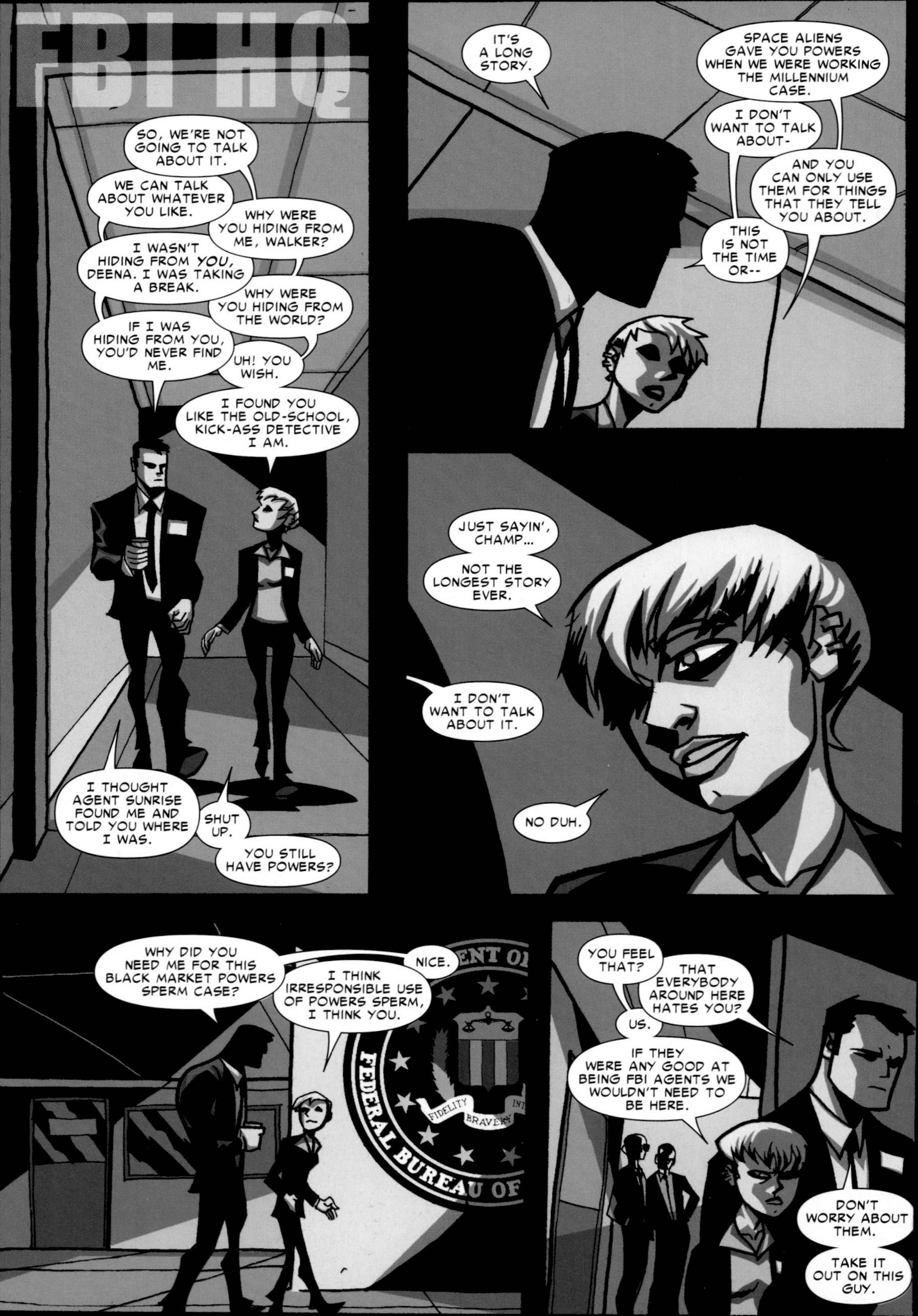
FBI HQ
SO, WE'RE NOT GOING TO TALK ABOUT IT.
WE CAN TALK ABOUT WHATEVER YOU LIKE.
WHY WERE YOU HIDING FROM ME, WALKER?
I WASN'T HIDING FROM YOU, DEENA. I WAS TAKING A BREAK.
WHY WERE YOU HIDING FROM THE WORLD?
IF I WAS HIDING FROM YOU, YOU'D NEVER FIND ME.
UH! YOU WISH.
I FOUND YOU LIKE THE OLD-SCHOOL, KICK-ASS DETECTIVE I AM.
I THOUGHT AGENT SUNRISE FOUND ME AND TOLD YOU WHERE I WAS.
SHUT UP.
YOU STILL HAVE POWERS?
IT'S A LONG STORY.
SPACE ALIENS GAVE YOU POWERS WHEN WE WERE WORKING THE MILLENNIUM CASE.
I DON'T WANT TO TALK ABOUT-
AND YOU CAN ONLY USE THEM FOR THINGS THAT THEY TELL YOU ABOUT.
THIS IS NOT THE TIME OR--
JUST SAYIN', CHAMP...
NOT THE LONGEST STORY EVER.
I DON'T WANT TO TALK ABOUT IT.
NO DUH.
WHY DID YOU NEED ME FOR THIS BLACK MARKET POWERS SPERM CASE?
NICE.
I THINK IRRESPONSIBLE USE OF POWERS SPERM, I THINK YOU.
FIDELITY BRAVERY
FEDERAL BUREAU OF
YOU FEEL THAT?
THAT EVERYBODY AROUND HERE HATES YOU?
US.
IF THEY WERE ANY GOOD AT BEING FBI AGENTS WE WOULDN'T NEED TO BE HERE.
DON'T WORRY ABOUT THEM.
TAKE IT OUT ON THIS GUY.

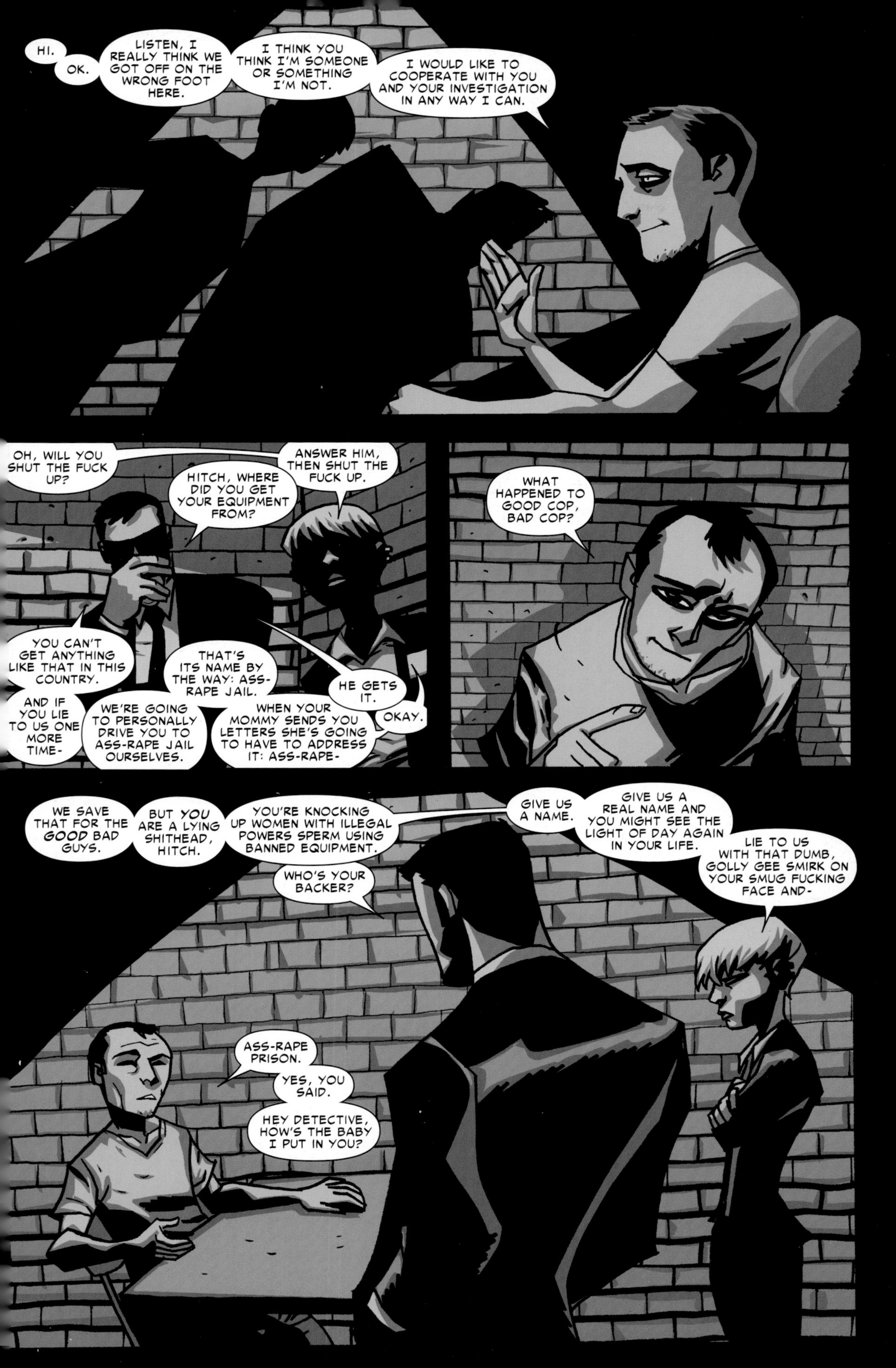
HI.
OK.
LISTEN, I REALLY THINK WE GOT OFF ON THE WRONG FOOT HERE.
I THINK YOU THINK I'M SOMEONE OR SOMETHING I'M NOT.
I WOULD LIKE TO COOPERATE WITH YOU AND YOUR INVESTIGATION IN ANY WAY I CAN.
OH, WILL YOU SHUT THE FUCK UP?
ANSWER HIM, THEN SHUT THE FUCK UP.
HITCH, WHERE DID YOU GET YOUR EQUIPMENT FROM?
YOU CAN'T GET ANYTHING LIKE THAT IN THIS COUNTRY.
AND IF YOU LIE TO US ONE MORE TIME-
WE'RE GOING TO PERSONALLY DRIVE YOU TO ASS-RAPE JAIL OURSELVES.
THAT'S ITS NAME BY THE WAY: ASS-RAPE JAIL.
WHEN YOUR MOMMY SENDS YOU LETTERS SHE'S GOING TO HAVE TO ADDRESS IT: ASS-RAPE-
HE GETS IT.
OKAY.
WHAT HAPPENED TO GOOD COP, BAD COP?
WE SAVE THAT FOR THE GOOD BAD GUYS.
BUT YOU ARE A LYING SHITHEAD, HITCH.
YOU'RE KNOCKING UP WOMEN WITH ILLEGAL POWERS SPERM USING BANNED EQUIPMENT.
WHO'S YOUR BACKER?
GIVE US A NAME.
GIVE US A REAL NAME AND YOU MIGHT SEE THE LIGHT OF DAY AGAIN IN YOUR LIFE.
LIE TO US WITH THAT DUMB, GOLLY GEE SMIRK ON YOUR SMUG FUCKING FACE AND-
ASS-RAPE PRISON.
YES, YOU SAID.
HEY DETECTIVE, HOW'S THE BABY I PUT IN YOU?

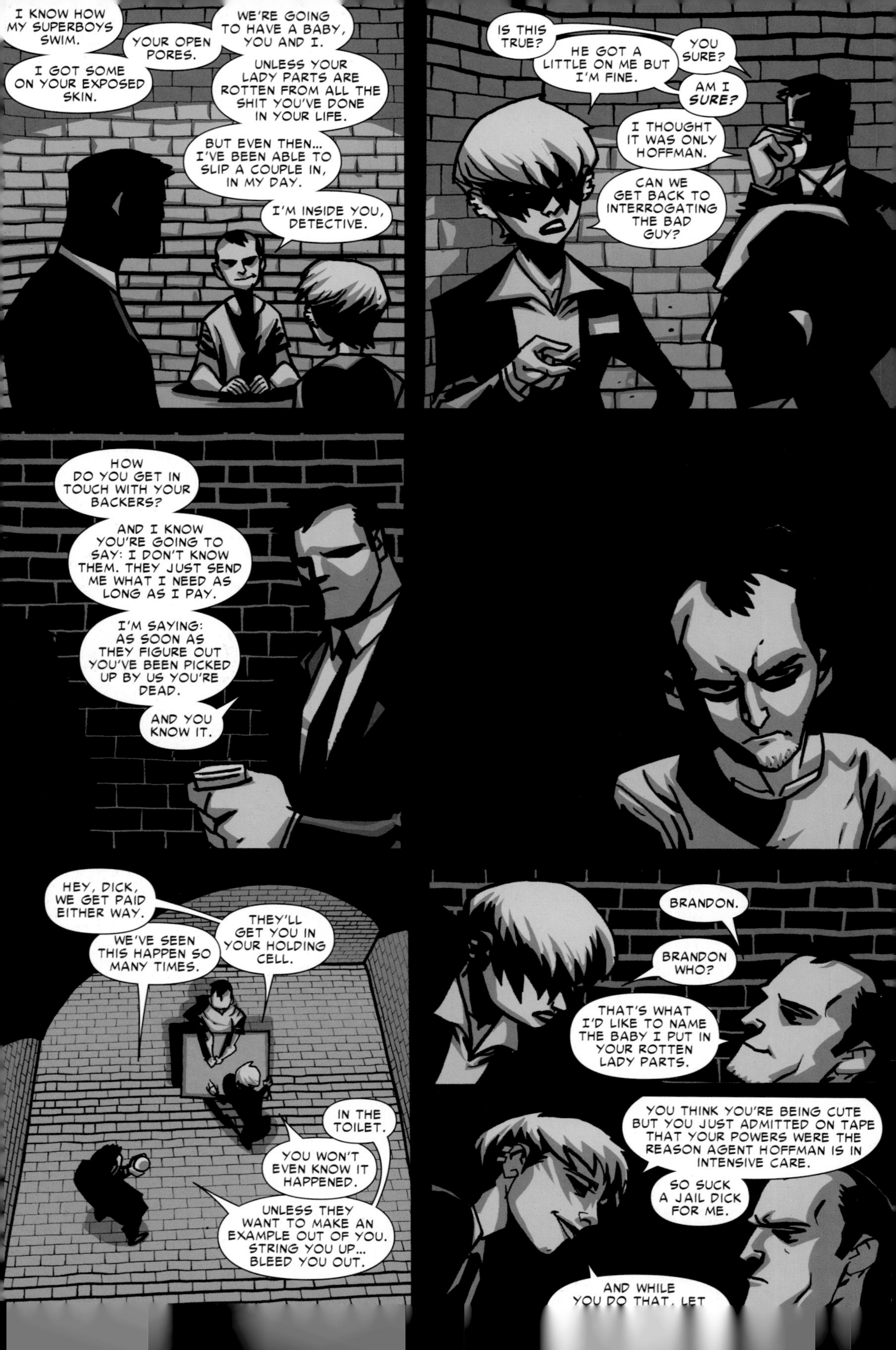
I KNOW HOW MY SUPERBOYS SWIM.
I GOT SOME ON YOUR EXPOSED SKIN.
YOUR OPEN PORES.
WE'RE GOING TO HAVE A BABY, YOU AND I.
UNLESS YOUR LADY PARTS ARE ROTTEN FROM ALL THE SHIT YOU'VE DONE IN YOUR LIFE.
BUT EVEN THEN... I'VE BEEN ABLE TO SLIP A COUPLE IN, IN MY DAY.
I'M INSIDE YOU, DETECTIVE.
IS THIS TRUE?
YOU SURE?
HE GOT A LITTLE ON ME BUT I'M FINE.
AM I SURE?
I THOUGHT IT WAS ONLY HOFFMAN.
CAN WE GET BACK TO INTERROGATING THE BAD GUY?
HOW DO YOU GET IN TOUCH WITH YOUR BACKERS?
AND I KNOW YOU'RE GOING TO SAY: I DON'T KNOW THEM. THEY JUST SEND ME WHAT I NEED AS LONG AS I PAY.
I'M SAYING: AS SOON AS THEY FIGURE OUT YOU'VE BEEN PICKED UP BY US YOU'RE DEAD.
AND YOU KNOW IT.
HEY, DICK, WE GET PAID EITHER WAY.
WE'VE SEEN THIS HAPPEN SO MANY TIMES.
THEY'LL GET YOU IN YOUR HOLDING CELL.
IN THE TOILET.
YOU WON'T EVEN KNOW IT HAPPENED.
UNLESS THEY WANT TO MAKE AN EXAMPLE OUT OF YOU. STRING YOU UP... BLEED YOU OUT.
BRANDON.
BRANDON WHO?
THAT'S WHAT I'D LIKE TO NAME THE BABY I PUT IN YOUR ROTTEN LADY PARTS.
YOU THINK YOU'RE BEING CUTE BUT YOU JUST ADMITTED ON TAPE THAT YOUR POWERS WERE THE REASON AGENT HOFFMAN IS IN INTENSIVE CARE.
SO SUCK A JAIL DICK FOR ME.
AND WHILE YOU DO THAT, LET

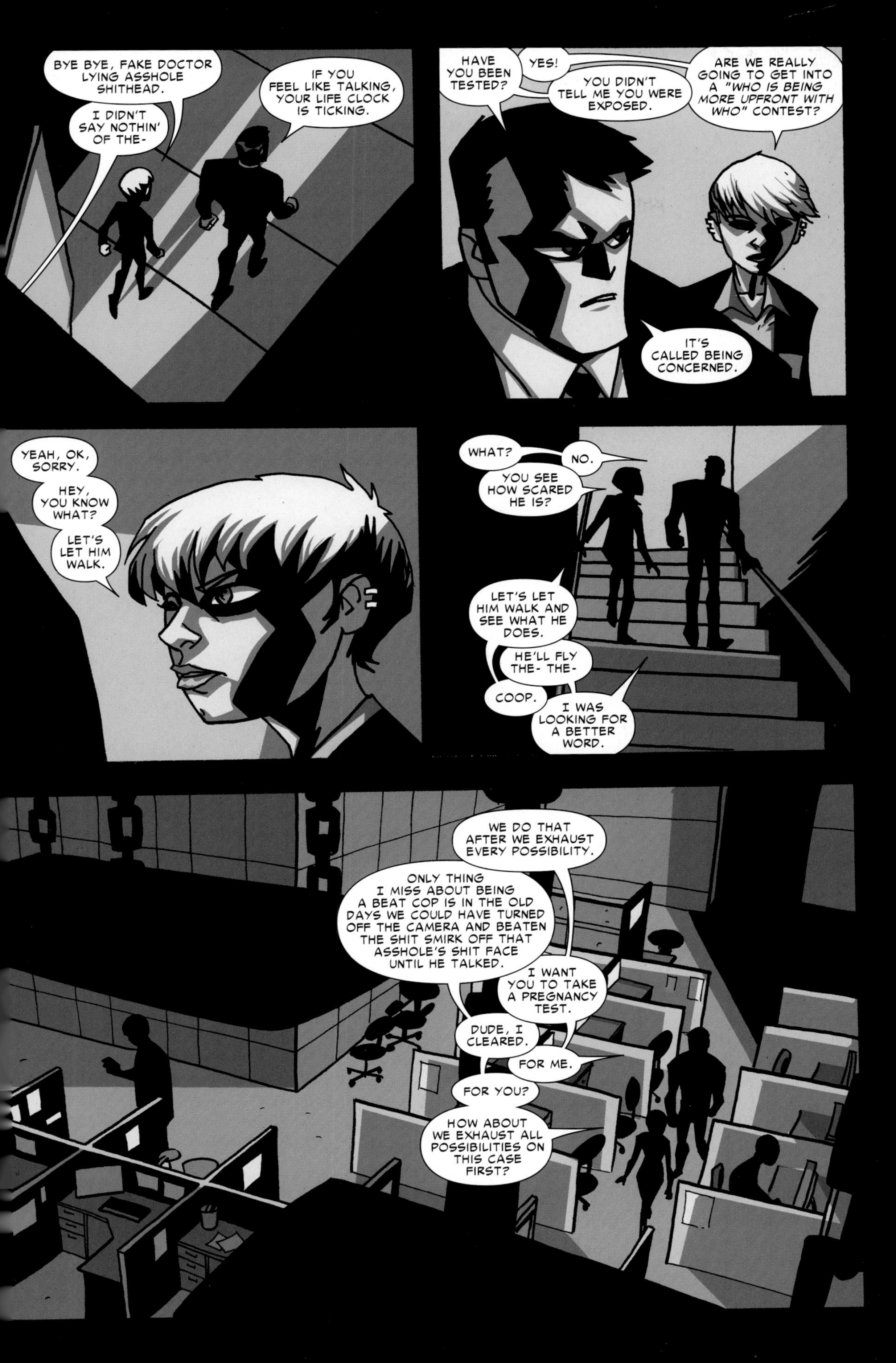
BYE BYE, FAKE DOCTOR LYING ASSHOLE SHITHEAD.
I DIDN'T SAY NOTHIN' OF THE-
IF YOU FEEL LIKE TALKING, YOUR LIFE CLOCK IS TICKING.
HAVE YOU BEEN TESTED?
YES!
YOU DIDN'T TELL ME YOU WERE EXPOSED.
ARE WE REALLY GOING TO GET INTO A "WHO IS BEING MORE UPFRONT WITH WHO" CONTEST?
IT'S CALLED BEING CONCERNED.
YEAH, OK, SORRY.
HEY, YOU KNOW WHAT?
LET'S LET HIM WALK.
WHAT?
NO.
YOU SEE HOW SCARED HE IS?
LET'S LET HIM WALK AND SEE WHAT HE DOES.
HE'LL FLY THE- THE-
COOP.
I WAS LOOKING FOR A BETTER WORD.
WE DO THAT AFTER WE EXHAUST EVERY POSSIBILITY.
ONLY THING I MISS ABOUT BEING A BEAT COP IS IN THE OLD DAYS WE COULD HAVE TURNED OFF THE CAMERA AND BEATEN THE SHIT SMIRK OFF THAT ASSHOLE'S SHIT FACE UNTIL HE TALKED.
I WANT YOU TO TAKE A PREGNANCY TEST.
DUDE, I CLEARED.
FOR ME.
FOR YOU?
HOW ABOUT WE EXHAUST ALL POSSIBILITIES ON THIS CASE FIRST?

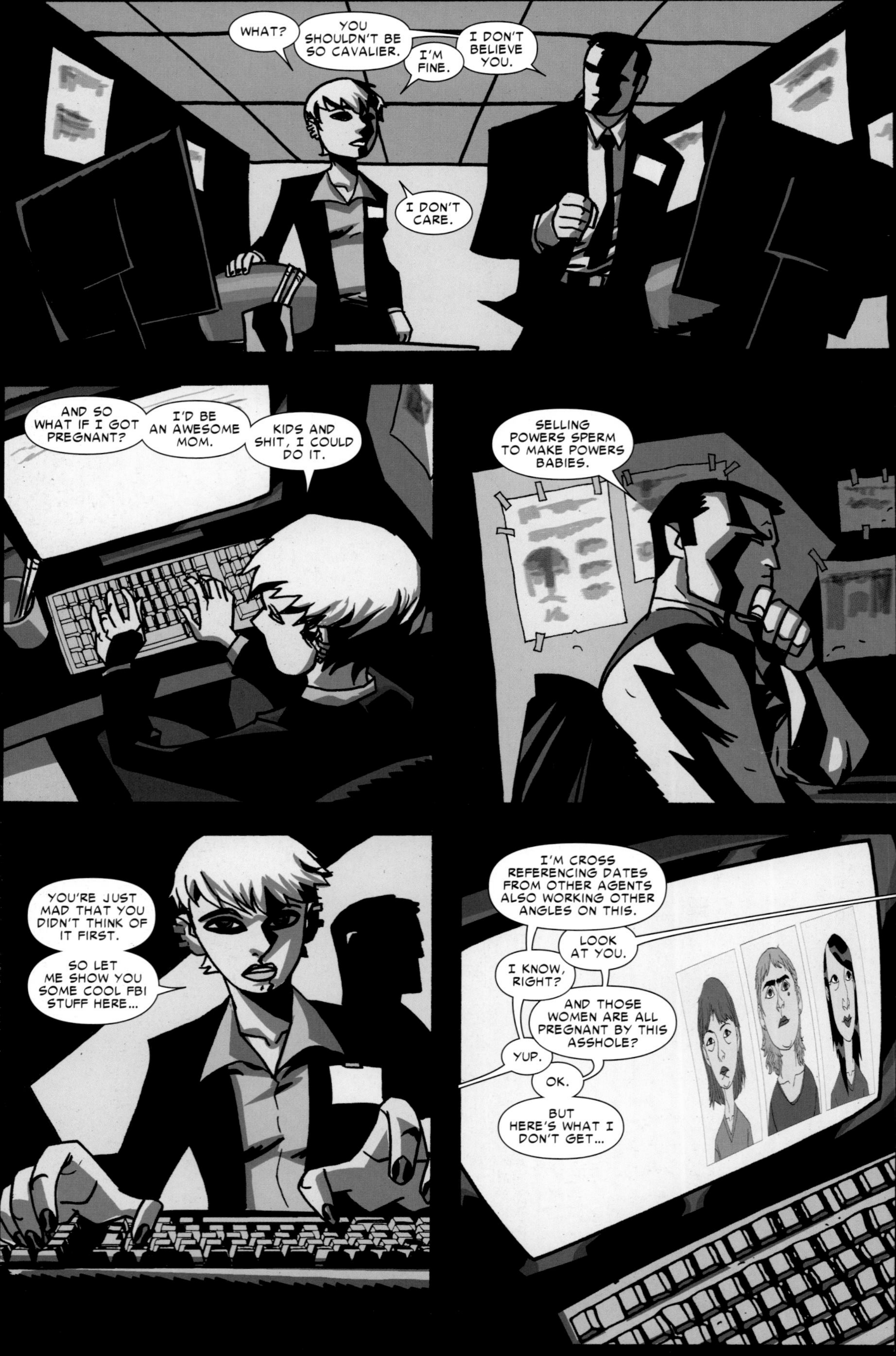
WHAT?
YOU SHOULDN'T BE SO CAVALIER.
I'M FINE.
I DON'T BELIEVE YOU.
I DON'T CARE.
AND SO WHAT IF I GOT PREGNANT?
I'D BE AN AWESOME MOM.
KIDS AND SHIT, I COULD DO IT.
SELLING POWERS SPERM TO MAKE POWERS BABIES.
YOU'RE JUST MAD THAT YOU DIDN'T THINK OF IT FIRST.
SO LET ME SHOW YOU SOME COOL FBI STUFF HERE...
I'M CROSS REFERENCING DATES FROM OTHER AGENTS ALSO WORKING OTHER ANGLES ON THIS.
LOOK AT YOU.
I KNOW, RIGHT?
AND THOSE WOMEN ARE ALL PREGNANT BY THIS ASSHOLE?
YUP.
OK.
BUT HERE'S WHAT I DON'T GET...

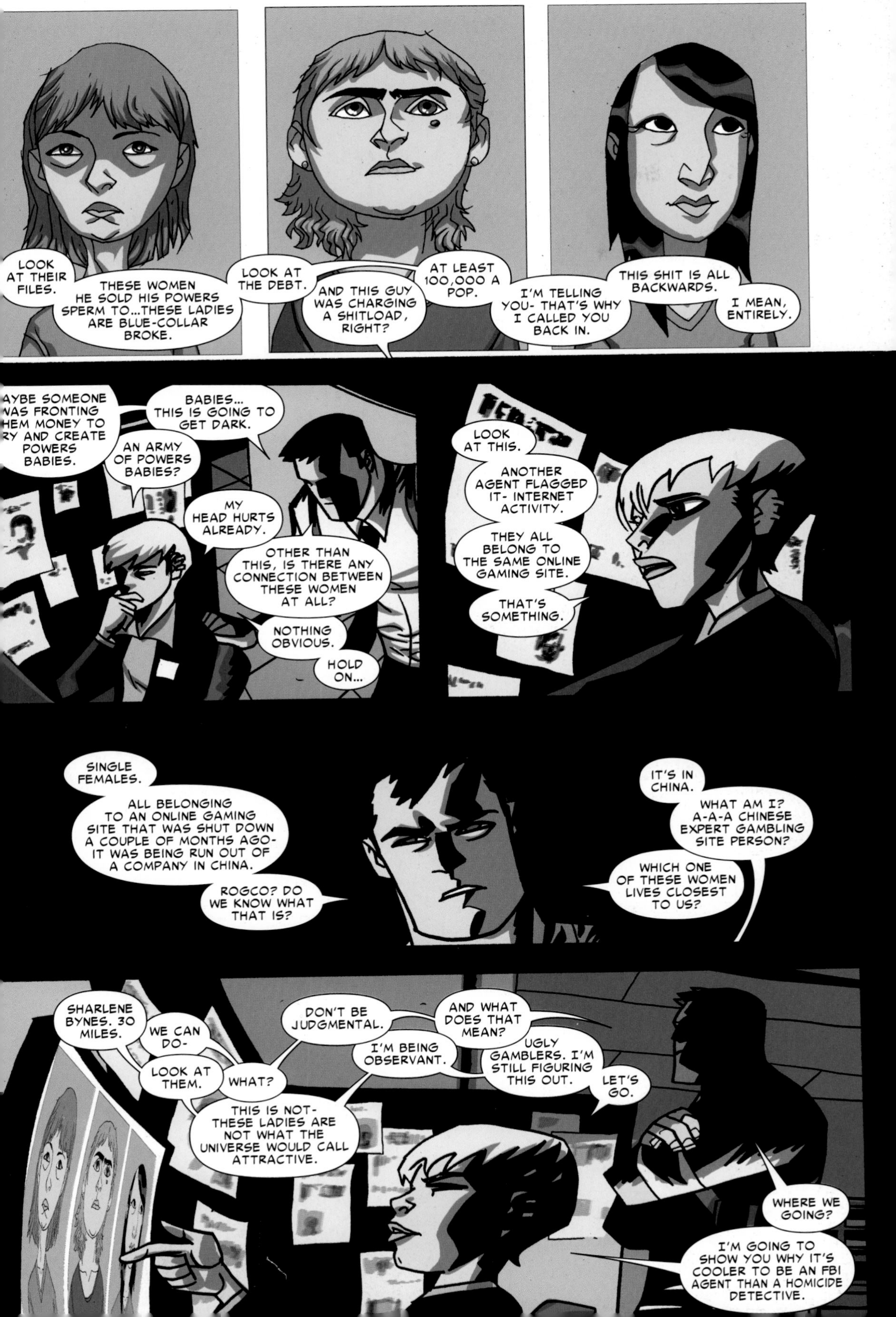

LOOK AT THEIR FILES.
THESE WOMEN HE SOLD HIS POWERS SPERM TO...THESE LADIES ARE BLUE-COLLAR BROKE.
LOOK AT THE DEBT.
AND THIS GUY WAS CHARGING A SHITLOAD, RIGHT?
AT LEAST 100,000 A POP.
I'M TELLING YOU- THAT'S WHY I CALLED YOU BACK IN.
THIS SHIT IS ALL BACKWARDS.
I MEAN, ENTIRELY.
AYBE SOMEONE VAS FRONTING HEM MONEY TO RY AND CREATE POWERS BABIES.
BABIES... THIS IS GOING TO GET DARK.
AN ARMY OF POWERS BABIES?
MY HEAD HURTS ALREADY.
OTHER THAN THIS, IS THERE ANY CONNECTION BETWEEN THESE WOMEN AT ALL?
NOTHING OBVIOUS.
HOLD ON...
LOOK AT THIS.
ANOTHER AGENT FLAGGED IT- INTERNET ACTIVITY.
THEY ALL BELONG TO THE SAME ONLINE GAMING SITE.
THAT'S SOMETHING.
SINGLE FEMALES.
ALL BELONGING TO AN ONLINE GAMING SITE THAT WAS SHUT DOWN A COUPLE OF MONTHS AGO- IT WAS BEING RUN OUT OF A COMPANY IN CHINA.
ROGCO? DO WE KNOW WHAT THAT IS?
IT'S IN CHINA.
WHAT AM I? A-A-A CHINESE EXPERT GAMBLING SITE PERSON?
WHICH ONE OF THESE WOMEN LIVES CLOSEST TO US?
SHARLENE BYNES. 30 MILES.
WE CAN DO-
LOOK AT THEM.
WHAT?
THIS IS NOT- THESE LADIES ARE NOT WHAT THE UNIVERSE WOULD CALL ATTRACTIVE.
DON'T BE JUDGMENTAL.
I'M BEING OBSERVANT.
AND WHAT DOES THAT MEAN?
UGLY GAMBLERS. I'M STILL FIGURING THIS OUT.
LET'S GO.
WHERE WE GOING?
I'M GOING TO SHOW YOU WHY IT'S COOLER TO BE AN FBI AGENT THAN A HOMICIDE DETECTIVE.

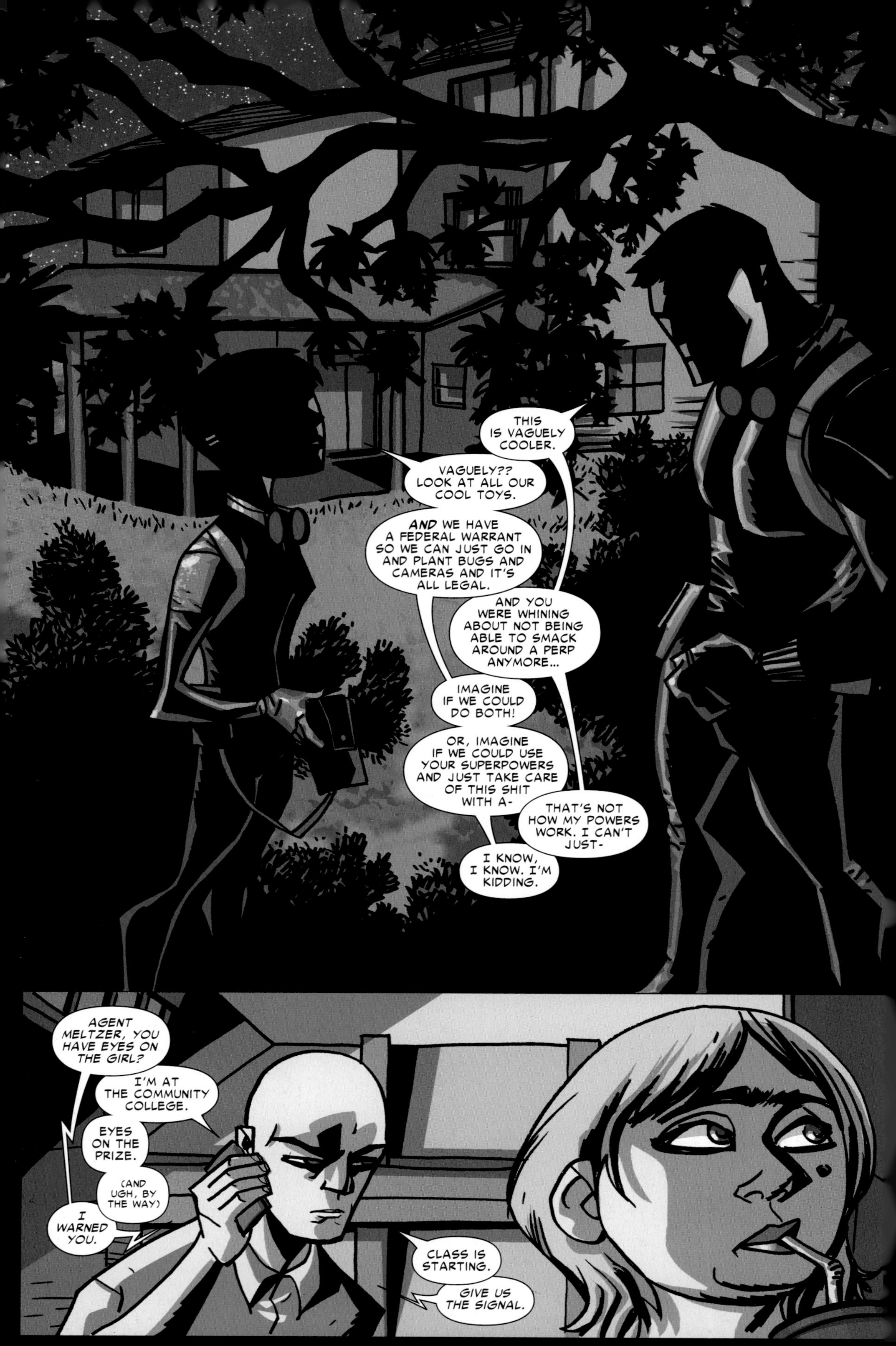
THIS IS VAGUELY COOLER.
VAGUELY?? LOOK AT ALL OUR COOL TOYS.
AND WE HAVE A FEDERAL WARRANT SO WE CAN JUST GO IN AND PLANT BUGS AND CAMERAS AND IT'S ALL LEGAL.
AND YOU WERE WHINING ABOUT NOT BEING ABLE TO SMACK AROUND A PERP ANYMORE...
IMAGINE IF WE COULD DO BOTH!
OR, IMAGINE IF WE COULD USE YOUR SUPERPOWERS AND JUST TAKE CARE OF THIS SHIT WITH A-
THAT'S NOT HOW MY POWERS WORK. I CAN'T JUST-
I KNOW, I KNOW. I'M KIDDING.
AGENT MELTZER, YOU HAVE EYES ON THE GIRL?
I'M AT THE COMMUNITY COLLEGE.
EYES ON THE PRIZE.
(AND UGH, BY THE WAY)
I WARNED YOU.
CLASS IS STARTING.
GIVE US THE SIGNAL.

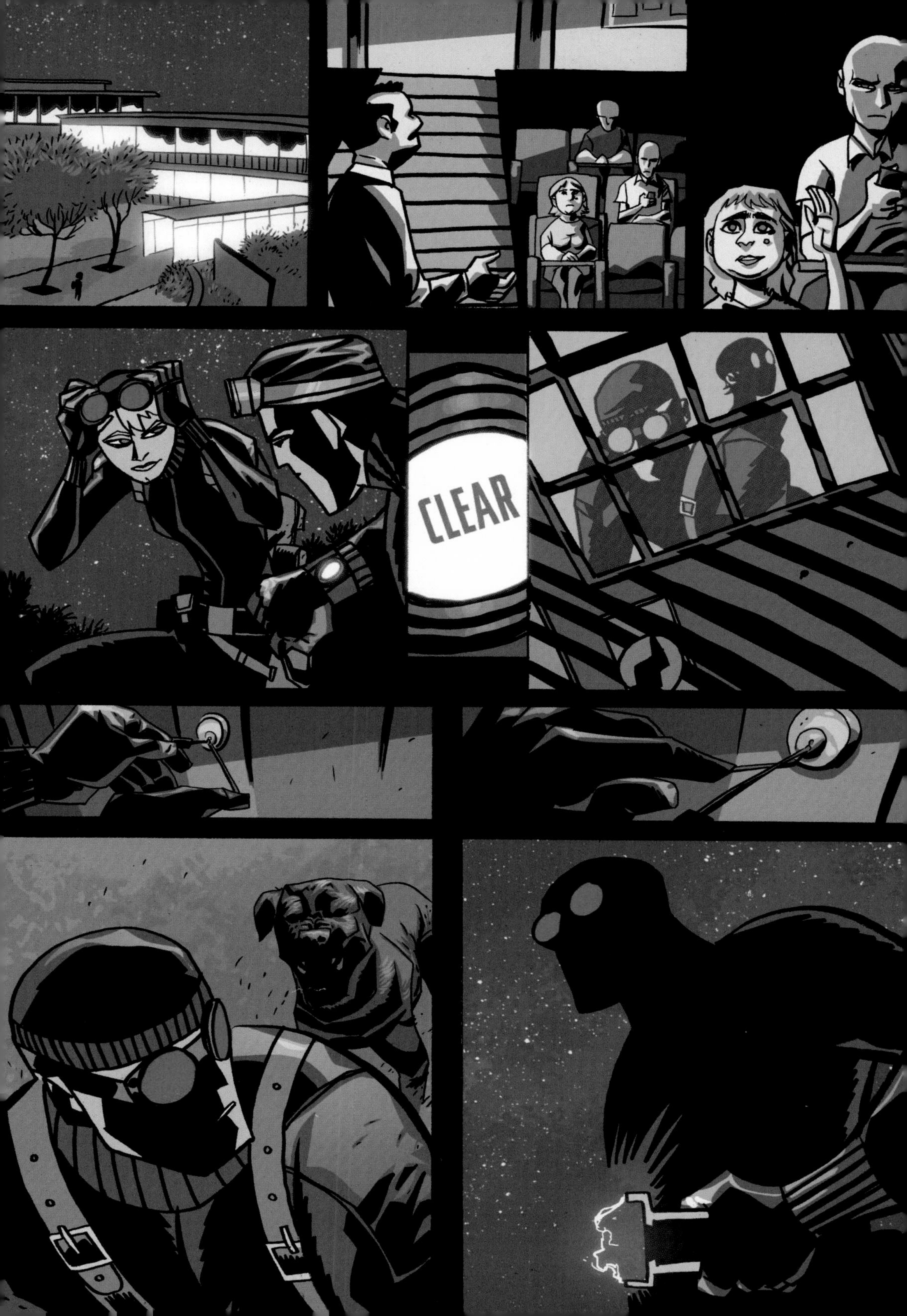
CLEAR

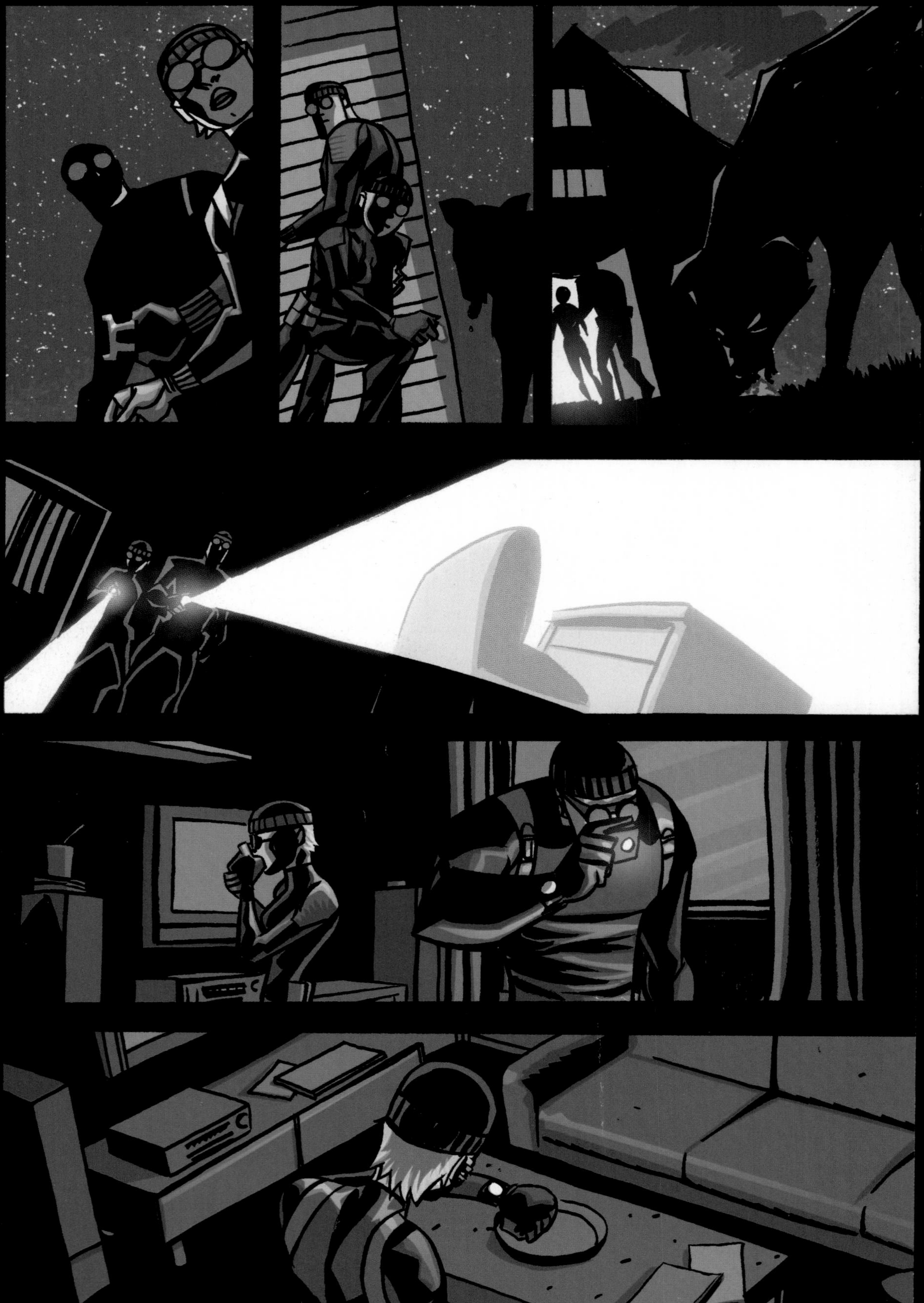

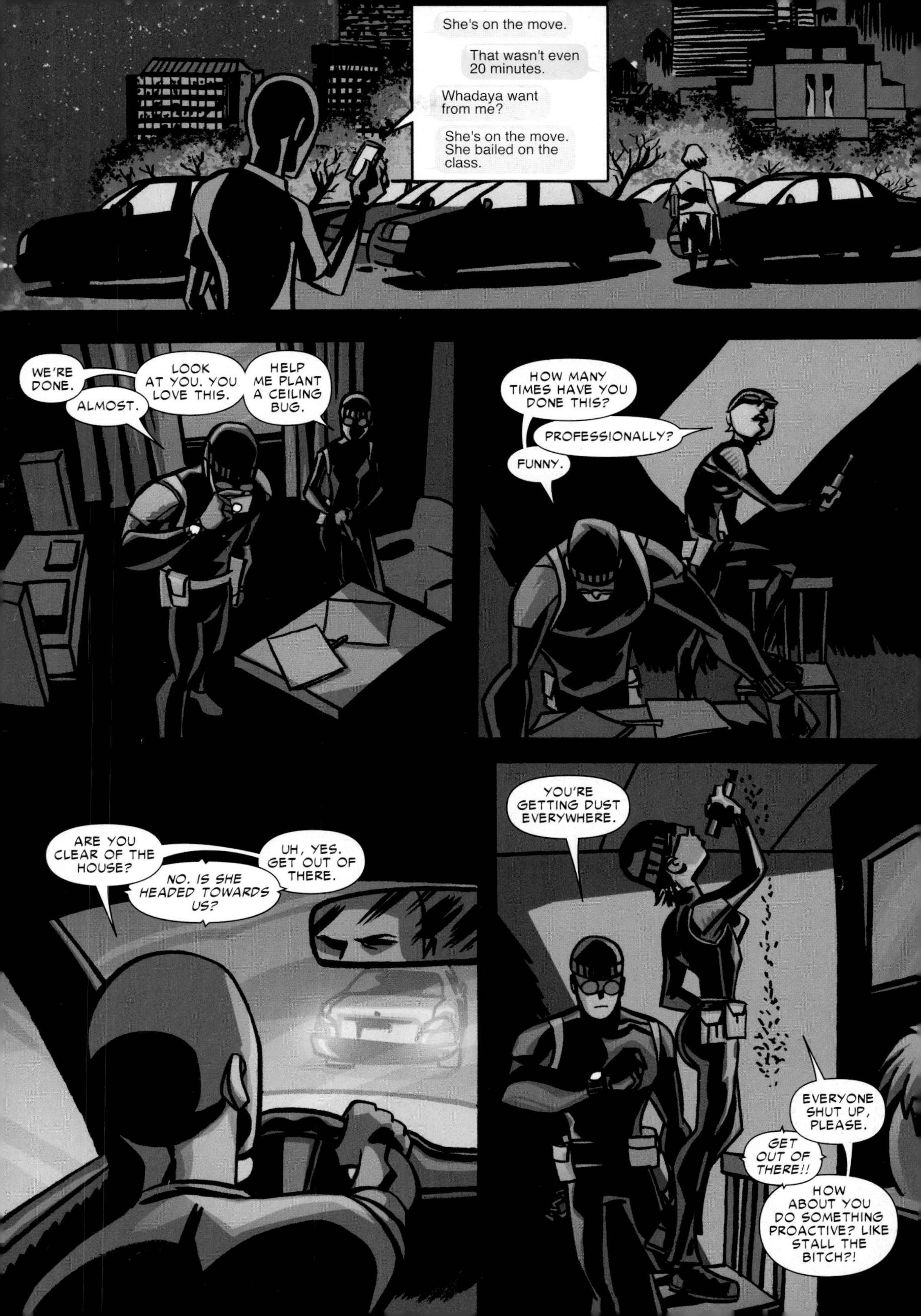
She's on the move.
That wasn't even 20 minutes.
Whadaya want from me?
She's on the move. She bailed on the class.
WE'RE DONE.
LOOK AT YOU. YOU LOVE THIS.
ALMOST.
HELP ME PLANT A CEILING BUG.
HOW MANY TIMES HAVE YOU DONE THIS?
PROFESSIONALLY?
FUNNY.
ARE YOU CLEAR OF THE HOUSE?
UH, YES. GET OUT OF THERE.
NO. IS SHE HEADED TOWARDS US?
YOU'RE GETTING DUST EVERYWHERE.
EVERYONE SHUT UP, PLEASE.
GET OUT OF THERE!!
HOW ABOUT YOU DO SOMETHING PROACTIVE? LIKE STALL THE BITCH?!

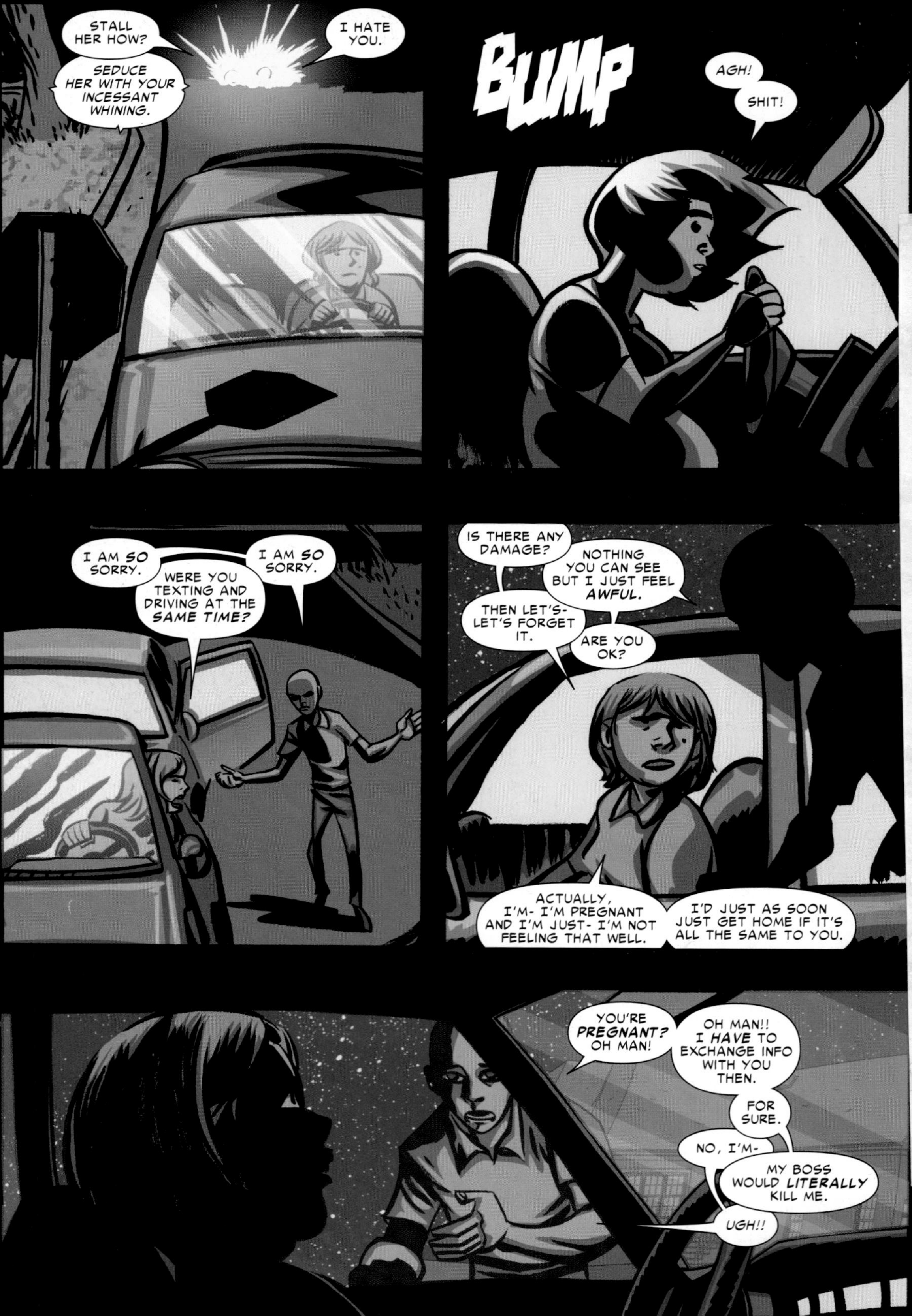
STALL HER HOW?
SEDUCE HER WITH YOUR INCESSANT WHINING.
I HATE YOU.
BUMP
AGH!
SHIT!
I AM SO SORRY.
WERE YOU TEXTING AND DRIVING AT THE SAME TIME?
I AM SO SORRY.
IS THERE ANY DAMAGE?
NOTHING YOU CAN SEE BUT I JUST FEEL AWFUL.
THEN LET'S- LET'S FORGET IT.
ARE YOU OK?
ACTUALLY, I'M- I'M PREGNANT AND I'M JUST- I'M NOT FEELING THAT WELL.
I'D JUST AS SOON JUST GET HOME IF IT'S ALL THE SAME TO YOU.
YOU'RE PREGNANT? OH MAN!
OH MAN!! I HAVE TO EXCHANGE INFO WITH YOU THEN.
FOR SURE.
NO, I'M-
MY BOSS WOULD LITERALLY KILL ME.
UGH!!

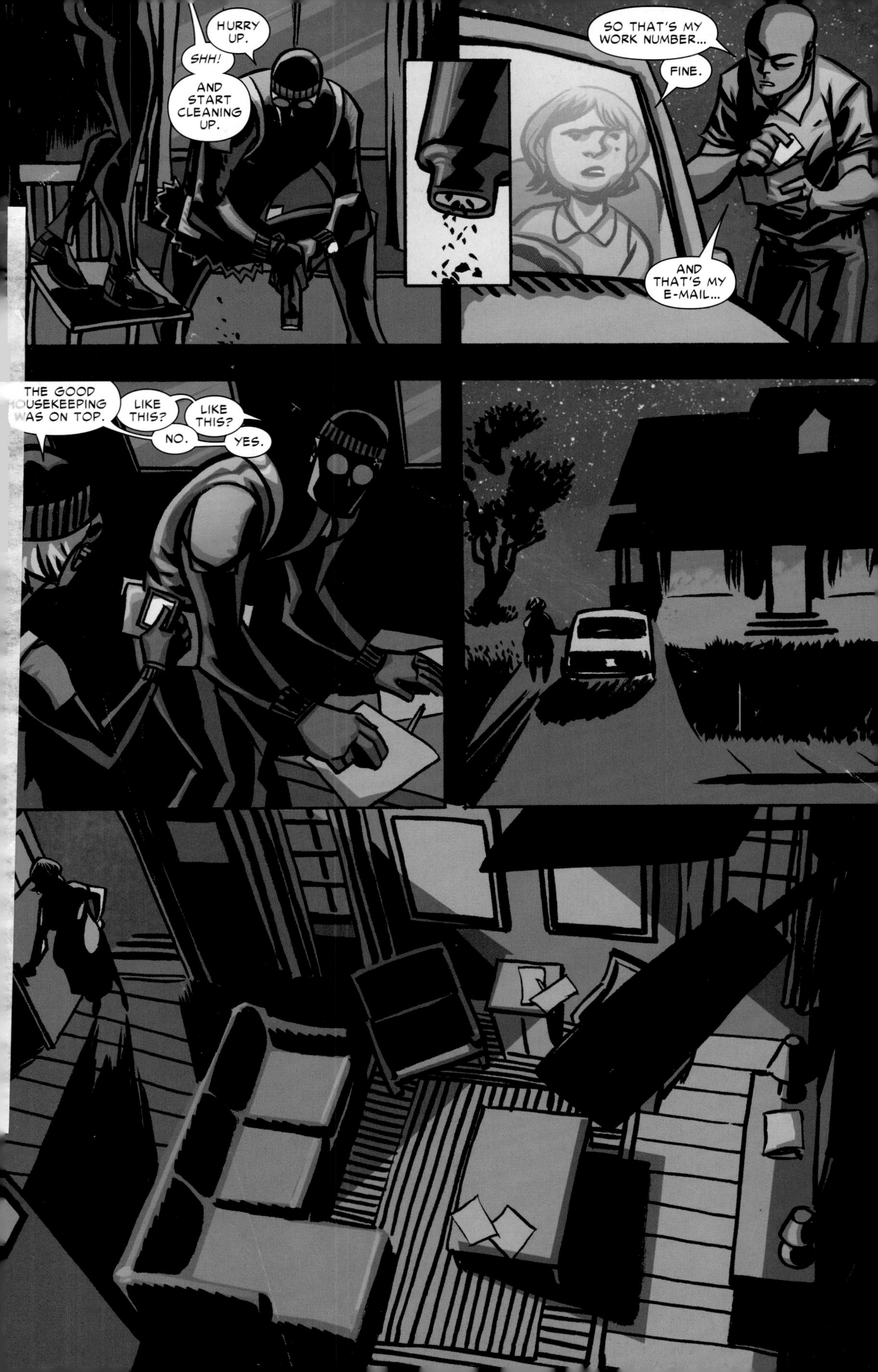
HURRY UP.
SHH!
AND START CLEANING UP.
SO THAT'S MY WORK NUMBER...
FINE.
AND THAT'S MY E-MAIL...
THE GOOD HOUSEKEEPING WAS ON TOP.
LIKE THIS?
NO.
LIKE THIS?
YES.

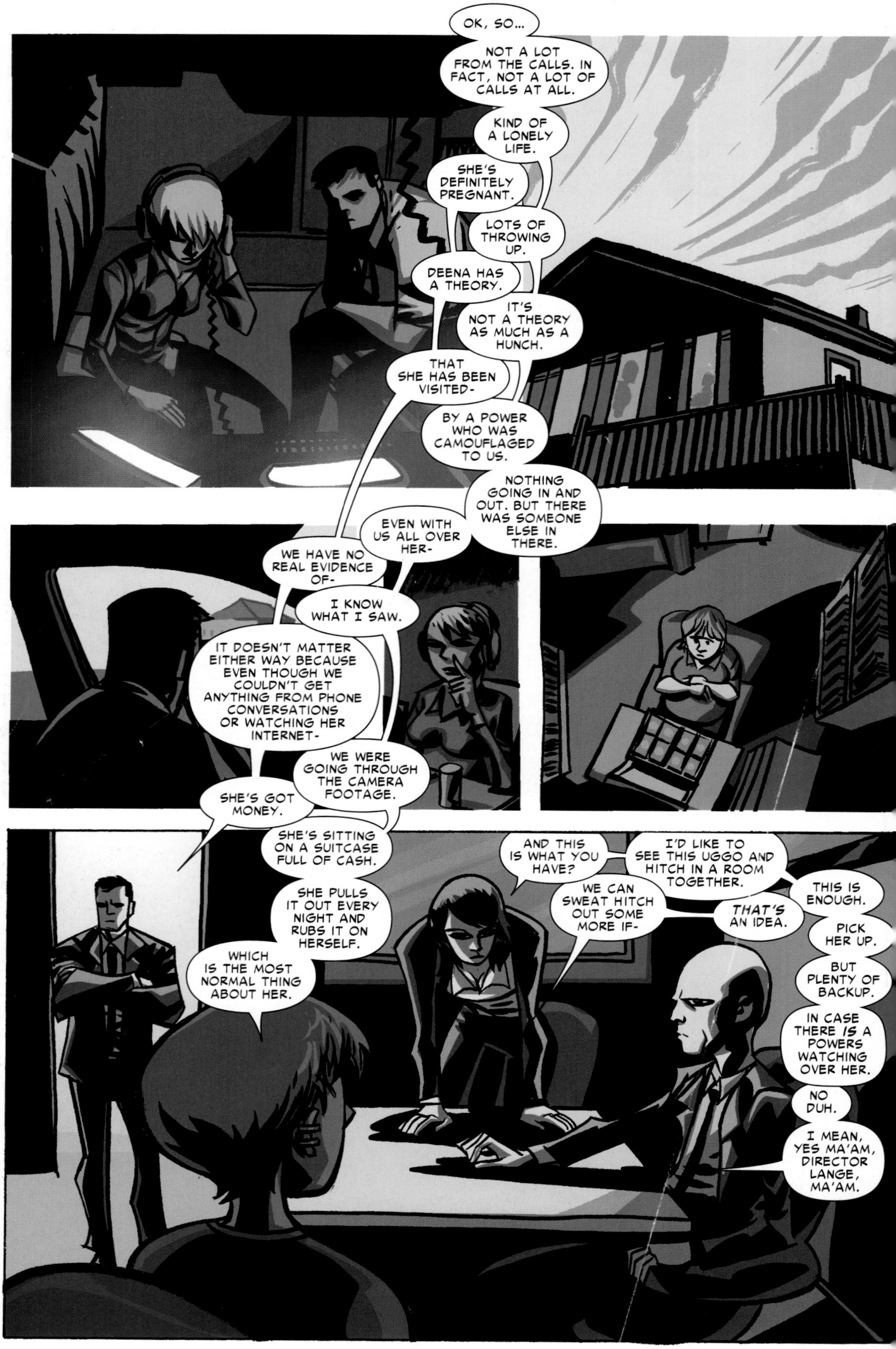
OK, SO...
NOT A LOT FROM THE CALLS. IN FACT, NOT A LOT OF CALLS AT ALL.
KIND OF A LONELY LIFE.
SHE'S DEFINITELY PREGNANT.
LOTS OF THROWING UP.
DEENA HAS A THEORY.
IT'S NOT A THEORY AS MUCH AS A HUNCH.
THAT SHE HAS BEEN VISITED-
BY A POWER WHO WAS CAMOUFLAGED TO US.
NOTHING GOING IN AND OUT. BUT THERE WAS SOMEONE ELSE IN THERE.
EVEN WITH US ALL OVER HER-
WE HAVE NO REAL EVIDENCE OF-
I KNOW WHAT I SAW.
IT DOESN'T MATTER EITHER WAY BECAUSE EVEN THOUGH WE COULDN'T GET ANYTHING FROM PHONE CONVERSATIONS OR WATCHING HER INTERNET-
WE WERE GOING THROUGH THE CAMERA FOOTAGE.
SHE'S GOT MONEY.
SHE'S SITTING ON A SUITCASE FULL OF CASH.
SHE PULLS IT OUT EVERY NIGHT AND RUBS IT ON HERSELF.
WHICH IS THE MOST NORMAL THING ABOUT HER.
AND THIS IS WHAT YOU HAVE?
I'D LIKE TO SEE THIS UGGO AND HITCH IN A ROOM TOGETHER.
WE CAN SWEAT HITCH OUT SOME MORE IF-
THAT'S AN IDEA.
THIS IS ENOUGH.
PICK HER UP.
BUT PLENTY OF BACKUP.
IN CASE THERE *IS* A POWERS WATCHING OVER HER.
NO DUH.
I MEAN, YES MA'AM, DIRECTOR LANGE, MA'AM.

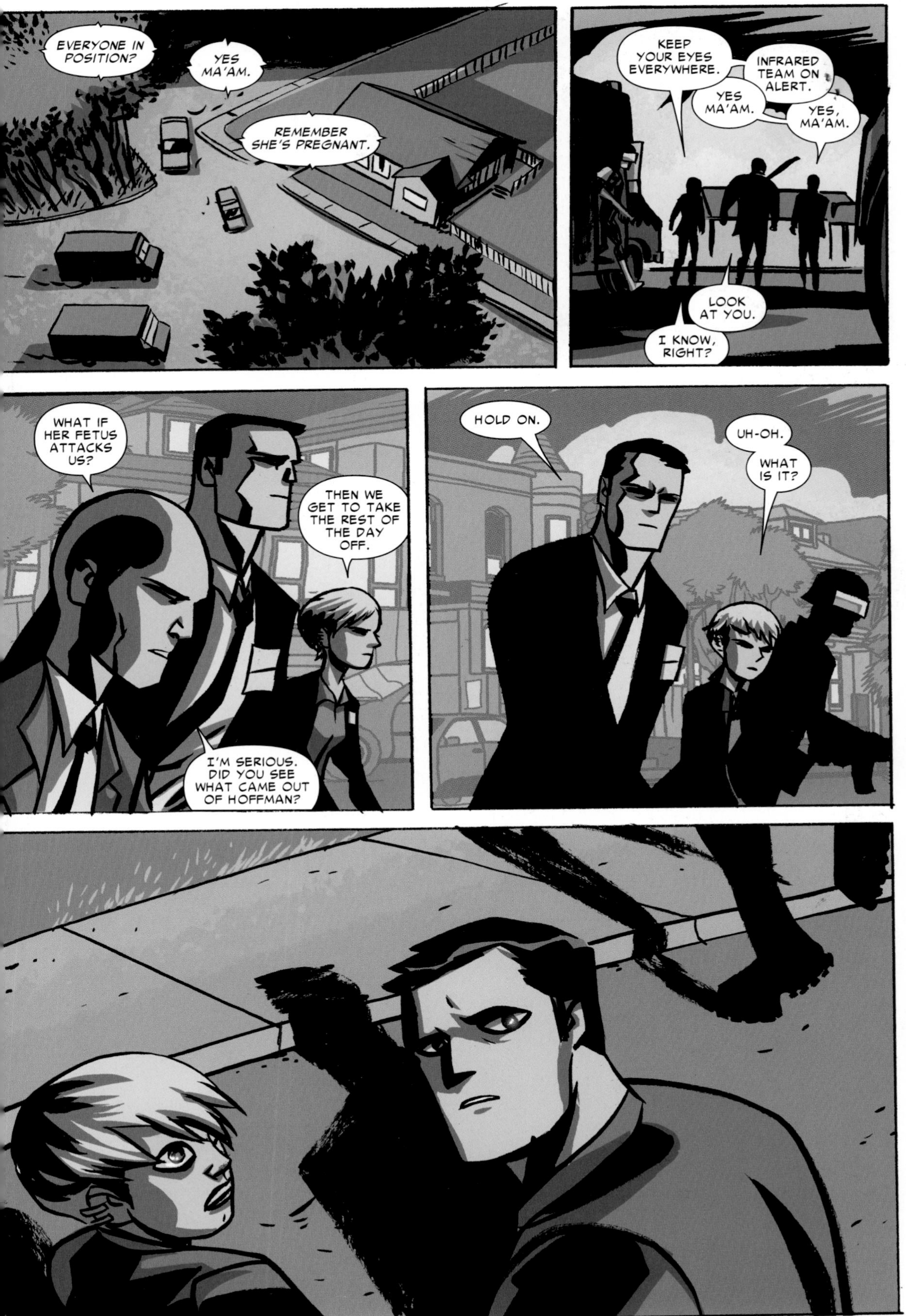

EVERYONE IN POSITION?
YES MA'AM.
REMEMBER SHE'S PREGNANT.
KEEP YOUR EYES EVERYWHERE.
INFRARED TEAM ON ALERT.
YES MA'AM.
YES, MA'AM.
LOOK AT YOU.
I KNOW, RIGHT?
WHAT IF HER FETUS ATTACKS US?
THEN WE GET TO TAKE THE REST OF THE DAY OFF.
I'M SERIOUS. DID YOU SEE WHAT CAME OUT OF HOFFMAN?
HOLD ON.
UH-OH.
WHAT IS IT?

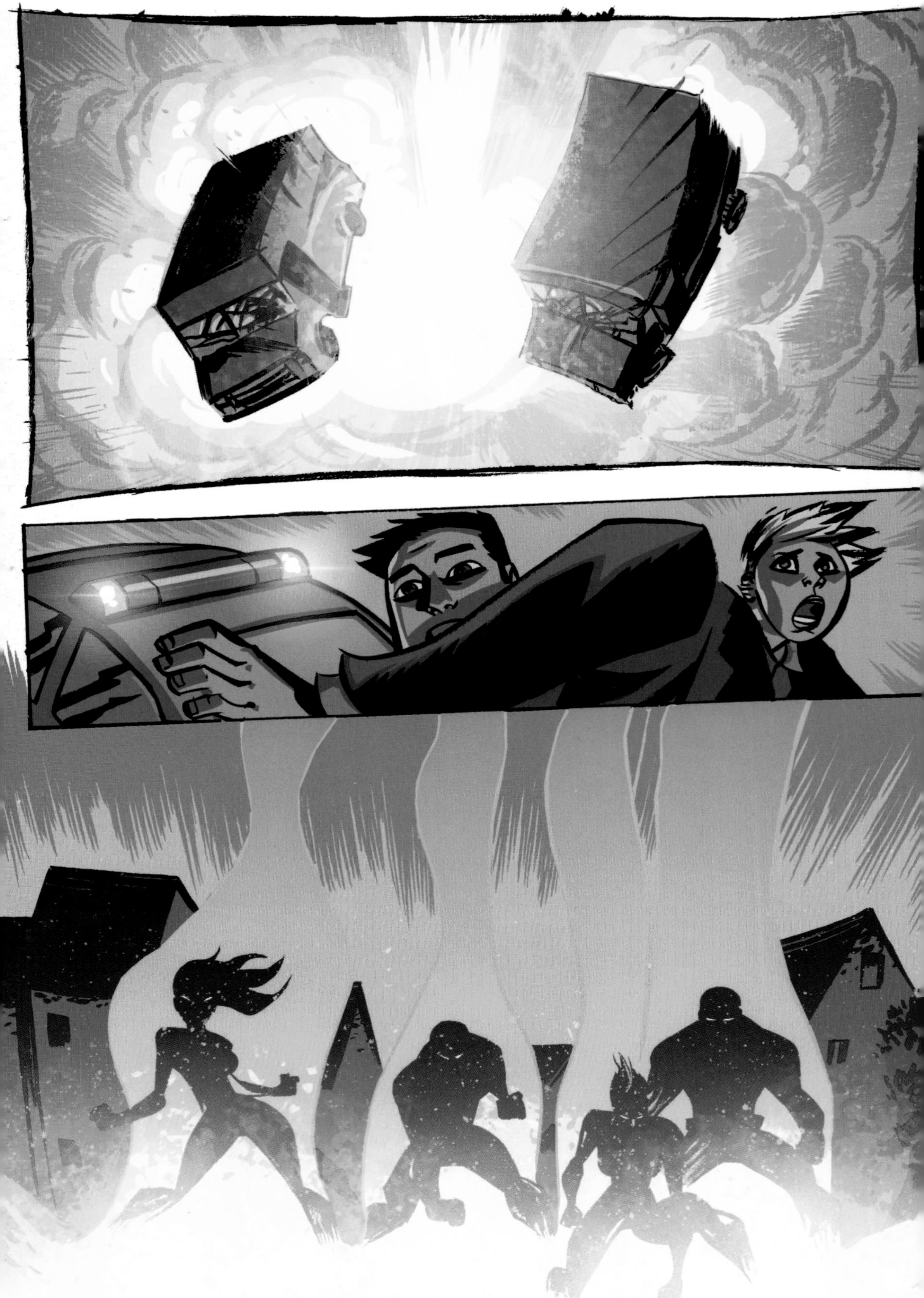

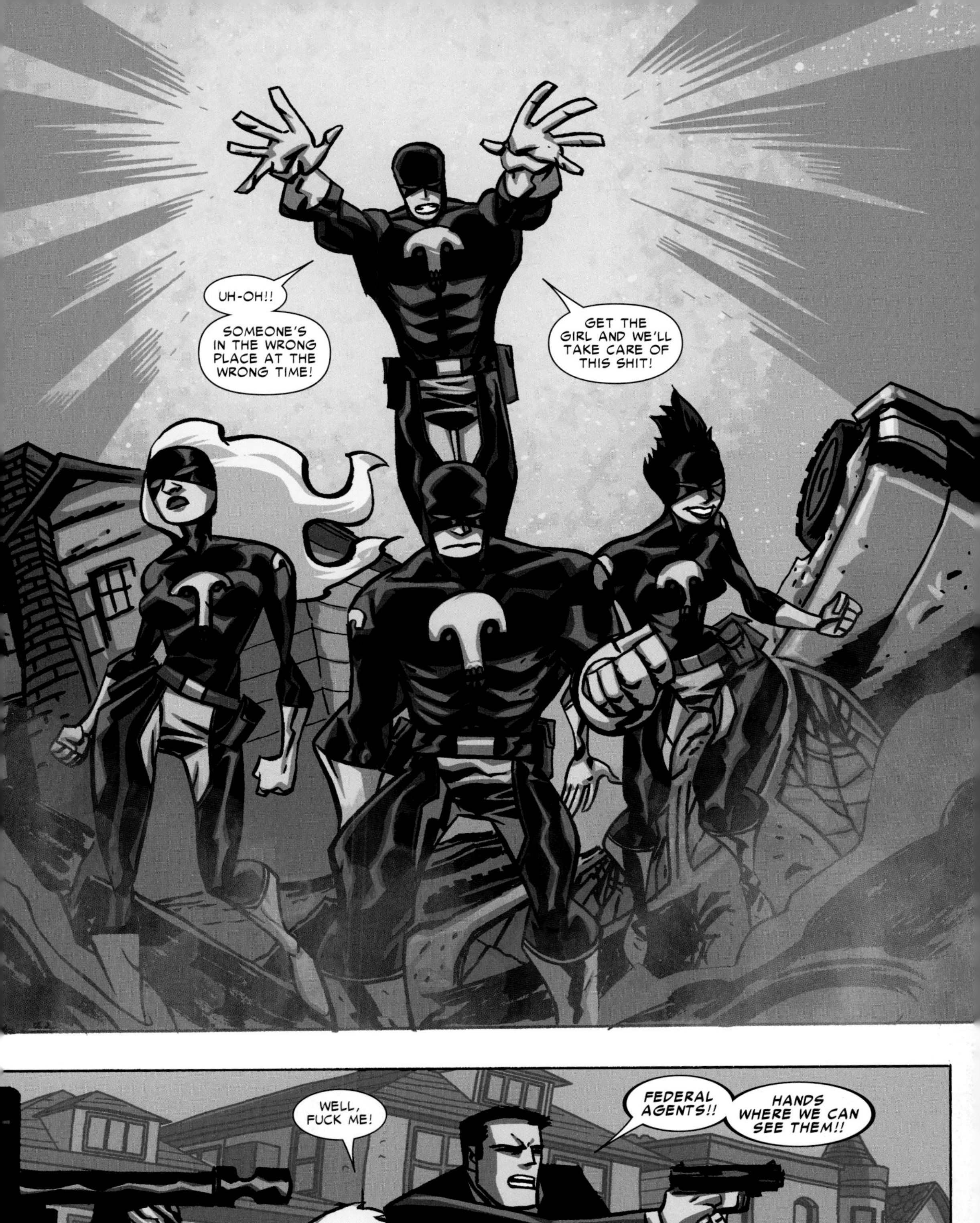
UH-OH!!
SOMEONE'S IN THE WRONG PLACE AT THE WRONG TIME!
GET THE GIRL AND WE'LL TAKE CARE OF THIS SHIT!

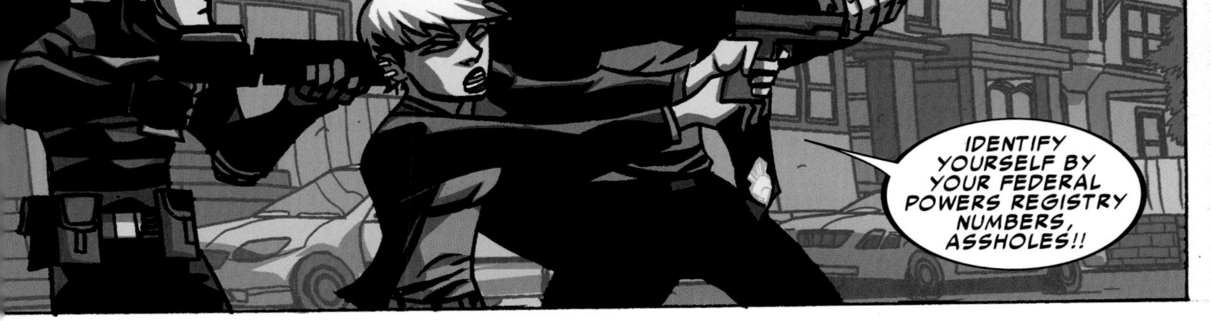
WELL, FUCK ME!
FEDERAL AGENTS!!
HANDS WHERE WE CAN SEE THEM!!
IDENTIFY YOURSELF BY YOUR FEDERAL POWERS REGISTRY NUMBERS, ASSHOLES!!

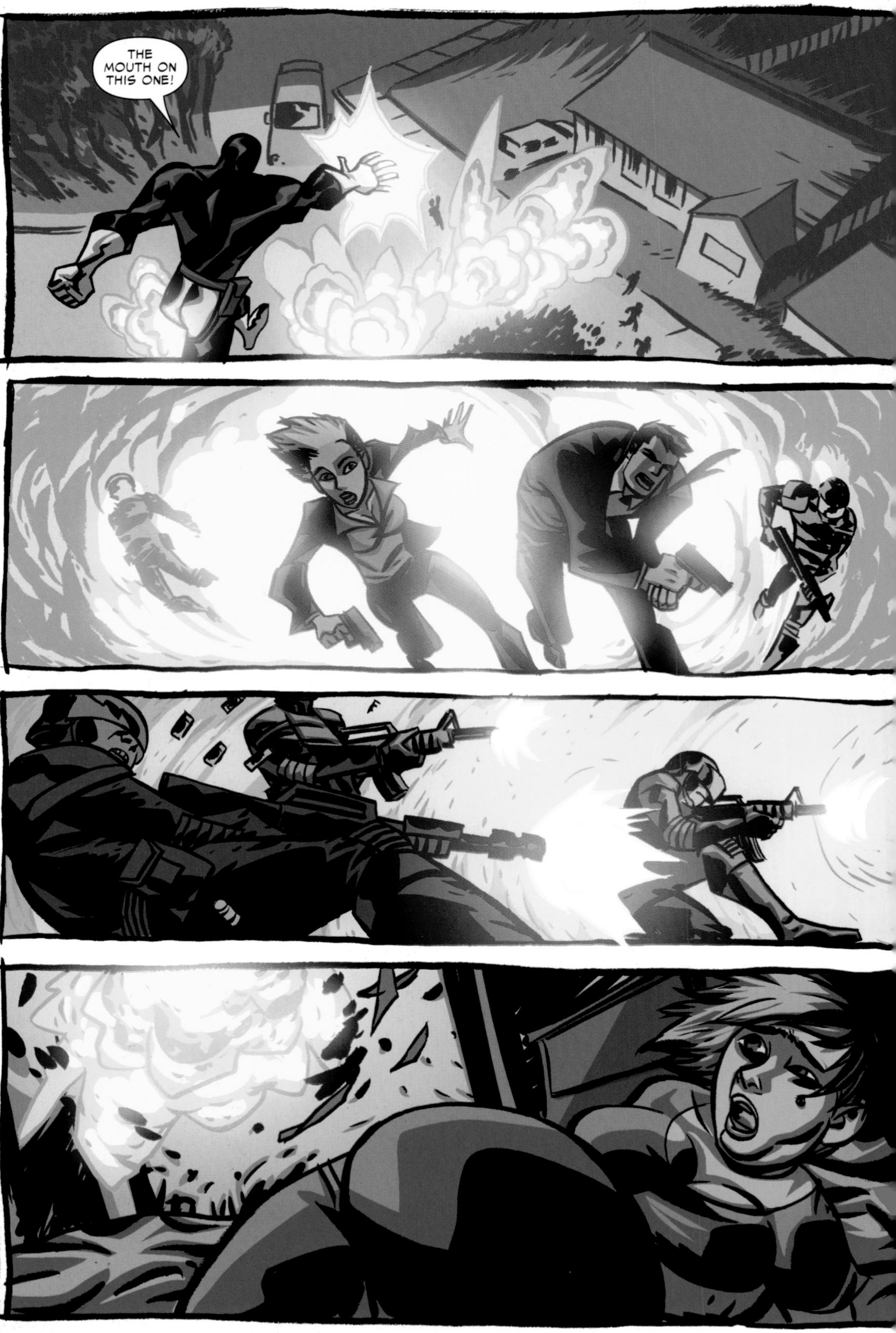
THE MOUTH ON THIS ONE!

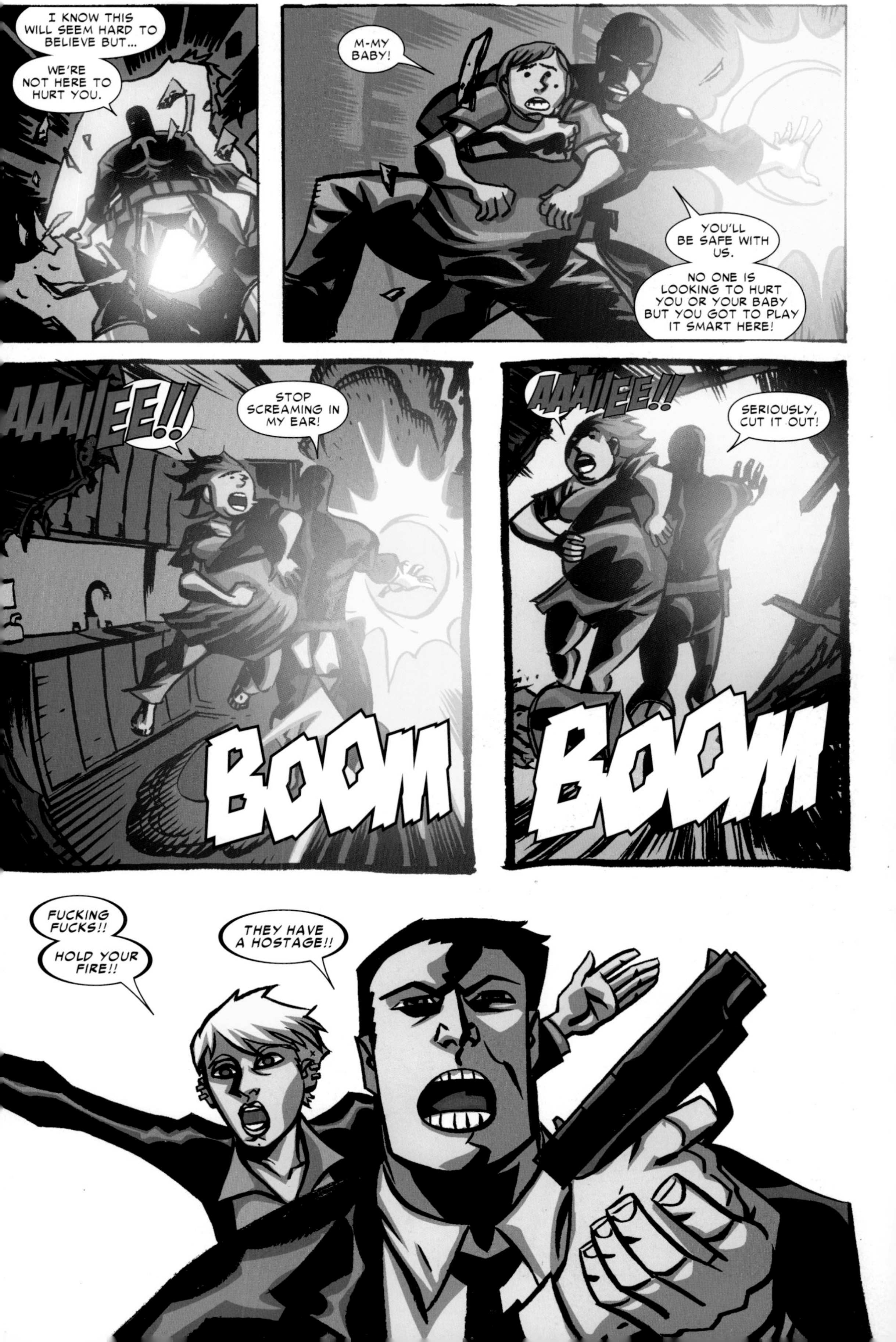
I KNOW THIS WILL SEEM HARD TO BELIEVE BUT...
WE'RE NOT HERE TO HURT YOU.
M-MY BABY!
YOU'LL BE SAFE WITH US.
NO ONE IS LOOKING TO HURT YOU OR YOUR BABY BUT YOU GOT TO PLAY IT SMART HERE!
AAAIIEE!!
STOP SCREAMING IN MY EAR!
BOOM
AAAIIEE!!
SERIOUSLY, CUT IT OUT!
BOOM
FUCKING FUCKS!!
HOLD YOUR FIRE!!
THEY HAVE A HOSTAGE!!

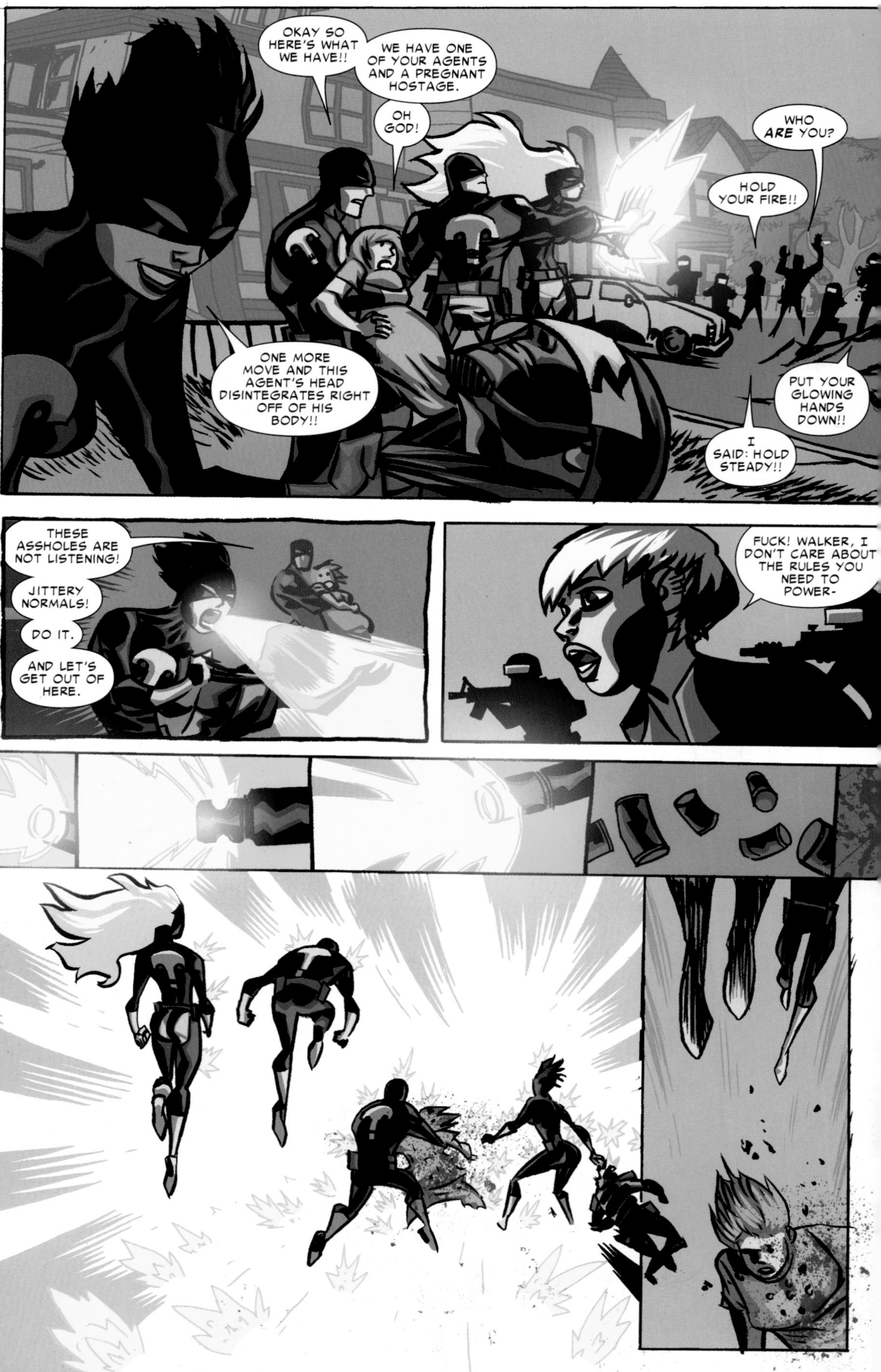

OKAY SO HERE'S WHAT WE HAVE!!
WE HAVE ONE OF YOUR AGENTS AND A PREGNANT HOSTAGE.
OH GOD!
WHO *ARE* YOU?
HOLD YOUR FIRE!!
ONE MORE MOVE AND THIS AGENT'S HEAD DISINTEGRATES RIGHT OFF OF HIS BODY!!
PUT YOUR GLOWING HANDS DOWN!!
I SAID: HOLD STEADY!!
THESE ASSHOLES ARE NOT LISTENING!
JITTERY NORMALS!
DO IT.
AND LET'S GET OUT OF HERE.
FUCK! WALKER, I DON'T CARE ABOUT THE RULES YOU NEED TO POWER-

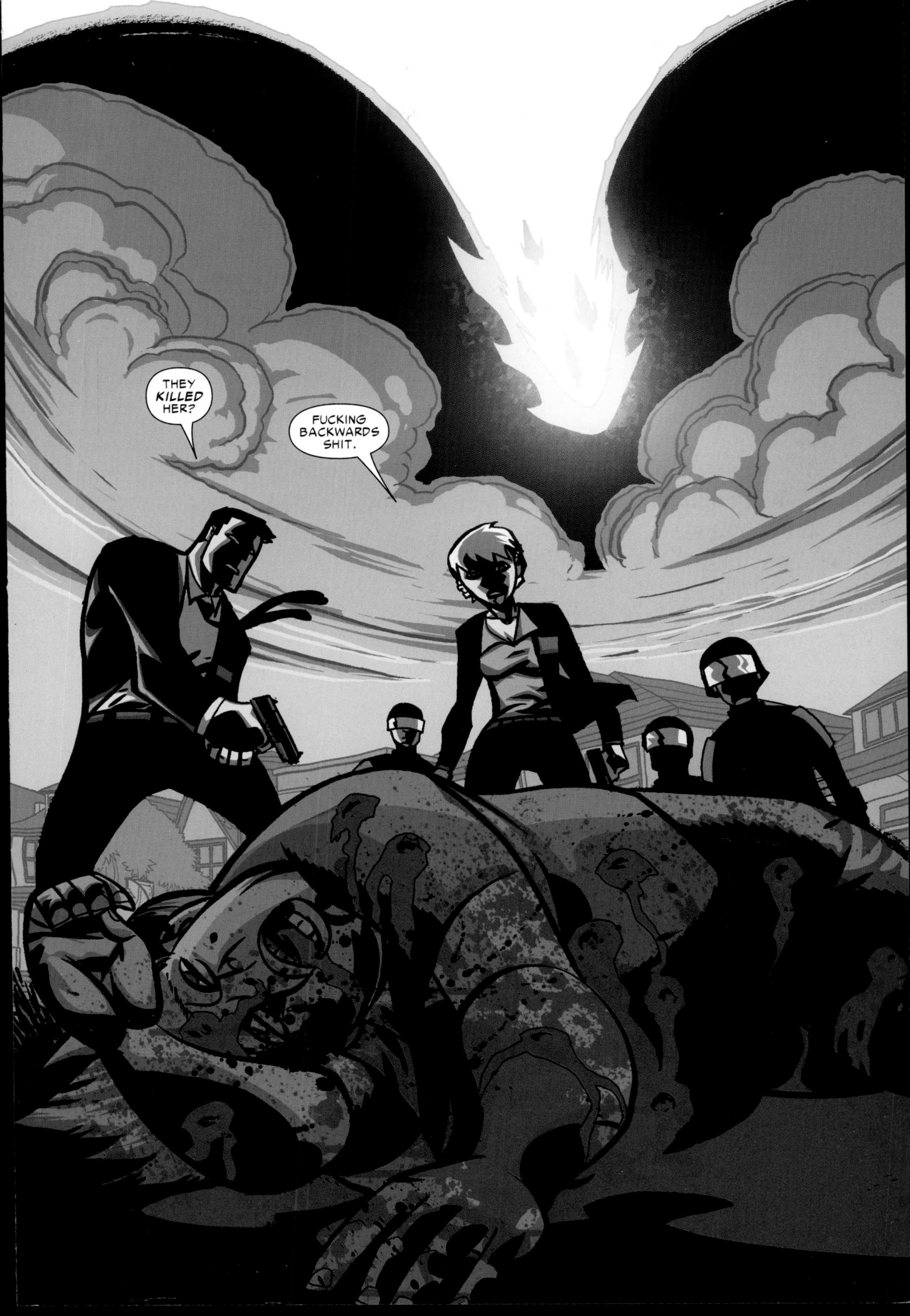
THEY *KILLED* HER?
FUCKING BACKWARDS SHIT.

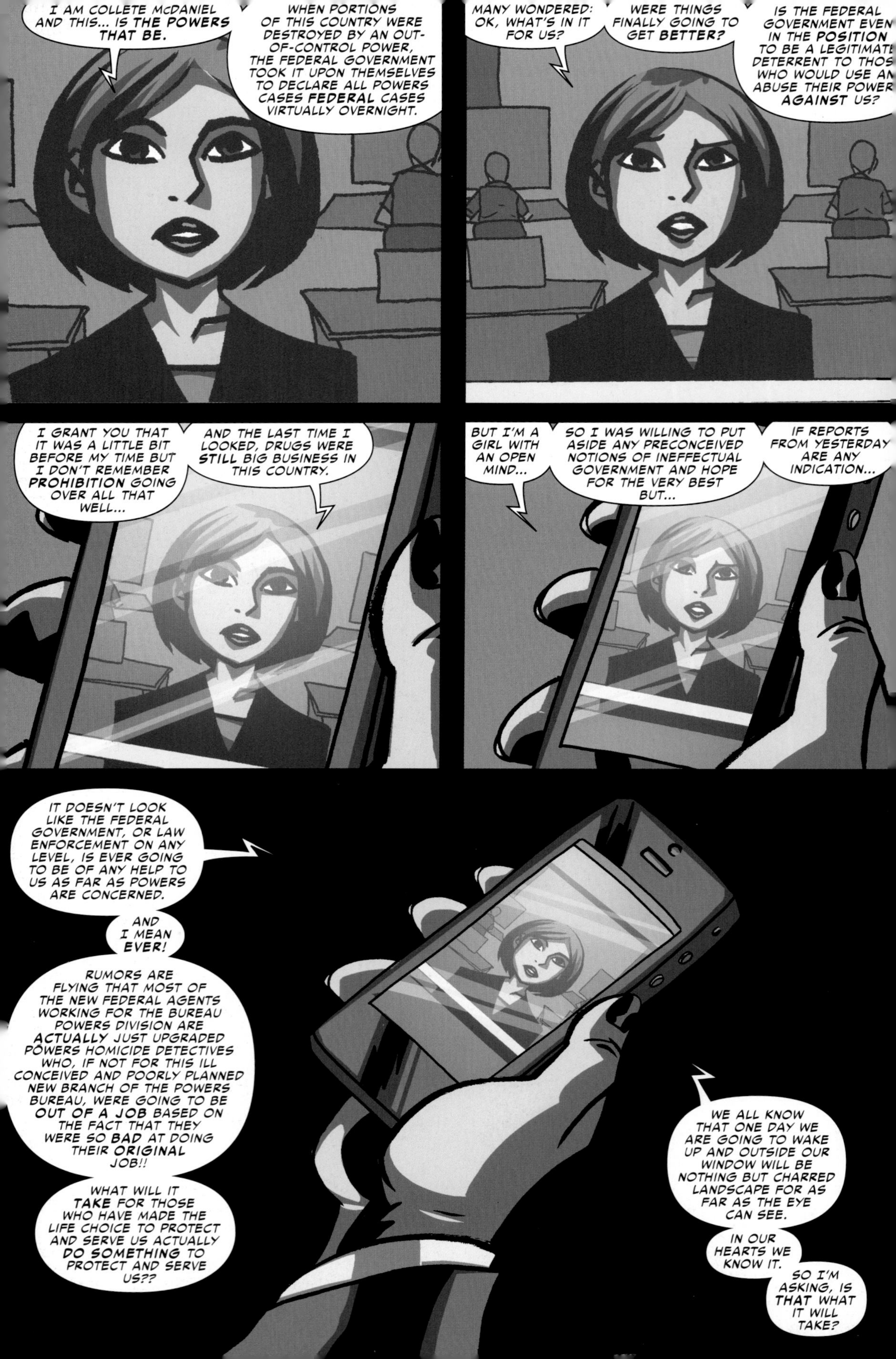
I AM COLLETE McDANIEL AND THIS... IS THE POWERS THAT BE.
WHEN PORTIONS OF THIS COUNTRY WERE DESTROYED BY AN OUT-OF-CONTROL POWER, THE FEDERAL GOVERNMENT TOOK IT UPON THEMSELVES TO DECLARE ALL POWERS CASES FEDERAL CASES VIRTUALLY OVERNIGHT.
MANY WONDERED: OK, WHAT'S IN IT FOR US?
WERE THINGS FINALLY GOING TO GET BETTER?
IS THE FEDERAL GOVERNMENT EVEN IN THE POSITION TO BE A LEGITIMATE DETERRENT TO THOSE WHO WOULD USE AND ABUSE THEIR POWER AGAINST US?
I GRANT YOU THAT IT WAS A LITTLE BIT BEFORE MY TIME BUT I DON'T REMEMBER PROHIBITION GOING OVER ALL THAT WELL...
AND THE LAST TIME I LOOKED, DRUGS WERE STILL BIG BUSINESS IN THIS COUNTRY.
BUT I'M A GIRL WITH AN OPEN MIND...
SO I WAS WILLING TO PUT ASIDE ANY PRECONCEIVED NOTIONS OF INEFFECTUAL GOVERNMENT AND HOPE FOR THE VERY BEST BUT...
IF REPORTS FROM YESTERDAY ARE ANY INDICATION...
IT DOESN'T LOOK LIKE THE FEDERAL GOVERNMENT, OR LAW ENFORCEMENT ON ANY LEVEL, IS EVER GOING TO BE OF ANY HELP TO US AS FAR AS POWERS ARE CONCERNED.
AND I MEAN EVER!
RUMORS ARE FLYING THAT MOST OF THE NEW FEDERAL AGENTS WORKING FOR THE BUREAU POWERS DIVISION ARE ACTUALLY JUST UPGRADED POWERS HOMICIDE DETECTIVES WHO, IF NOT FOR THIS ILL CONCEIVED AND POORLY PLANNED NEW BRANCH OF THE POWERS BUREAU, WERE GOING TO BE OUT OF A JOB BASED ON THE FACT THAT THEY WERE SO BAD AT DOING THEIR ORIGINAL JOB!!
WHAT WILL IT TAKE FOR THOSE WHO HAVE MADE THE LIFE CHOICE TO PROTECT AND SERVE US ACTUALLY DO SOMETHING TO PROTECT AND SERVE US??
WE ALL KNOW THAT ONE DAY WE ARE GOING TO WAKE UP AND OUTSIDE OUR WINDOW WILL BE NOTHING BUT CHARRED LANDSCAPE FOR AS FAR AS THE EYE CAN SEE.
IN OUR HEARTS WE KNOW IT.
SO I'M ASKING, IS THAT WHAT IT WILL TAKE?

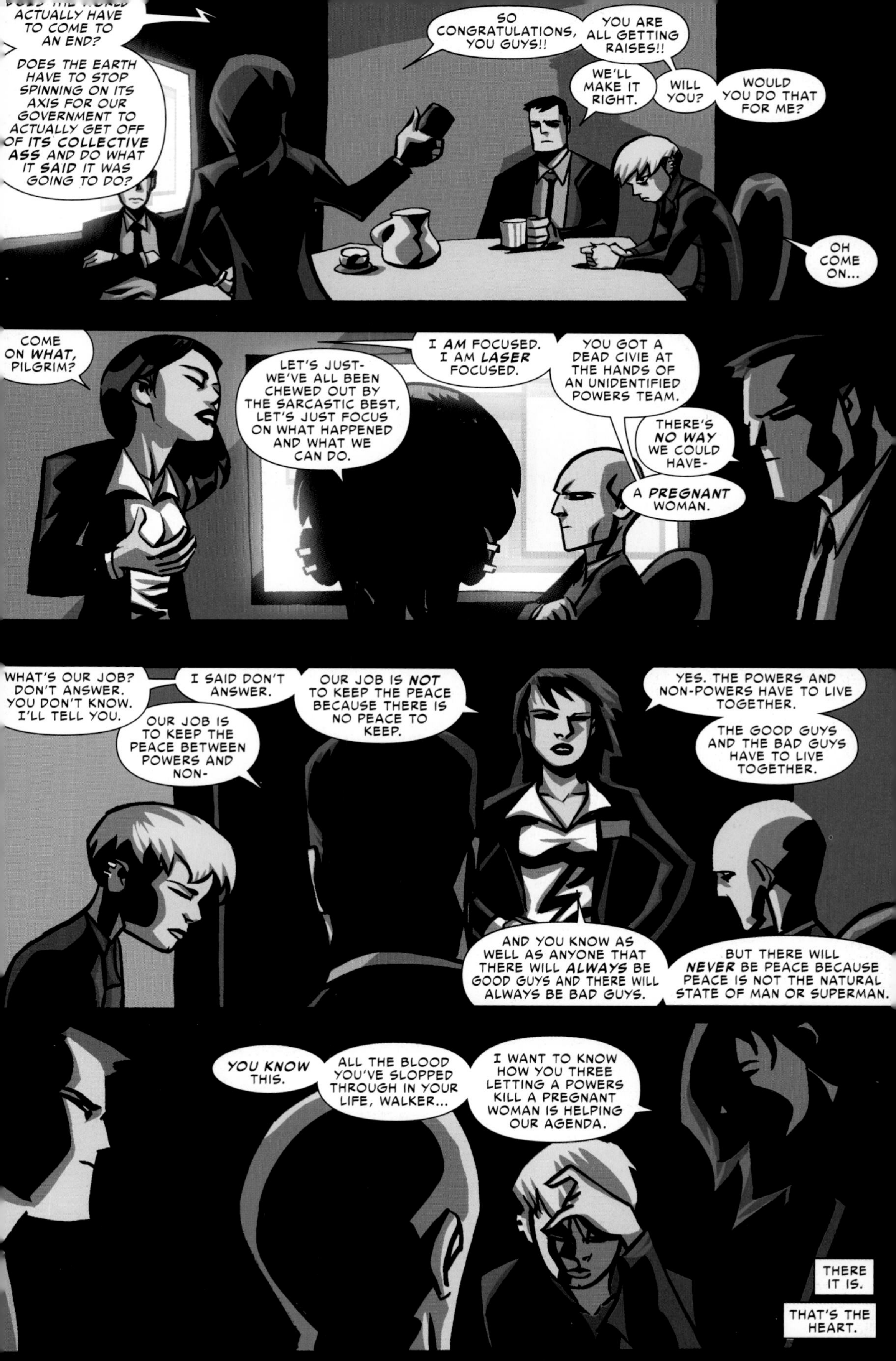
ACTUALLY HAVE TO COME TO AN END?
DOES THE EARTH HAVE TO STOP SPINNING ON ITS AXIS FOR OUR GOVERNMENT TO ACTUALLY GET OFF OF ITS COLLECTIVE ASS AND DO WHAT IT SAID IT WAS GOING TO DO?
SO CONGRATULATIONS, YOU GUYS!!
YOU ARE ALL GETTING RAISES!!
WE'LL MAKE IT RIGHT.
WILL YOU?
WOULD YOU DO THAT FOR ME?
OH COME ON...
COME ON WHAT, PILGRIM?
LET'S JUST- WE'VE ALL BEEN CHEWED OUT BY THE SARCASTIC BEST, LET'S JUST FOCUS ON WHAT HAPPENED AND WHAT WE CAN DO.
I AM FOCUSED. I AM LASER FOCUSED.
YOU GOT A DEAD CIVIE AT THE HANDS OF AN UNIDENTIFIED POWERS TEAM.
THERE'S NO WAY WE COULD HAVE-
A PREGNANT WOMAN.
WHAT'S OUR JOB? DON'T ANSWER. YOU DON'T KNOW. I'LL TELL YOU.
I SAID DON'T ANSWER.
OUR JOB IS TO KEEP THE PEACE BETWEEN POWERS AND NON-
OUR JOB IS NOT TO KEEP THE PEACE BECAUSE THERE IS NO PEACE TO KEEP.
YES. THE POWERS AND NON-POWERS HAVE TO LIVE TOGETHER.
THE GOOD GUYS AND THE BAD GUYS HAVE TO LIVE TOGETHER.
AND YOU KNOW AS WELL AS ANYONE THAT THERE WILL ALWAYS BE GOOD GUYS AND THERE WILL ALWAYS BE BAD GUYS.
BUT THERE WILL NEVER BE PEACE BECAUSE PEACE IS NOT THE NATURAL STATE OF MAN OR SUPERMAN.
YOU KNOW THIS.
ALL THE BLOOD YOU'VE SLOPPED THROUGH IN YOUR LIFE, WALKER...
I WANT TO KNOW HOW YOU THREE LETTING A POWERS KILL A PREGNANT WOMAN IS HELPING OUR AGENDA.
THERE IT IS.
THAT'S THE HEART.

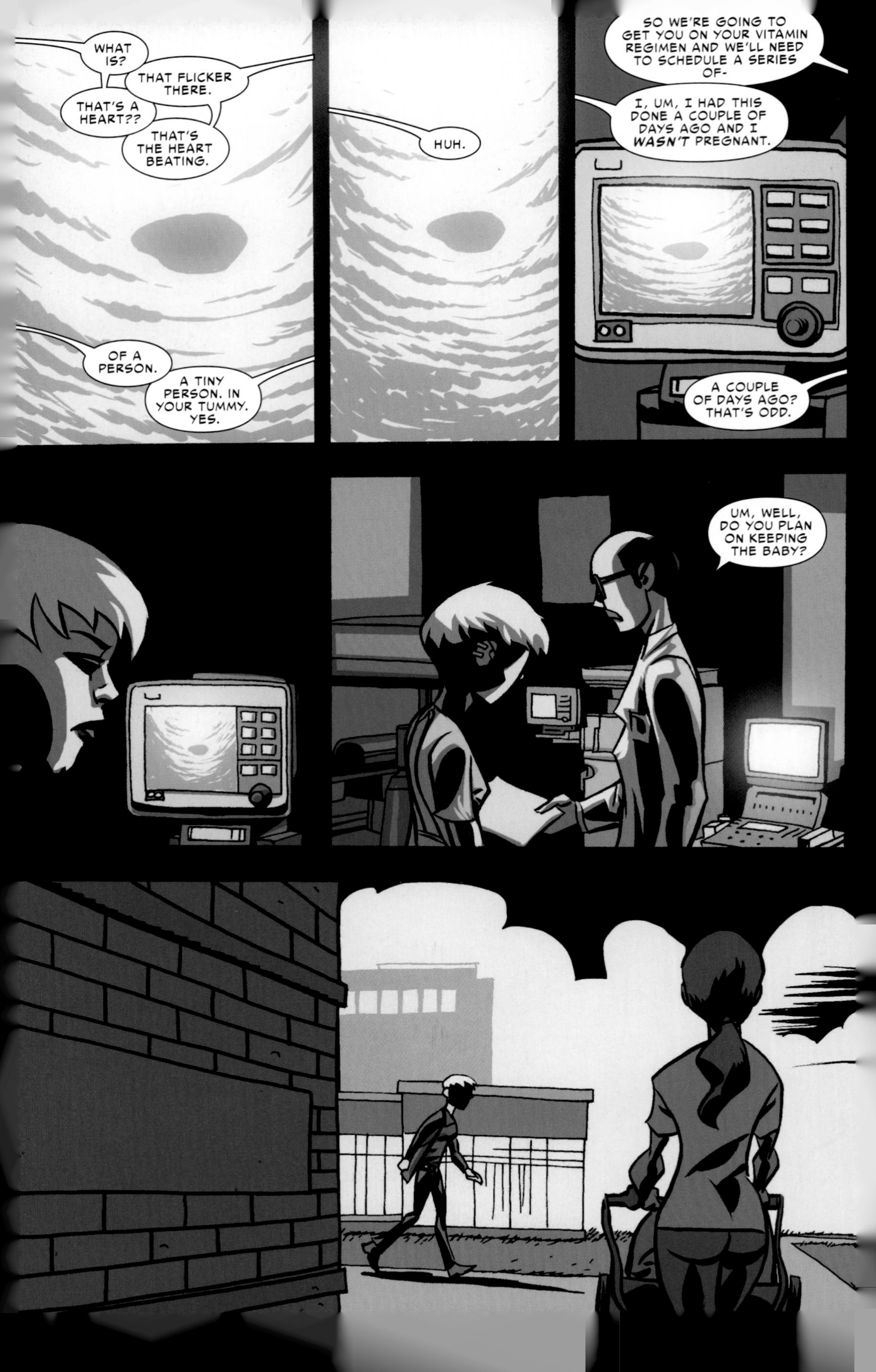
WHAT IS?
THAT FLICKER THERE.
THAT'S A HEART??
THAT'S THE HEART BEATING.
OF A PERSON.
A TINY PERSON. IN YOUR TUMMY. YES.
HUH.
SO WE'RE GOING TO GET YOU ON YOUR VITAMIN REGIMEN AND WE'LL NEED TO SCHEDULE A SERIES OF-
I, UM, I HAD THIS DONE A COUPLE OF DAYS AGO AND I WASN'T PREGNANT.
A COUPLE OF DAYS AGO? THAT'S ODD.
UM, WELL, DO YOU PLAN ON KEEPING THE BABY?

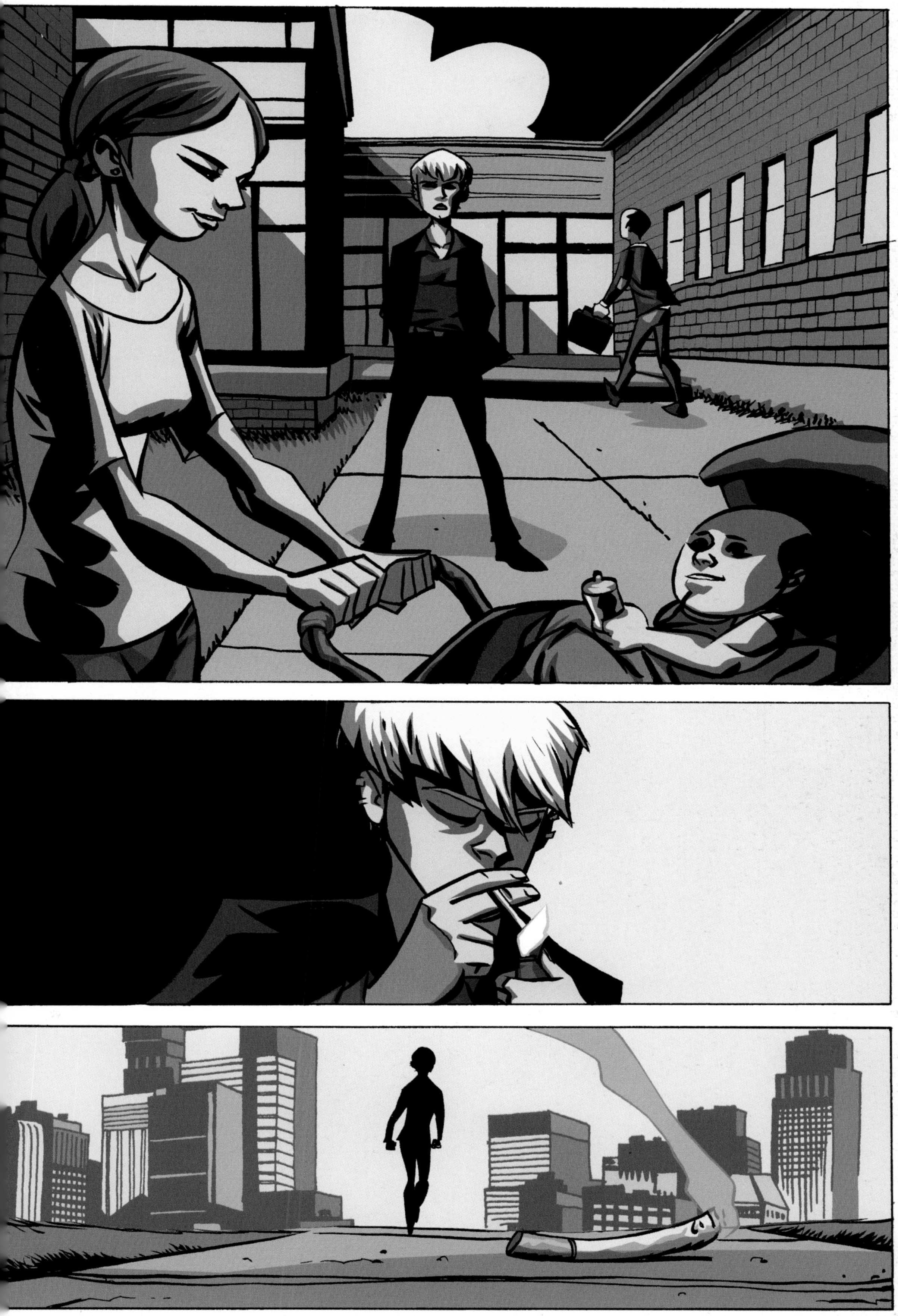

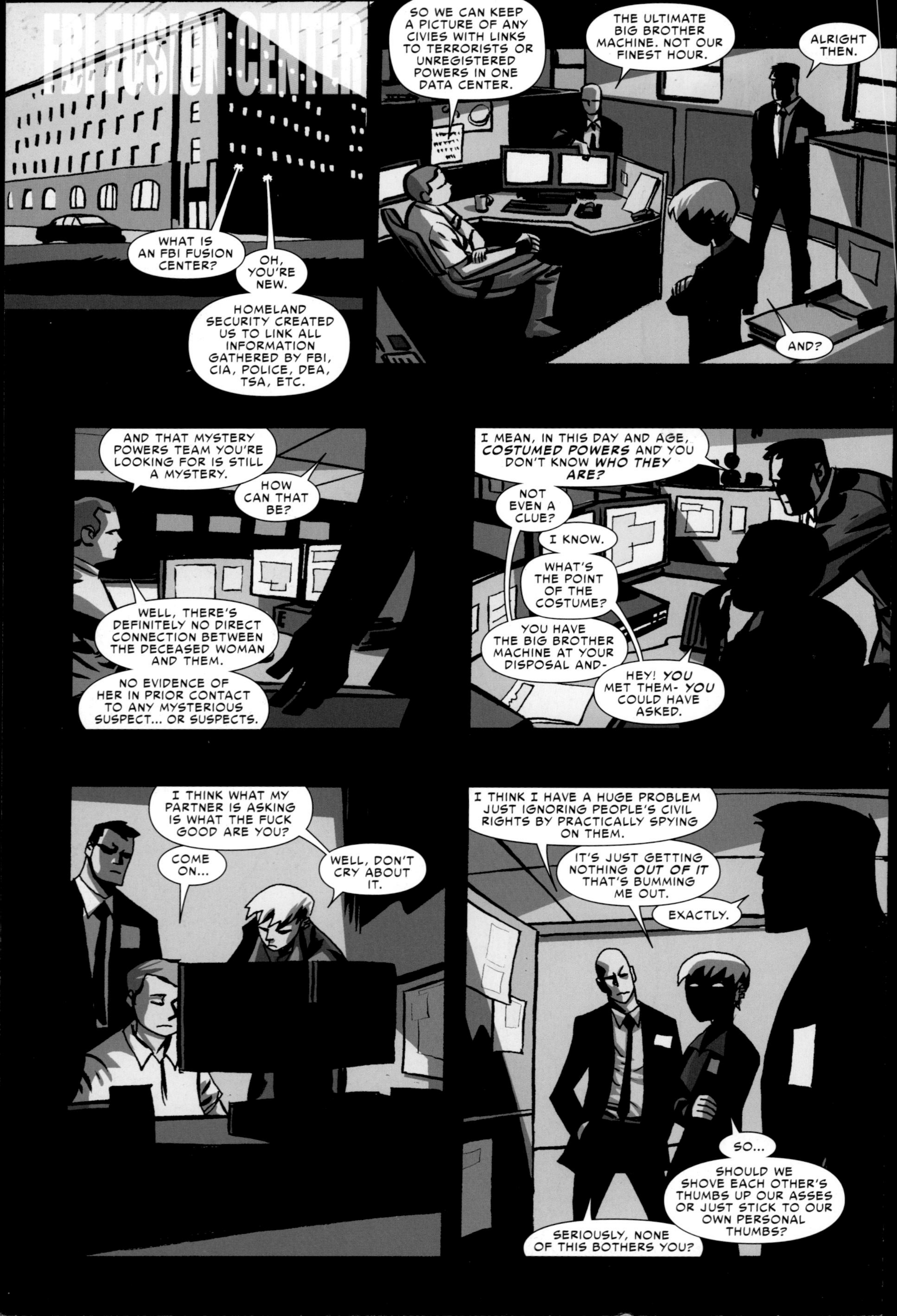
FBI FUSION CENTER
WHAT IS AN FBI FUSION CENTER?
OH, YOU'RE NEW.
HOMELAND SECURITY CREATED US TO LINK ALL INFORMATION GATHERED BY FBI, CIA, POLICE, DEA, TSA, ETC.
SO WE CAN KEEP A PICTURE OF ANY CIVIES WITH LINKS TO TERRORISTS OR UNREGISTERED POWERS IN ONE DATA CENTER.
THE ULTIMATE BIG BROTHER MACHINE. NOT OUR FINEST HOUR.
ALRIGHT THEN.
AND?
AND THAT MYSTERY POWERS TEAM YOU'RE LOOKING FOR IS STILL A MYSTERY.
HOW CAN THAT BE?
WELL, THERE'S DEFINITELY NO DIRECT CONNECTION BETWEEN THE DECEASED WOMAN AND THEM.
NO EVIDENCE OF HER IN PRIOR CONTACT TO ANY MYSTERIOUS SUSPECT... OR SUSPECTS.
I MEAN, IN THIS DAY AND AGE, COSTUMED POWERS AND YOU DON'T KNOW WHO THEY ARE?
NOT EVEN A CLUE?
I KNOW.
WHAT'S THE POINT OF THE COSTUME?
YOU HAVE THE BIG BROTHER MACHINE AT YOUR DISPOSAL AND-
HEY! YOU MET THEM- YOU COULD HAVE ASKED.
I THINK WHAT MY PARTNER IS ASKING IS WHAT THE FUCK GOOD ARE YOU?
COME ON...
WELL, DON'T CRY ABOUT IT.
I THINK I HAVE A HUGE PROBLEM JUST IGNORING PEOPLE'S CIVIL RIGHTS BY PRACTICALLY SPYING ON THEM.
IT'S JUST GETTING NOTHING OUT OF IT THAT'S BUMMING ME OUT.
EXACTLY.
SO...
SHOULD WE SHOVE EACH OTHER'S THUMBS UP OUR ASSES OR JUST STICK TO OUR OWN PERSONAL THUMBS?
SERIOUSLY, NONE OF THIS BOTHERS YOU?

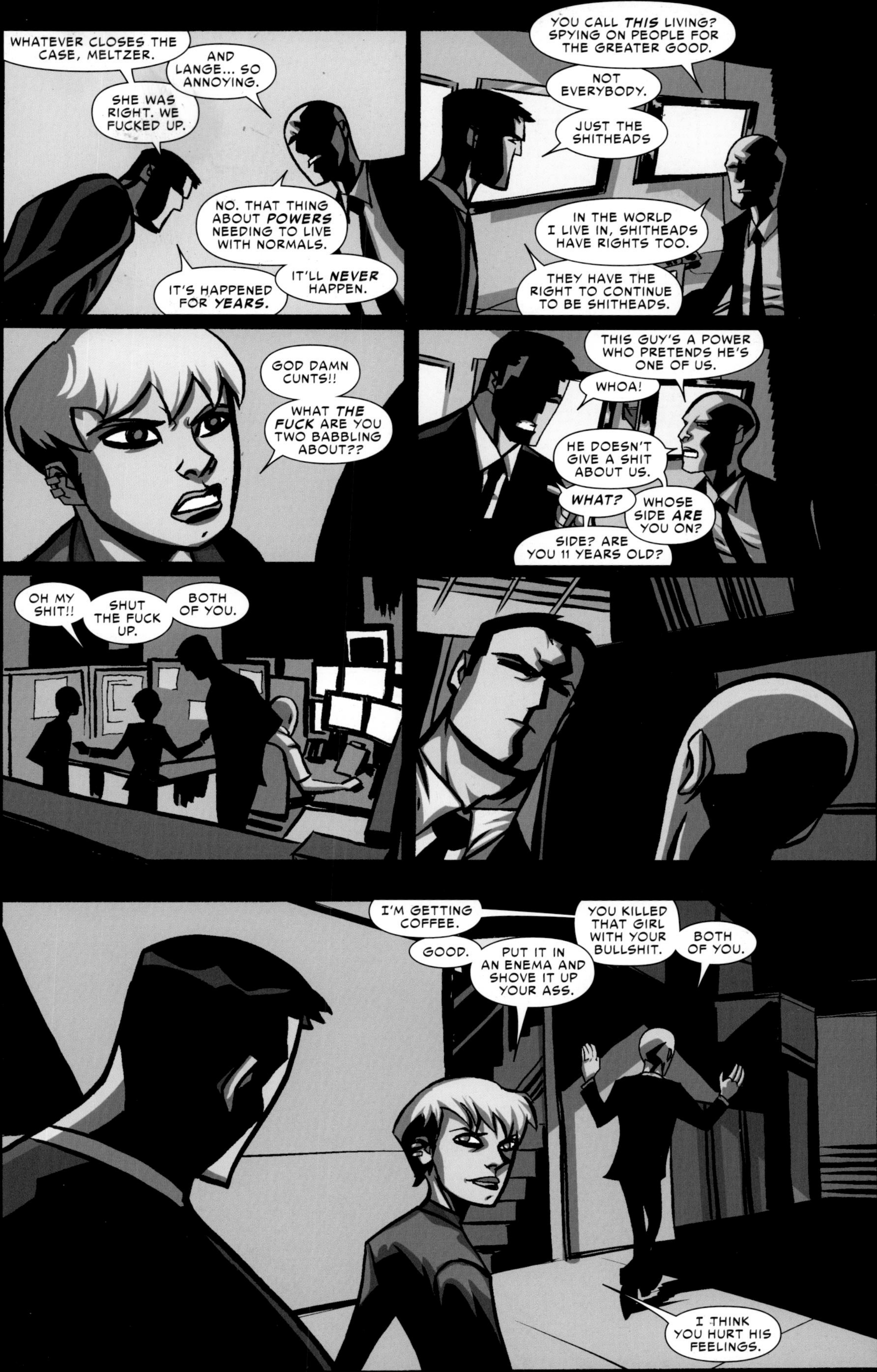
WHATEVER CLOSES THE CASE, MELTZER.
AND LANGE... SO ANNOYING.
SHE WAS RIGHT. WE FUCKED UP.
NO. THAT THING ABOUT POWERS NEEDING TO LIVE WITH NORMALS.
IT'LL NEVER HAPPEN.
IT'S HAPPENED FOR YEARS.
YOU CALL THIS LIVING? SPYING ON PEOPLE FOR THE GREATER GOOD.
NOT EVERYBODY.
JUST THE SHITHEADS
IN THE WORLD I LIVE IN, SHITHEADS HAVE RIGHTS TOO.
THEY HAVE THE RIGHT TO CONTINUE TO BE SHITHEADS.
GOD DAMN CUNTS!!
WHAT THE FUCK ARE YOU TWO BABBLING ABOUT??
THIS GUY'S A POWER WHO PRETENDS HE'S ONE OF US.
WHOA!
HE DOESN'T GIVE A SHIT ABOUT US.
WHAT?
WHOSE SIDE ARE YOU ON?
SIDE? ARE YOU 11 YEARS OLD?
OH MY SHIT!!
SHUT THE FUCK UP.
BOTH OF YOU.
I'M GETTING COFFEE.
YOU KILLED THAT GIRL WITH YOUR BULLSHIT.
BOTH OF YOU.
GOOD.
PUT IT IN AN ENEMA AND SHOVE IT UP YOUR ASS.
I THINK YOU HURT HIS FEELINGS.

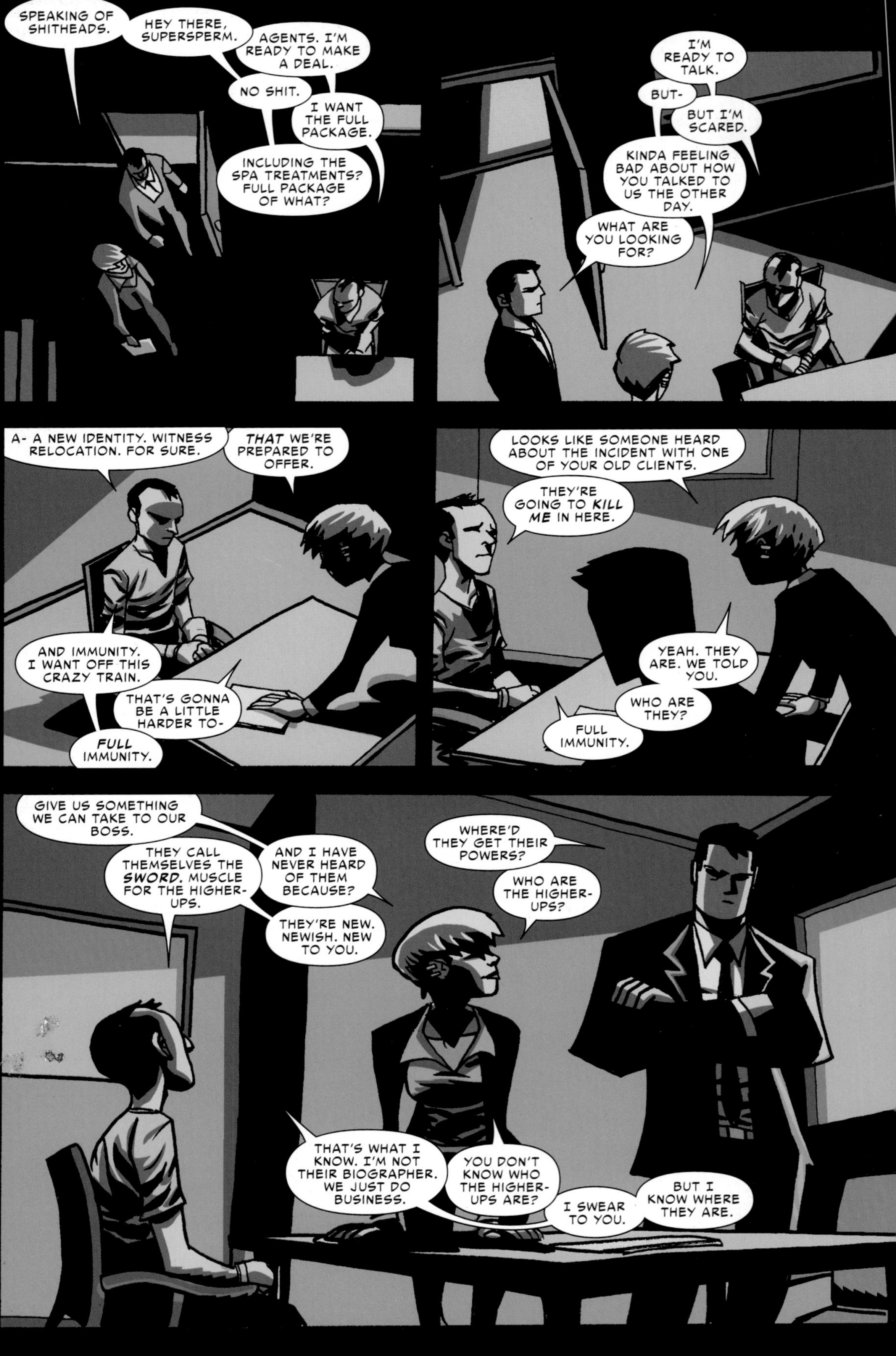
SPEAKING OF SHITHEADS.
HEY THERE, SUPERSPERM.
AGENTS. I'M READY TO MAKE A DEAL.
NO SHIT.
I WANT THE FULL PACKAGE.
INCLUDING THE SPA TREATMENTS? FULL PACKAGE OF WHAT?
I'M READY TO TALK.
BUT-
BUT I'M SCARED.
KINDA FEELING BAD ABOUT HOW YOU TALKED TO US THE OTHER DAY.
WHAT ARE YOU LOOKING FOR?
A- A NEW IDENTITY. WITNESS RELOCATION. FOR SURE.
THAT WE'RE PREPARED TO OFFER.
AND IMMUNITY. I WANT OFF THIS CRAZY TRAIN.
THAT'S GONNA BE A LITTLE HARDER TO-
FULL IMMUNITY.
LOOKS LIKE SOMEONE HEARD ABOUT THE INCIDENT WITH ONE OF YOUR OLD CLIENTS.
THEY'RE GOING TO *KILL ME* IN HERE.
YEAH. THEY ARE. WE TOLD YOU.
WHO ARE THEY?
FULL IMMUNITY.
GIVE US SOMETHING WE CAN TAKE TO OUR BOSS.
THEY CALL THEMSELVES THE *SWORD.* MUSCLE FOR THE HIGHER-UPS.
AND I HAVE NEVER HEARD OF THEM BECAUSE?
THEY'RE NEW. NEWISH. NEW TO YOU.
WHERE'D THEY GET THEIR POWERS?
WHO ARE THE HIGHER-UPS?
THAT'S WHAT I KNOW. I'M NOT THEIR BIOGRAPHER. WE JUST DO BUSINESS.
YOU DON'T KNOW WHO THE HIGHER-UPS ARE?
I SWEAR TO YOU.
BUT I KNOW WHERE THEY ARE.

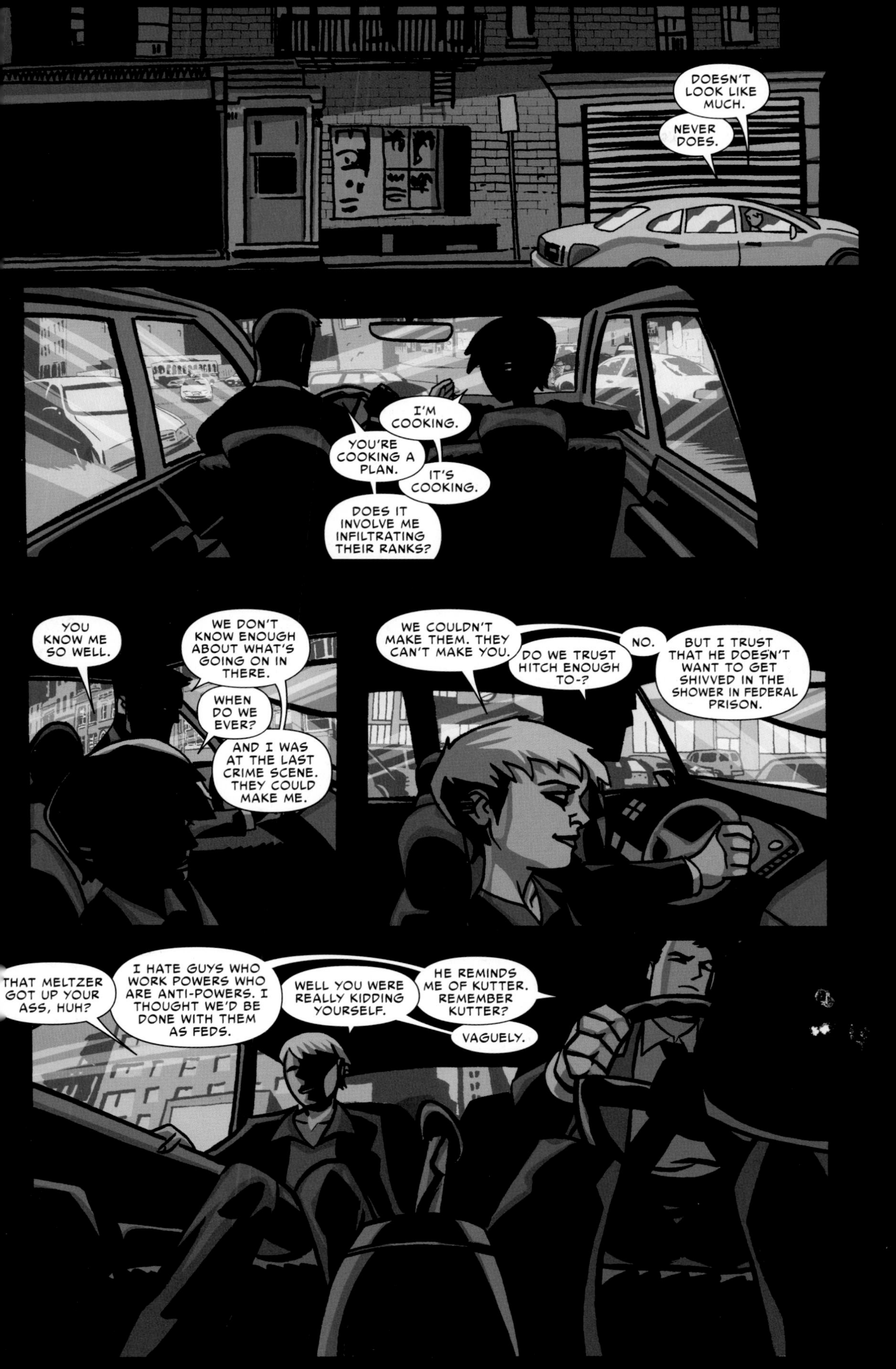
DOESN'T LOOK LIKE MUCH.
NEVER DOES.
I'M COOKING.
YOU'RE COOKING A PLAN.
IT'S COOKING.
DOES IT INVOLVE ME INFILTRATING THEIR RANKS?
YOU KNOW ME SO WELL.
WE DON'T KNOW ENOUGH ABOUT WHAT'S GOING ON IN THERE.
WHEN DO WE EVER?
AND I WAS AT THE LAST CRIME SCENE. THEY COULD MAKE ME.
WE COULDN'T MAKE THEM. THEY CAN'T MAKE YOU.
DO WE TRUST HITCH ENOUGH TO-?
NO.
BUT I TRUST THAT HE DOESN'T WANT TO GET SHIVVED IN THE SHOWER IN FEDERAL PRISON.
THAT MELTZER GOT UP YOUR ASS, HUH?
I HATE GUYS WHO WORK POWERS WHO ARE ANTI-POWERS. I THOUGHT WE'D BE DONE WITH THEM AS FEDS.
WELL YOU WERE REALLY KIDDING YOURSELF.
HE REMINDS ME OF KUTTER. REMEMBER KUTTER?
VAGUELY.

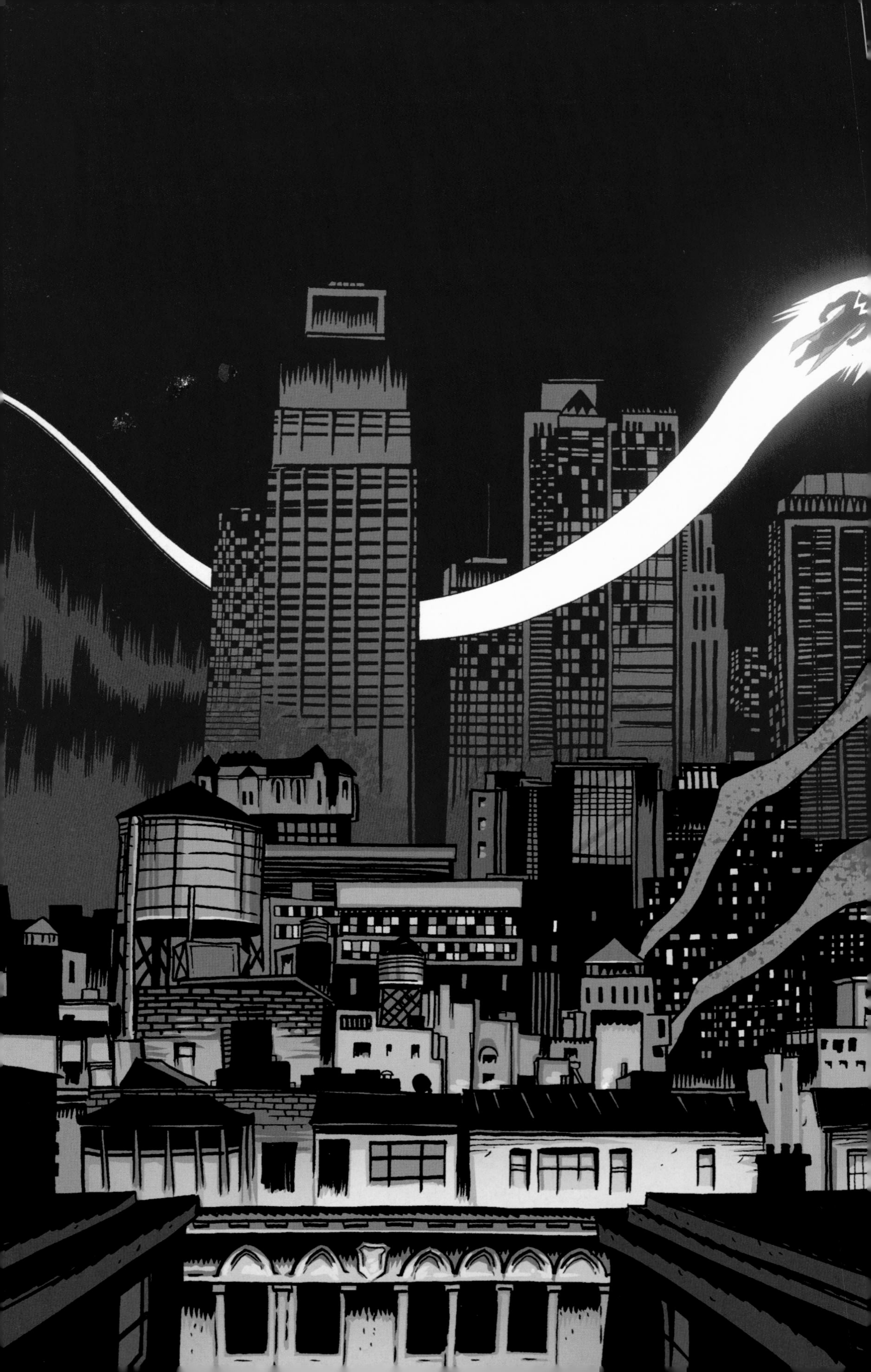

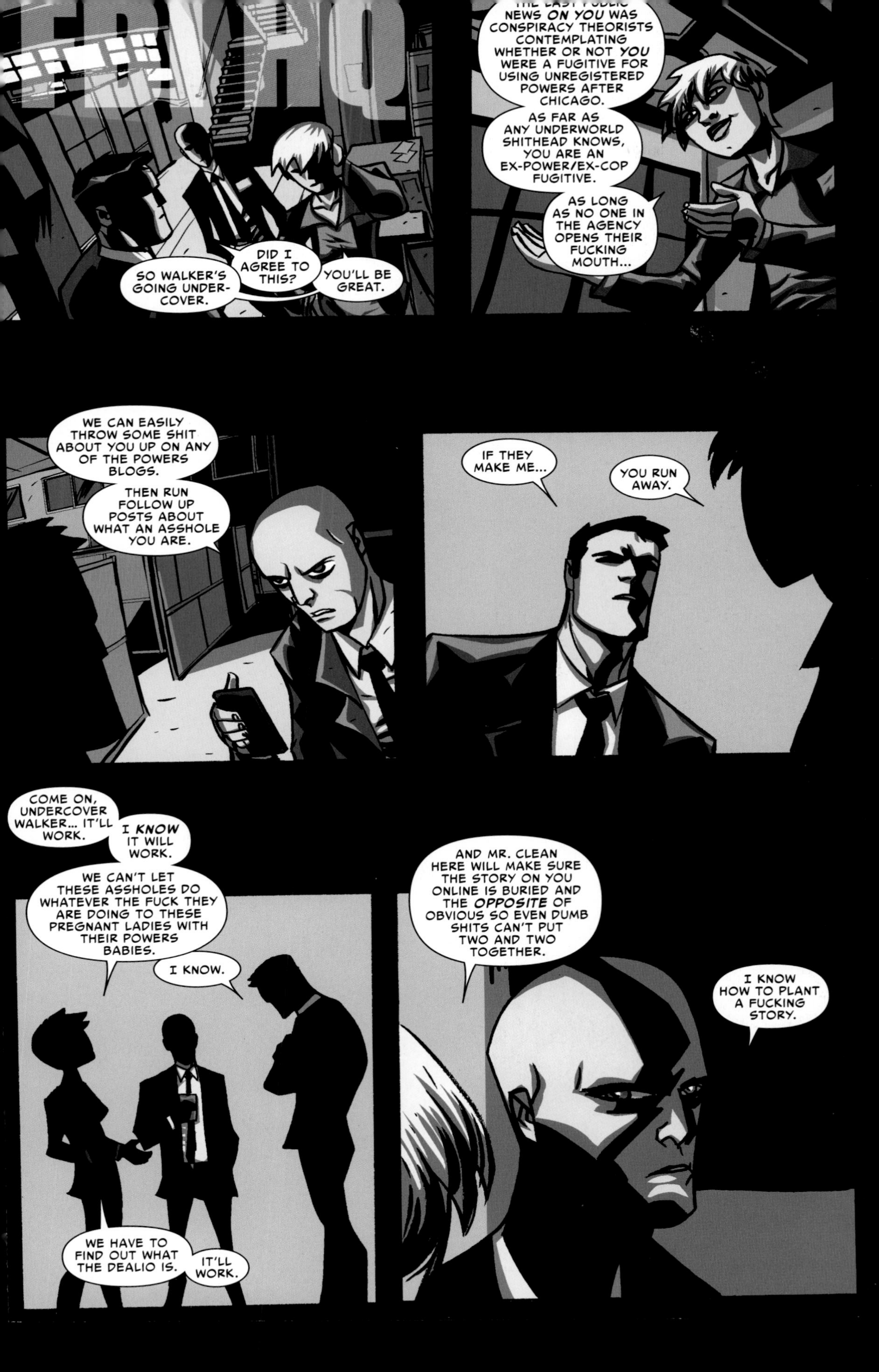
FBI HQ
SO WALKER'S GOING UNDER-COVER.
DID I AGREE TO THIS?
YOU'LL BE GREAT.
NEWS ON YOU WAS CONSPIRACY THEORISTS CONTEMPLATING WHETHER OR NOT YOU WERE A FUGITIVE FOR USING UNREGISTERED POWERS AFTER CHICAGO.
AS FAR AS ANY UNDERWORLD SHITHEAD KNOWS, YOU ARE AN EX-POWER/EX-COP FUGITIVE.
AS LONG AS NO ONE IN THE AGENCY OPENS THEIR FUCKING MOUTH...
WE CAN EASILY THROW SOME SHIT ABOUT YOU UP ON ANY OF THE POWERS BLOGS.
THEN RUN FOLLOW UP POSTS ABOUT WHAT AN ASSHOLE YOU ARE.
IF THEY MAKE ME...
YOU RUN AWAY.
COME ON, UNDERCOVER WALKER... IT'LL WORK.
I KNOW IT WILL WORK.
WE CAN'T LET THESE ASSHOLES DO WHATEVER THE FUCK THEY ARE DOING TO THESE PREGNANT LADIES WITH THEIR POWERS BABIES.
I KNOW.
WE HAVE TO FIND OUT WHAT THE DEALIO IS.
IT'LL WORK.
AND MR. CLEAN HERE WILL MAKE SURE THE STORY ON YOU ONLINE IS BURIED AND THE OPPOSITE OF OBVIOUS SO EVEN DUMB SHITS CAN'T PUT TWO AND TWO TOGETHER.
I KNOW HOW TO PLANT A FUCKING STORY.

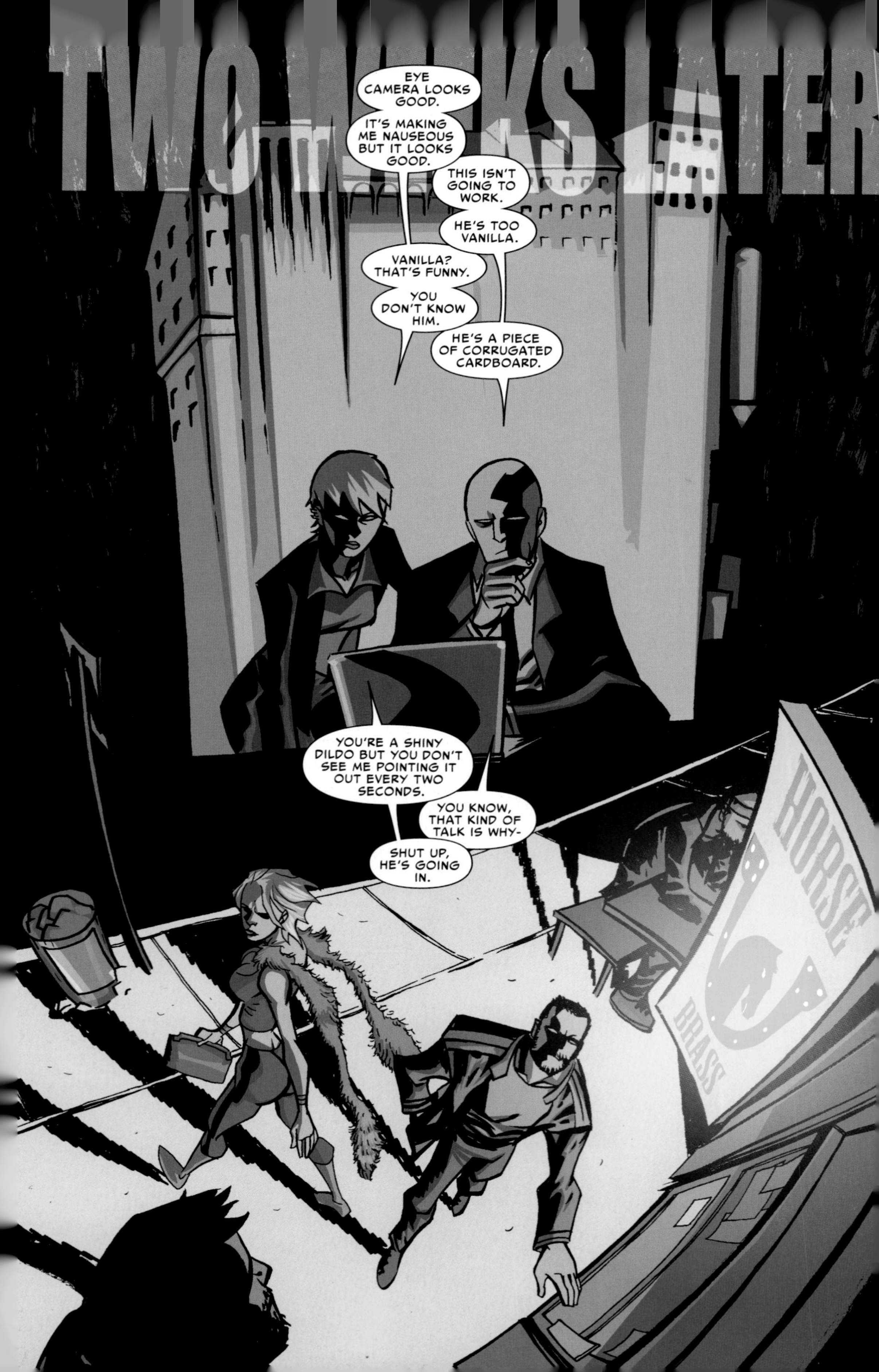
TWO WEEKS LATER
EYE CAMERA LOOKS GOOD.
IT'S MAKING ME NAUSEOUS BUT IT LOOKS GOOD.
THIS ISN'T GOING TO WORK.
HE'S TOO VANILLA.
VANILLA? THAT'S FUNNY.
YOU DON'T KNOW HIM.
HE'S A PIECE OF CORRUGATED CARDBOARD.
YOU'RE A SHINY DILDO BUT YOU DON'T SEE ME POINTING IT OUT EVERY TWO SECONDS.
YOU KNOW, THAT KIND OF TALK IS WHY-
SHUT UP, HE'S GOING IN.
HORSE
BRASS

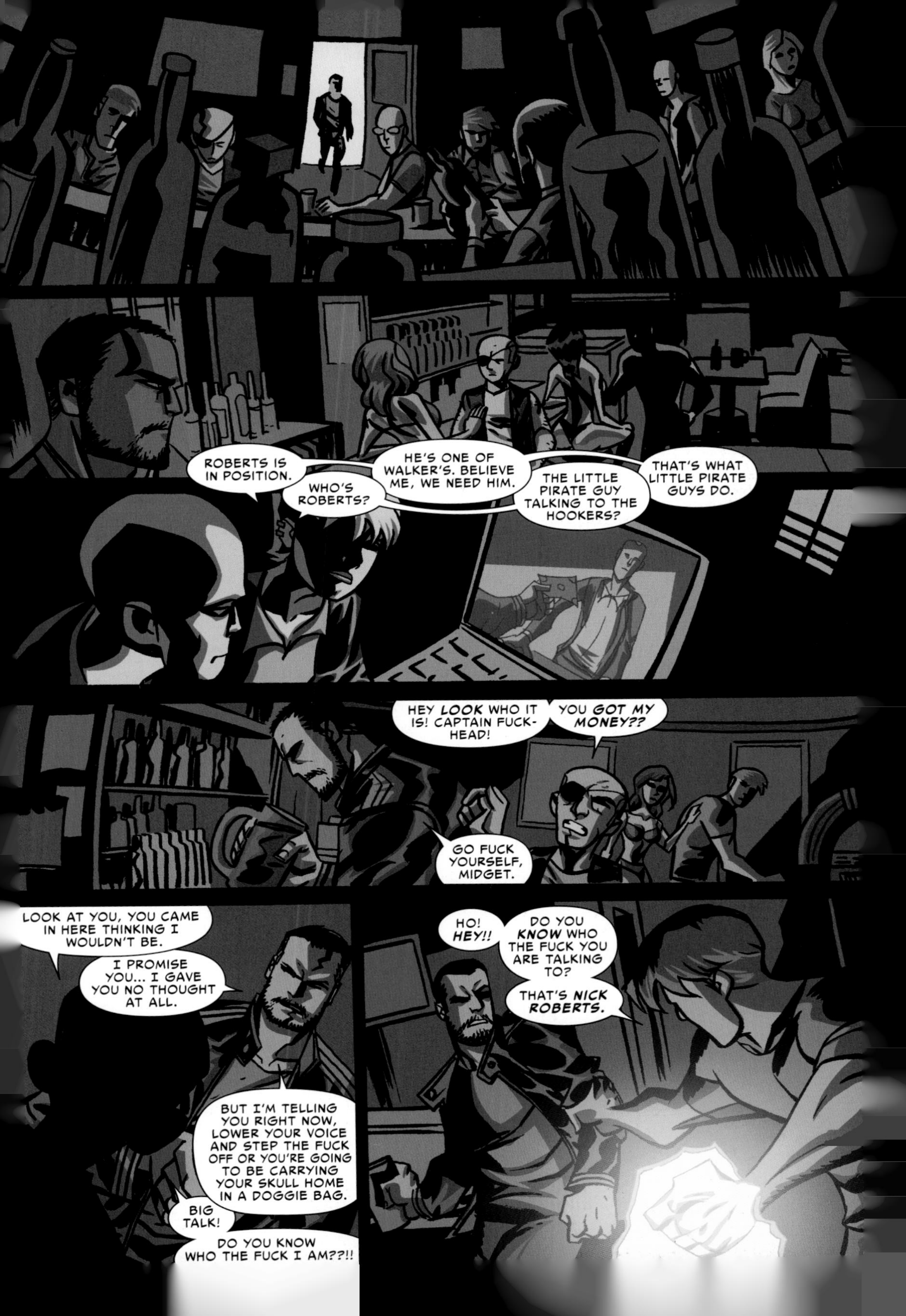
ROBERTS IS IN POSITION.
WHO'S ROBERTS?
HE'S ONE OF WALKER'S. BELIEVE ME, WE NEED HIM.
THE LITTLE PIRATE GUY TALKING TO THE HOOKERS?
THAT'S WHAT LITTLE PIRATE GUYS DO.
HEY LOOK WHO IT IS! CAPTAIN FUCK-HEAD!
YOU GOT MY MONEY??
GO FUCK YOURSELF, MIDGET.
LOOK AT YOU, YOU CAME IN HERE THINKING I WOULDN'T BE.
I PROMISE YOU... I GAVE YOU NO THOUGHT AT ALL.
BUT I'M TELLING YOU RIGHT NOW, LOWER YOUR VOICE AND STEP THE FUCK OFF OR YOU'RE GOING TO BE CARRYING YOUR SKULL HOME IN A DOGGIE BAG.
BIG TALK!
DO YOU KNOW WHO THE FUCK I AM??!!
HO! HEY!!
DO YOU KNOW WHO THE FUCK YOU ARE TALKING TO?
THAT'S NICK ROBERTS.

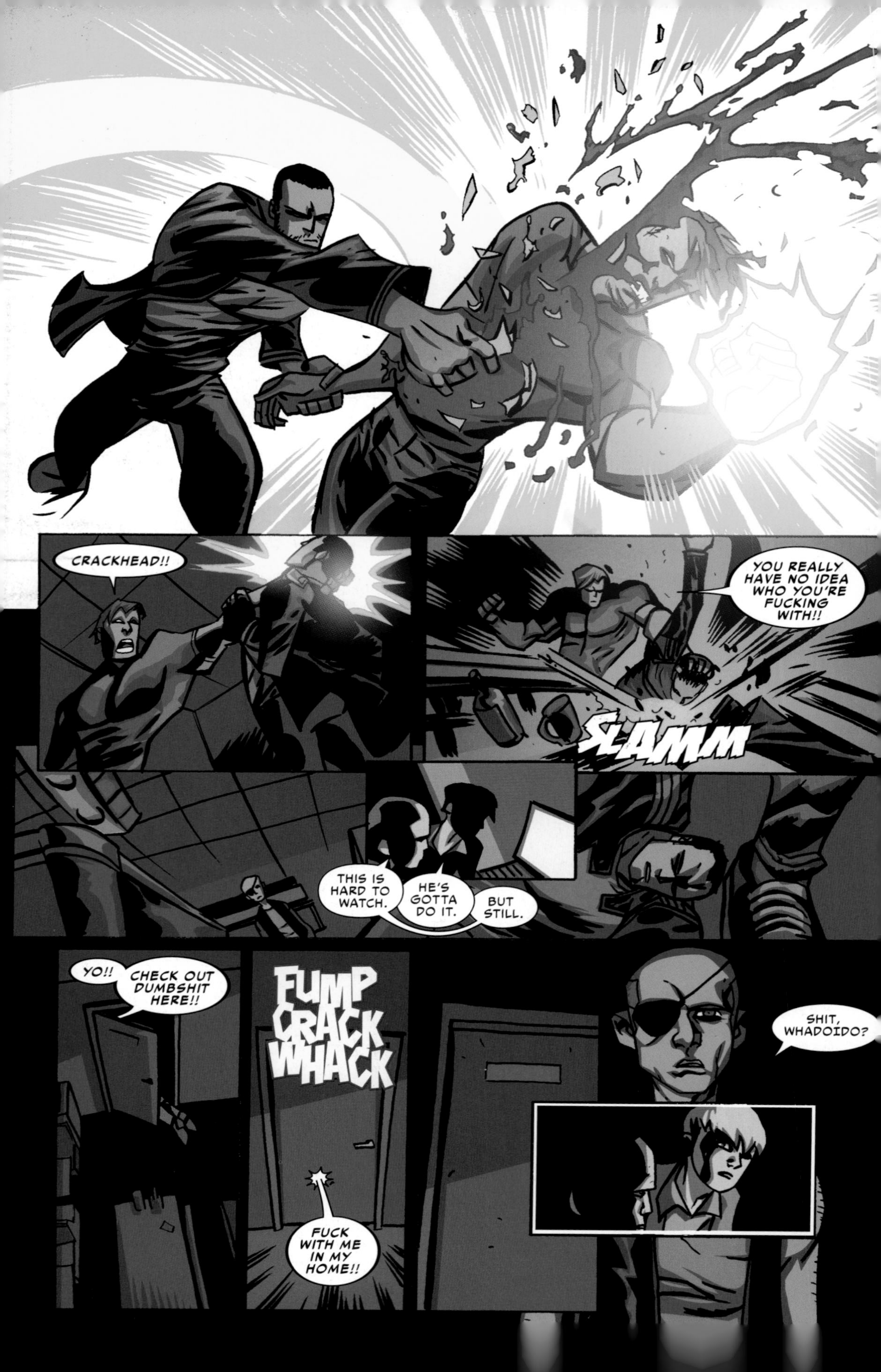
CRACKHEAD!!
YOU REALLY HAVE NO IDEA WHO YOU'RE FUCKING WITH!!
SLAMM
THIS IS HARD TO WATCH.
HE'S GOTTA DO IT.
BUT STILL.
YO!!
CHECK OUT DUMBSHIT HERE!!
FUMP CRACK WHACK
FUCK WITH ME IN MY HOME!!
SHIT, WHADOIDO?

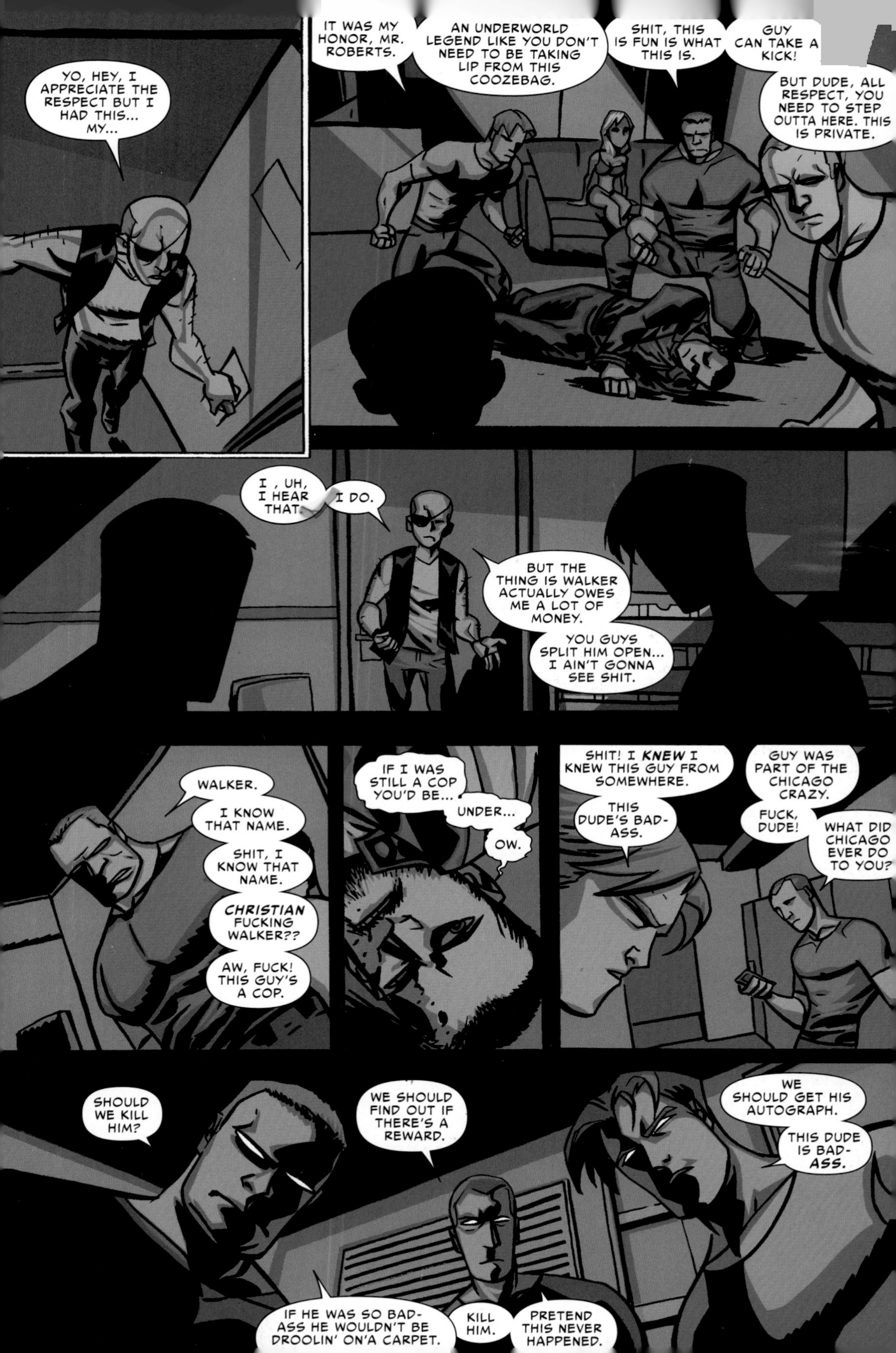
YO, HEY, I APPRECIATE THE RESPECT BUT I HAD THIS... MY...
IT WAS MY HONOR, MR. ROBERTS.
AN UNDERWORLD LEGEND LIKE YOU DON'T NEED TO BE TAKING LIP FROM THIS COOZEBAG.
SHIT, THIS IS FUN IS WHAT THIS IS.
GUY CAN TAKE A KICK!
BUT DUDE, ALL RESPECT, YOU NEED TO STEP OUTTA HERE. THIS IS PRIVATE.
I , UH, I HEAR THAT.
I DO.
BUT THE THING IS WALKER ACTUALLY OWES ME A LOT OF MONEY.
YOU GUYS SPLIT HIM OPEN... I AIN'T GONNA SEE SHIT.
WALKER.
I KNOW THAT NAME.
SHIT, I KNOW THAT NAME.
CHRISTIAN FUCKING WALKER??
AW, FUCK! THIS GUY'S A COP.
IF I WAS STILL A COP YOU'D BE...
UNDER...
OW.
SHIT! I *KNEW* I KNEW THIS GUY FROM SOMEWHERE.
THIS DUDE'S BAD-ASS.
GUY WAS PART OF THE CHICAGO CRAZY.
FUCK, DUDE!
WHAT DID CHICAGO EVER DO TO YOU?
SHOULD WE KILL HIM?
WE SHOULD FIND OUT IF THERE'S A REWARD.
WE SHOULD GET HIS AUTOGRAPH.
THIS DUDE IS BAD-*ASS.*
IF HE WAS SO BAD-ASS HE WOULDN'T BE DROOLIN' ON'A CARPET.
KILL HIM.
PRETEND THIS NEVER HAPPENED.

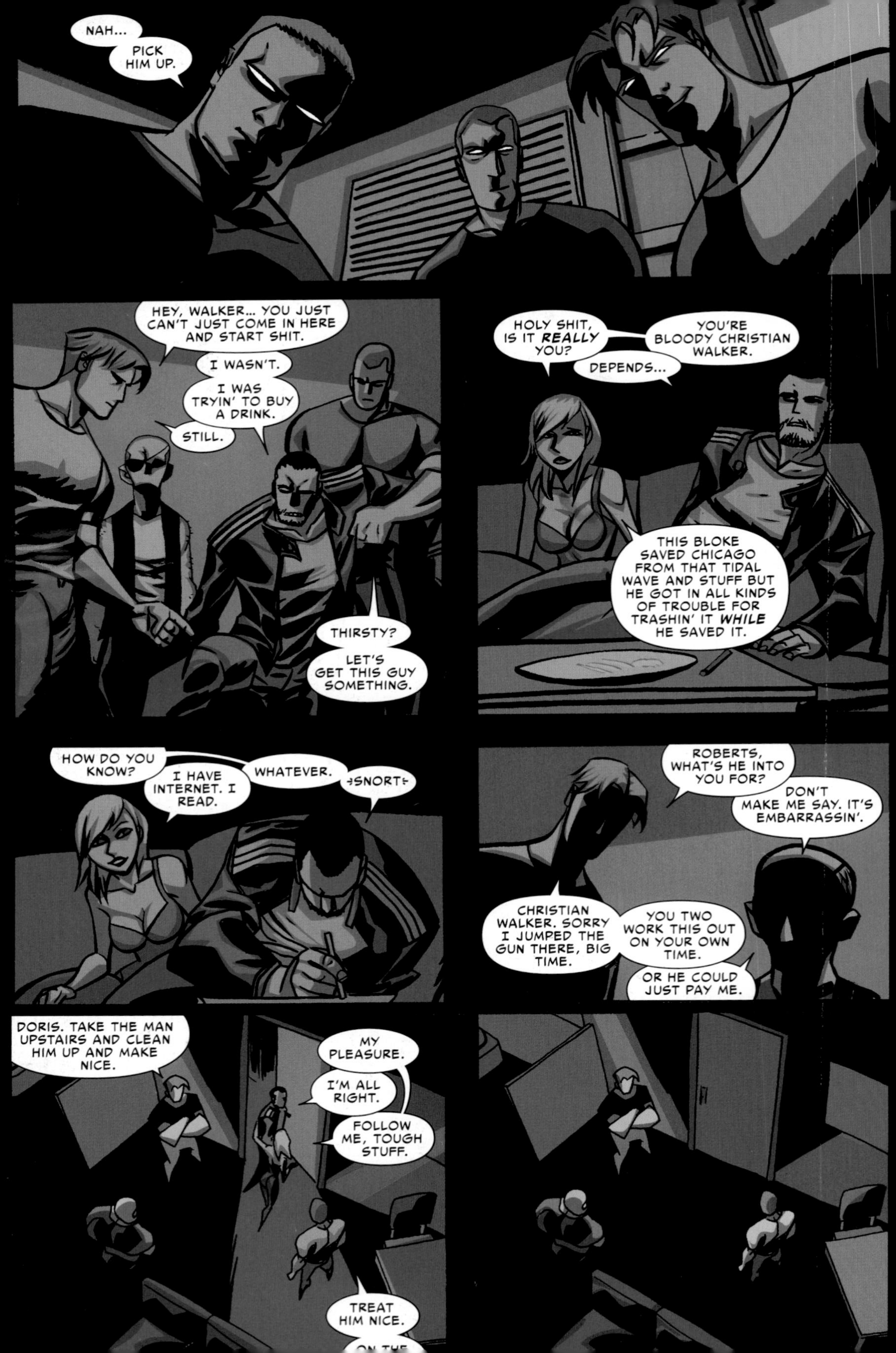
NAH...
PICK HIM UP.
HEY, WALKER... YOU JUST CAN'T JUST COME IN HERE AND START SHIT.
I WASN'T.
I WAS TRYIN' TO BUY A DRINK.
STILL.
THIRSTY?
LET'S GET THIS GUY SOMETHING.
HOLY SHIT, IS IT *REALLY* YOU?
YOU'RE BLOODY CHRISTIAN WALKER.
DEPENDS...
THIS BLOKE SAVED CHICAGO FROM THAT TIDAL WAVE AND STUFF BUT HE GOT IN ALL KINDS OF TROUBLE FOR TRASHIN' IT *WHILE* HE SAVED IT.
HOW DO YOU KNOW?
I HAVE INTERNET. I READ.
WHATEVER.
SNORT
ROBERTS, WHAT'S HE INTO YOU FOR?
DON'T MAKE ME SAY. IT'S EMBARRASSIN'.
CHRISTIAN WALKER. SORRY I JUMPED THE GUN THERE, BIG TIME.
YOU TWO WORK THIS OUT ON YOUR OWN TIME.
OR HE COULD JUST PAY ME.
DORIS. TAKE THE MAN UPSTAIRS AND CLEAN HIM UP AND MAKE NICE.
MY PLEASURE.
I'M ALL RIGHT.
FOLLOW ME, TOUGH STUFF.
TREAT HIM NICE.

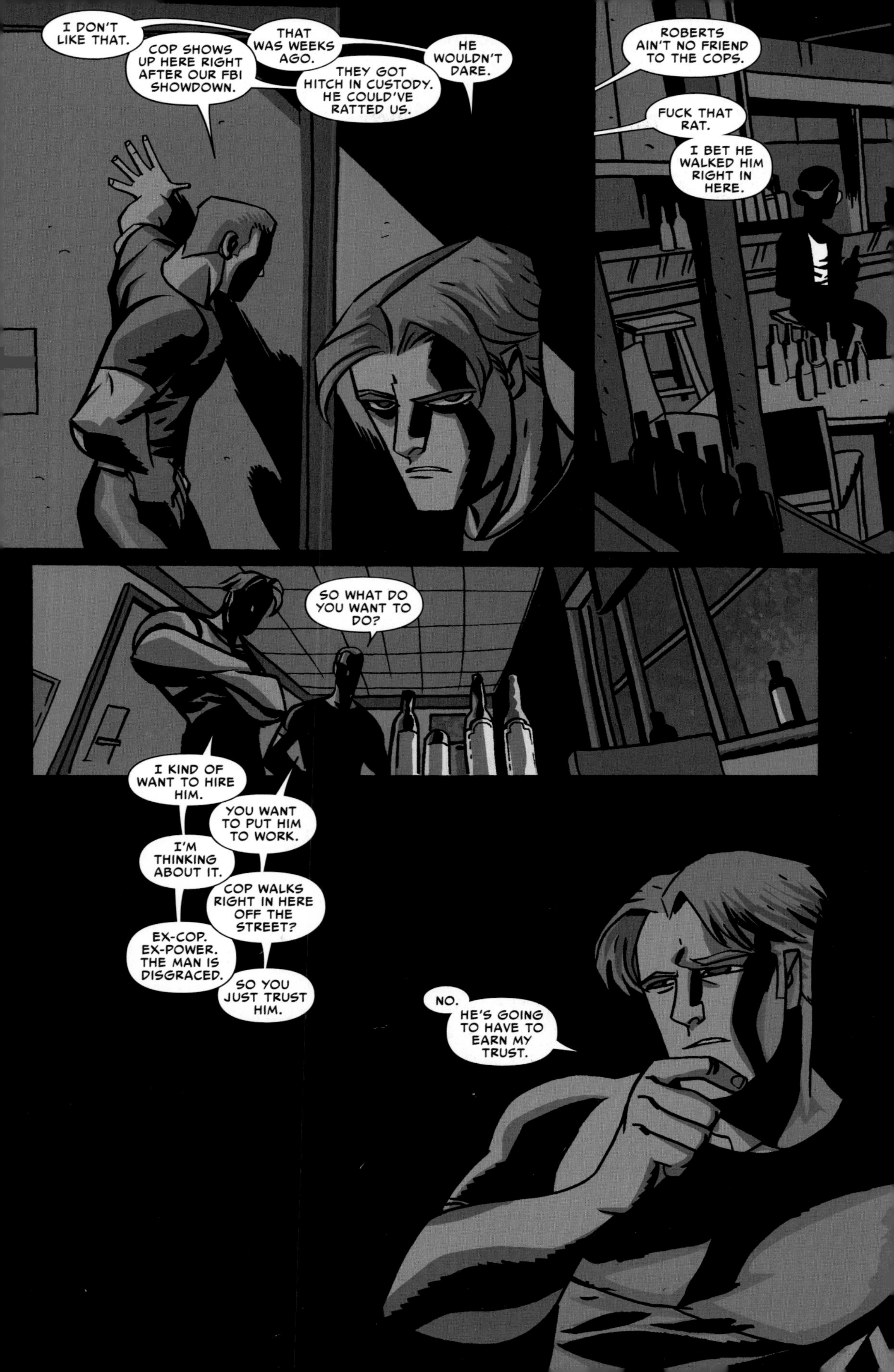
I DON'T LIKE THAT.
COP SHOWS UP HERE RIGHT AFTER OUR FBI SHOWDOWN.
THAT WAS WEEKS AGO.
THEY GOT HITCH IN CUSTODY. HE COULD'VE RATTED US.
HE WOULDN'T DARE.
ROBERTS AIN'T NO FRIEND TO THE COPS.
FUCK THAT RAT.
I BET HE WALKED HIM RIGHT IN HERE.
SO WHAT DO YOU WANT TO DO?
I KIND OF WANT TO HIRE HIM.
YOU WANT TO PUT HIM TO WORK.
I'M THINKING ABOUT IT.
COP WALKS RIGHT IN HERE OFF THE STREET?
EX-COP. EX-POWER. THE MAN IS DISGRACED.
SO YOU JUST TRUST HIM.
NO.
HE'S GOING TO HAVE TO EARN MY TRUST.

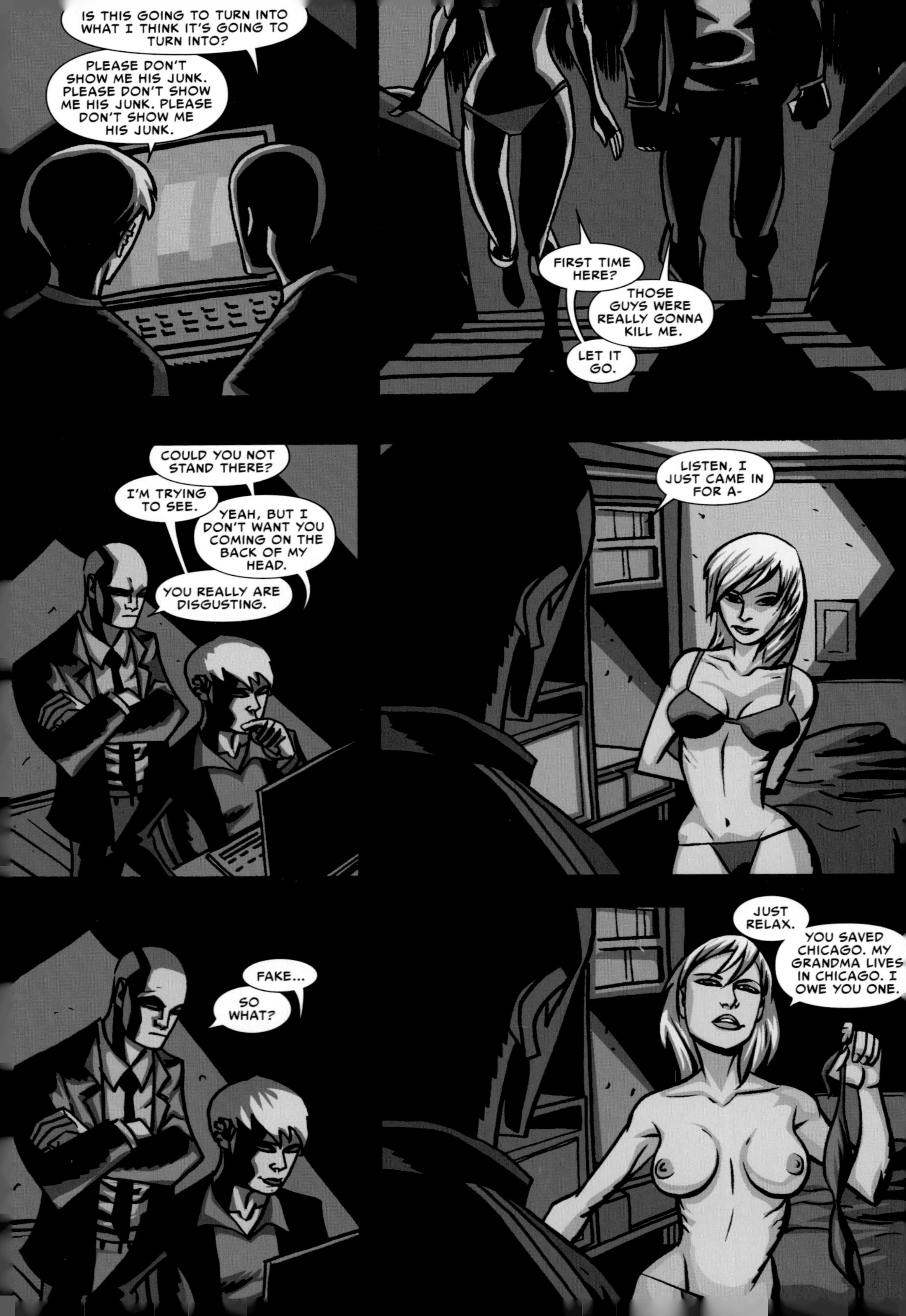
IS THIS GOING TO TURN INTO WHAT I THINK IT'S GOING TO TURN INTO?
PLEASE DON'T SHOW ME HIS JUNK. PLEASE DON'T SHOW ME HIS JUNK. PLEASE DON'T SHOW ME HIS JUNK.
FIRST TIME HERE?
THOSE GUYS WERE REALLY GONNA KILL ME.
LET IT GO.
COULD YOU NOT STAND THERE?
I'M TRYING TO SEE.
YEAH, BUT I DON'T WANT YOU COMING ON THE BACK OF MY HEAD.
YOU REALLY ARE DISGUSTING.
LISTEN, I JUST CAME IN FOR A-
FAKE...
SO WHAT?
JUST RELAX.
YOU SAVED CHICAGO. MY GRANDMA LIVES IN CHICAGO. I OWE YOU ONE.

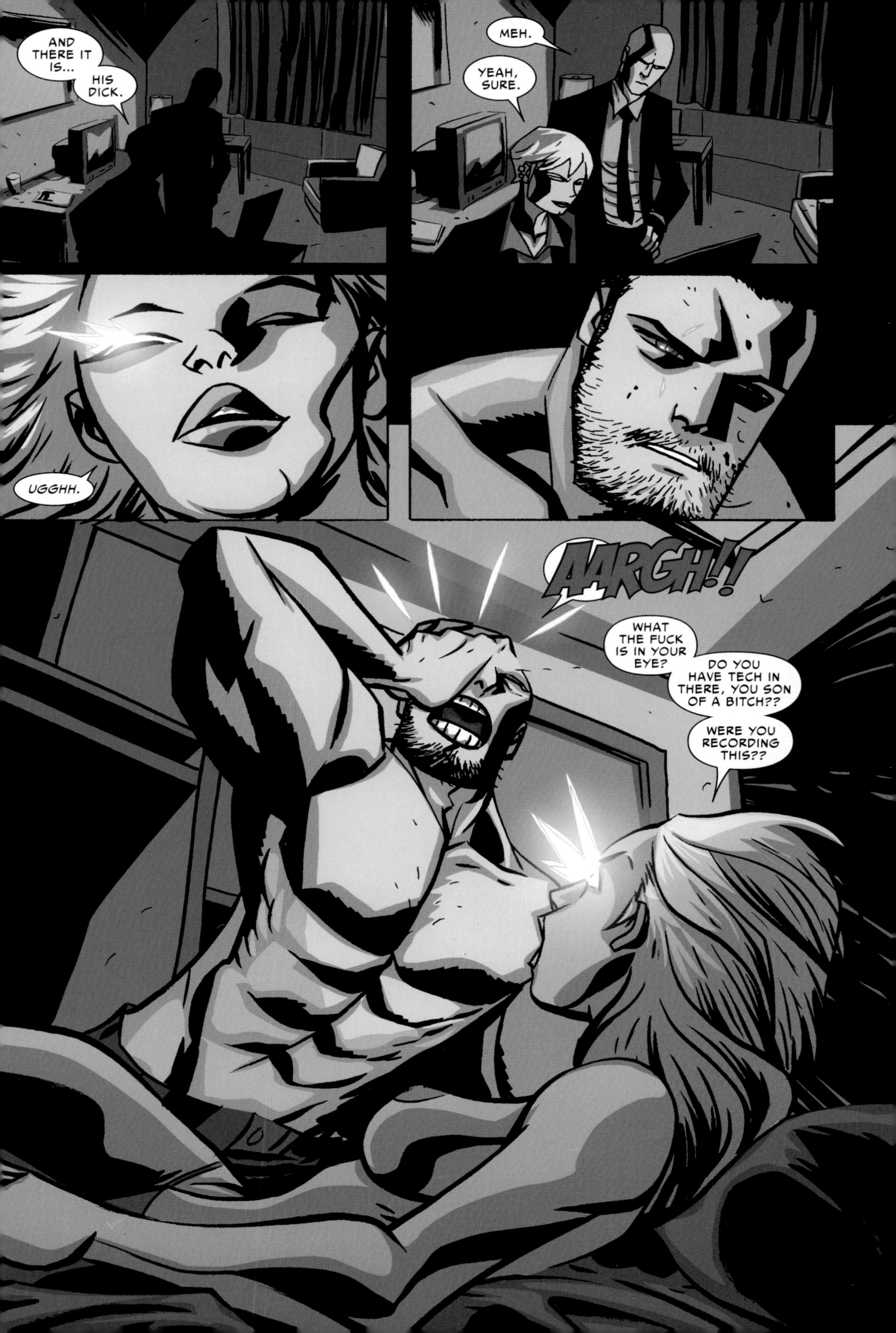
AND THERE IT IS...
HIS DICK.
MEH.
YEAH, SURE.
UGGHH.
AARGH!!
WHAT THE FUCK IS IN YOUR EYE?
DO YOU HAVE TECH IN THERE, YOU SON OF A BITCH??
WERE YOU RECORDING THIS??

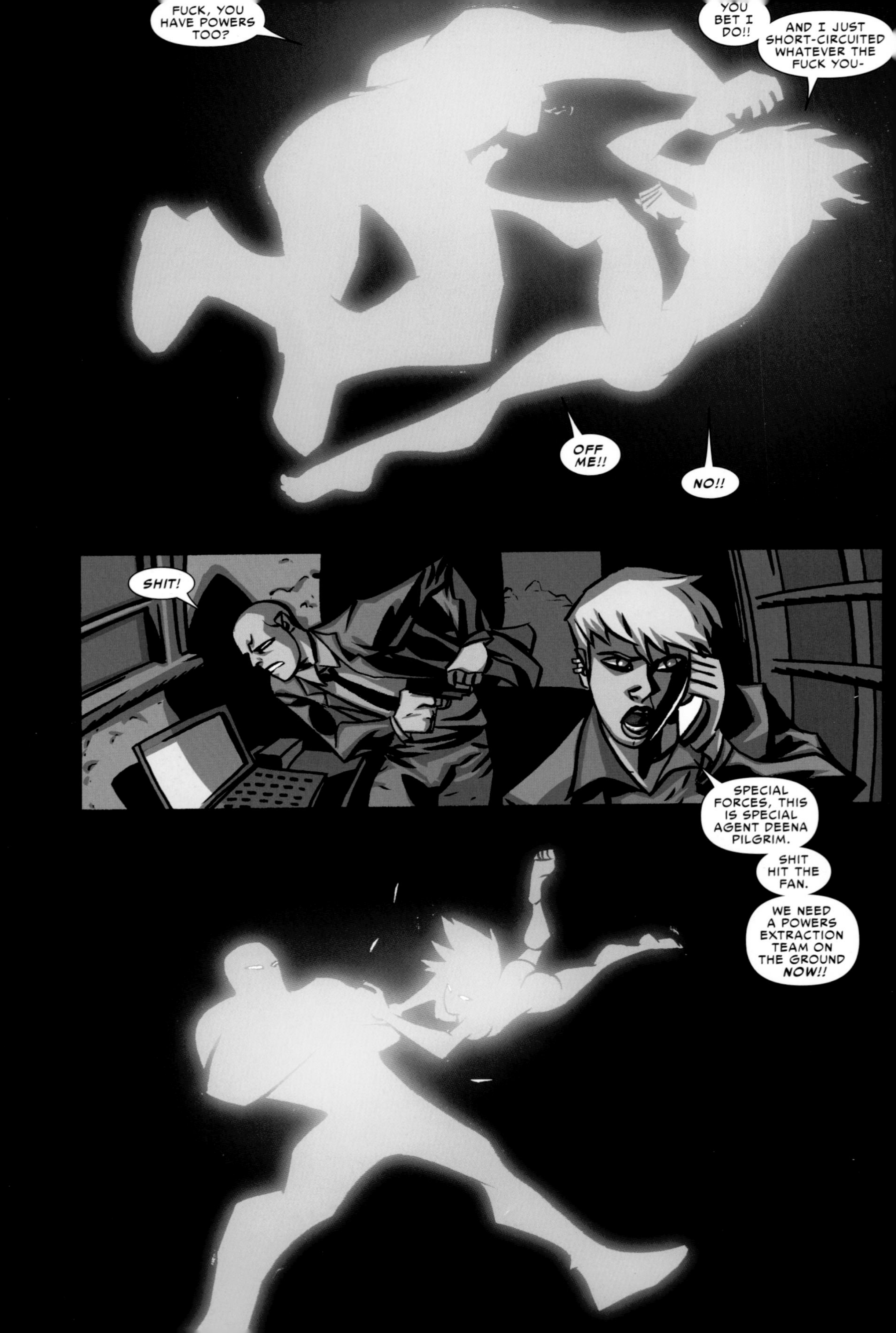
FUCK, YOU HAVE POWERS TOO?
YOU BET I DO!!
AND I JUST SHORT-CIRCUITED WHATEVER THE FUCK YOU-
OFF ME!!
NO!!
SHIT!
SPECIAL FORCES, THIS IS SPECIAL AGENT DEENA PILGRIM.
SHIT HIT THE FAN.
WE NEED A POWERS EXTRACTION TEAM ON THE GROUND NOW!!

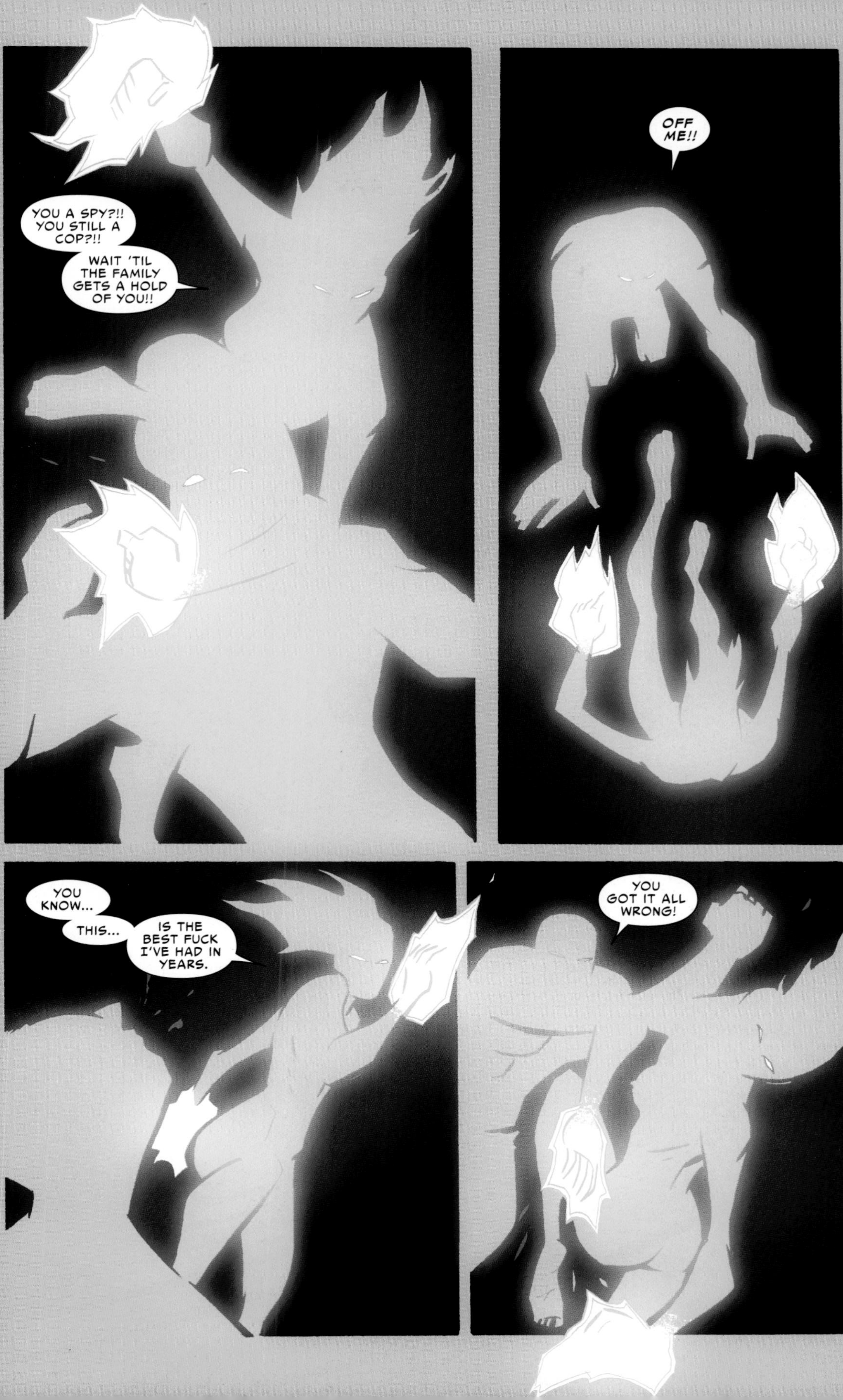
YOU A SPY?!! YOU STILL A COP?!!
WAIT 'TIL THE FAMILY GETS A HOLD OF YOU!!
OFF ME!!
YOU KNOW...
THIS...
IS THE BEST FUCK I'VE HAD IN YEARS.
YOU GOT IT ALL WRONG!

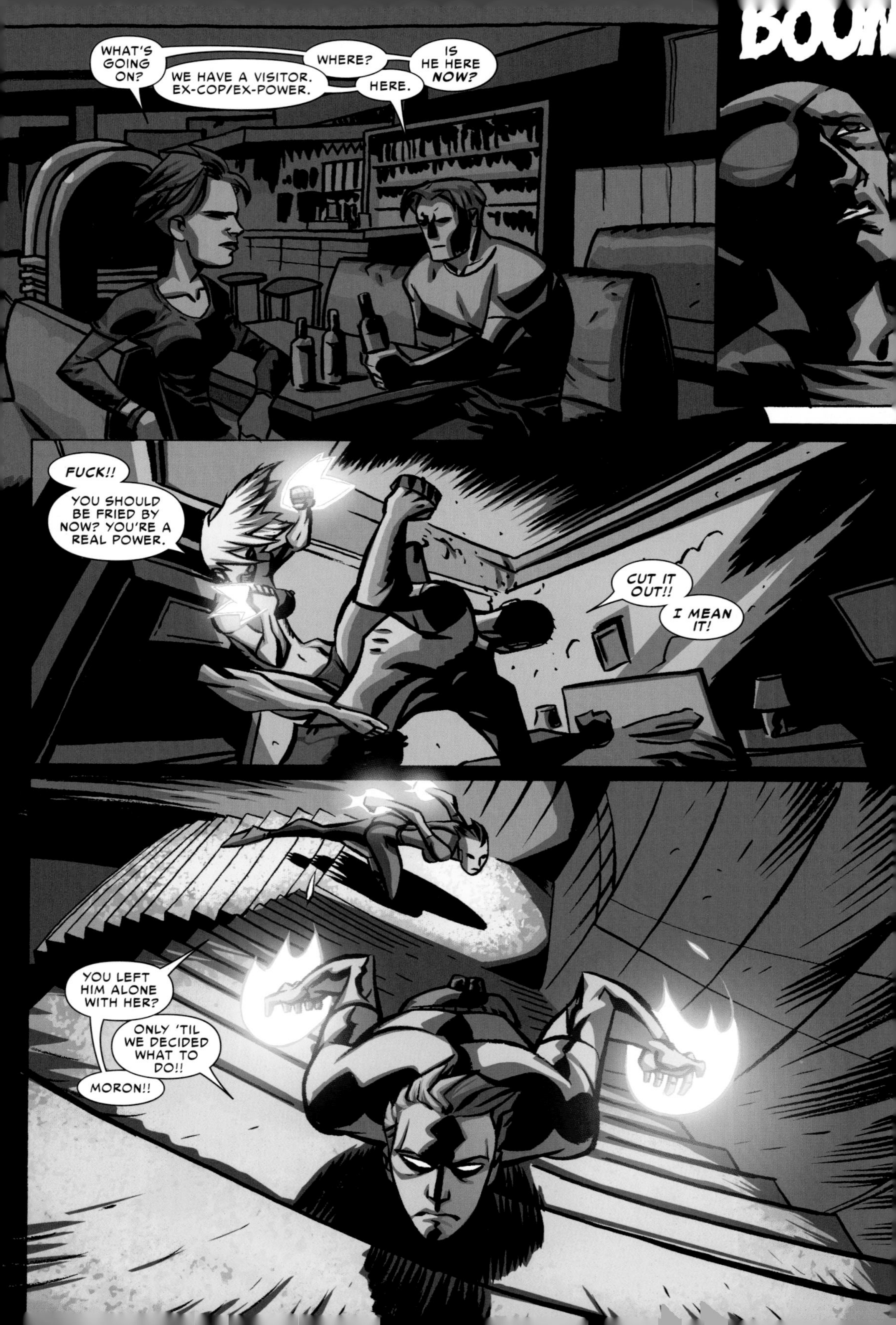
BOOM
WHAT'S GOING ON?
WE HAVE A VISITOR. EX-COP/EX-POWER.
WHERE?
HERE.
IS HE HERE NOW?
FUCK!!
YOU SHOULD BE FRIED BY NOW? YOU'RE A REAL POWER.
CUT IT OUT!!
I MEAN IT!
YOU LEFT HIM ALONE WITH HER?
ONLY 'TIL WE DECIDED WHAT TO DO!!
MORON!!

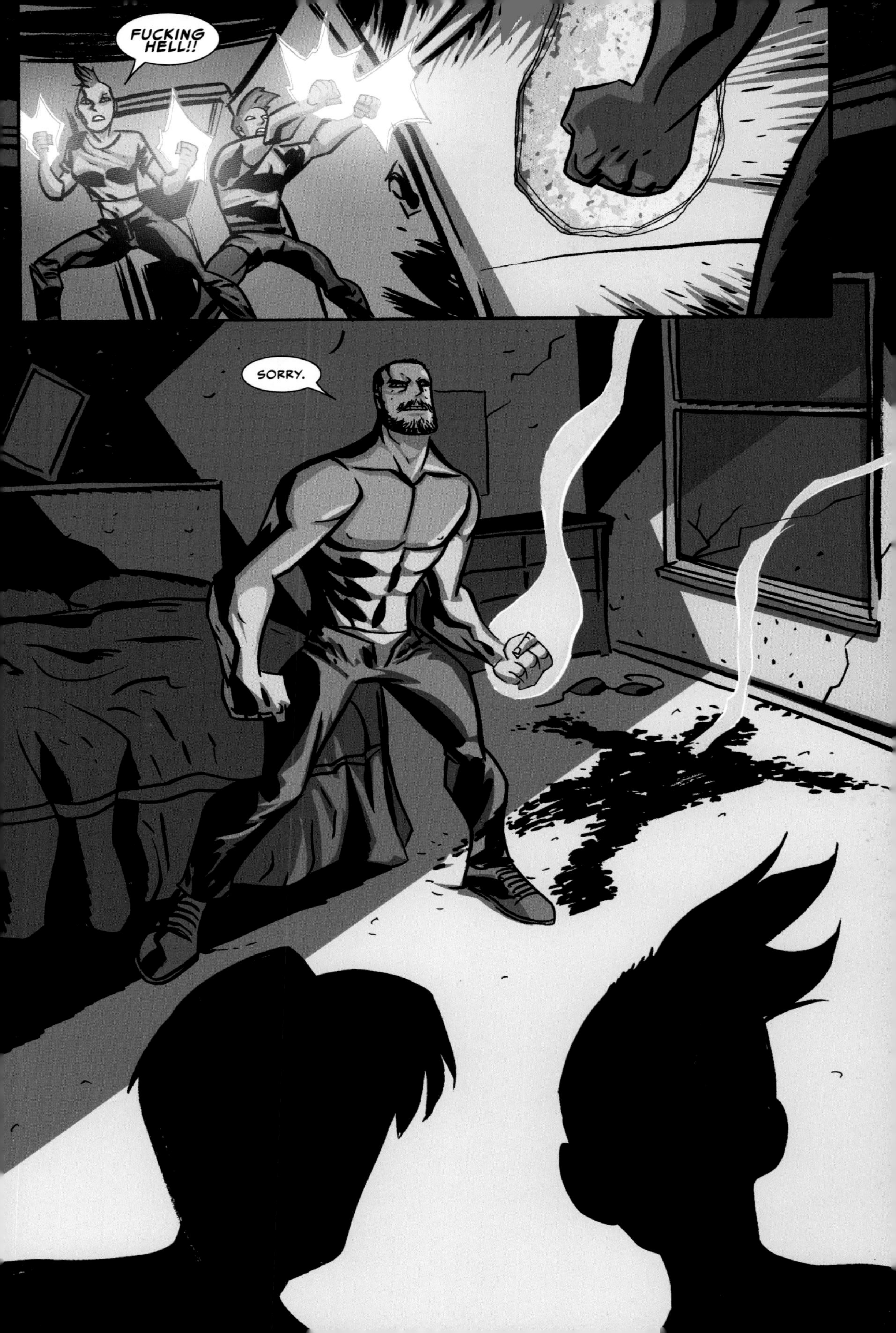
FUCKING HELL!!
SORRY.

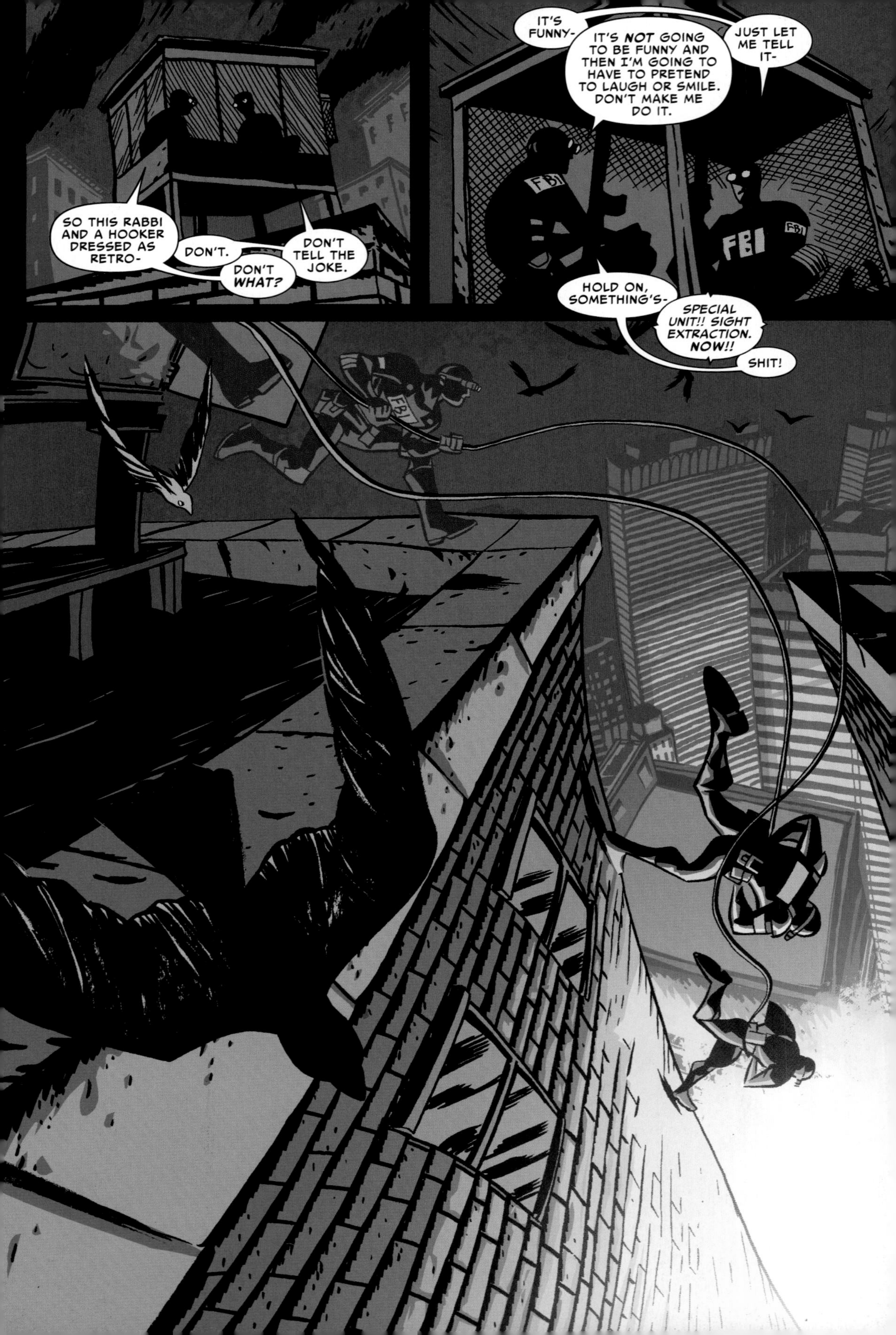
SO THIS RABBI AND A HOOKER DRESSED AS RETRO-
DON'T.
DON'T WHAT?
DON'T TELL THE JOKE.
IT'S FUNNY-
IT'S NOT GOING TO BE FUNNY AND THEN I'M GOING TO HAVE TO PRETEND TO LAUGH OR SMILE. DON'T MAKE ME DO IT.
JUST LET ME TELL IT-
FBI
FBI
FBI
HOLD ON, SOMETHING'S-
SPECIAL UNIT!! SIGHT EXTRACTION. NOW!!
SHIT!
FBI

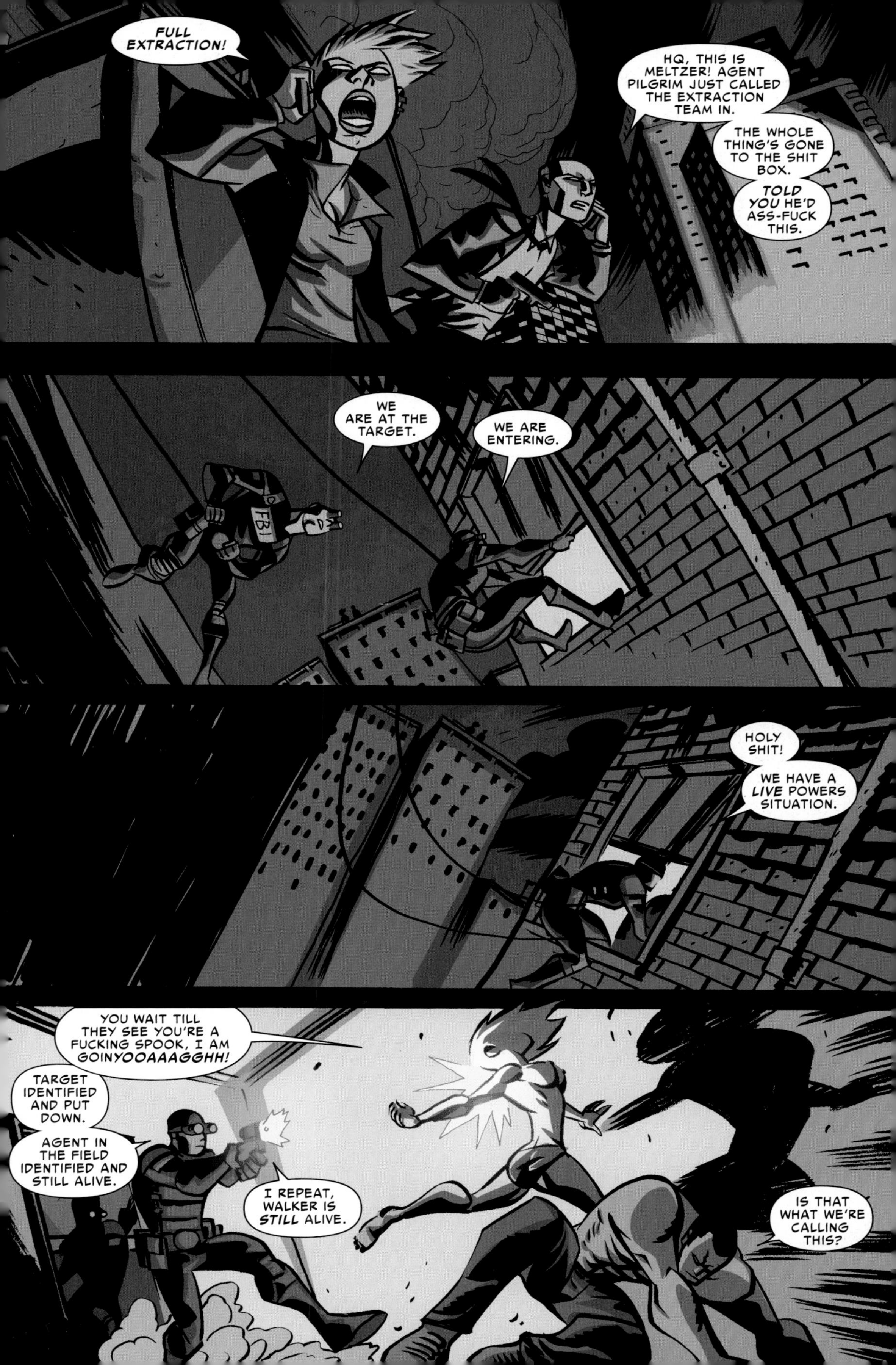
FULL EXTRACTION!
HQ, THIS IS MELTZER! AGENT PILGRIM JUST CALLED THE EXTRACTION TEAM IN.
THE WHOLE THING'S GONE TO THE SHIT BOX.
TOLD YOU HE'D ASS-FUCK THIS.
WE ARE AT THE TARGET.
WE ARE ENTERING.
HOLY SHIT!
WE HAVE A LIVE POWERS SITUATION.
YOU WAIT TILL THEY SEE YOU'RE A FUCKING SPOOK, I AM GOINYOOAAAGGHH!
TARGET IDENTIFIED AND PUT DOWN.
AGENT IN THE FIELD IDENTIFIED AND STILL ALIVE.
I REPEAT, WALKER IS STILL ALIVE.
IS THAT WHAT WE'RE CALLING THIS?
FBI

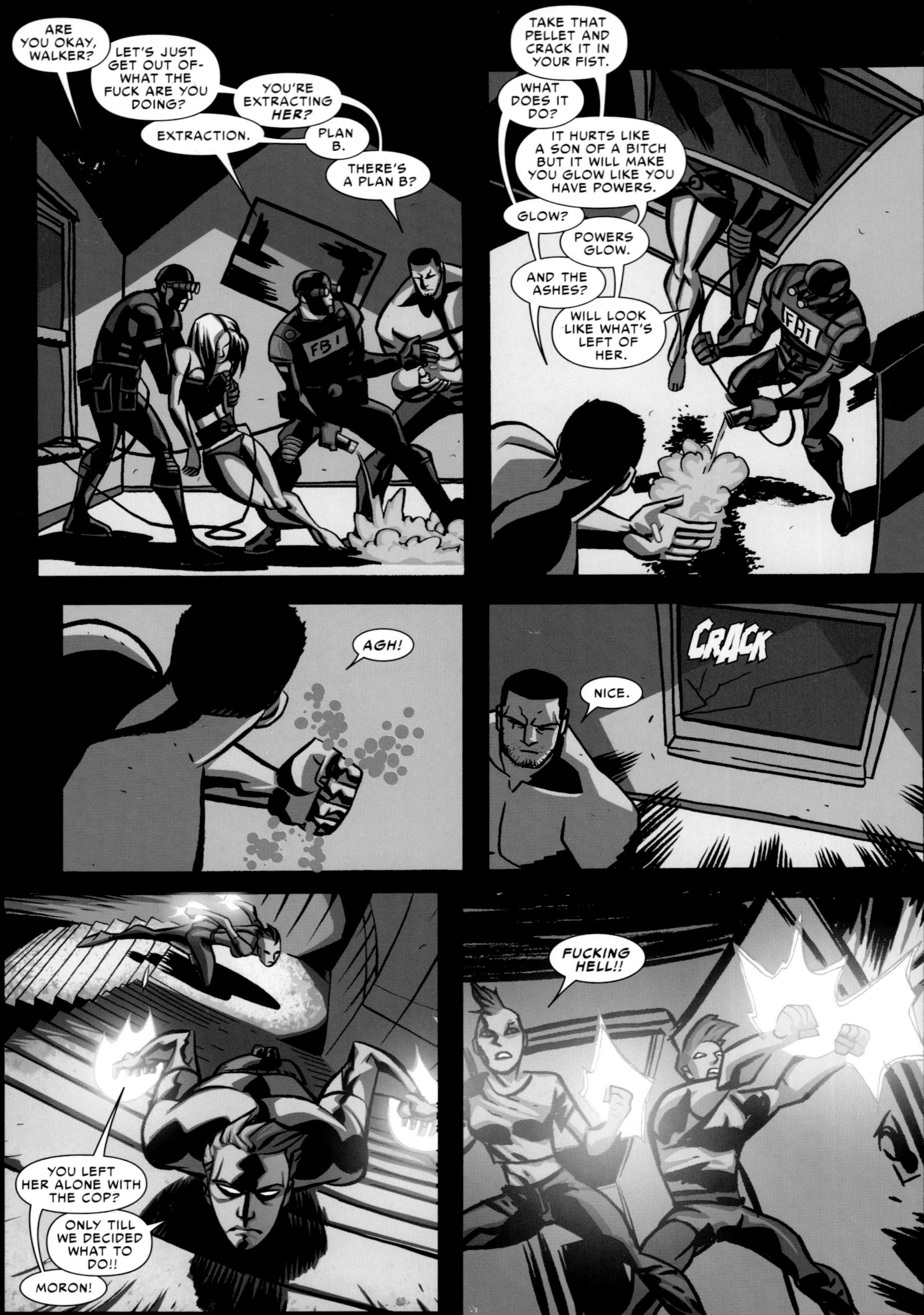

ARE YOU OKAY, WALKER?
LET'S JUST GET OUT OF- WHAT THE FUCK ARE YOU DOING?
YOU'RE EXTRACTING *HER?*
EXTRACTION.
PLAN B.
THERE'S A PLAN B?
TAKE THAT PELLET AND CRACK IT IN YOUR FIST.
WHAT DOES IT DO?
IT HURTS LIKE A SON OF A BITCH BUT IT WILL MAKE YOU GLOW LIKE YOU HAVE POWERS.
GLOW?
POWERS GLOW.
AND THE ASHES?
WILL LOOK LIKE WHAT'S LEFT OF HER.
AGH!
CRACK
NICE.
YOU LEFT HER ALONE WITH THE COP?
ONLY TILL WE DECIDED WHAT TO DO!!
MORON!
FUCKING HELL!!

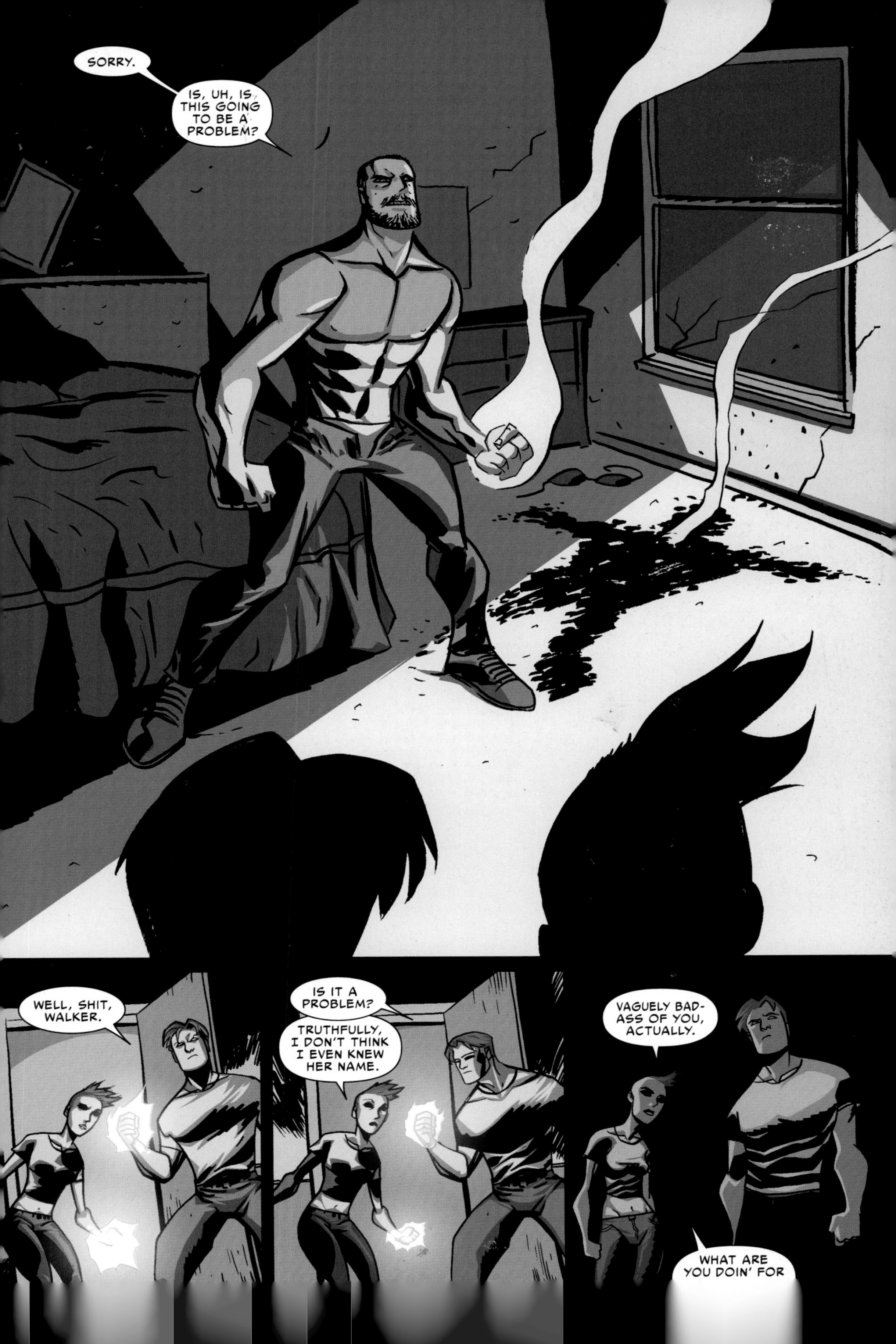
SORRY.
IS, UH, IS THIS GOING TO BE A PROBLEM?
WELL, SHIT, WALKER.
IS IT A PROBLEM?
TRUTHFULLY, I DON'T THINK I EVEN KNEW HER NAME.
VAGUELY BAD-ASS OF YOU, ACTUALLY.
WHAT ARE YOU DOIN' FOR

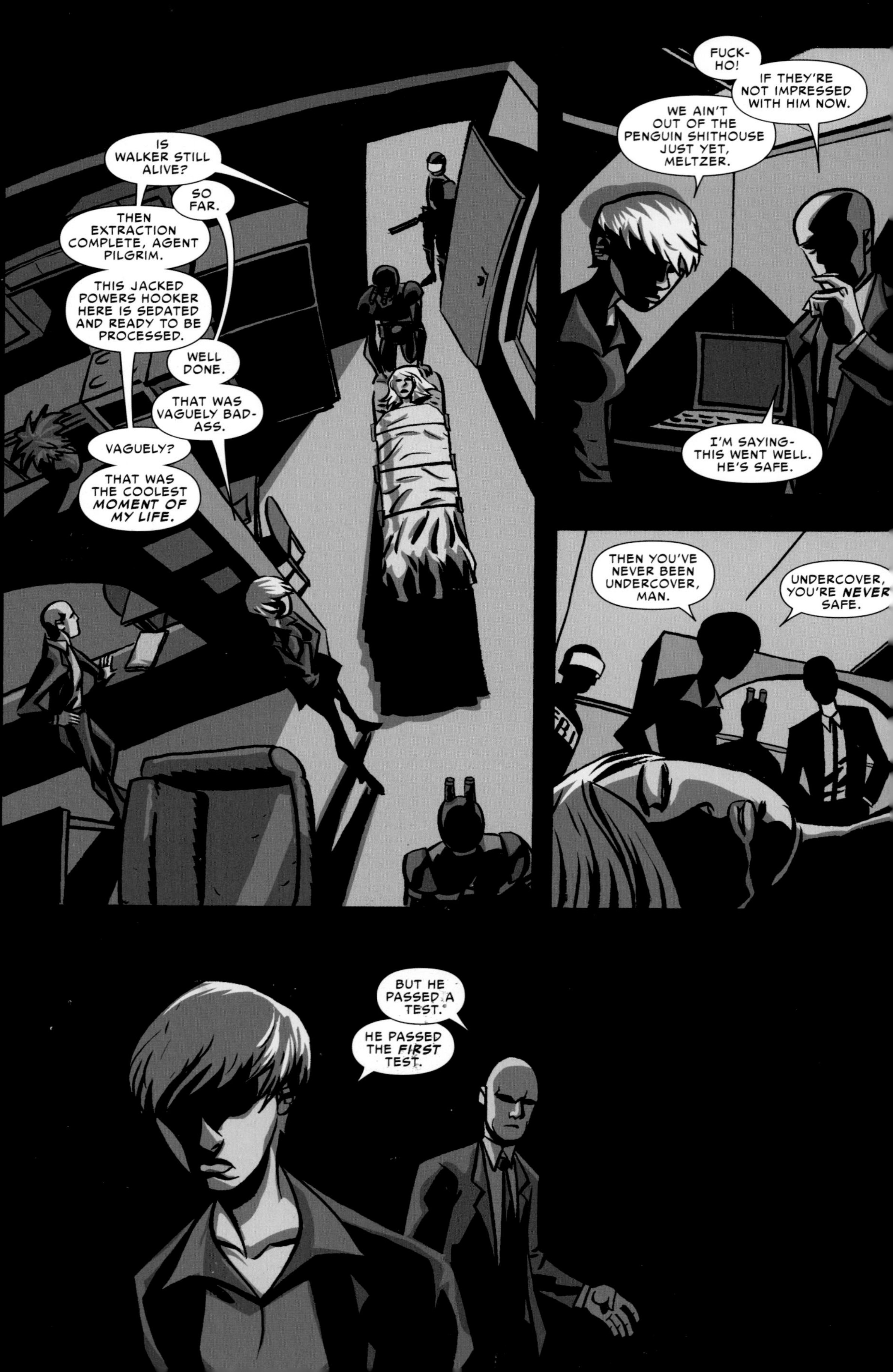
IS WALKER STILL ALIVE?
SO FAR.
THEN EXTRACTION COMPLETE, AGENT PILGRIM.
THIS JACKED POWERS HOOKER HERE IS SEDATED AND READY TO BE PROCESSED.
WELL DONE.
THAT WAS VAGUELY BAD-ASS.
VAGUELY?
THAT WAS THE COOLEST *MOMENT OF MY LIFE.*
FUCK-HO!
IF THEY'RE NOT IMPRESSED WITH HIM NOW.
WE AIN'T OUT OF THE PENGUIN SHITHOUSE JUST YET, MELTZER.
I'M SAYING-THIS WENT WELL. HE'S SAFE.
THEN YOU'VE NEVER BEEN UNDERCOVER, MAN.
UNDERCOVER, YOU'RE *NEVER* SAFE.
BUT HE PASSED A TEST.
HE PASSED THE *FIRST* TEST.

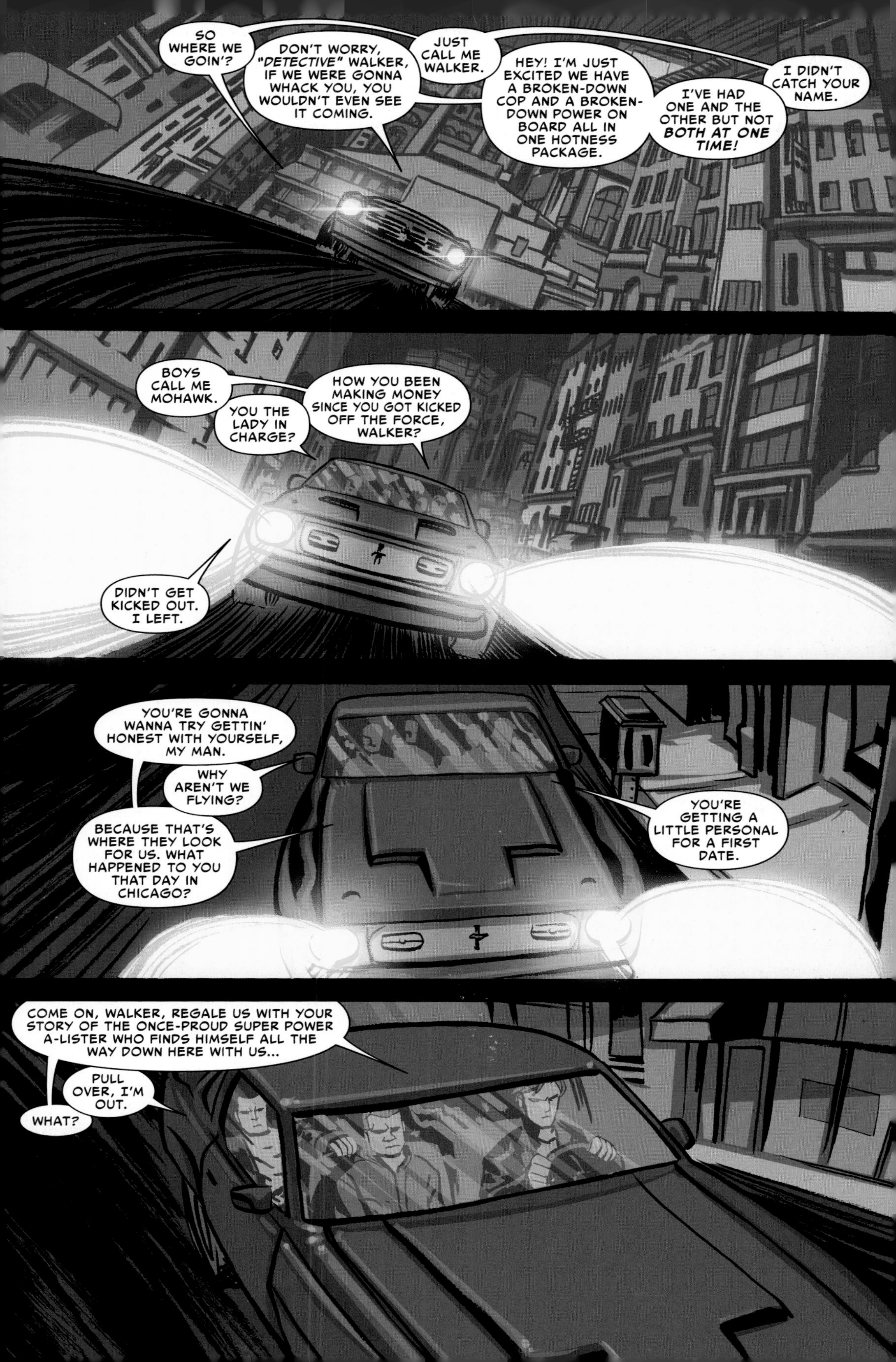
SO WHERE WE GOIN'?
DON'T WORRY, "*DETECTIVE*" WALKER, IF WE WERE GONNA WHACK YOU, YOU WOULDN'T EVEN SEE IT COMING.
JUST CALL ME WALKER.
HEY! I'M JUST EXCITED WE HAVE A BROKEN-DOWN COP AND A BROKEN-DOWN POWER ON BOARD ALL IN ONE HOTNESS PACKAGE.
I DIDN'T CATCH YOUR NAME.
I'VE HAD ONE AND THE OTHER BUT NOT *BOTH AT ONE TIME!*
BOYS CALL ME MOHAWK.
YOU THE LADY IN CHARGE?
HOW YOU BEEN MAKING MONEY SINCE YOU GOT KICKED OFF THE FORCE, WALKER?
DIDN'T GET KICKED OUT. I LEFT.
YOU'RE GONNA WANNA TRY GETTIN' HONEST WITH YOURSELF, MY MAN.
WHY AREN'T WE FLYING?
BECAUSE THAT'S WHERE THEY LOOK FOR US. WHAT HAPPENED TO YOU THAT DAY IN CHICAGO?
YOU'RE GETTING A LITTLE PERSONAL FOR A FIRST DATE.
COME ON, WALKER, REGALE US WITH YOUR STORY OF THE ONCE-PROUD SUPER POWER A-LISTER WHO FINDS HIMSELF ALL THE WAY DOWN HERE WITH US...
PULL OVER, I'M OUT.
WHAT?

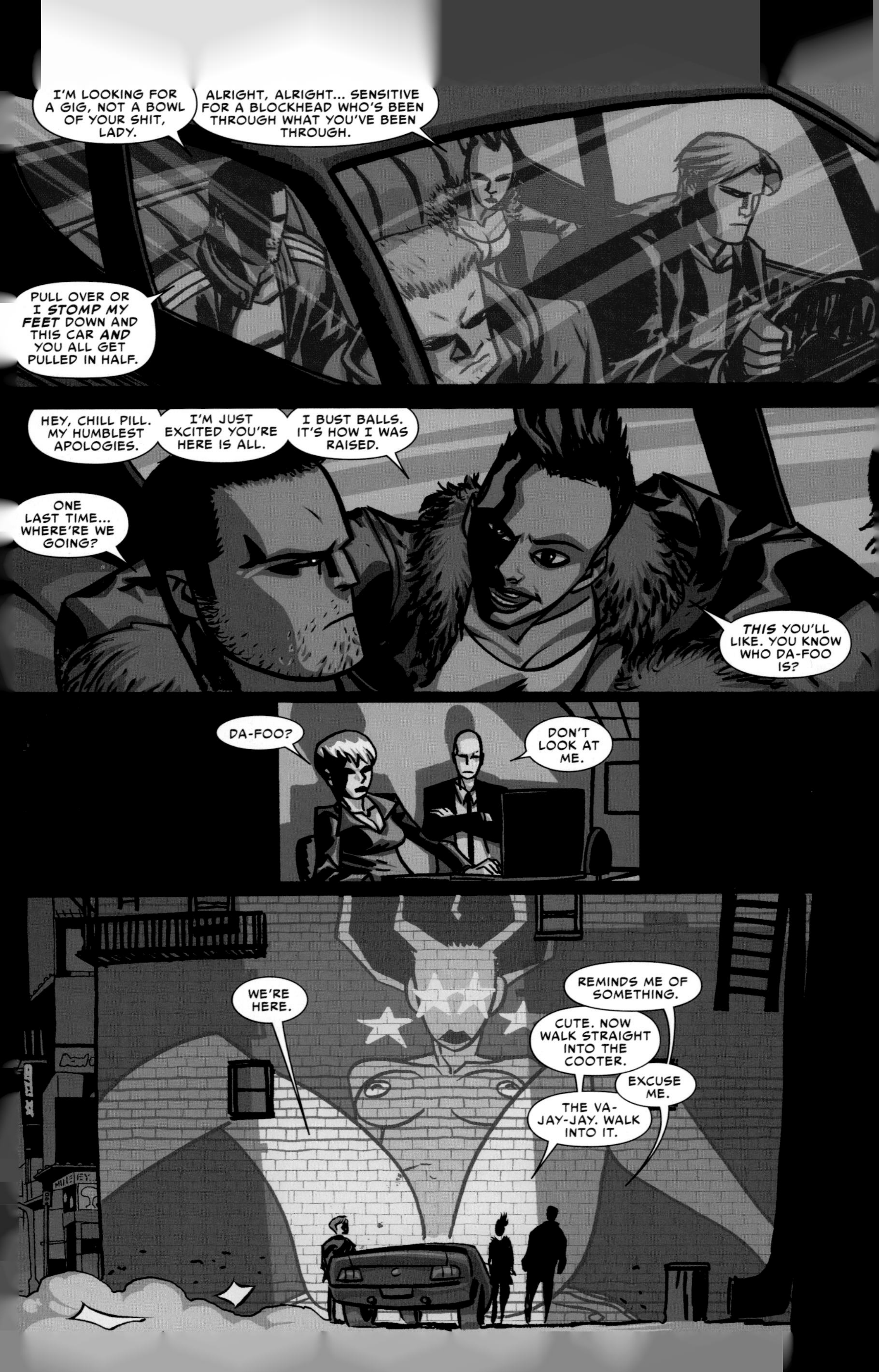
I'M LOOKING FOR A GIG, NOT A BOWL OF YOUR SHIT, LADY.
ALRIGHT, ALRIGHT... SENSITIVE FOR A BLOCKHEAD WHO'S BEEN THROUGH WHAT YOU'VE BEEN THROUGH.
PULL OVER OR I STOMP MY FEET DOWN AND THIS CAR AND YOU ALL GET PULLED IN HALF.
HEY, CHILL PILL. MY HUMBLEST APOLOGIES.
I'M JUST EXCITED YOU'RE HERE IS ALL.
I BUST BALLS. IT'S HOW I WAS RAISED.
ONE LAST TIME... WHERE'RE WE GOING?
THIS YOU'LL LIKE. YOU KNOW WHO DA-FOO IS?
DA-FOO?
DON'T LOOK AT ME.
WE'RE HERE.
REMINDS ME OF SOMETHING.
CUTE. NOW WALK STRAIGHT INTO THE COOTER.
EXCUSE ME.
THE VA-JAY-JAY. WALK INTO IT.

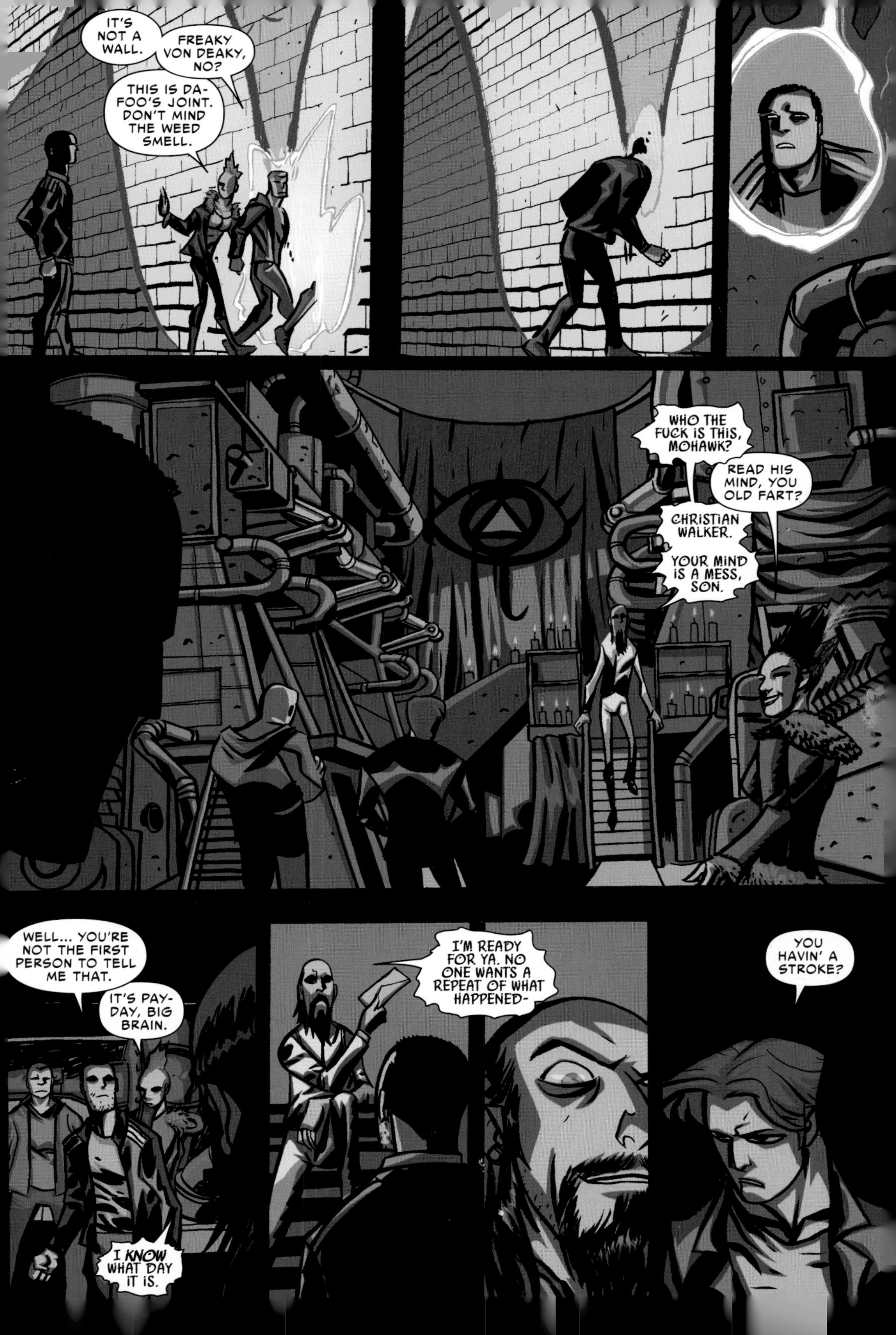
IT'S NOT A WALL.
FREAKY VON DEAKY, NO?
THIS IS DA-FOO'S JOINT. DON'T MIND THE WEED SMELL.
WHO THE FUCK IS THIS, MOHAWK?
READ HIS MIND, YOU OLD FART?
CHRISTIAN WALKER.
YOUR MIND IS A MESS, SON.
WELL... YOU'RE NOT THE FIRST PERSON TO TELL ME THAT.
IT'S PAY-DAY, BIG BRAIN.
I KNOW WHAT DAY IT IS.
I'M READY FOR YA. NO ONE WANTS A REPEAT OF WHAT HAPPENED-
YOU HAVIN' A STROKE?

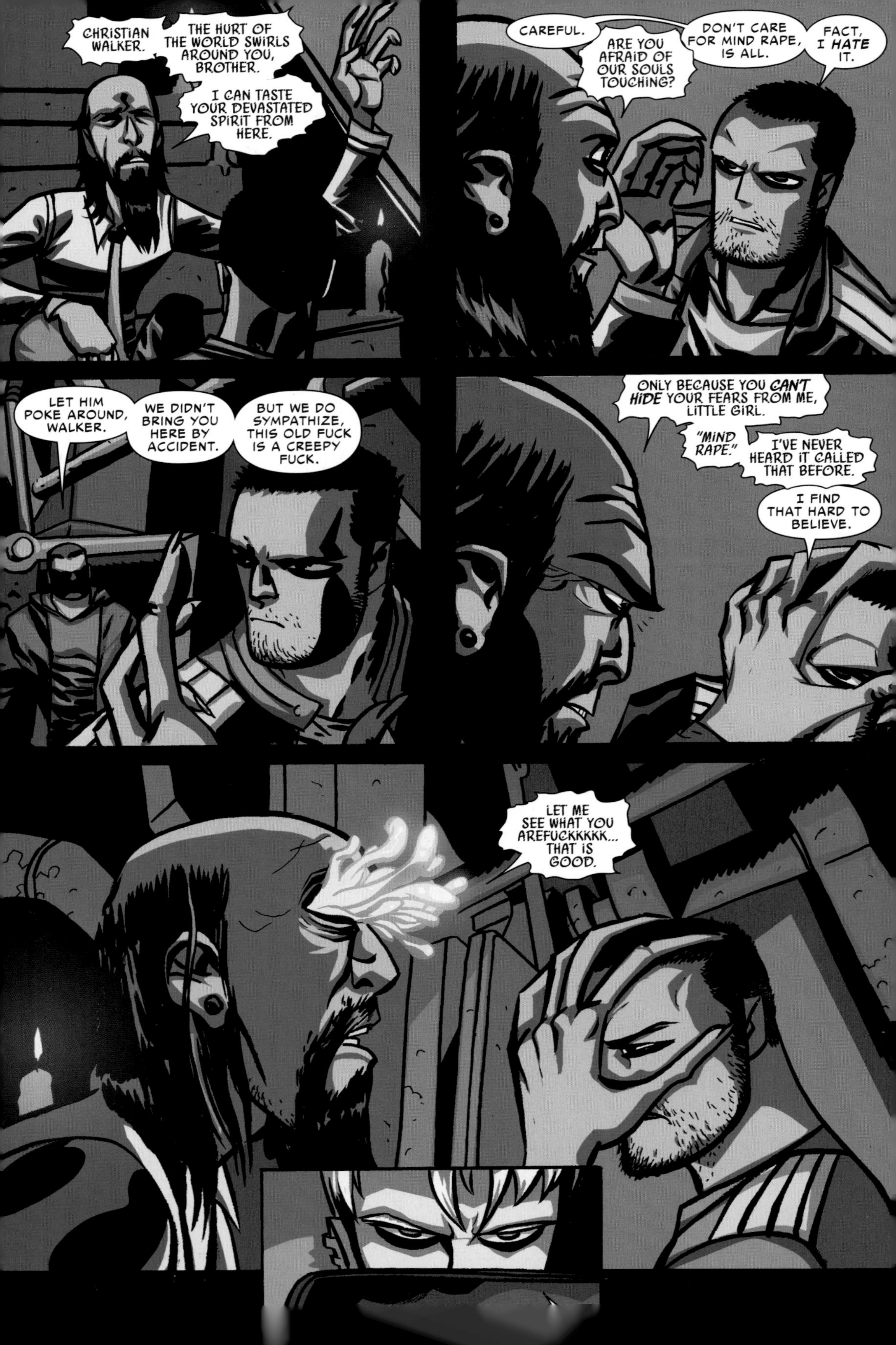
CHRISTIAN WALKER.
THE HURT OF THE WORLD SWIRLS AROUND YOU, BROTHER.
I CAN TASTE YOUR DEVASTATED SPIRIT FROM HERE.
CAREFUL.
ARE YOU AFRAID OF OUR SOULS TOUCHING?
DON'T CARE FOR MIND RAPE, IS ALL.
FACT, I *HATE* IT.
LET HIM POKE AROUND, WALKER.
WE DIDN'T BRING YOU HERE BY ACCIDENT.
BUT WE DO SYMPATHIZE, THIS OLD FUCK IS A CREEPY FUCK.
ONLY BECAUSE YOU *CAN'T HIDE* YOUR FEARS FROM ME, LITTLE GIRL.
"MIND RAPE."
I'VE NEVER HEARD IT CALLED THAT BEFORE.
I FIND THAT HARD TO BELIEVE.
LET ME SEE WHAT YOU AREFUCKKKKK... THAT IS GOOD.

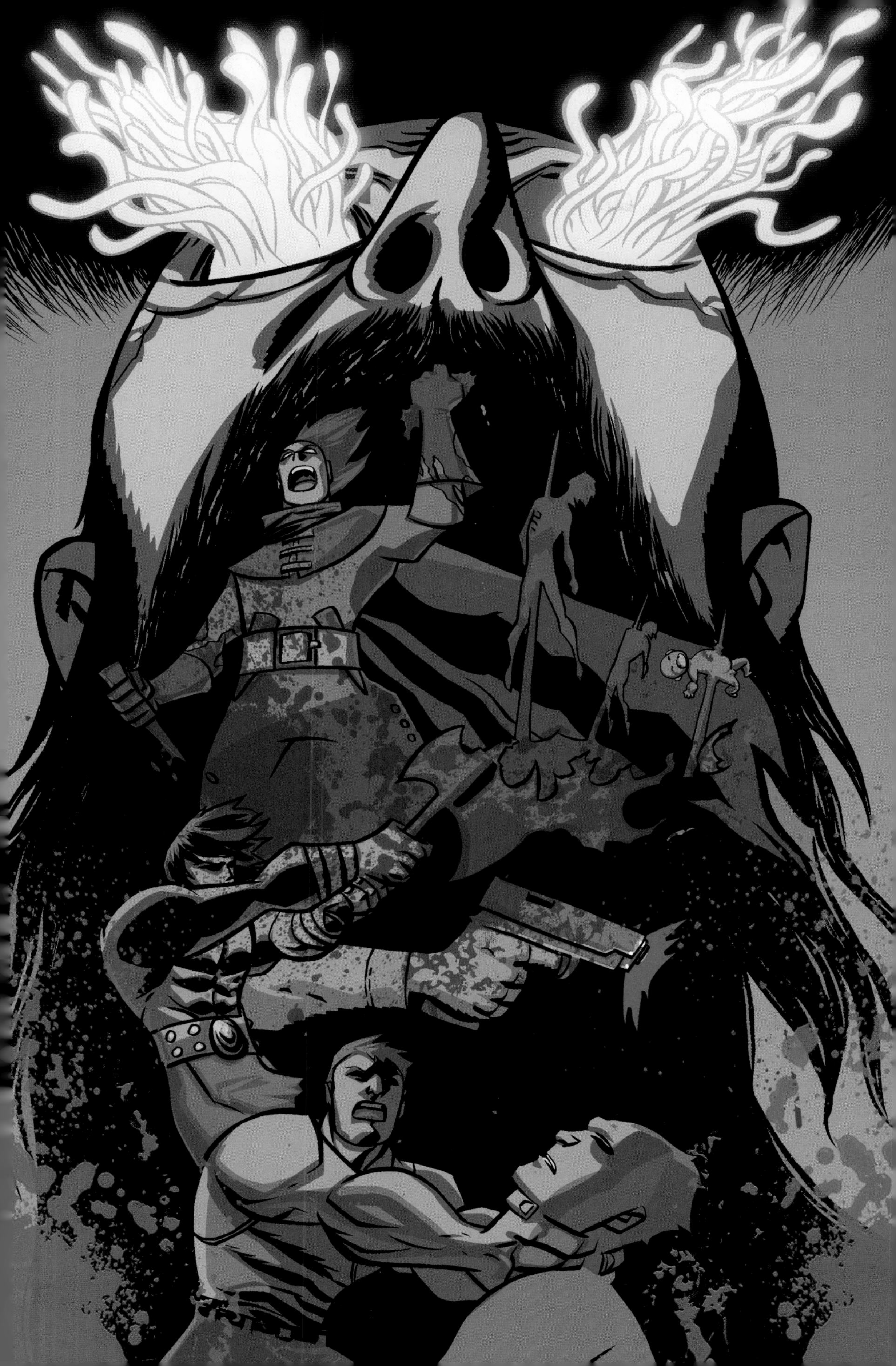

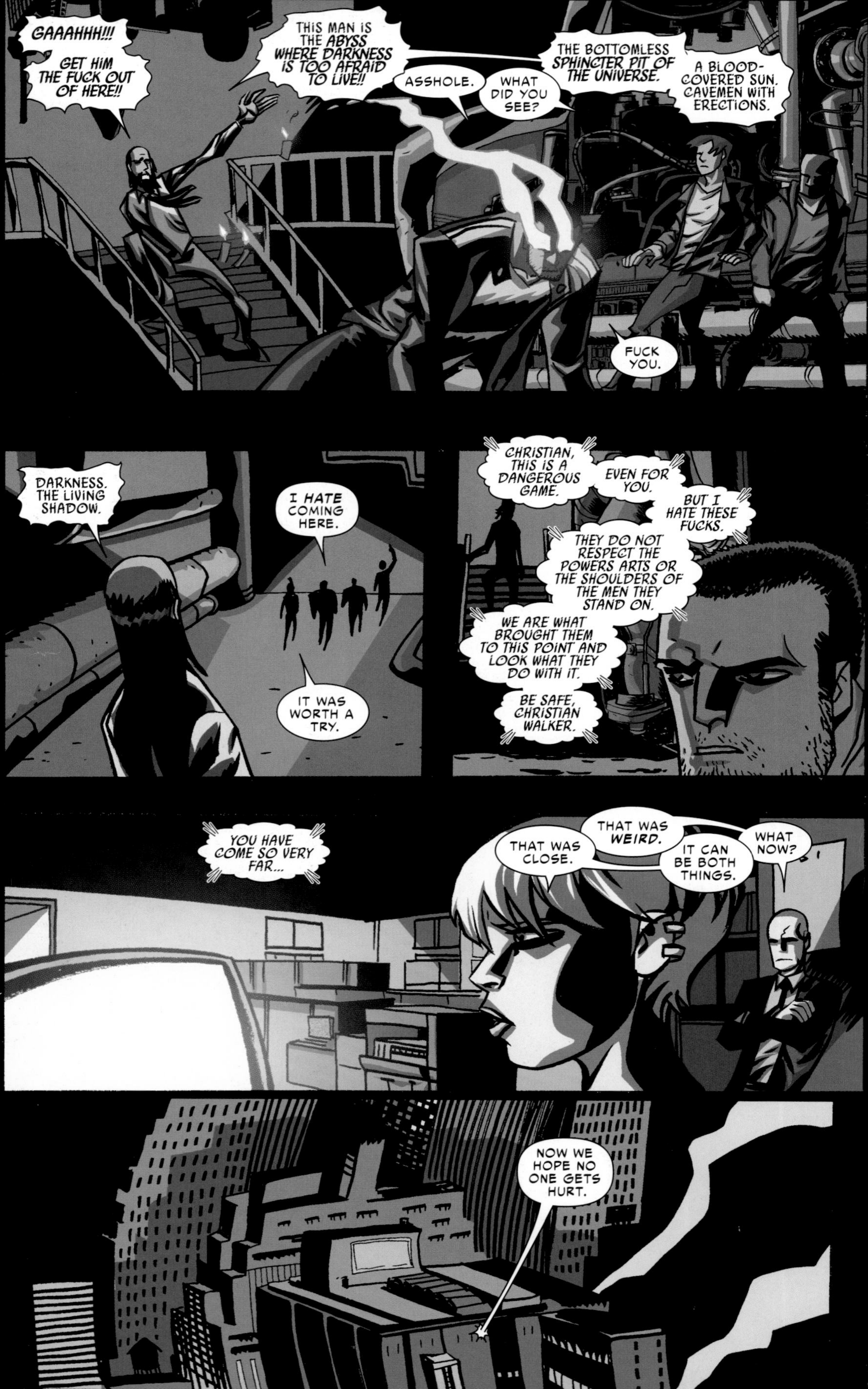
GAAAHHH!!! GET HIM THE FUCK OUT OF HERE!!
THIS MAN IS THE ABYSS WHERE DARKNESS IS TOO AFRAID TO LIVE!!
ASSHOLE.
WHAT DID YOU SEE?
THE BOTTOMLESS SPHINCTER PIT OF THE UNIVERSE.
A BLOOD-COVERED SUN. CAVEMEN WITH ERECTIONS.
FUCK YOU.
DARKNESS. THE LIVING SHADOW.
I HATE COMING HERE.
IT WAS WORTH A TRY.
CHRISTIAN, THIS IS A DANGEROUS GAME.
EVEN FOR YOU.
BUT I HATE THESE FUCKS.
THEY DO NOT RESPECT THE POWERS ARTS OR THE SHOULDERS OF THE MEN THEY STAND ON.
WE ARE WHAT BROUGHT THEM TO THIS POINT AND LOOK WHAT THEY DO WITH IT.
BE SAFE, CHRISTIAN WALKER.
YOU HAVE COME SO VERY FAR...
THAT WAS CLOSE.
THAT WAS WEIRD.
IT CAN BE BOTH THINGS.
WHAT NOW?
NOW WE HOPE NO ONE GETS HURT.

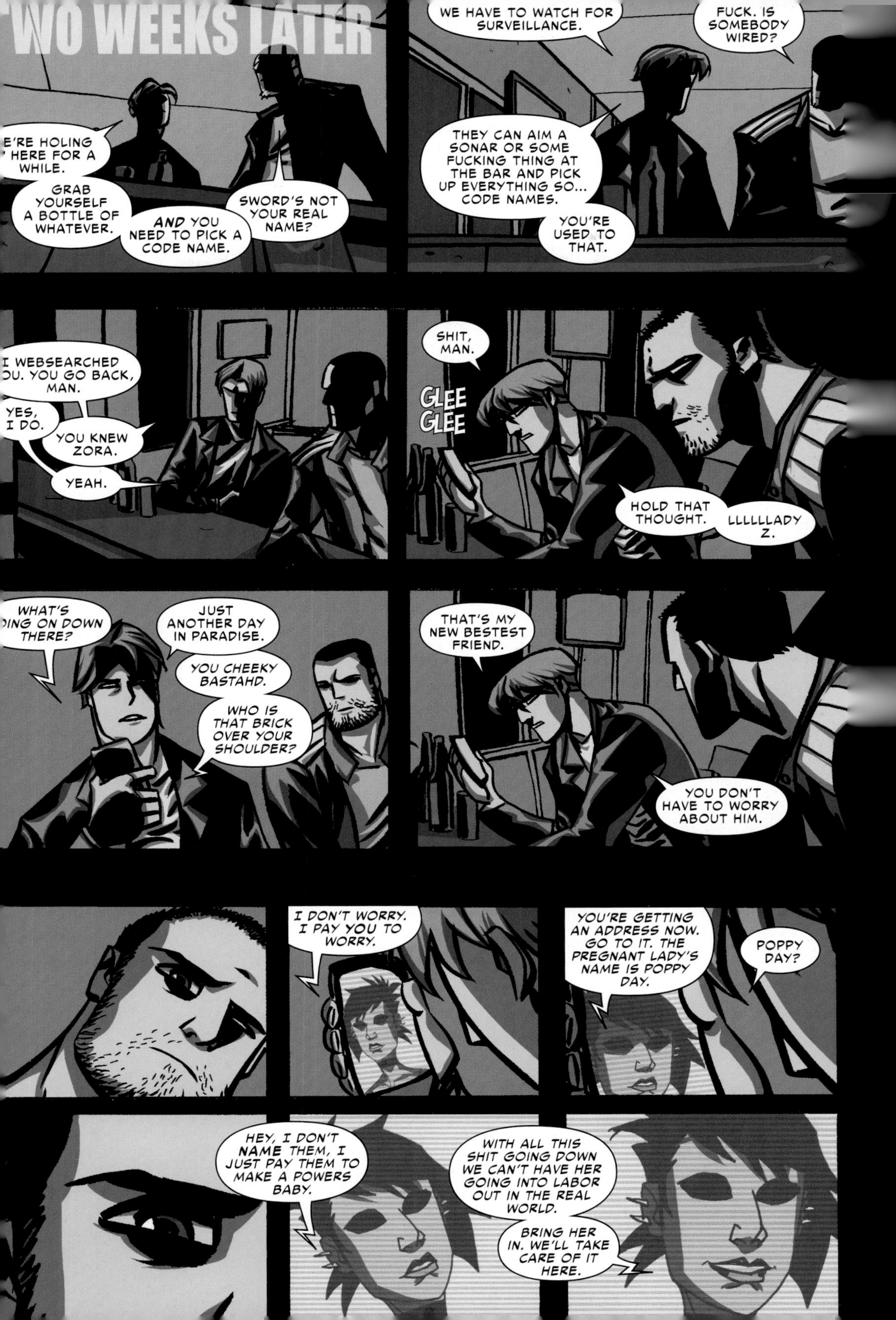
WO WEEKS LATER
E'RE HOLING HERE FOR A WHILE.
GRAB YOURSELF A BOTTLE OF WHATEVER.
AND YOU NEED TO PICK A CODE NAME.
SWORD'S NOT YOUR REAL NAME?
WE HAVE TO WATCH FOR SURVEILLANCE.
FUCK. IS SOMEBODY WIRED?
THEY CAN AIM A SONAR OR SOME FUCKING THING AT THE BAR AND PICK UP EVERYTHING SO... CODE NAMES.
YOU'RE USED TO THAT.
I WEBSEARCHED OU. YOU GO BACK, MAN.
YES, I DO.
YOU KNEW ZORA.
YEAH.
SHIT, MAN.
GLEE GLEE
HOLD THAT THOUGHT.
LLLLLLADY Z.
WHAT'S OING ON DOWN THERE?
JUST ANOTHER DAY IN PARADISE.
YOU CHEEKY BASTAHD.
WHO IS THAT BRICK OVER YOUR SHOULDER?
THAT'S MY NEW BESTEST FRIEND.
YOU DON'T HAVE TO WORRY ABOUT HIM.
I DON'T WORRY. I PAY YOU TO WORRY.
YOU'RE GETTING AN ADDRESS NOW. GO TO IT. THE PREGNANT LADY'S NAME IS POPPY DAY.
POPPY DAY?
HEY, I DON'T NAME THEM, I JUST PAY THEM TO MAKE A POWERS BABY.
WITH ALL THIS SHIT GOING DOWN WE CAN'T HAVE HER GOING INTO LABOR OUT IN THE REAL WORLD.
BRING HER IN. WE'LL TAKE CARE OF IT HERE.

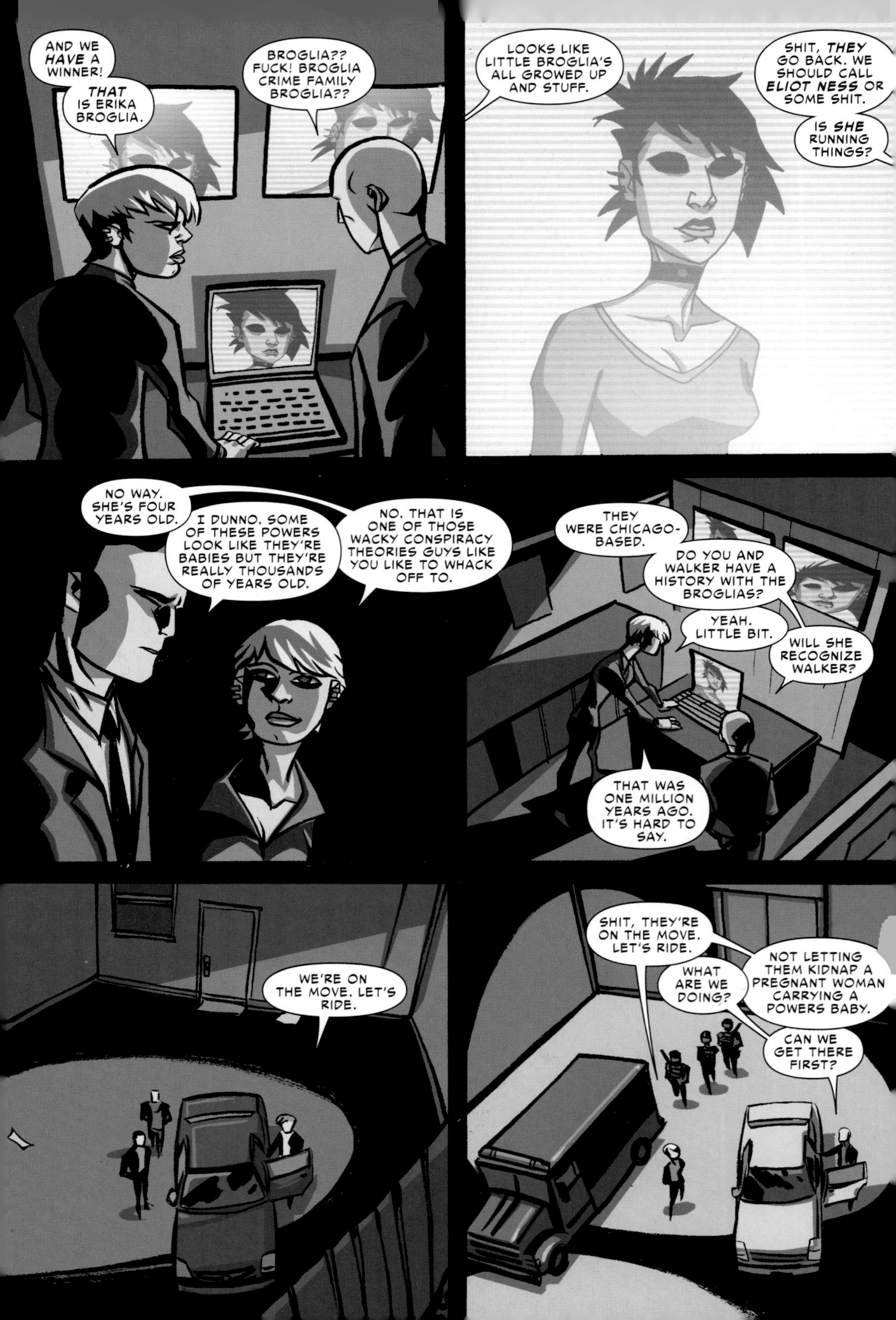
AND WE HAVE A WINNER!
THAT IS ERIKA BROGLIA.
BROGLIA?? FUCK! BROGLIA CRIME FAMILY BROGLIA??
LOOKS LIKE LITTLE BROGLIA'S ALL GROWED UP AND STUFF.
SHIT, THEY GO BACK. WE SHOULD CALL ELIOT NESS OR SOME SHIT.
IS SHE RUNNING THINGS?
NO WAY. SHE'S FOUR YEARS OLD.
I DUNNO. SOME OF THESE POWERS LOOK LIKE THEY'RE BABIES BUT THEY'RE REALLY THOUSANDS OF YEARS OLD.
NO. THAT IS ONE OF THOSE WACKY CONSPIRACY THEORIES GUYS LIKE YOU LIKE TO WHACK OFF TO.
THEY WERE CHICAGO-BASED.
DO YOU AND WALKER HAVE A HISTORY WITH THE BROGLIAS?
YEAH. LITTLE BIT.
WILL SHE RECOGNIZE WALKER?
THAT WAS ONE MILLION YEARS AGO. IT'S HARD TO SAY.
WE'RE ON THE MOVE. LET'S RIDE.
SHIT, THEY'RE ON THE MOVE. LET'S RIDE.
WHAT ARE WE DOING?
NOT LETTING THEM KIDNAP A PREGNANT WOMAN CARRYING A POWERS BABY.
CAN WE GET THERE FIRST?

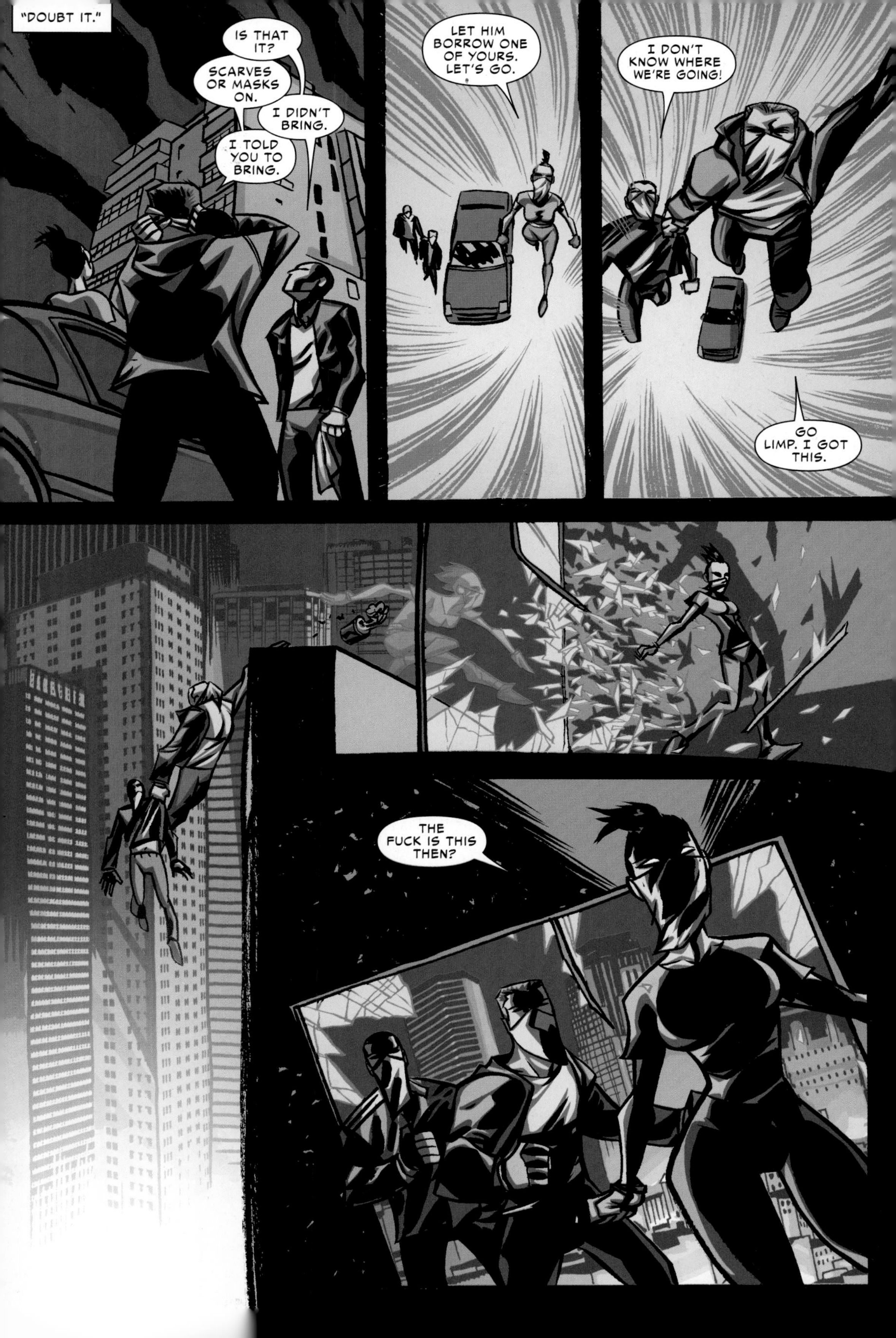
"DOUBT IT."
IS THAT IT?
SCARVES OR MASKS ON.
I DIDN'T BRING.
I TOLD YOU TO BRING.
LET HIM BORROW ONE OF YOURS. LET'S GO.
I DON'T KNOW WHERE WE'RE GOING!
GO LIMP. I GOT THIS.
THE FUCK IS THIS THEN?

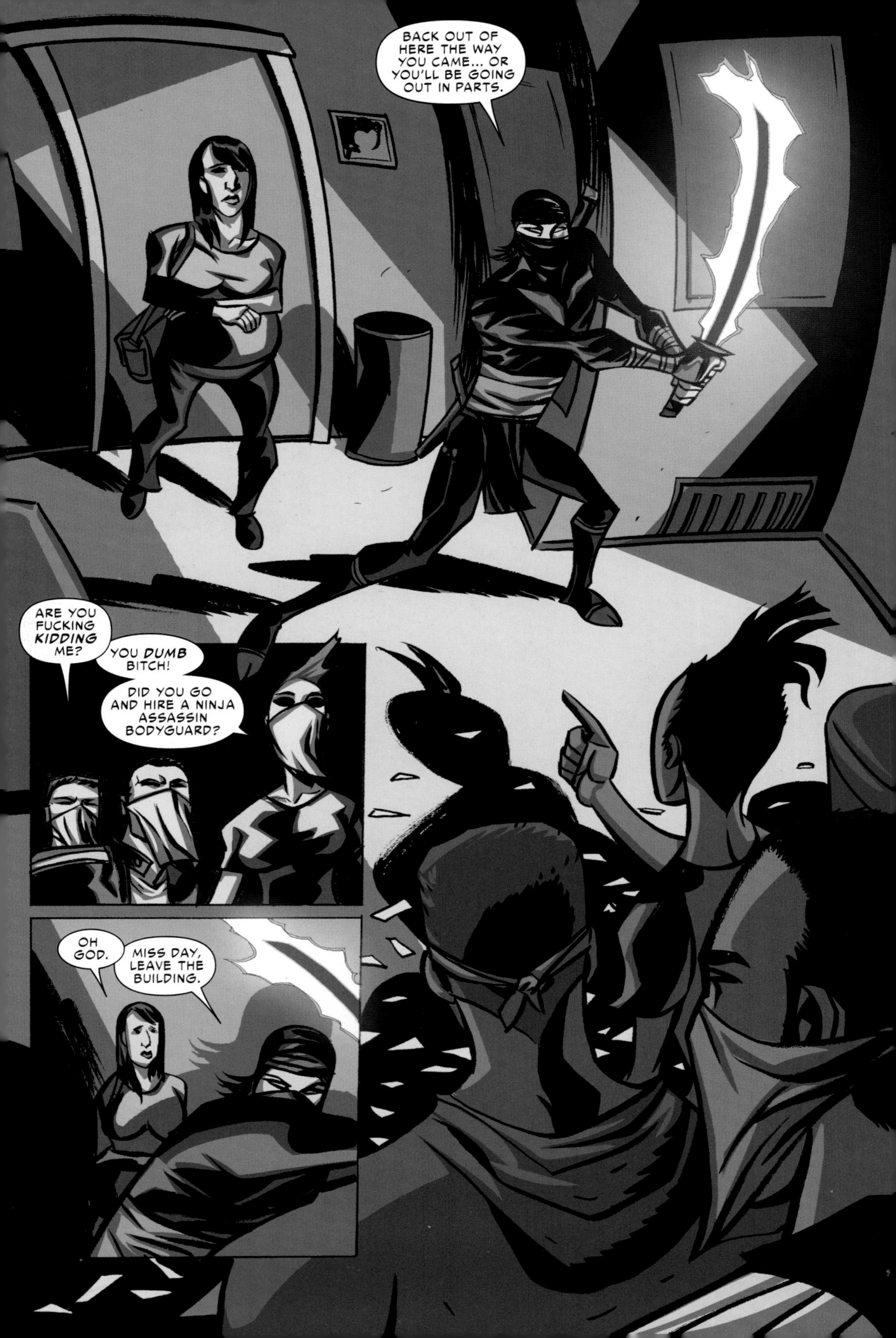
BACK OUT OF HERE THE WAY YOU CAME... OR YOU'LL BE GOING OUT IN PARTS.
ARE YOU FUCKING *KIDDING* ME?
YOU *DUMB* BITCH!
DID YOU GO AND HIRE A NINJA ASSASSIN BODYGUARD?
OH GOD.
MISS DAY, LEAVE THE BUILDING.

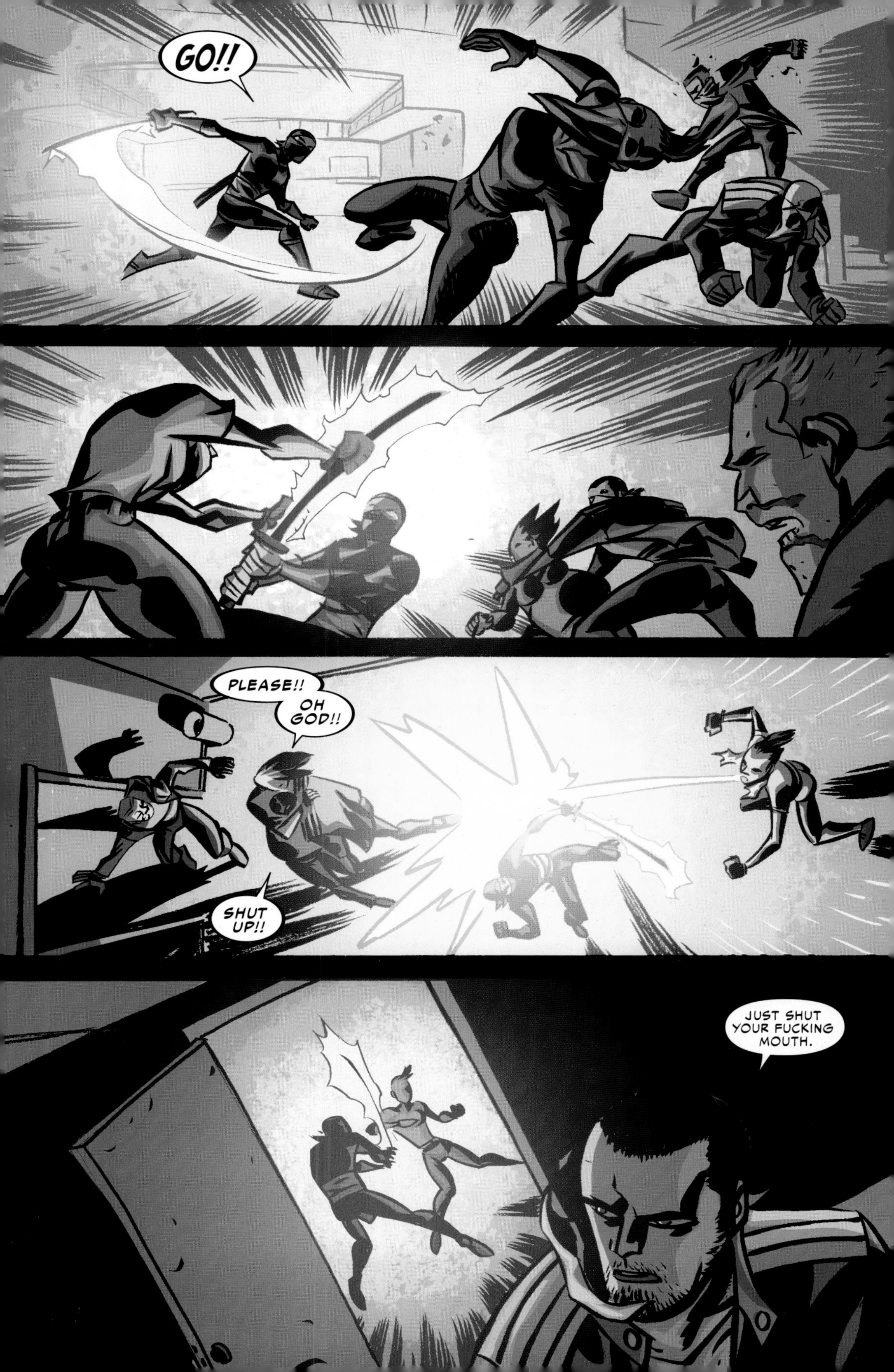

GO!!
PLEASE!!
OH GOD!!
SHUT UP!!
JUST SHUT YOUR FUCKING MOUTH.

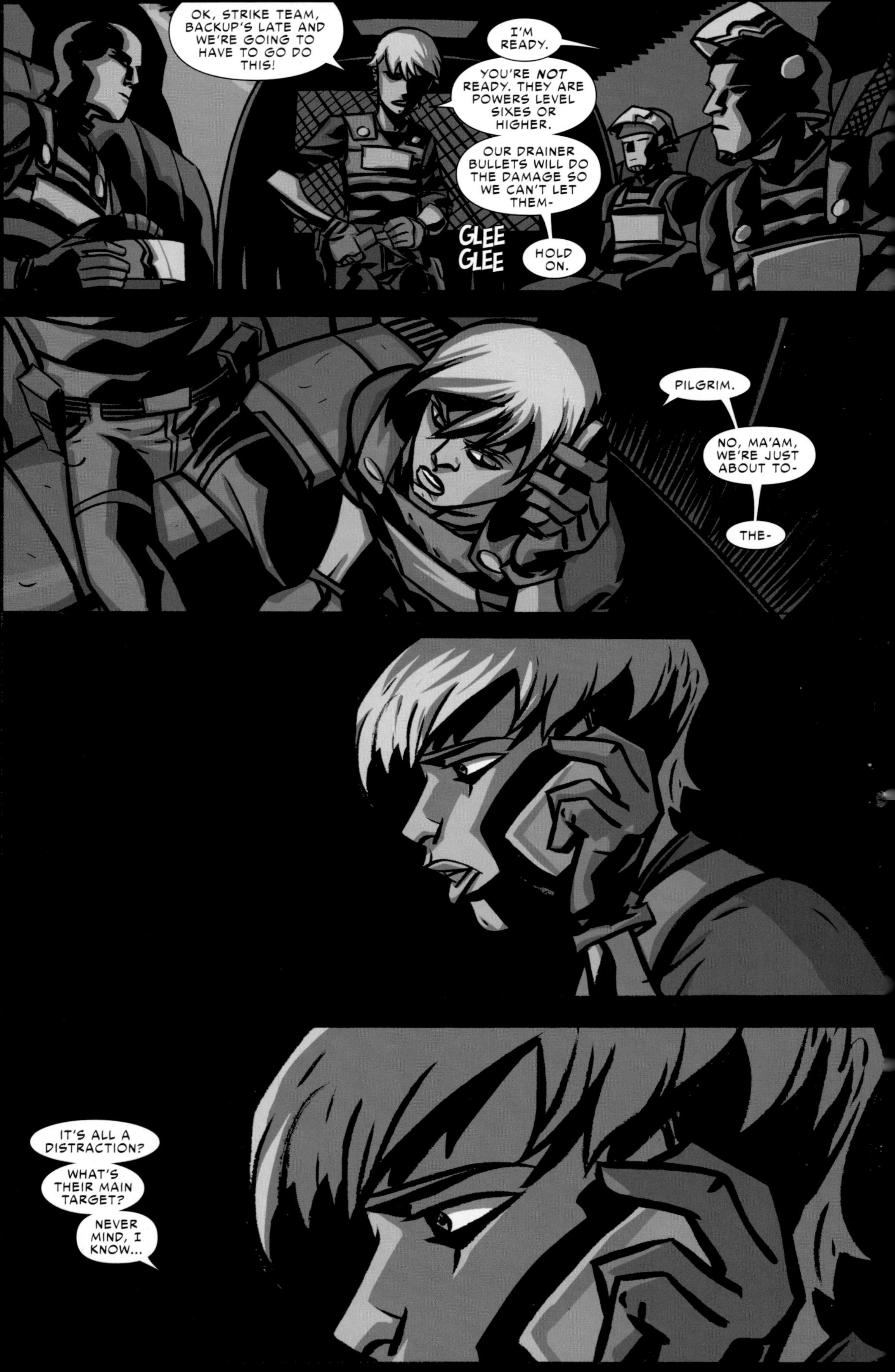
OK, STRIKE TEAM, BACKUP'S LATE AND WE'RE GOING TO HAVE TO GO DO THIS!
I'M READY.
YOU'RE *NOT* READY. THEY ARE POWERS LEVEL SIXES OR HIGHER.
OUR DRAINER BULLETS WILL DO THE DAMAGE SO WE CAN'T LET THEM-
GLEE GLEE
HOLD ON.
PILGRIM.
NO, MA'AM, WE'RE JUST ABOUT TO-
THE-
IT'S ALL A DISTRACTION?
WHAT'S THEIR MAIN TARGET?
NEVER MIND, I KNOW...

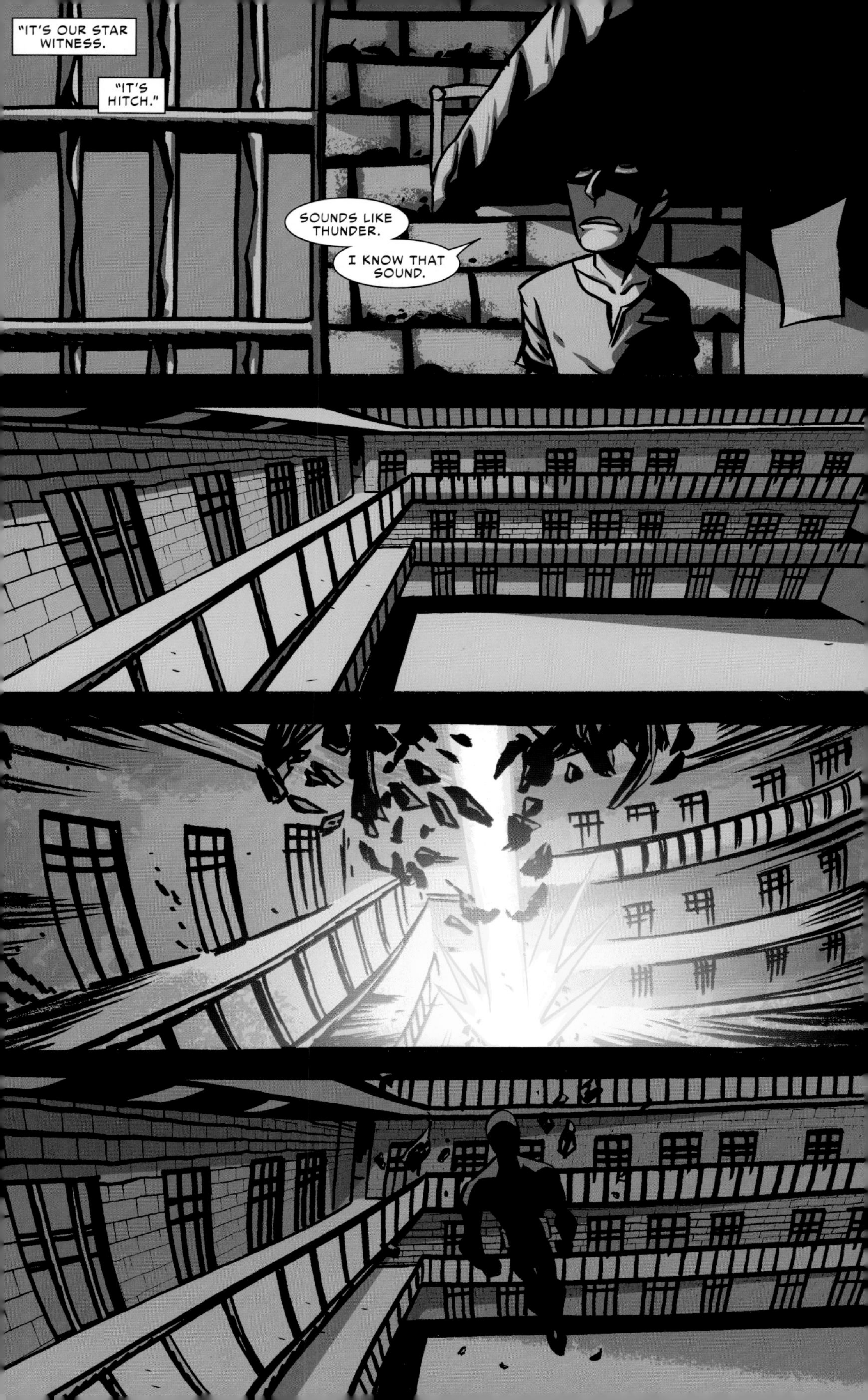
"IT'S OUR STAR WITNESS.
"IT'S HITCH."
SOUNDS LIKE THUNDER.
I KNOW THAT SOUND.

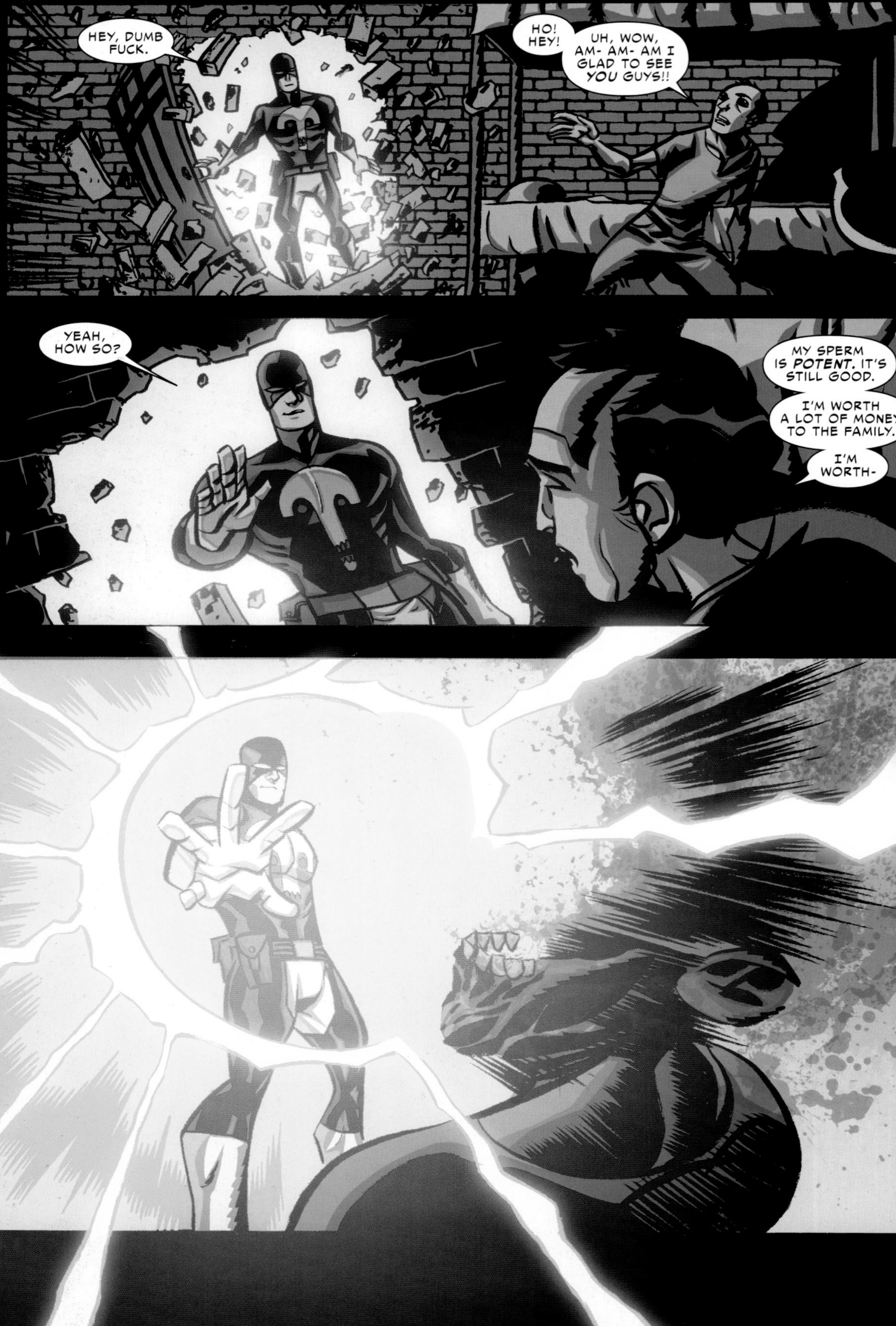
HEY, DUMB FUCK.
HO! HEY!
UH, WOW, AM- AM- AM I GLAD TO SEE YOU GUYS!!
YEAH, HOW SO?
MY SPERM IS POTENT. IT'S STILL GOOD.
I'M WORTH A LOT OF MONEY TO THE FAMILY.
I'M WORTH-

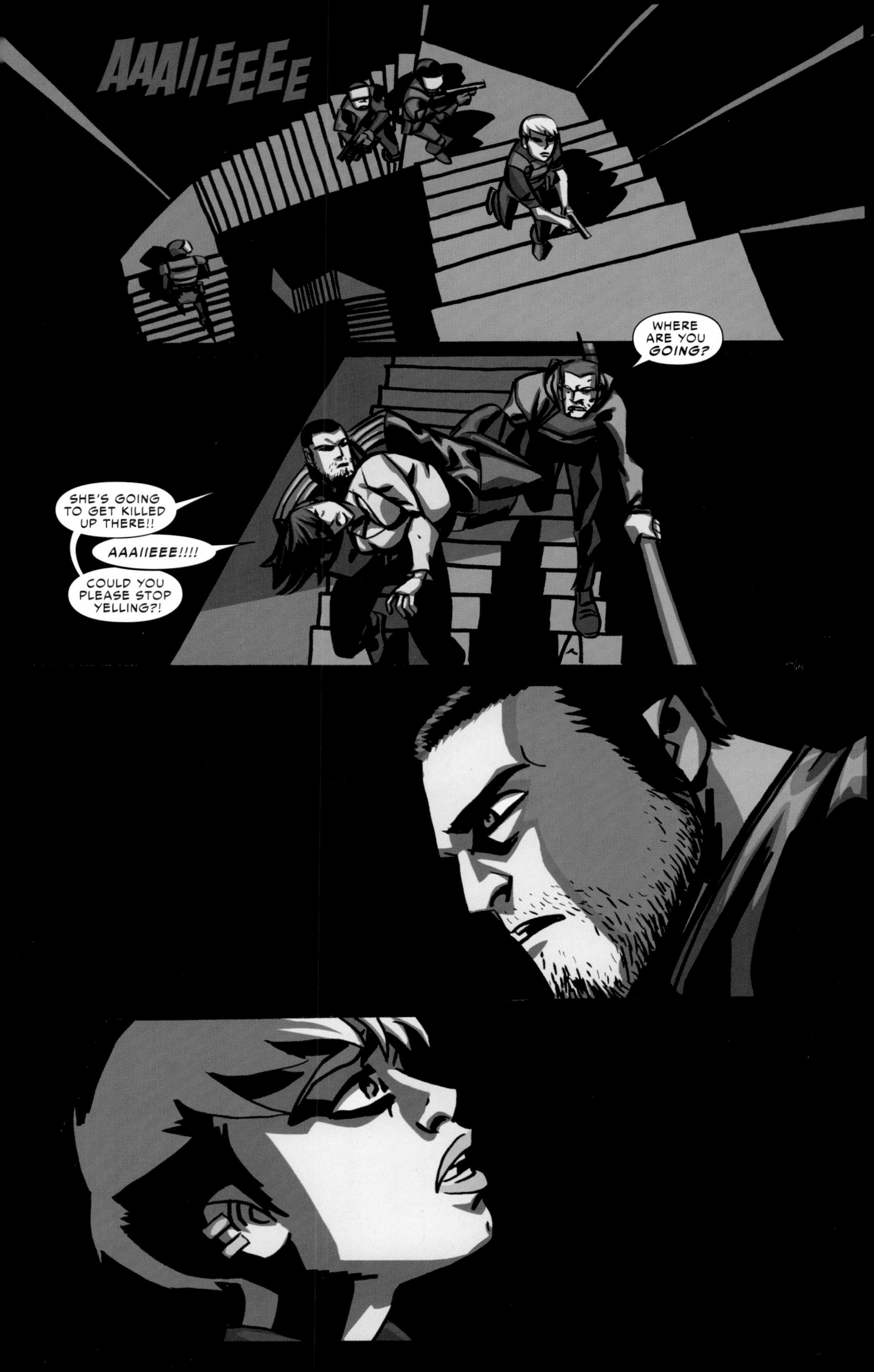
AAAIIEEEE
WHERE ARE YOU GOING?
SHE'S GOING TO GET KILLED UP THERE!!
AAAIIEEE!!!!
COULD YOU PLEASE STOP YELLING?!

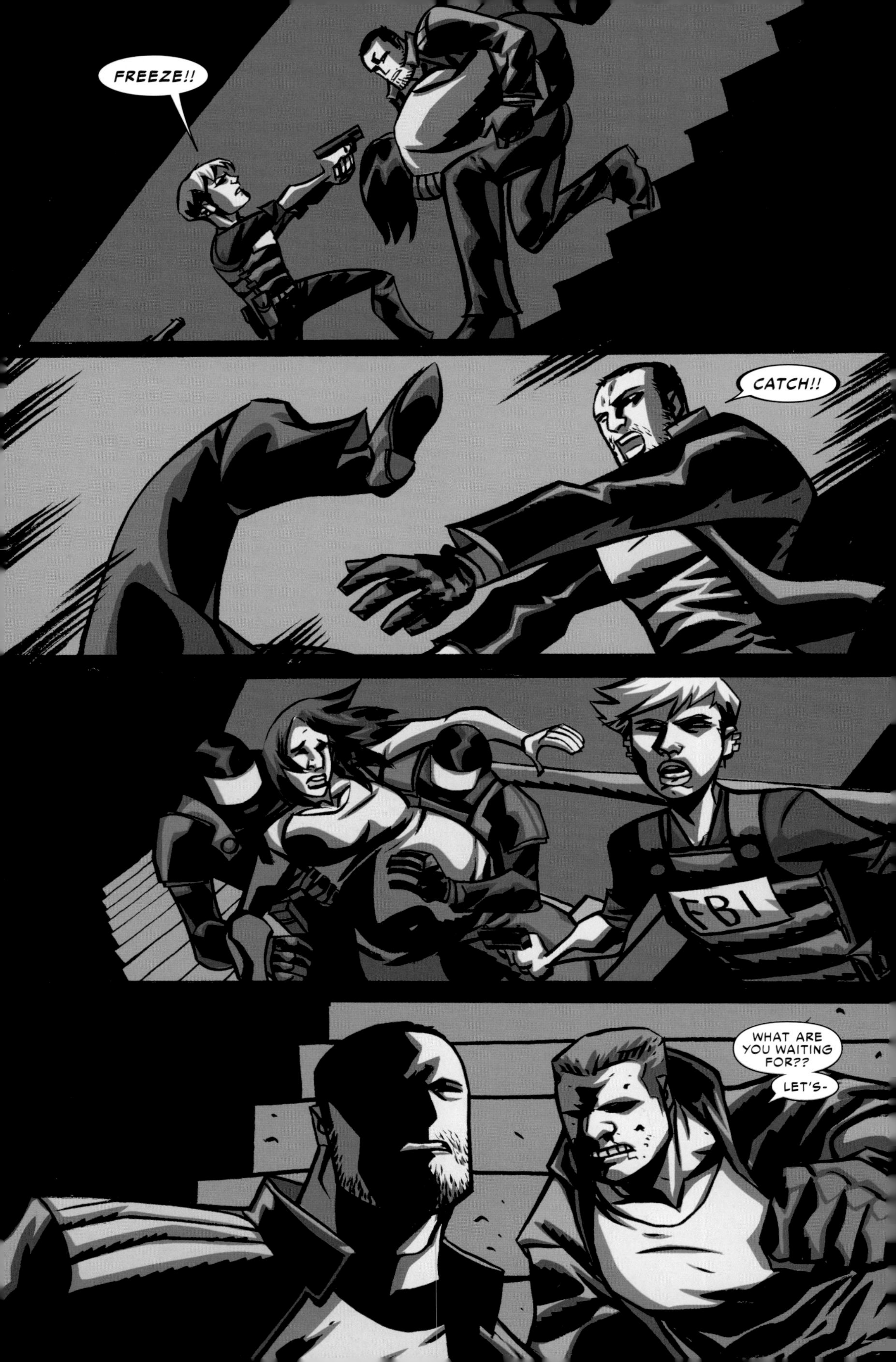
FREEZE!!
CATCH!!
FBI
WHAT ARE YOU WAITING FOR??
LET'S-

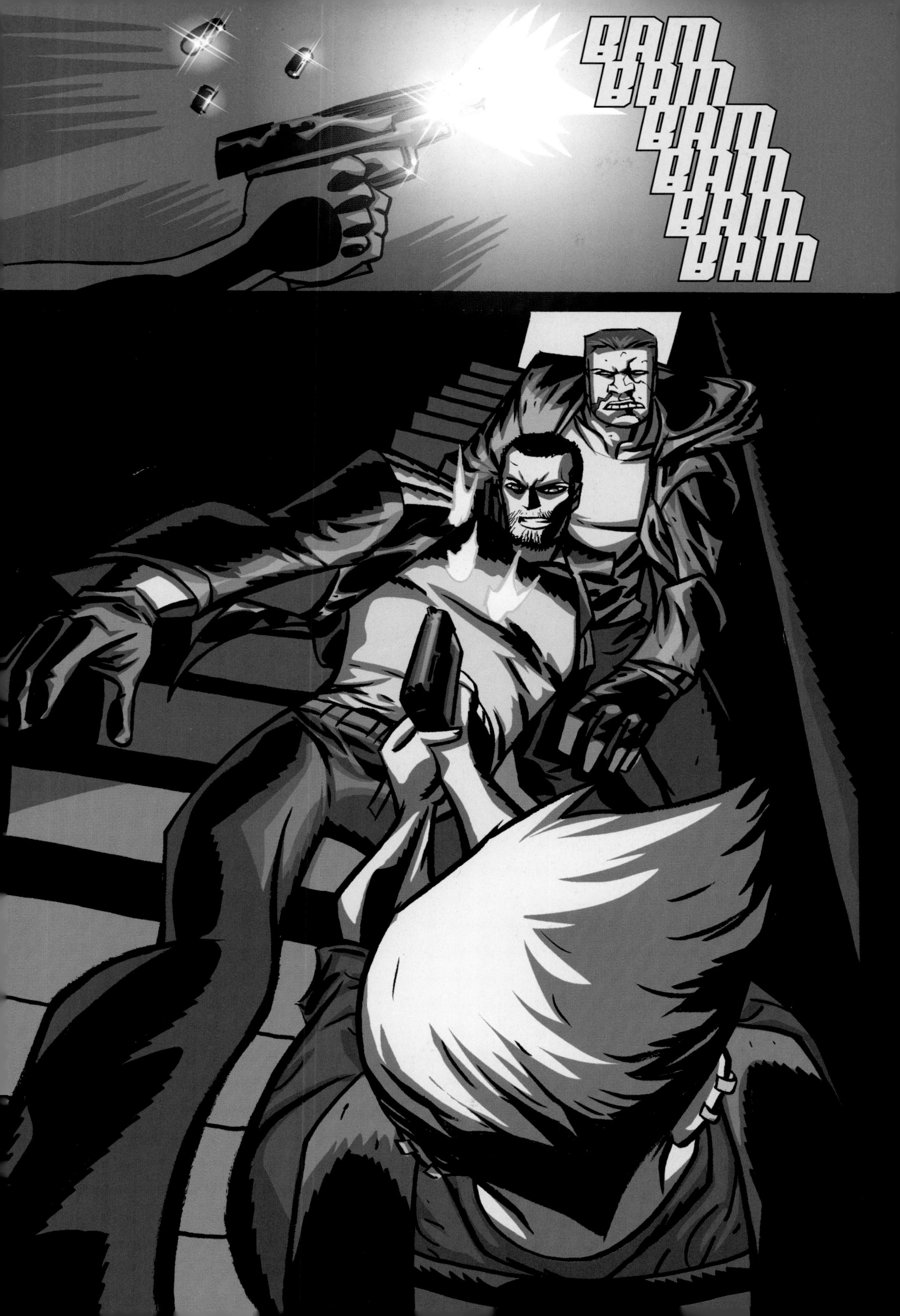
BAM
BAM
BAM
BAM
BAM
BAM

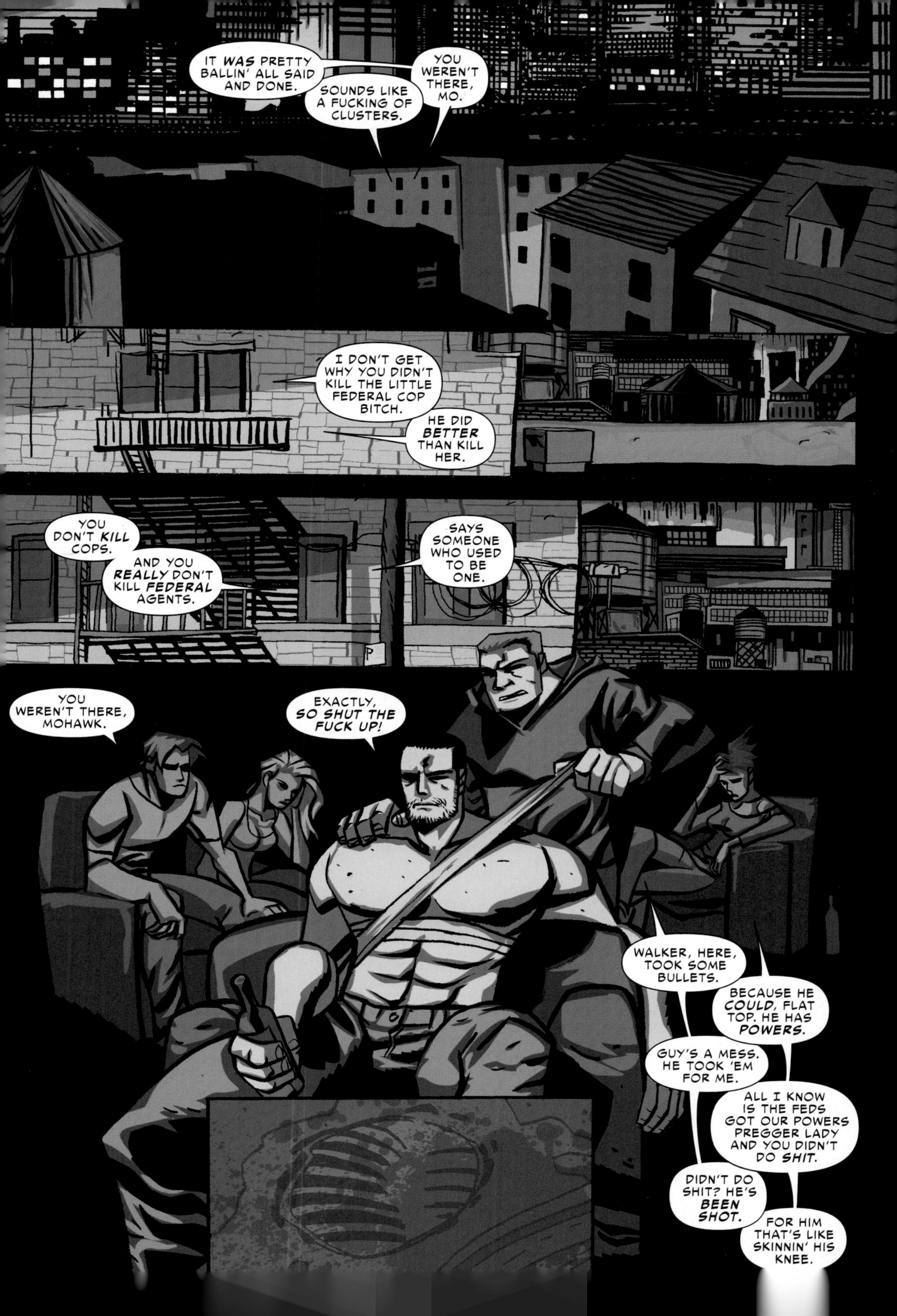

IT WAS PRETTY BALLIN' ALL SAID AND DONE.
YOU WEREN'T THERE, MO.
SOUNDS LIKE A FUCKING OF CLUSTERS.
I DON'T GET WHY YOU DIDN'T KILL THE LITTLE FEDERAL COP BITCH.
HE DID BETTER THAN KILL HER.
YOU DON'T KILL COPS.
AND YOU REALLY DON'T KILL FEDERAL AGENTS.
SAYS SOMEONE WHO USED TO BE ONE.
YOU WEREN'T THERE, MOHAWK.
EXACTLY, SO SHUT THE FUCK UP!
WALKER, HERE, TOOK SOME BULLETS.
BECAUSE HE COULD, FLAT TOP. HE HAS POWERS.
GUY'S A MESS. HE TOOK 'EM FOR ME.
ALL I KNOW IS THE FEDS GOT OUR POWERS PREGGER LADY AND YOU DIDN'T DO SHIT.
DIDN'T DO SHIT? HE'S BEEN SHOT.
FOR HIM THAT'S LIKE SKINNIN' HIS KNEE.

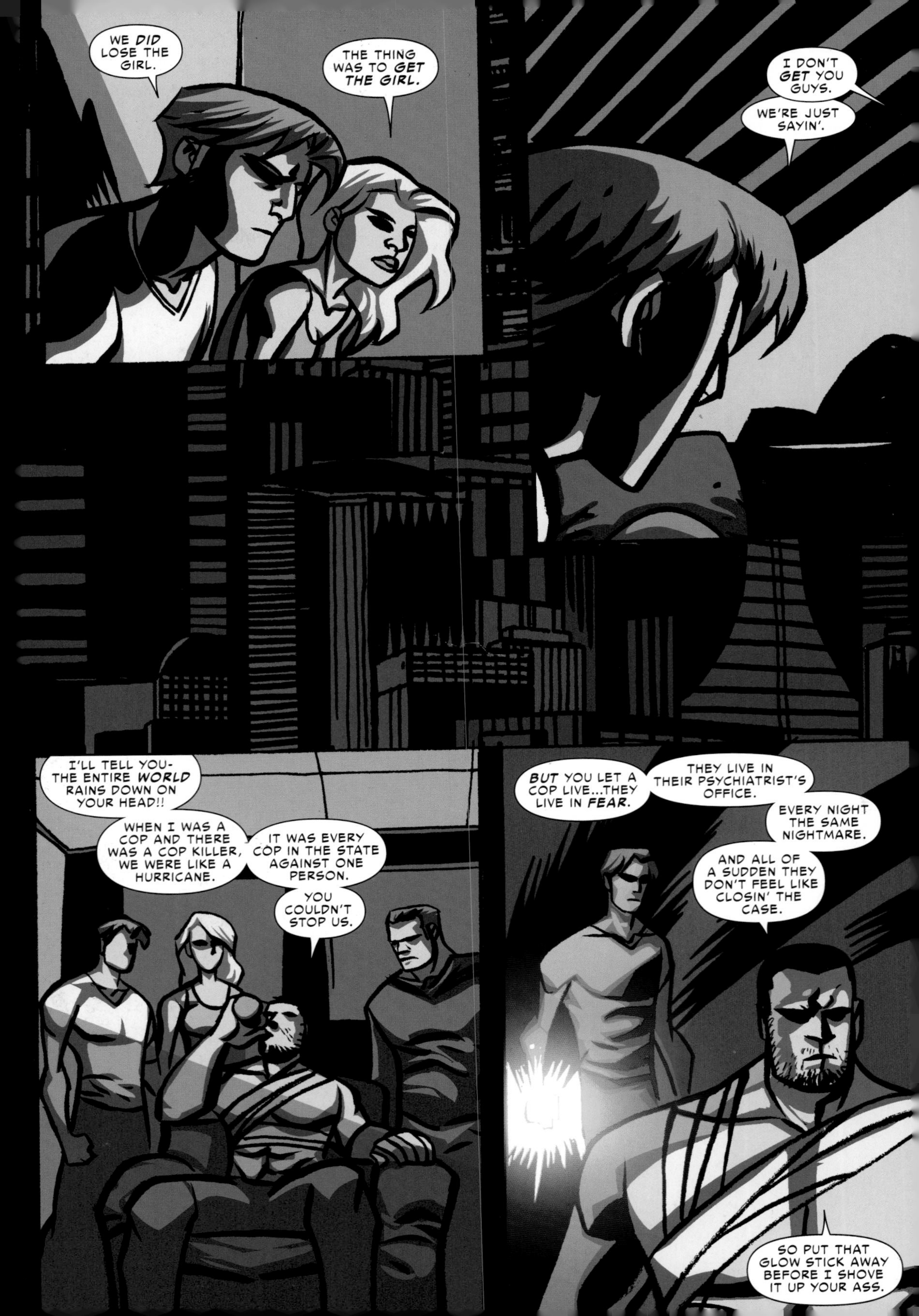
WE DID LOSE THE GIRL.
THE THING WAS TO GET THE GIRL.
I DON'T GET YOU GUYS.
WE'RE JUST SAYIN'.
I'LL TELL YOU- THE ENTIRE WORLD RAINS DOWN ON YOUR HEAD!!
WHEN I WAS A COP AND THERE WAS A COP KILLER, WE WERE LIKE A HURRICANE.
IT WAS EVERY COP IN THE STATE AGAINST ONE PERSON.
YOU COULDN'T STOP US.
BUT YOU LET A COP LIVE...THEY LIVE IN FEAR.
THEY LIVE IN THEIR PSYCHIATRIST'S OFFICE.
EVERY NIGHT THE SAME NIGHTMARE.
AND ALL OF A SUDDEN THEY DON'T FEEL LIKE CLOSIN' THE CASE.
SO PUT THAT GLOW STICK AWAY BEFORE I SHOVE IT UP YOUR ASS.

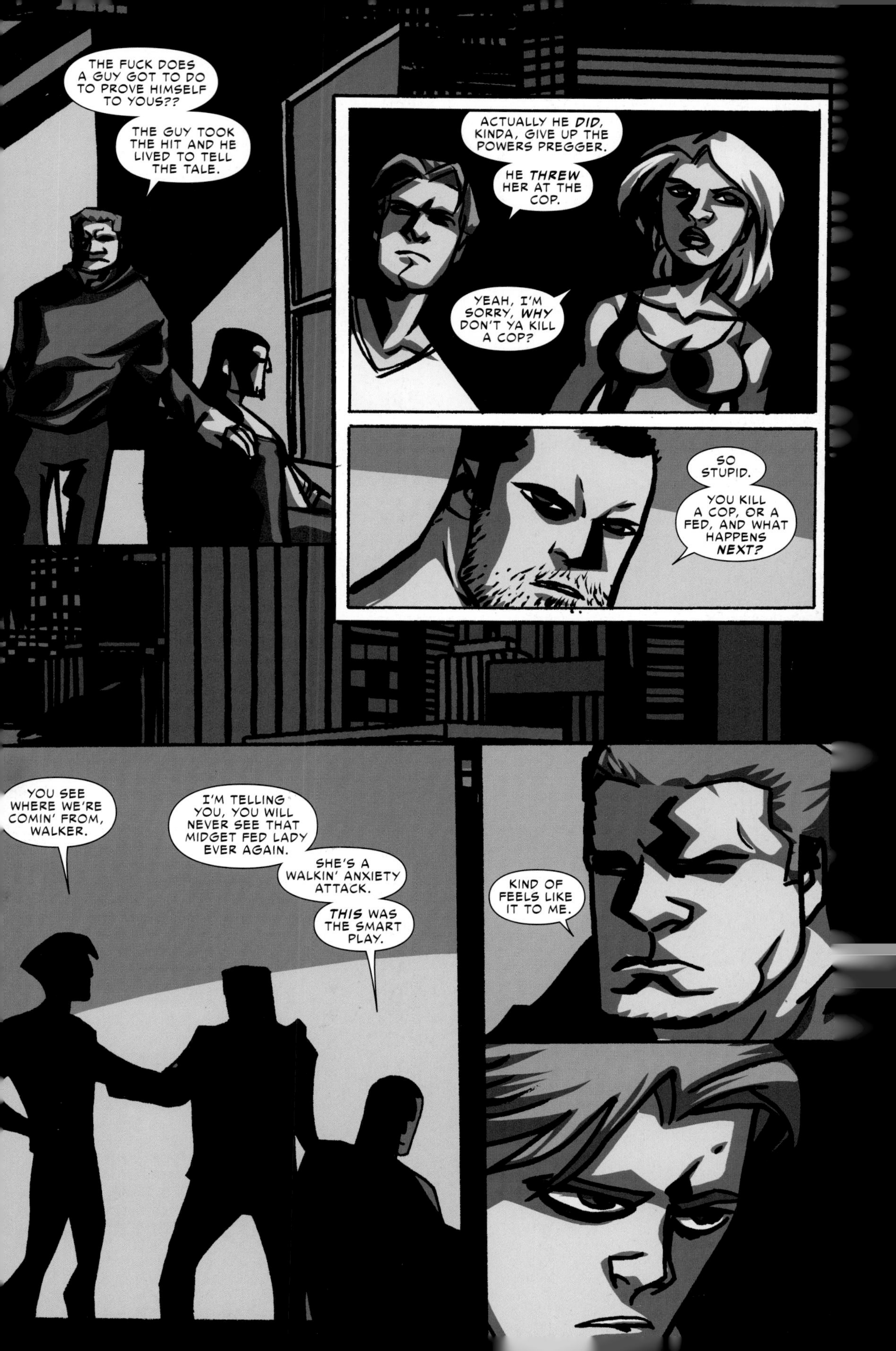
THE FUCK DOES A GUY GOT TO DO TO PROVE HIMSELF TO YOUS??
THE GUY TOOK THE HIT AND HE LIVED TO TELL THE TALE.
ACTUALLY HE *DID*, KINDA, GIVE UP THE POWERS PREGGER.
HE *THREW* HER AT THE COP.
YEAH, I'M SORRY, *WHY* DON'T YA KILL A COP?
SO STUPID.
YOU KILL A COP, OR A FED, AND WHAT HAPPENS *NEXT?*
YOU SEE WHERE WE'RE COMIN' FROM, WALKER.
I'M TELLING YOU, YOU WILL NEVER SEE THAT MIDGET FED LADY EVER AGAIN.
SHE'S A WALKIN' ANXIETY ATTACK.
THIS WAS THE SMART PLAY.
KIND OF FEELS LIKE IT TO ME.

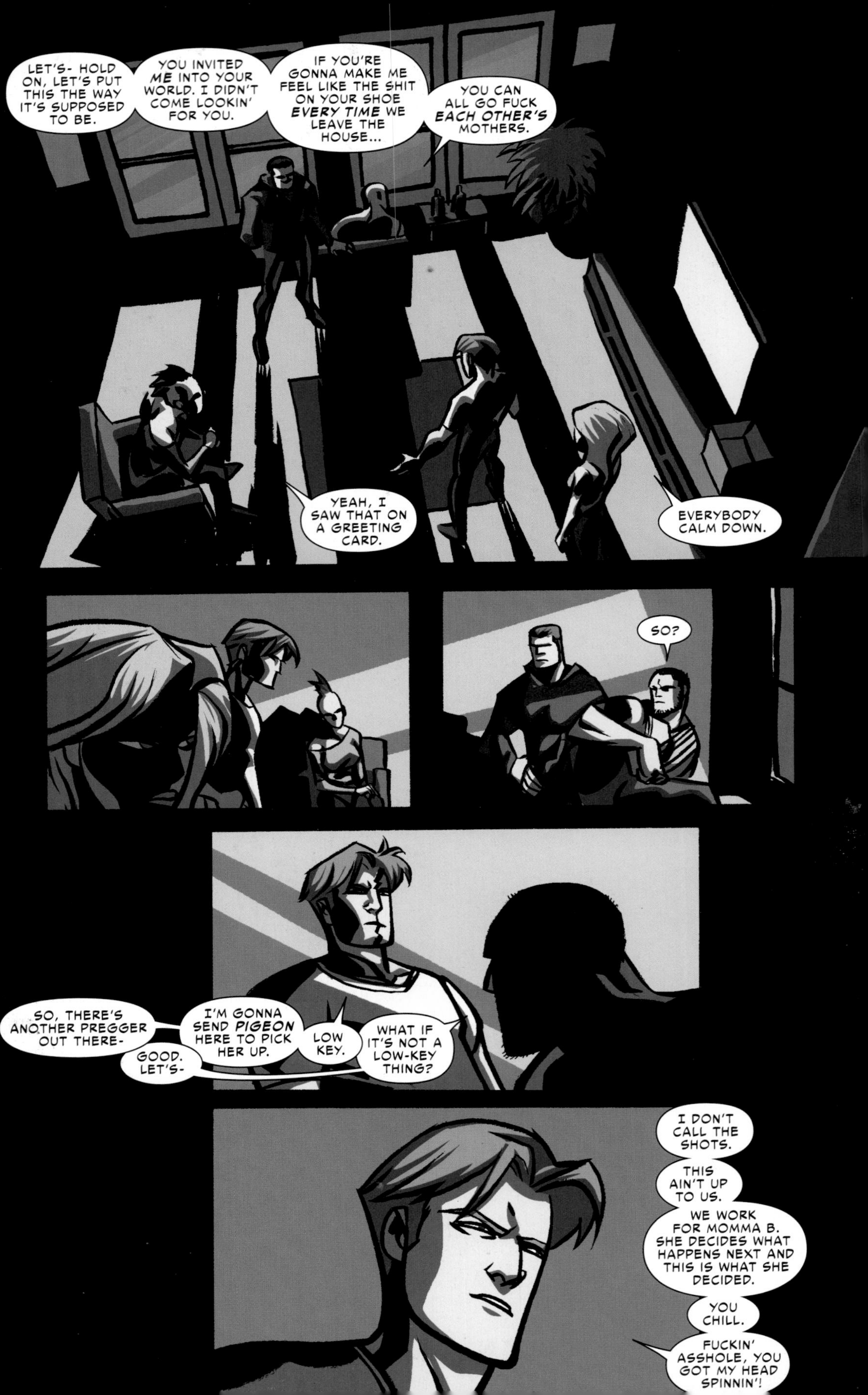
LET'S- HOLD ON, LET'S PUT THIS THE WAY IT'S SUPPOSED TO BE.
YOU INVITED *ME* INTO YOUR WORLD. I DIDN'T COME LOOKIN' FOR YOU.
IF YOU'RE GONNA MAKE ME FEEL LIKE THE SHIT ON YOUR SHOE *EVERY TIME* WE LEAVE THE HOUSE...
YOU CAN ALL GO FUCK *EACH OTHER'S* MOTHERS.
YEAH, I SAW THAT ON A GREETING CARD.
EVERYBODY CALM DOWN.
SO?
SO, THERE'S ANOTHER PREGGER OUT THERE-
GOOD. LET'S-
I'M GONNA SEND *PIGEON* HERE TO PICK HER UP.
LOW KEY.
WHAT IF IT'S NOT A LOW-KEY THING?
I DON'T CALL THE SHOTS.
THIS AIN'T UP TO US.
WE WORK FOR MOMMA B. SHE DECIDES WHAT HAPPENS NEXT AND THIS IS WHAT SHE DECIDED.
YOU CHILL.
FUCKIN' ASSHOLE, YOU GOT MY HEAD SPINNIN'!

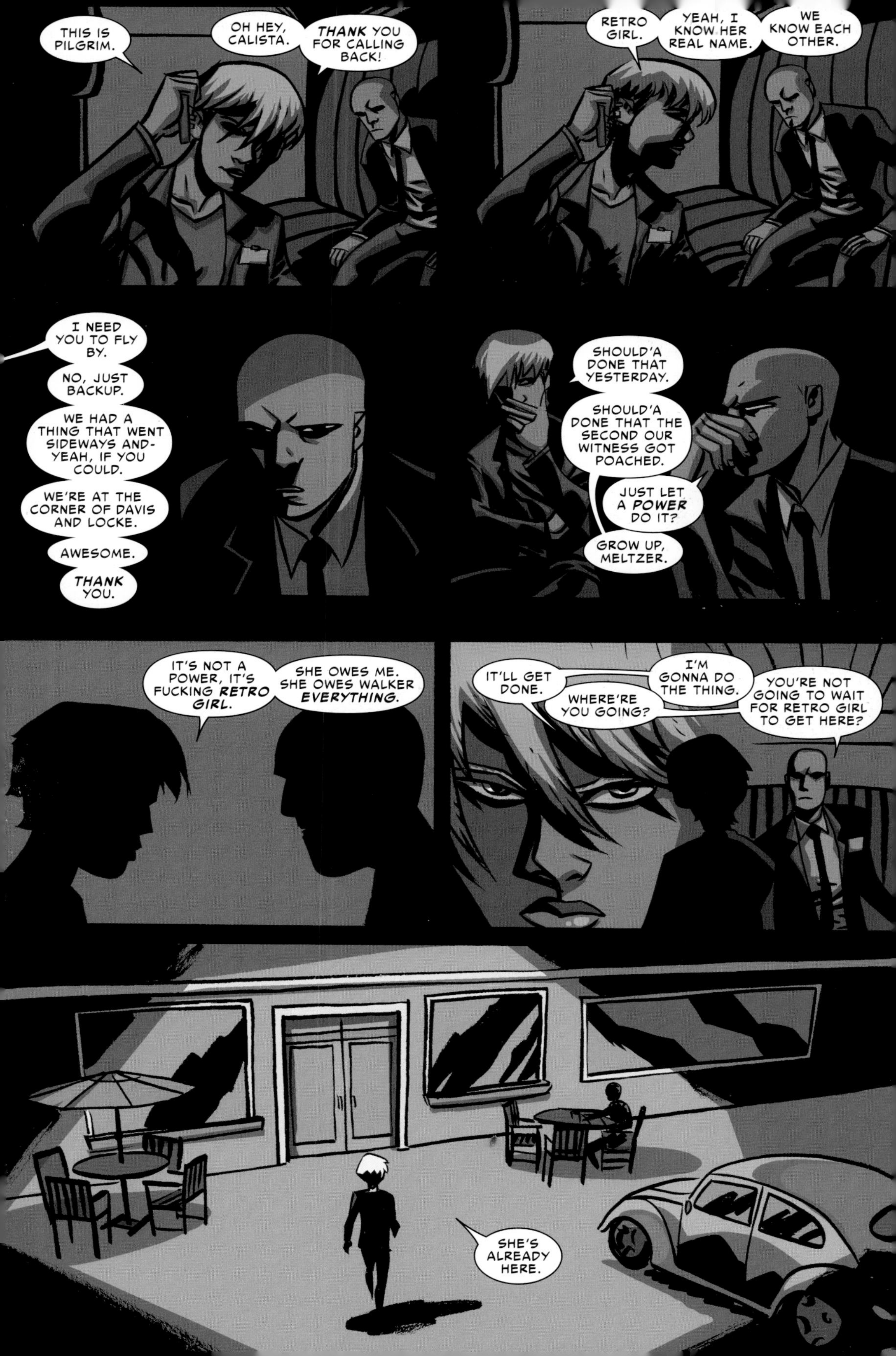

THIS IS PILGRIM.
OH HEY, CALISTA.
THANK YOU FOR CALLING BACK!
RETRO GIRL.
YEAH, I KNOW HER REAL NAME.
WE KNOW EACH OTHER.
I NEED YOU TO FLY BY.
NO, JUST BACKUP.
WE HAD A THING THAT WENT SIDEWAYS AND- YEAH, IF YOU COULD.
WE'RE AT THE CORNER OF DAVIS AND LOCKE.
AWESOME.
THANK YOU.
SHOULD'A DONE THAT YESTERDAY.
SHOULD'A DONE THAT THE SECOND OUR WITNESS GOT POACHED.
JUST LET A POWER DO IT?
GROW UP, MELTZER.
IT'S NOT A POWER, IT'S FUCKING RETRO GIRL.
SHE OWES ME. SHE OWES WALKER EVERYTHING.
IT'LL GET DONE.
WHERE'RE YOU GOING?
I'M GONNA DO THE THING.
YOU'RE NOT GOING TO WAIT FOR RETRO GIRL TO GET HERE?
SHE'S ALREADY HERE.

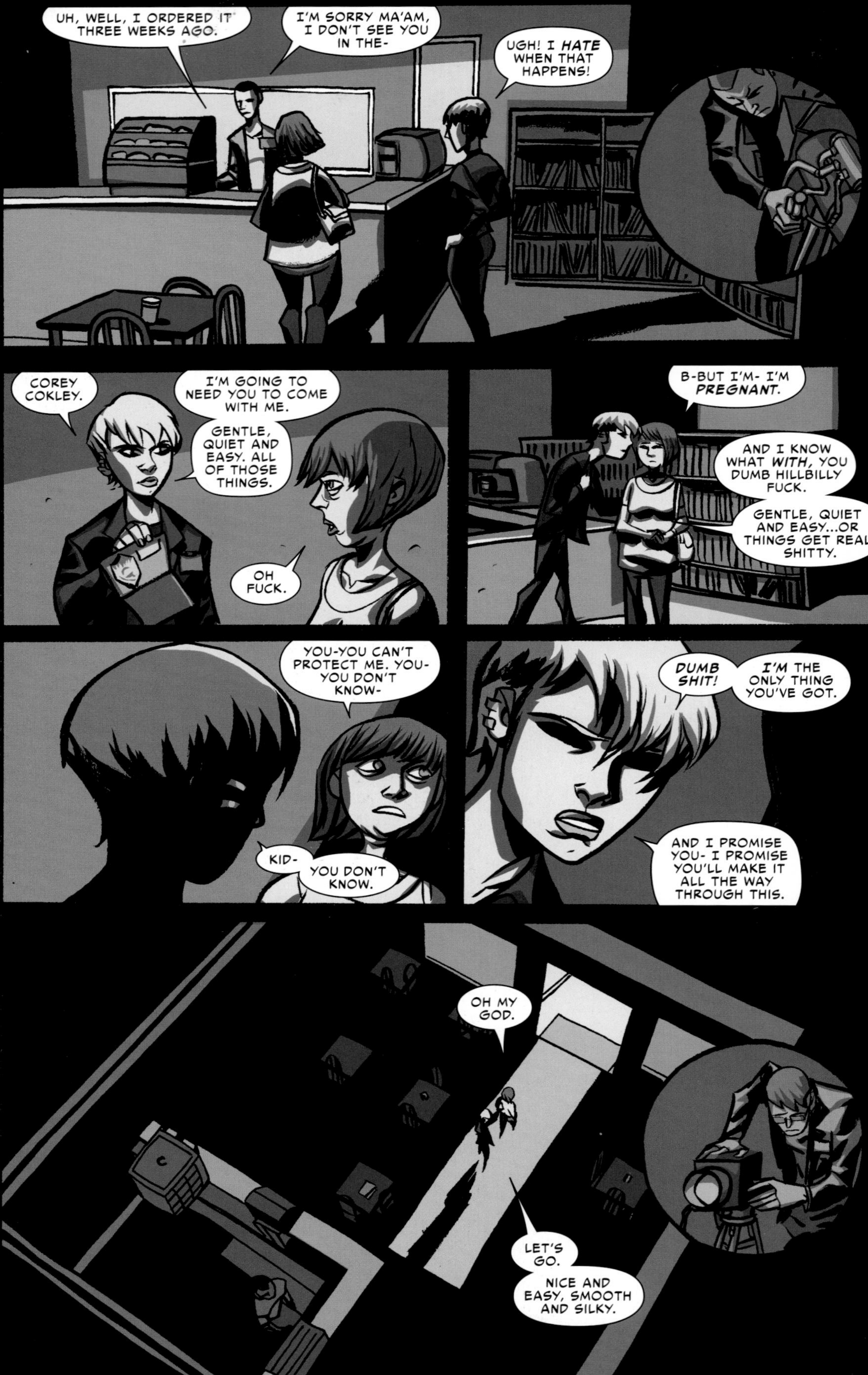

UH, WELL, I ORDERED IT THREE WEEKS AGO.
I'M SORRY MA'AM, I DON'T SEE YOU IN THE-
UGH! I HATE WHEN THAT HAPPENS!
COREY COKLEY.
I'M GOING TO NEED YOU TO COME WITH ME.
GENTLE, QUIET AND EASY. ALL OF THOSE THINGS.
OH FUCK.
B-BUT I'M- I'M PREGNANT.
AND I KNOW WHAT WITH, YOU DUMB HILLBILLY FUCK.
GENTLE, QUIET AND EASY...OR THINGS GET REAL SHITTY.
YOU-YOU CAN'T PROTECT ME. YOU-YOU DON'T KNOW-
KID-
YOU DON'T KNOW.
DUMB SHIT!
I'M THE ONLY THING YOU'VE GOT.
AND I PROMISE YOU- I PROMISE YOU'LL MAKE IT ALL THE WAY THROUGH THIS.
OH MY GOD.
LET'S GO.
NICE AND EASY, SMOOTH AND SILKY.

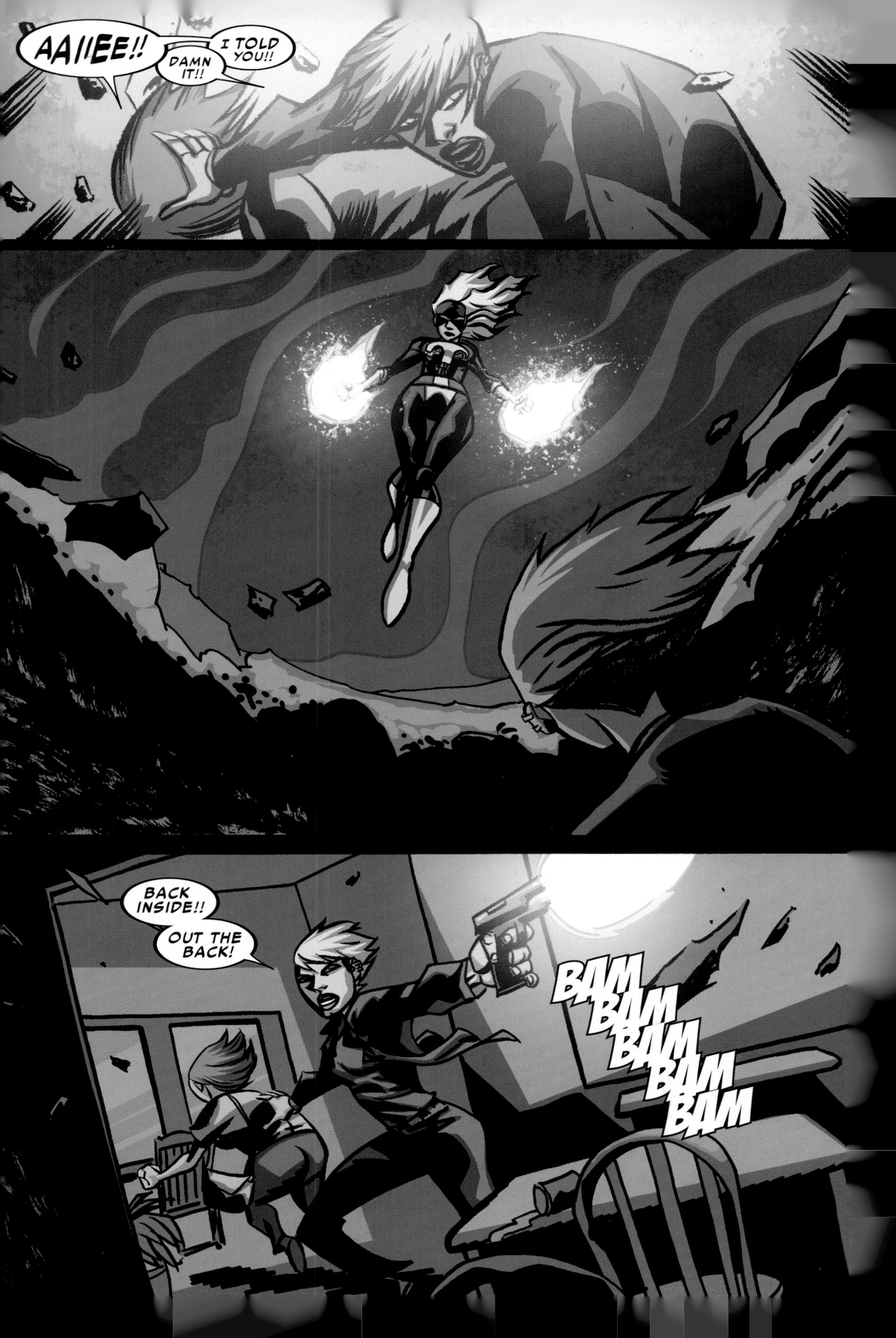
AAIIEE!!
DAMN IT!!
I TOLD YOU!!
BACK INSIDE!!
OUT THE BACK!
BAM BAM BAM BAM BAM

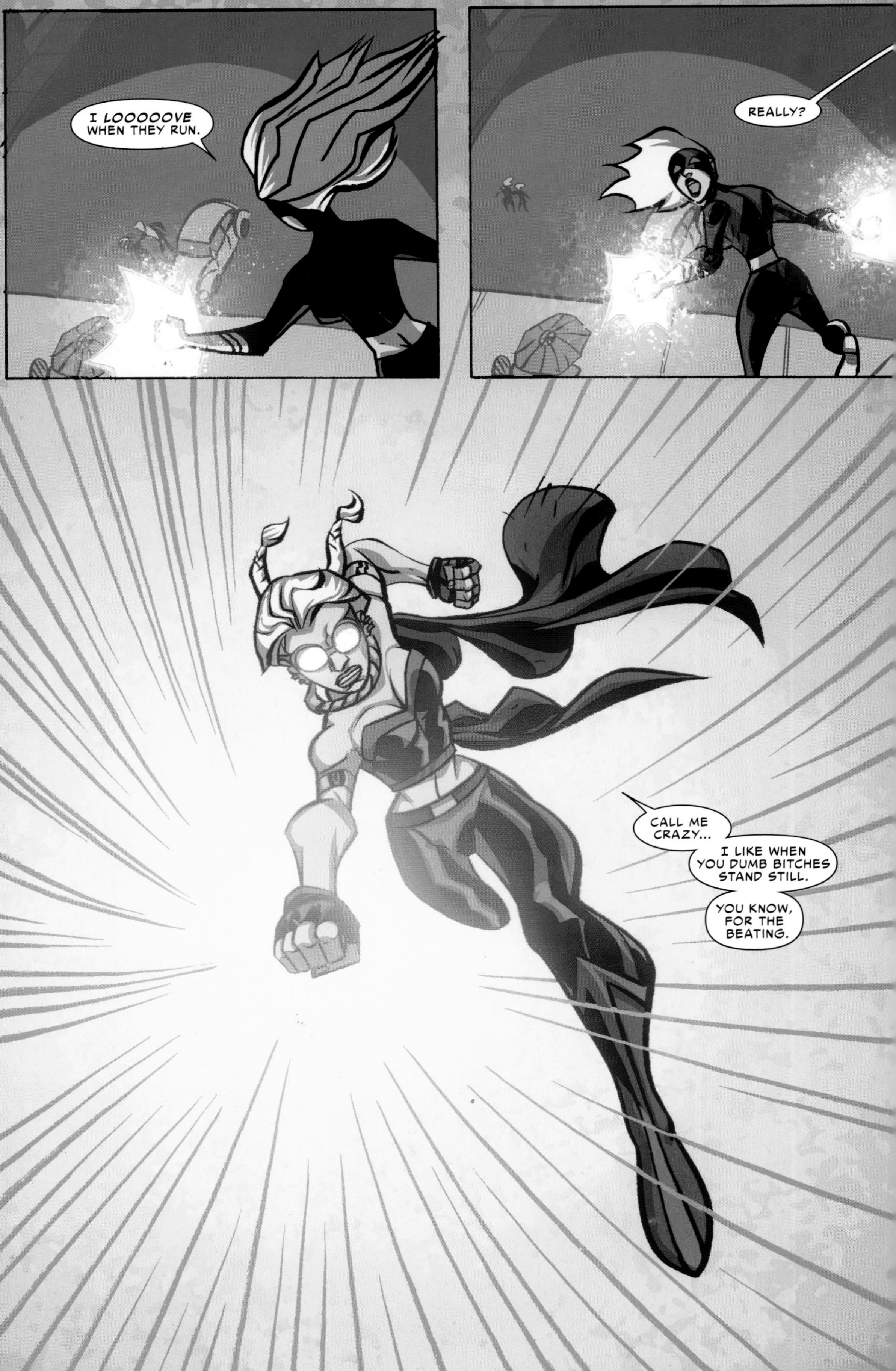
I LOOOOOVE WHEN THEY RUN.
REALLY?
CALL ME CRAZY...
I LIKE WHEN YOU DUMB BITCHES STAND STILL.
YOU KNOW, FOR THE BEATING.

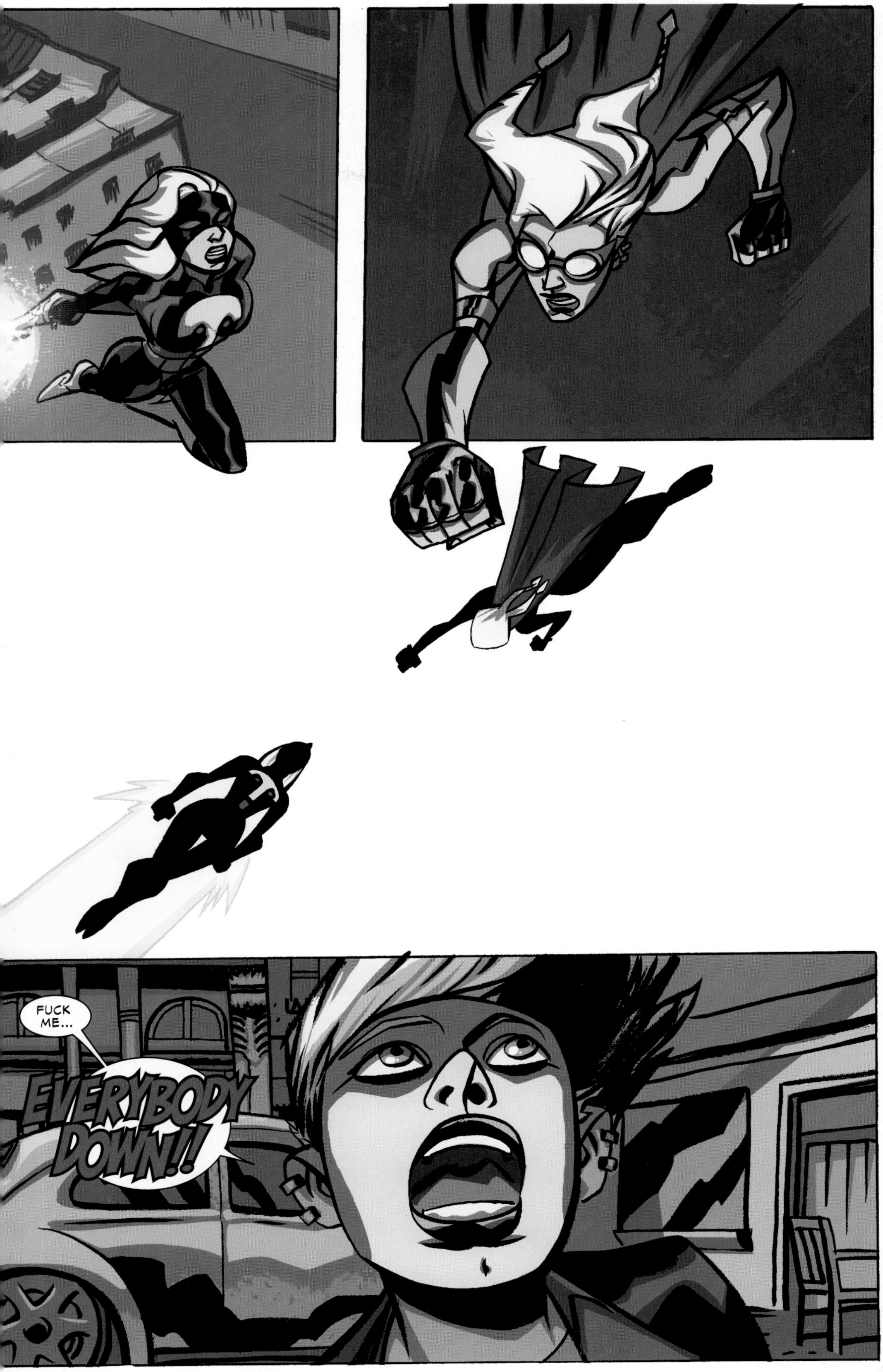
FUCK ME...
EVERYBODY DOWN!!

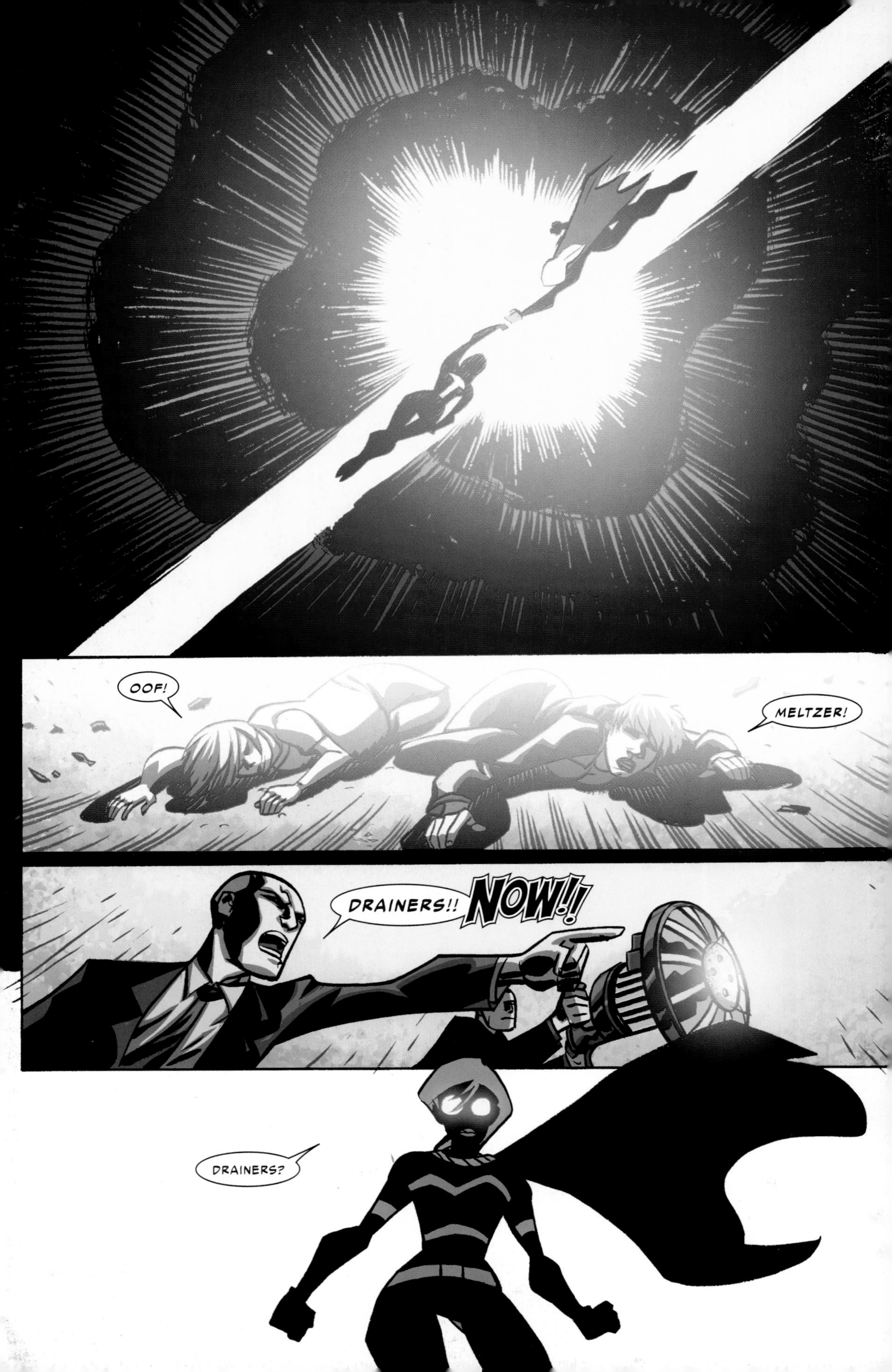
OOF!
MELTZER!
DRAINERS!! NOW!!
DRAINERS?

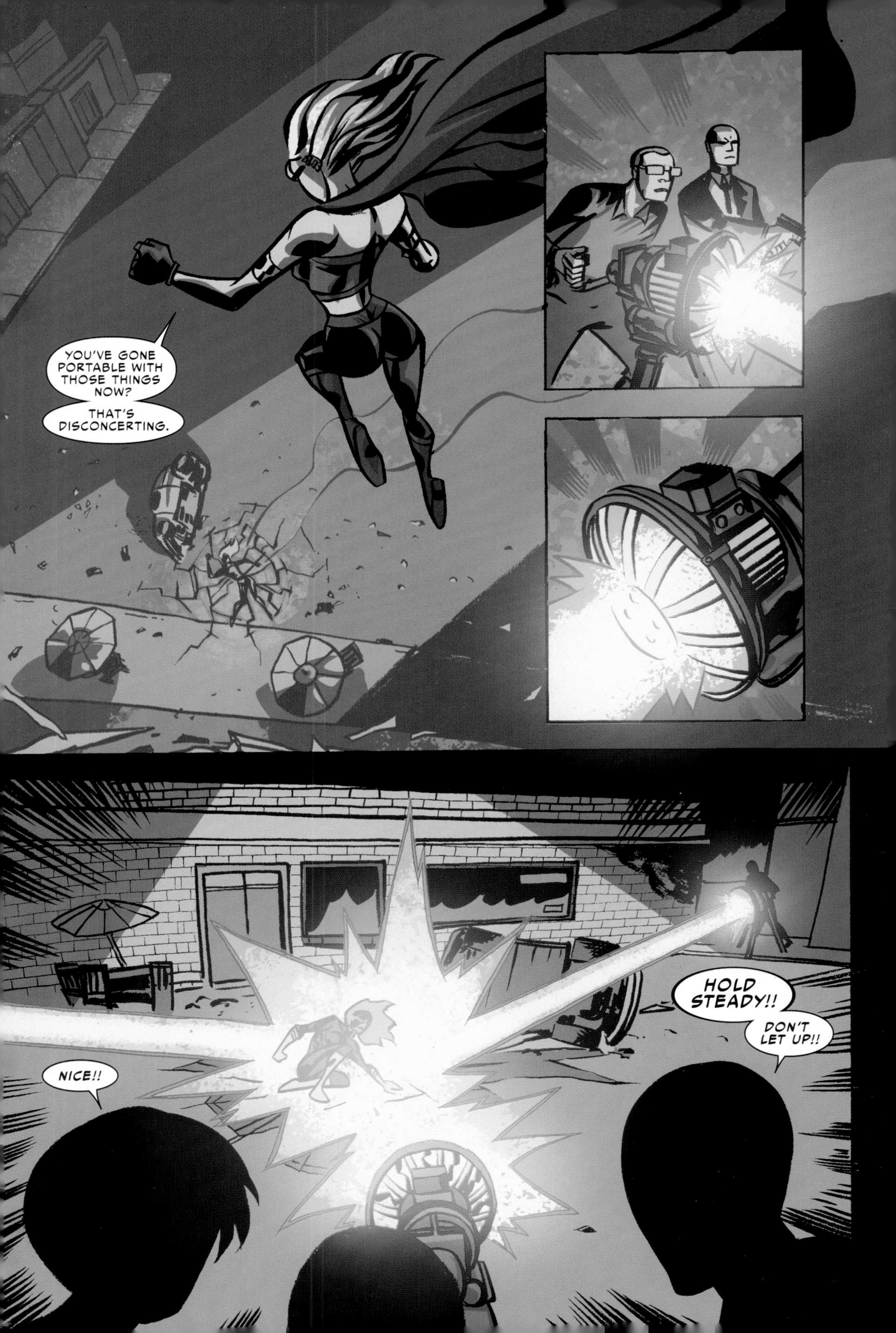
YOU'VE GONE PORTABLE WITH THOSE THINGS NOW?
THAT'S DISCONCERTING.
HOLD STEADY!!
DON'T LET UP!!
NICE!!

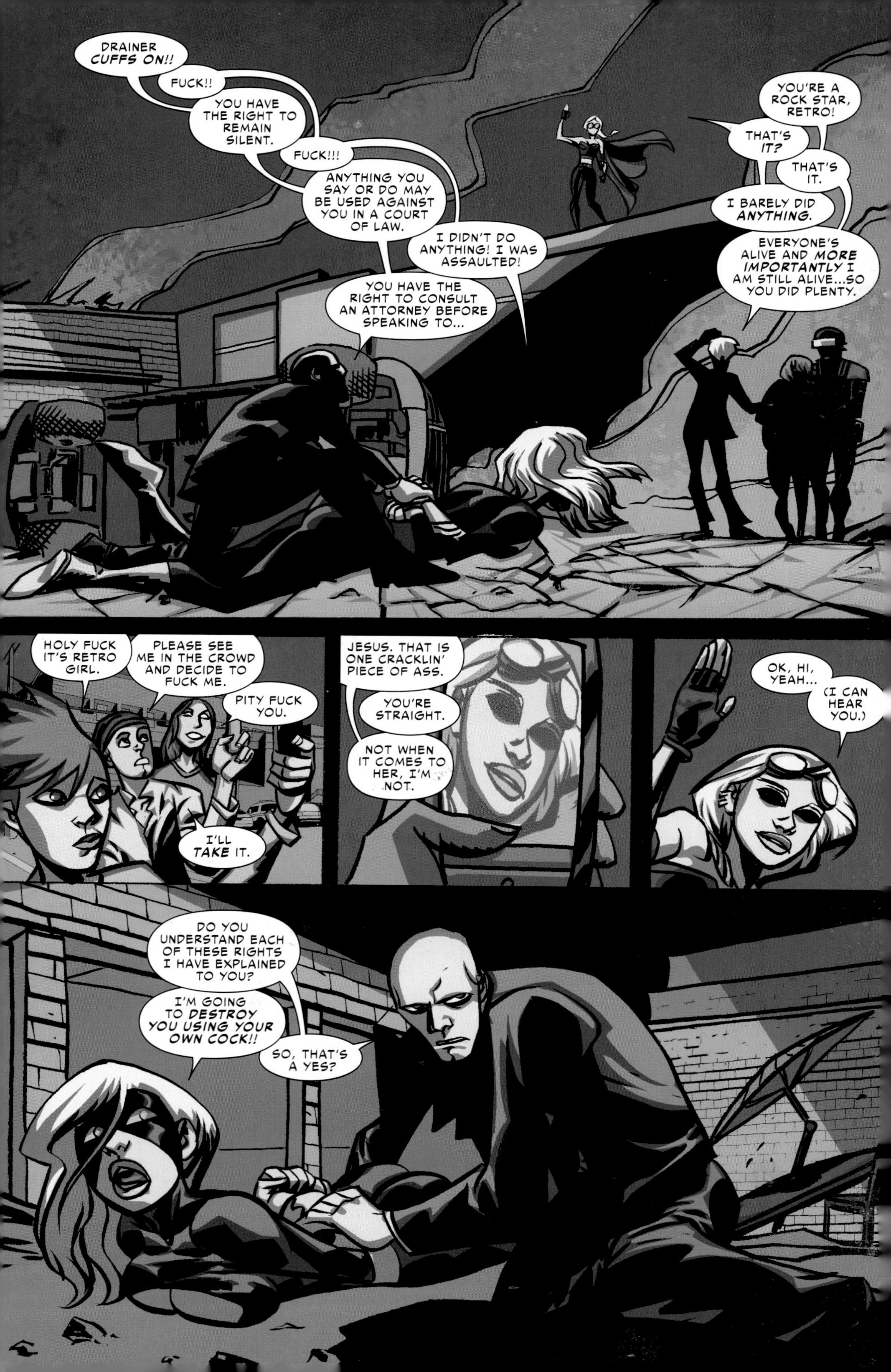
DRAINER *CUFFS ON!!*
FUCK!!
YOU HAVE THE RIGHT TO REMAIN SILENT.
FUCK!!!
ANYTHING YOU SAY OR DO MAY BE USED AGAINST YOU IN A COURT OF LAW.
I DIDN'T DO ANYTHING! I WAS ASSAULTED!
YOU HAVE THE RIGHT TO CONSULT AN ATTORNEY BEFORE SPEAKING TO...
YOU'RE A ROCK STAR, RETRO!
THAT'S *IT?*
THAT'S IT.
I BARELY DID *ANYTHING.*
EVERYONE'S ALIVE AND *MORE IMPORTANTLY* I AM STILL ALIVE...SO YOU DID PLENTY.
HOLY FUCK IT'S RETRO GIRL.
PLEASE SEE ME IN THE CROWD AND DECIDE TO FUCK ME.
PITY FUCK YOU.
I'LL *TAKE* IT.
JESUS. THAT IS ONE CRACKLIN' PIECE OF ASS.
YOU'RE STRAIGHT.
NOT WHEN IT COMES TO HER, I'M NOT.
OK, HI, YEAH...
(I CAN HEAR YOU.)
DO YOU UNDERSTAND EACH OF THESE RIGHTS I HAVE EXPLAINED TO YOU?
I'M GOING TO *DESTROY YOU USING YOUR OWN COCK!!*
SO, THAT'S A YES?

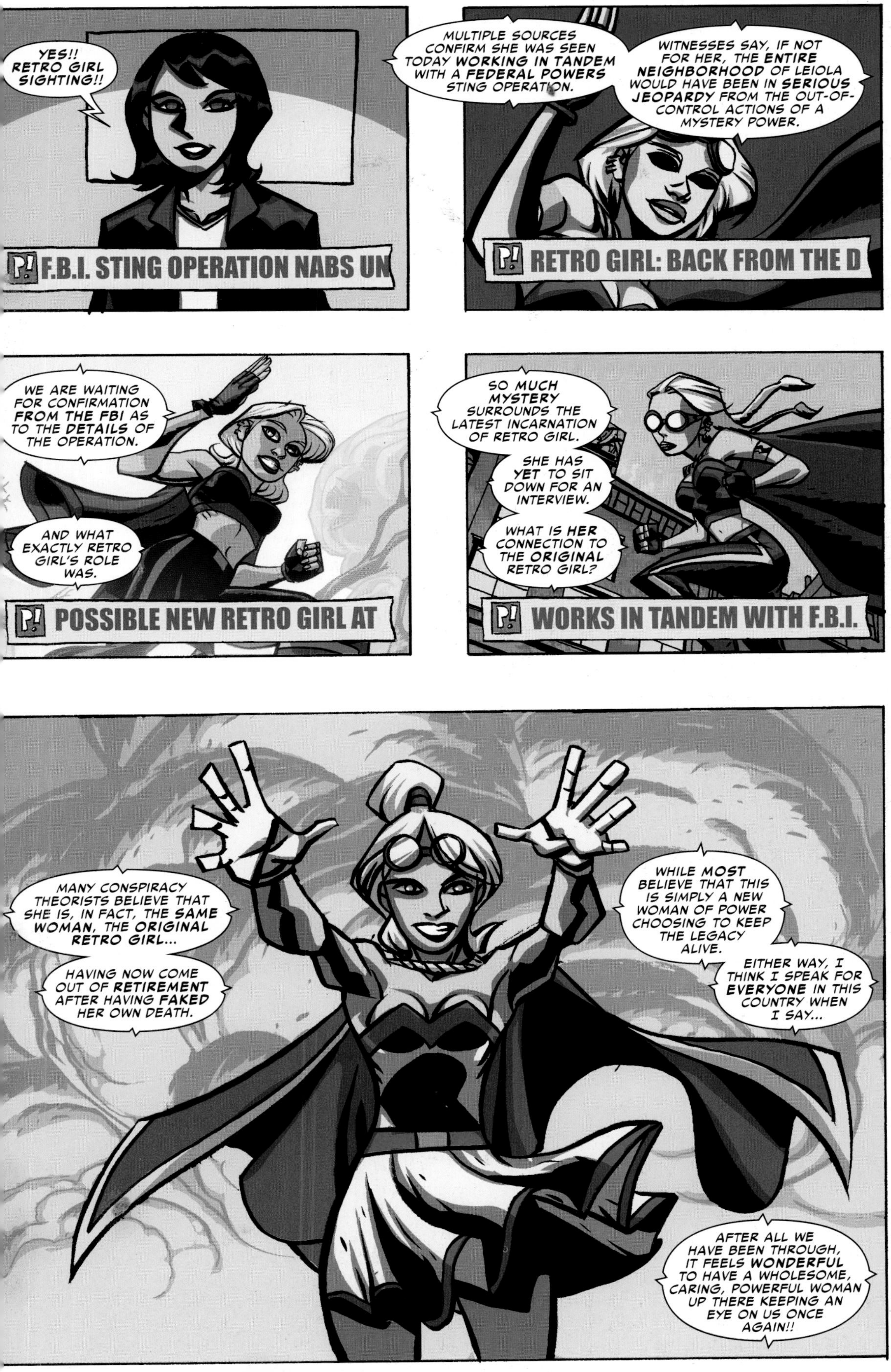
YES!! RETRO GIRL SIGHTING!!
F.B.I. STING OPERATION NABS UN
MULTIPLE SOURCES CONFIRM SHE WAS SEEN TODAY WORKING IN TANDEM WITH A FEDERAL POWERS STING OPERATION.
WITNESSES SAY, IF NOT FOR HER, THE ENTIRE NEIGHBORHOOD OF LEIOLA WOULD HAVE BEEN IN SERIOUS JEOPARDY FROM THE OUT-OF-CONTROL ACTIONS OF A MYSTERY POWER.
RETRO GIRL: BACK FROM THE D
WE ARE WAITING FOR CONFIRMATION FROM THE FBI AS TO THE DETAILS OF THE OPERATION.
AND WHAT EXACTLY RETRO GIRL'S ROLE WAS.
POSSIBLE NEW RETRO GIRL AT
SO MUCH MYSTERY SURROUNDS THE LATEST INCARNATION OF RETRO GIRL.
SHE HAS YET TO SIT DOWN FOR AN INTERVIEW.
WHAT IS HER CONNECTION TO THE ORIGINAL RETRO GIRL?
WORKS IN TANDEM WITH F.B.I.
MANY CONSPIRACY THEORISTS BELIEVE THAT SHE IS, IN FACT, THE SAME WOMAN, THE ORIGINAL RETRO GIRL...
HAVING NOW COME OUT OF RETIREMENT AFTER HAVING FAKED HER OWN DEATH.
WHILE MOST BELIEVE THAT THIS IS SIMPLY A NEW WOMAN OF POWER CHOOSING TO KEEP THE LEGACY ALIVE.
EITHER WAY, I THINK I SPEAK FOR EVERYONE IN THIS COUNTRY WHEN I SAY...
AFTER ALL WE HAVE BEEN THROUGH, IT FEELS WONDERFUL TO HAVE A WHOLESOME, CARING, POWERFUL WOMAN UP THERE KEEPING AN EYE ON US ONCE AGAIN!!

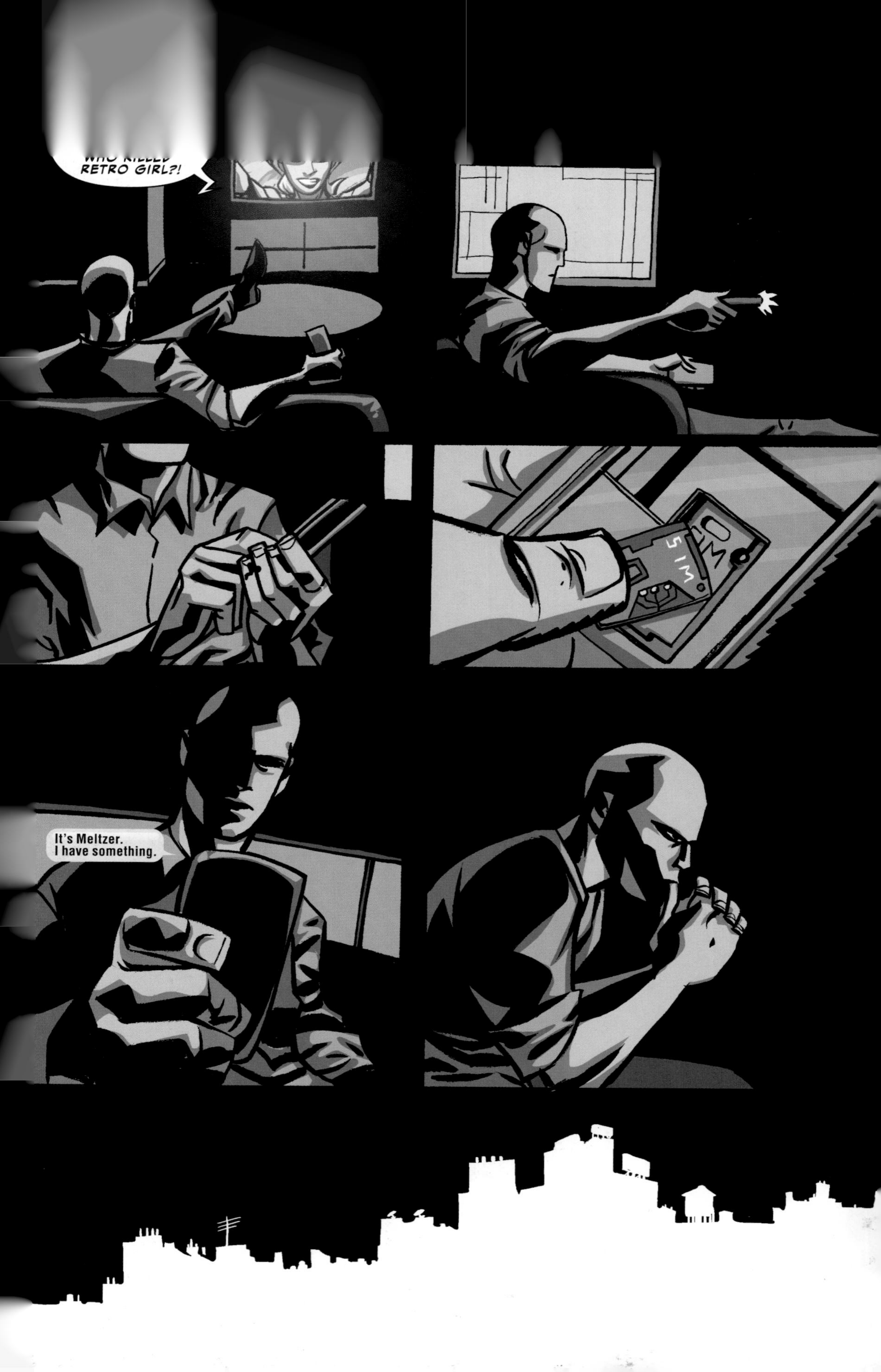
RETRO GIRL?!
It's Meltzer.
I have something.

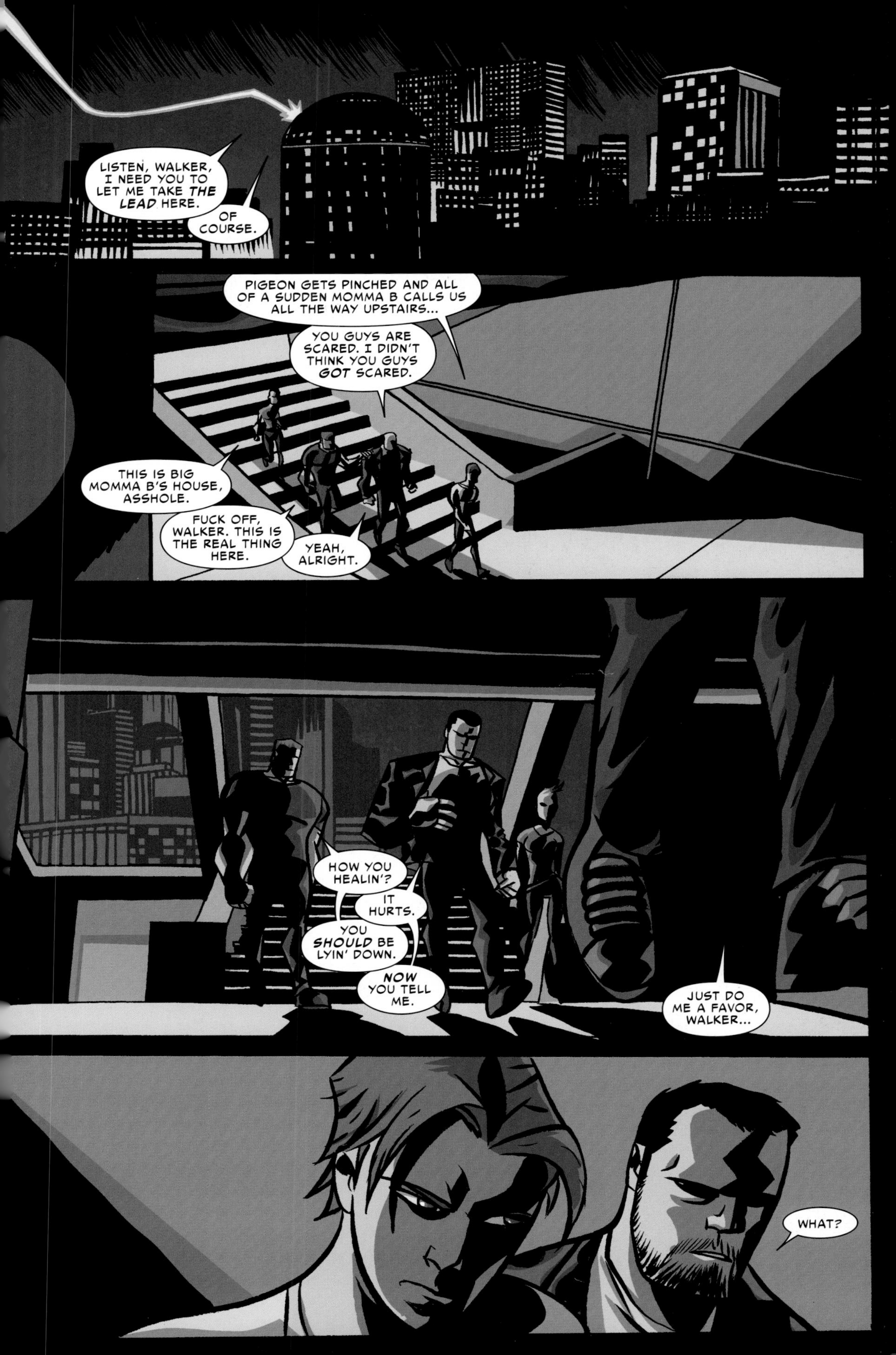
LISTEN, WALKER, I NEED YOU TO LET ME TAKE *THE LEAD* HERE.
OF COURSE.
PIGEON GETS PINCHED AND ALL OF A SUDDEN MOMMA B CALLS US ALL THE WAY UPSTAIRS...
YOU GUYS ARE SCARED. I DIDN'T THINK YOU GUYS *GOT* SCARED.
THIS IS BIG MOMMA B'S HOUSE, ASSHOLE.
FUCK OFF, WALKER. THIS IS THE REAL THING HERE.
YEAH, ALRIGHT.
HOW YOU HEALIN'?
IT HURTS.
YOU *SHOULD* BE LYIN' DOWN.
NOW YOU TELL ME.
JUST DO ME A FAVOR, WALKER...
WHAT?

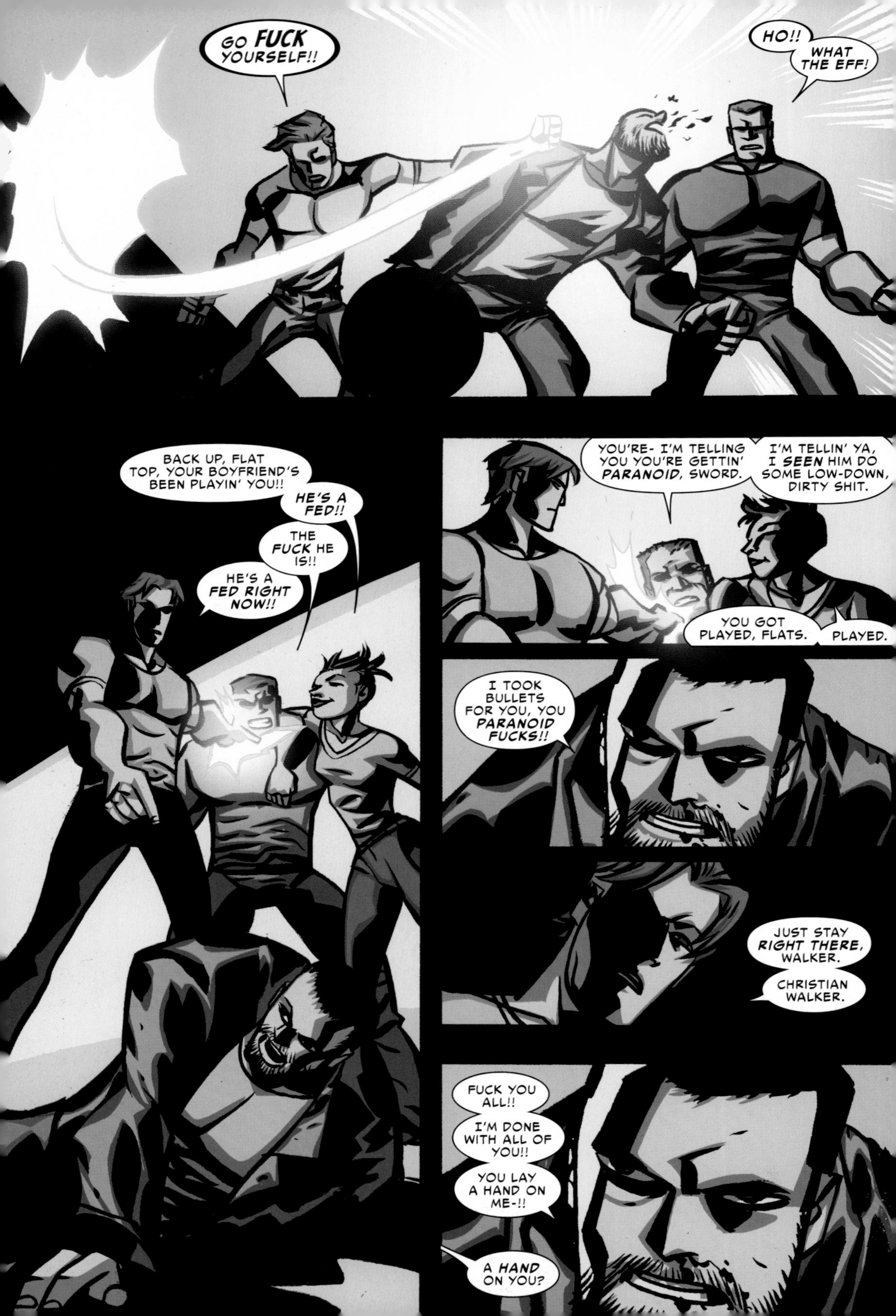
GO FUCK YOURSELF!!
HO!! WHAT THE EFF!
BACK UP, FLAT TOP, YOUR BOYFRIEND'S BEEN PLAYIN' YOU!!
HE'S A FED!!
THE FUCK HE IS!!
HE'S A FED RIGHT NOW!!
YOU'RE- I'M TELLING YOU YOU'RE GETTIN' PARANOID, SWORD.
I'M TELLIN' YA, I SEEN HIM DO SOME LOW-DOWN, DIRTY SHIT.
YOU GOT PLAYED, FLATS.
PLAYED.
I TOOK BULLETS FOR YOU, YOU PARANOID FUCKS!!
JUST STAY RIGHT THERE, WALKER.
CHRISTIAN WALKER.
FUCK YOU ALL!!
I'M DONE WITH ALL OF YOU!!
YOU LAY A HAND ON ME-!!
A HAND ON YOU?

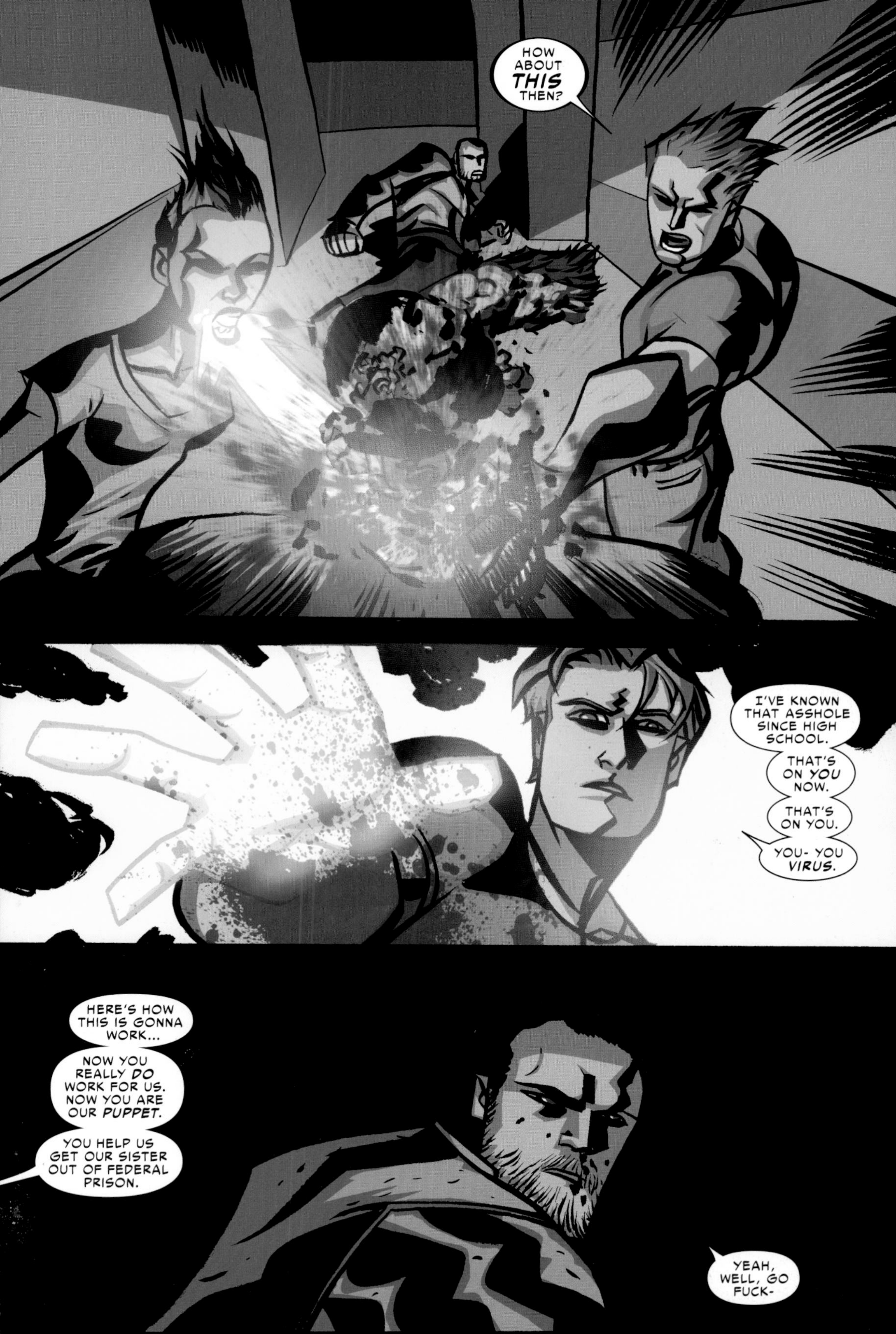
HOW ABOUT THIS THEN?
I'VE KNOWN THAT ASSHOLE SINCE HIGH SCHOOL.
THAT'S ON YOU NOW.
THAT'S ON YOU.
YOU- YOU VIRUS.
HERE'S HOW THIS IS GONNA WORK...
NOW YOU REALLY DO WORK FOR US. NOW YOU ARE OUR PUPPET.
YOU HELP US GET OUR SISTER OUT OF FEDERAL PRISON.
YEAH, WELL, GO FUCK-

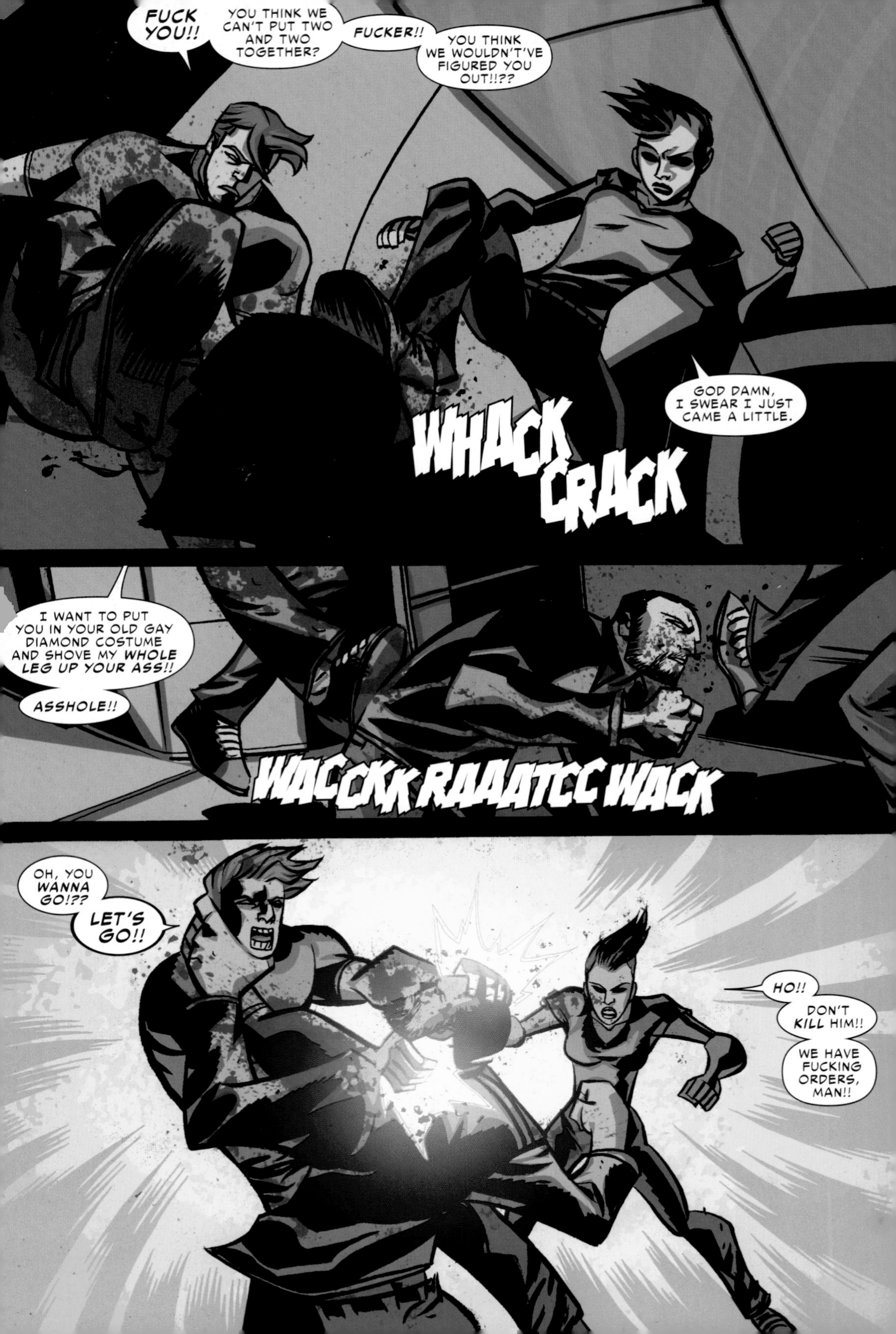
FUCK YOU!!
YOU THINK WE CAN'T PUT TWO AND TWO TOGETHER?
FUCKER!!
YOU THINK WE WOULDN'T'VE FIGURED YOU OUT!!??
GOD DAMN, I SWEAR I JUST CAME A LITTLE.
WHACK
CRACK
I WANT TO PUT YOU IN YOUR OLD GAY DIAMOND COSTUME AND SHOVE MY WHOLE LEG UP YOUR ASS!!
ASSHOLE!!
WACCKK RAAATCC WACK
OH, YOU WANNA GO!??
LET'S GO!!
HO!!
DON'T KILL HIM!!
WE HAVE FUCKING ORDERS, MAN!!

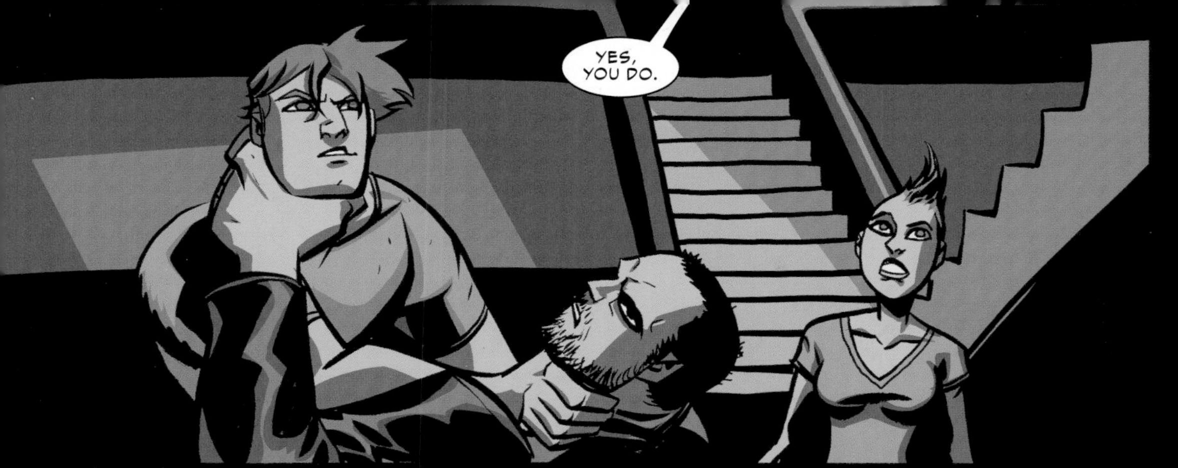
YES, YOU DO.

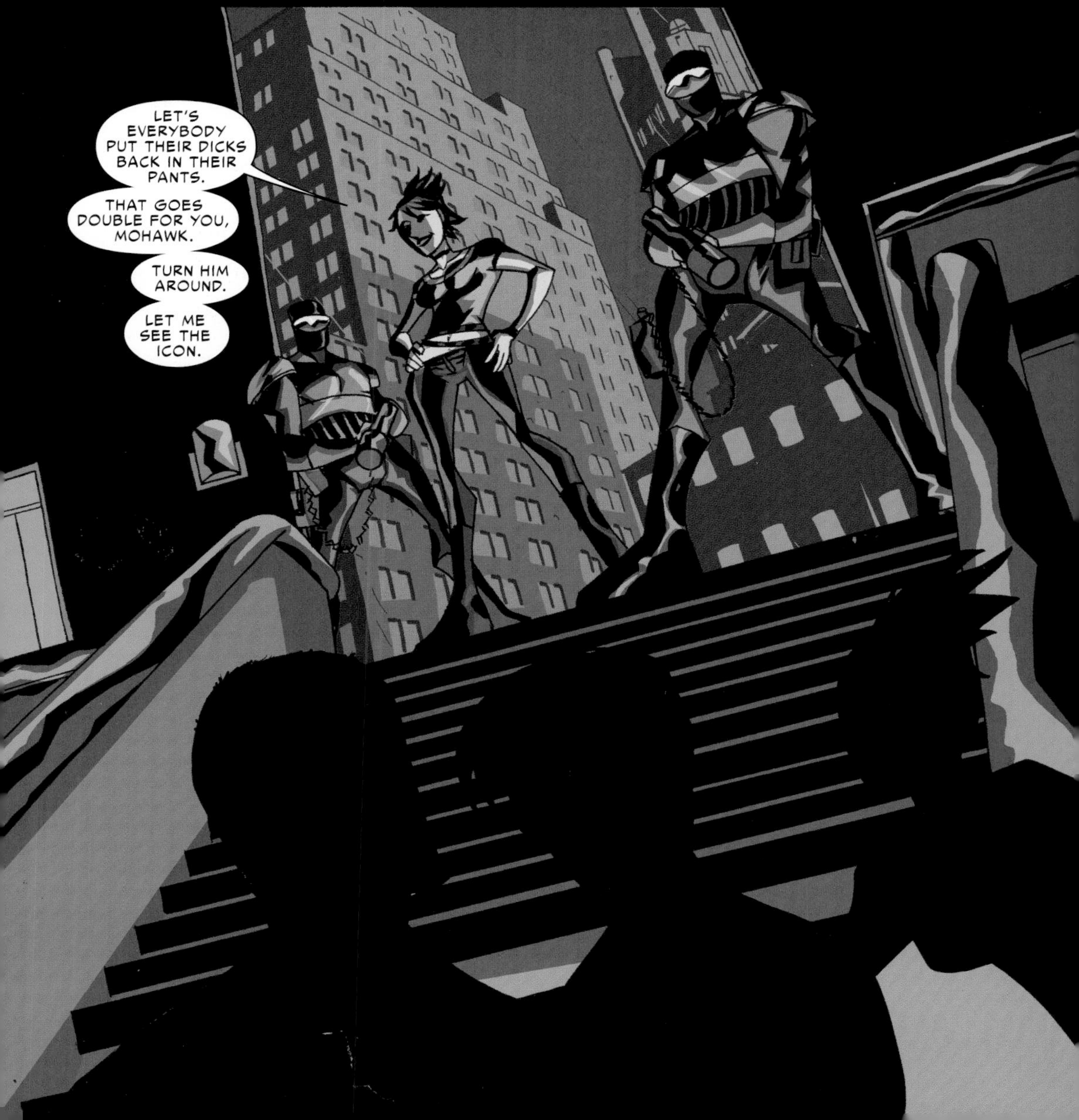
LET'S EVERYBODY PUT THEIR DICKS BACK IN THEIR PANTS.
THAT GOES DOUBLE FOR YOU, MOHAWK.
TURN HIM AROUND.
LET ME SEE THE ICON.

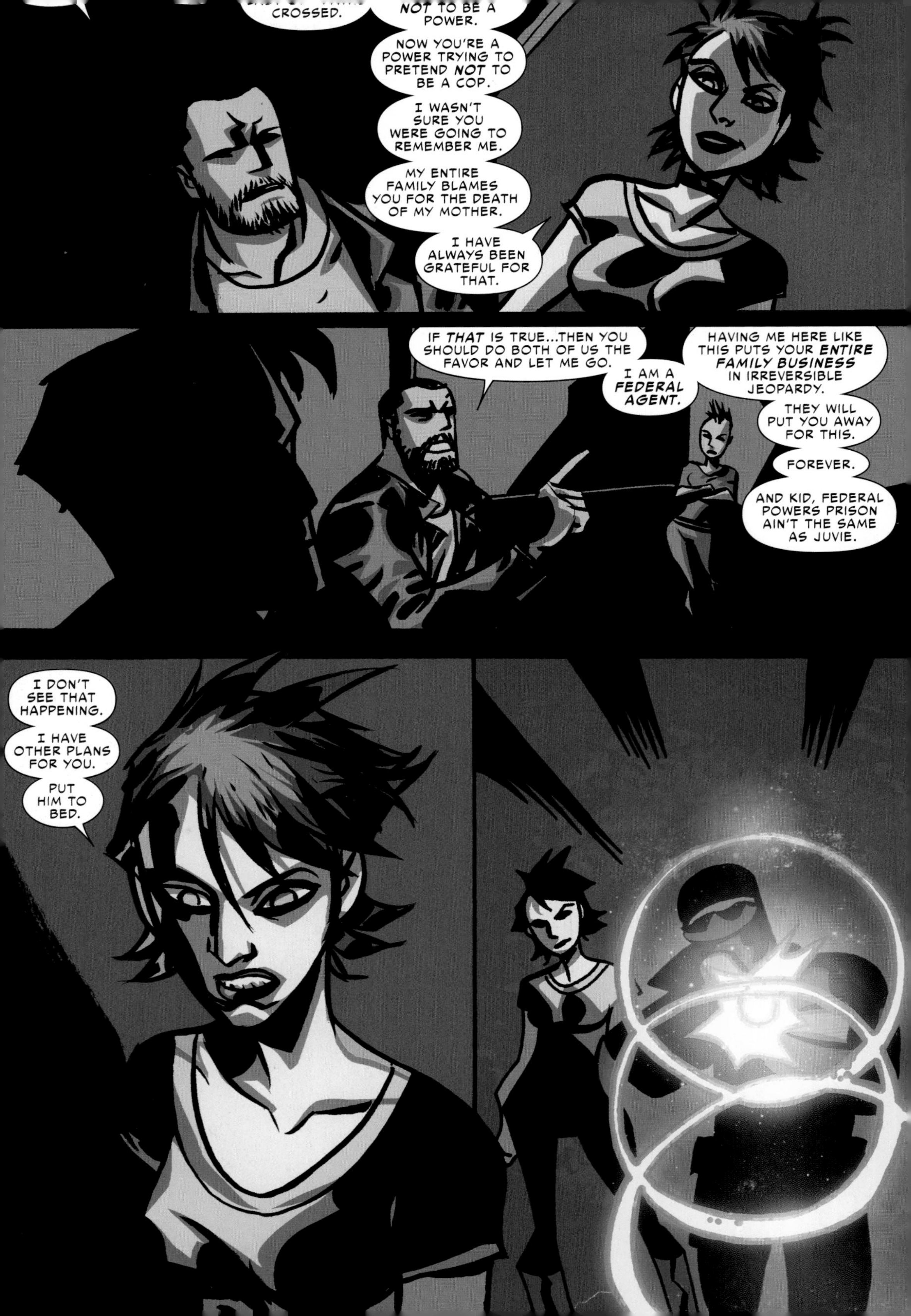
CROSSED.
NOT TO BE A POWER.
NOW YOU'RE A POWER TRYING TO PRETEND NOT TO BE A COP.
I WASN'T SURE YOU WERE GOING TO REMEMBER ME.
MY ENTIRE FAMILY BLAMES YOU FOR THE DEATH OF MY MOTHER.
I HAVE ALWAYS BEEN GRATEFUL FOR THAT.
IF THAT IS TRUE...THEN YOU SHOULD DO BOTH OF US THE FAVOR AND LET ME GO.
I AM A FEDERAL AGENT.
HAVING ME HERE LIKE THIS PUTS YOUR ENTIRE FAMILY BUSINESS IN IRREVERSIBLE JEOPARDY.
THEY WILL PUT YOU AWAY FOR THIS.
FOREVER.
AND KID, FEDERAL POWERS PRISON AIN'T THE SAME AS JUVIE.
I DON'T SEE THAT HAPPENING.
I HAVE OTHER PLANS FOR YOU.
PUT HIM TO BED.

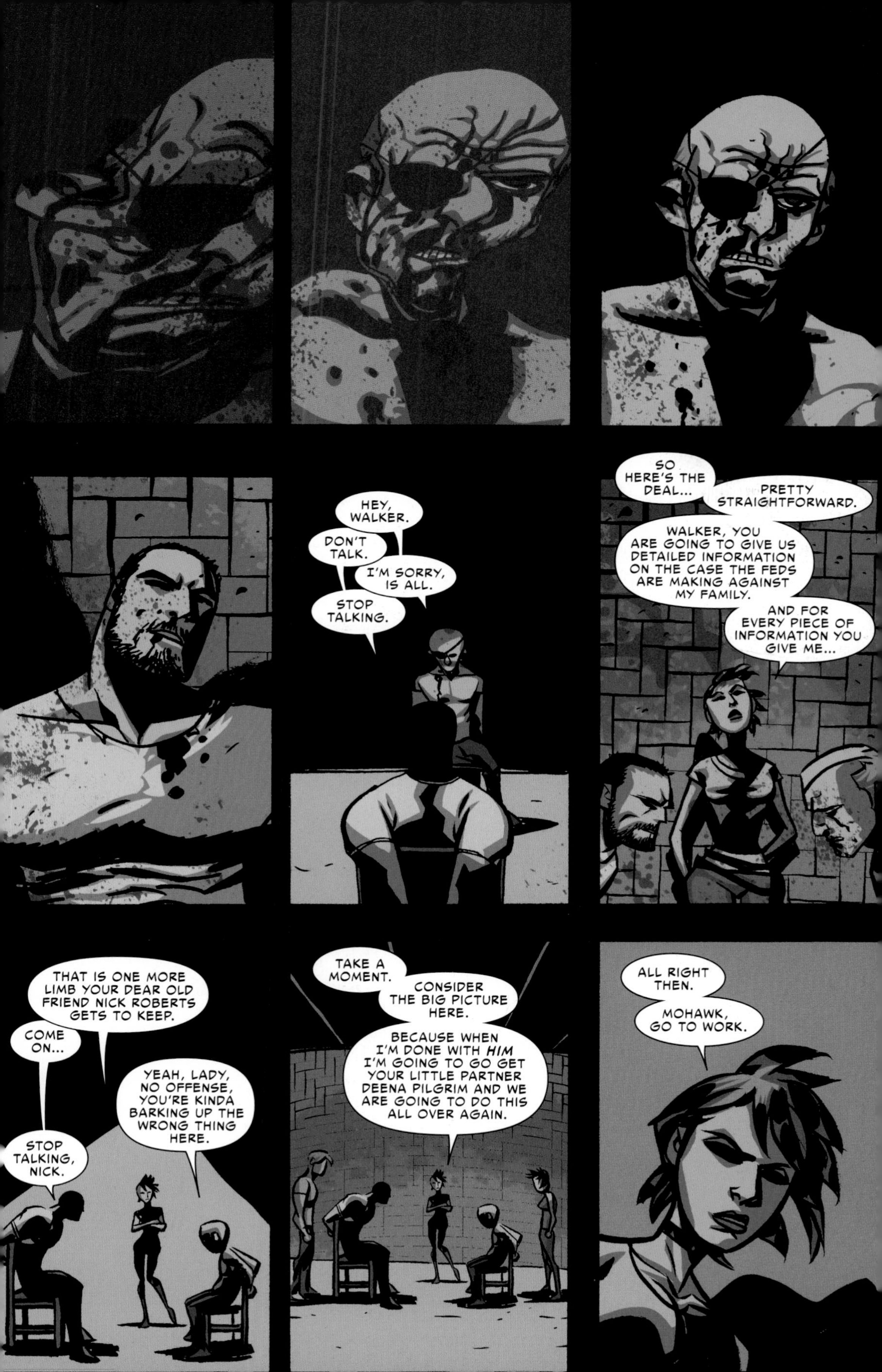
HEY, WALKER.
DON'T TALK.
I'M SORRY, IS ALL.
STOP TALKING.
SO HERE'S THE DEAL...
PRETTY STRAIGHTFORWARD.
WALKER, YOU ARE GOING TO GIVE US DETAILED INFORMATION ON THE CASE THE FEDS ARE MAKING AGAINST MY FAMILY.
AND FOR EVERY PIECE OF INFORMATION YOU GIVE ME...
THAT IS ONE MORE LIMB YOUR DEAR OLD FRIEND NICK ROBERTS GETS TO KEEP.
COME ON...
STOP TALKING, NICK.
YEAH, LADY, NO OFFENSE, YOU'RE KINDA BARKING UP THE WRONG THING HERE.
TAKE A MOMENT.
CONSIDER THE BIG PICTURE HERE.
BECAUSE WHEN I'M DONE WITH *HIM* I'M GOING TO GO GET YOUR LITTLE PARTNER DEENA PILGRIM AND WE ARE GOING TO DO THIS ALL OVER AGAIN.
ALL RIGHT THEN.
MOHAWK, GO TO WORK.

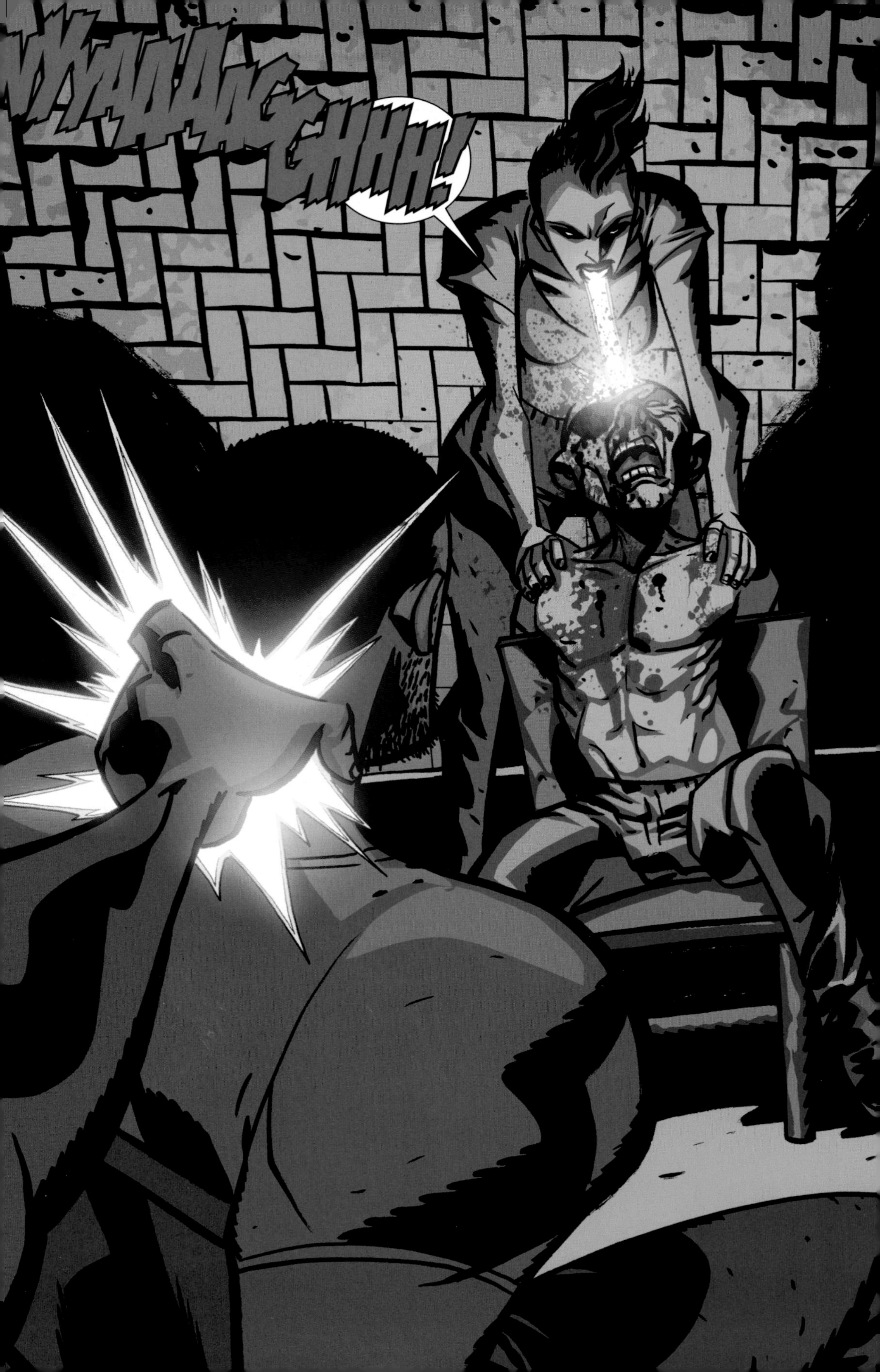
WAAAAGHHH!

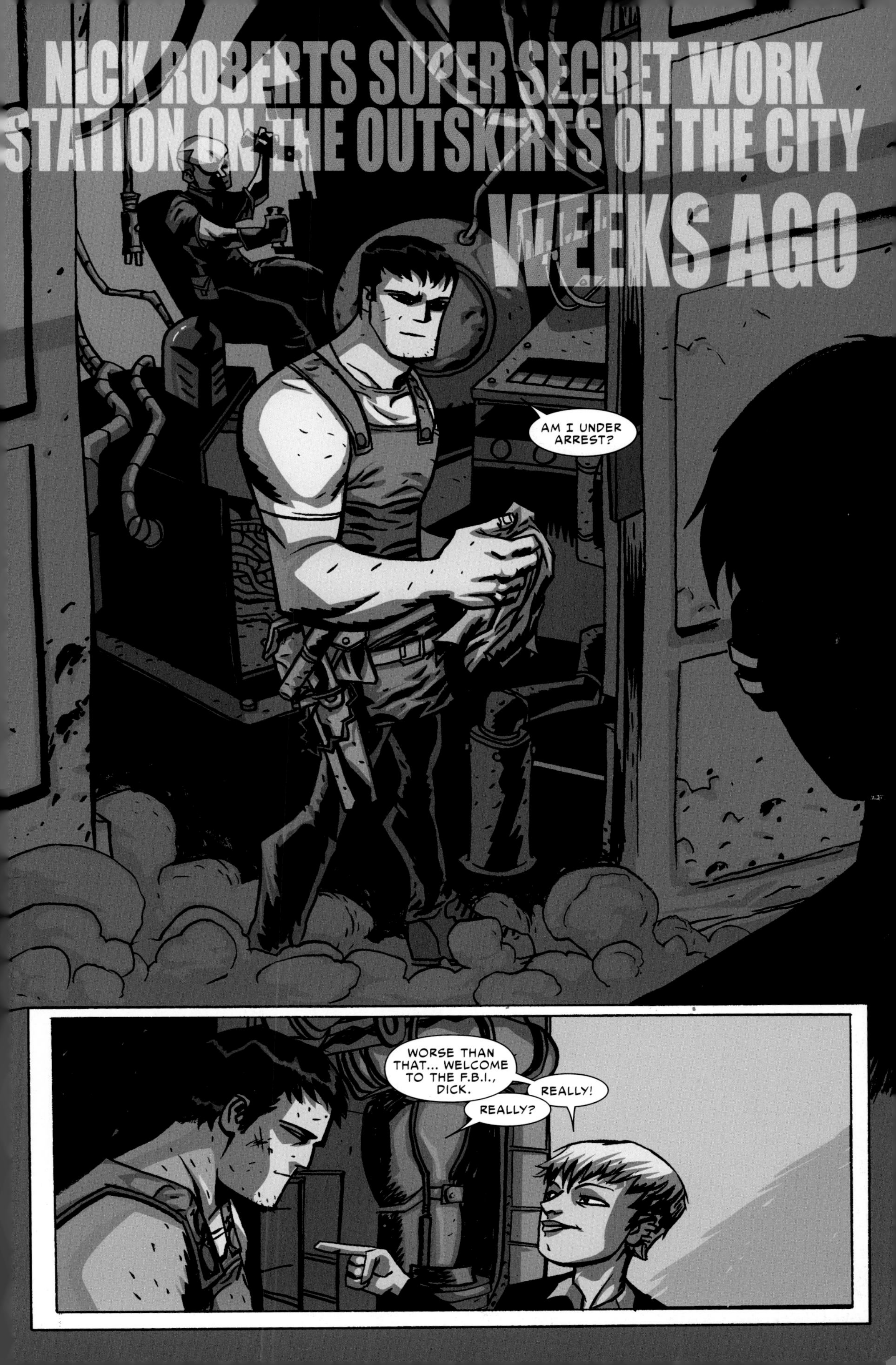
NICK ROBERTS SUPER SECRET WORK STATION ON THE OUTSKIRTS OF THE CITY
WEEKS AGO
AM I UNDER ARREST?
WORSE THAN THAT... WELCOME TO THE F.B.I., DICK.
REALLY?
REALLY!

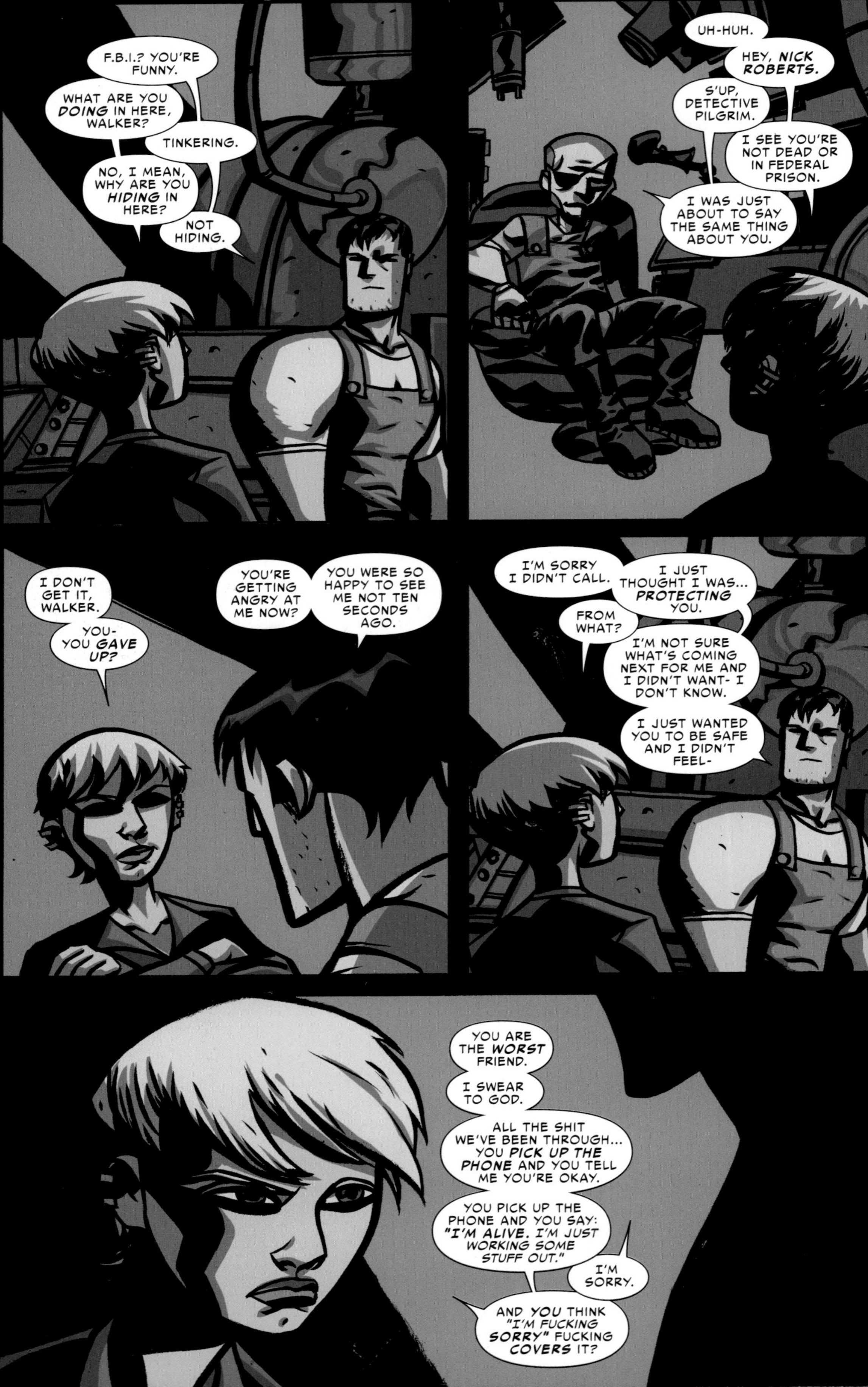

F.B.I.? YOU'RE FUNNY.
WHAT ARE YOU DOING IN HERE, WALKER?
TINKERING.
NO, I MEAN, WHY ARE YOU HIDING IN HERE?
NOT HIDING.
UH-HUH.
HEY, NICK ROBERTS.
S'UP, DETECTIVE PILGRIM.
I SEE YOU'RE NOT DEAD OR IN FEDERAL PRISON.
I WAS JUST ABOUT TO SAY THE SAME THING ABOUT YOU.
I DON'T GET IT, WALKER.
YOU- YOU GAVE UP?
YOU'RE GETTING ANGRY AT ME NOW?
YOU WERE SO HAPPY TO SEE ME NOT TEN SECONDS AGO.
I'M SORRY I DIDN'T CALL.
I JUST THOUGHT I WAS... PROTECTING YOU.
FROM WHAT?
I'M NOT SURE WHAT'S COMING NEXT FOR ME AND I DIDN'T WANT- I DON'T KNOW.
I JUST WANTED YOU TO BE SAFE AND I DIDN'T FEEL-
YOU ARE THE WORST FRIEND.
I SWEAR TO GOD.
ALL THE SHIT WE'VE BEEN THROUGH... YOU PICK UP THE PHONE AND YOU TELL ME YOU'RE OKAY.
YOU PICK UP THE PHONE AND YOU SAY: "I'M ALIVE. I'M JUST WORKING SOME STUFF OUT."
I'M SORRY.
AND YOU THINK "I'M FUCKING SORRY" FUCKING COVERS IT?

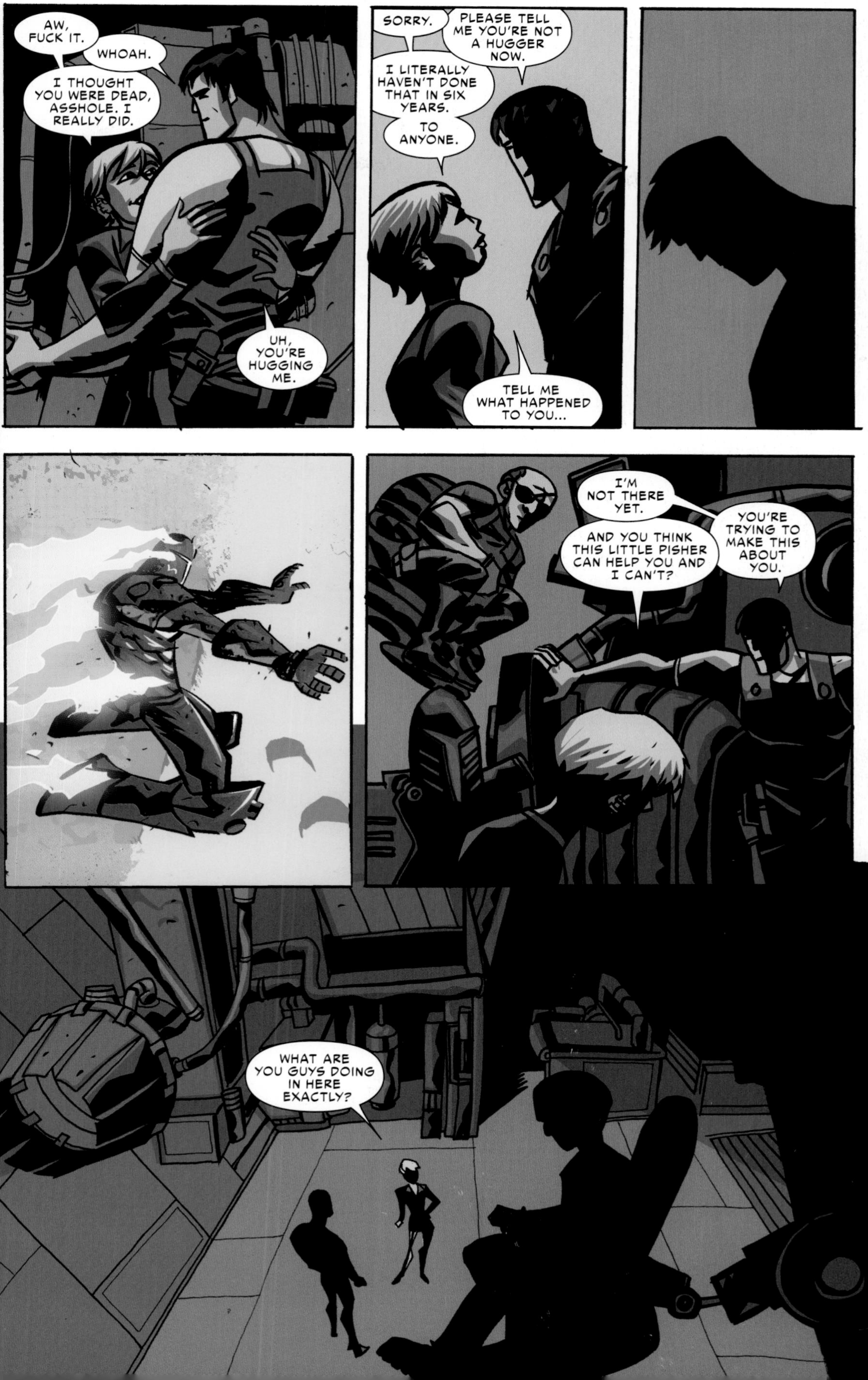
AW, FUCK IT.
WHOAH.
I THOUGHT YOU WERE DEAD, ASSHOLE. I REALLY DID.
UH, YOU'RE HUGGING ME.
SORRY.
PLEASE TELL ME YOU'RE NOT A HUGGER NOW.
I LITERALLY HAVEN'T DONE THAT IN SIX YEARS.
TO ANYONE.
TELL ME WHAT HAPPENED TO YOU...
I'M NOT THERE YET.
AND YOU THINK THIS LITTLE PISHER CAN HELP YOU AND I CAN'T?
YOU'RE TRYING TO MAKE THIS ABOUT YOU.
WHAT ARE YOU GUYS DOING IN HERE EXACTLY?

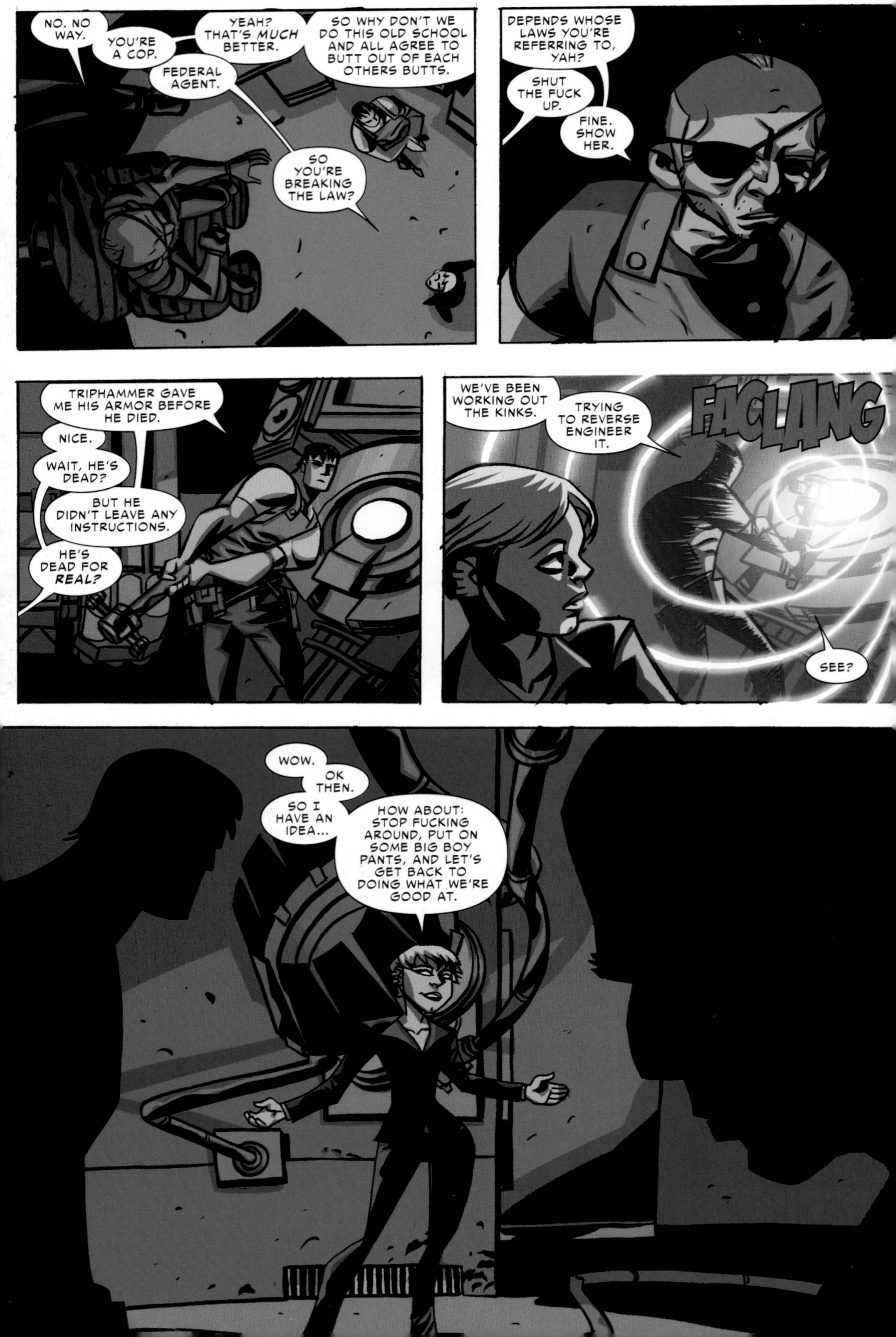
NO. NO WAY.
YOU'RE A COP.
YEAH? THAT'S *MUCH* BETTER.
SO WHY DON'T WE DO THIS OLD SCHOOL AND ALL AGREE TO BUTT OUT OF EACH OTHERS BUTTS.
FEDERAL AGENT.
SO YOU'RE BREAKING THE LAW?
DEPENDS WHOSE LAWS YOU'RE REFERRING TO, YAH?
SHUT THE FUCK UP.
FINE. SHOW HER.
TRIPHAMMER GAVE ME HIS ARMOR BEFORE HE DIED.
NICE.
WAIT, HE'S DEAD?
BUT HE DIDN'T LEAVE ANY INSTRUCTIONS.
HE'S DEAD FOR ***REAL?***
WE'VE BEEN WORKING OUT THE KINKS.
TRYING TO REVERSE ENGINEER IT.
FACLANG
SEE?
WOW.
OK THEN.
SO I HAVE AN IDEA...
HOW ABOUT: STOP FUCKING AROUND, PUT ON SOME BIG BOY PANTS, AND LET'S GET BACK TO DOING WHAT WE'RE GOOD AT.

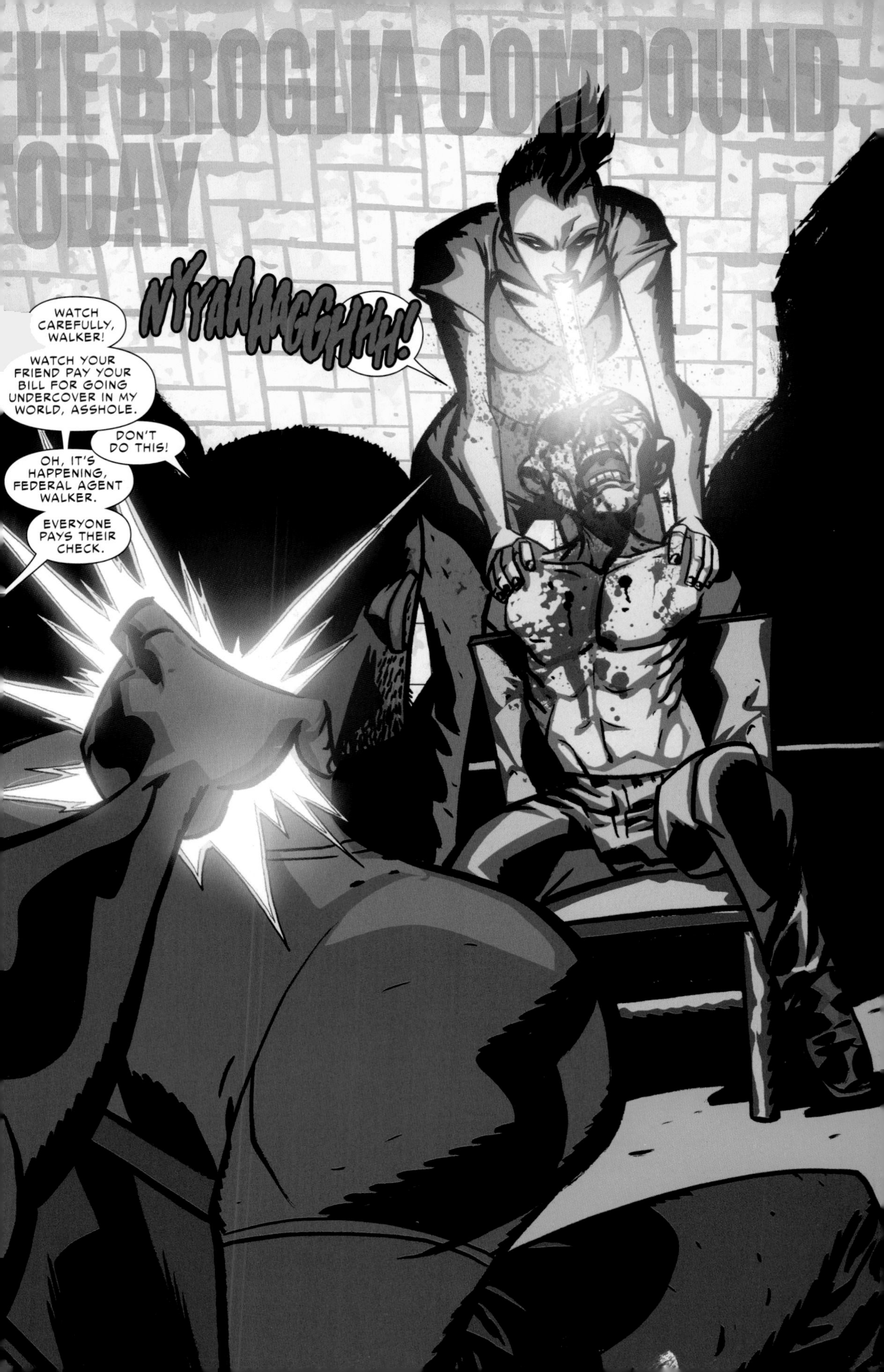
THE BROGLIA COMPOUND
TODAY
NYYAAAAAGGHHH!
WATCH CAREFULLY, WALKER!
WATCH YOUR FRIEND PAY YOUR BILL FOR GOING UNDERCOVER IN MY WORLD, ASSHOLE.
DON'T DO THIS!
OH, IT'S HAPPENING, FEDERAL AGENT WALKER.
EVERYONE PAYS THEIR CHECK.

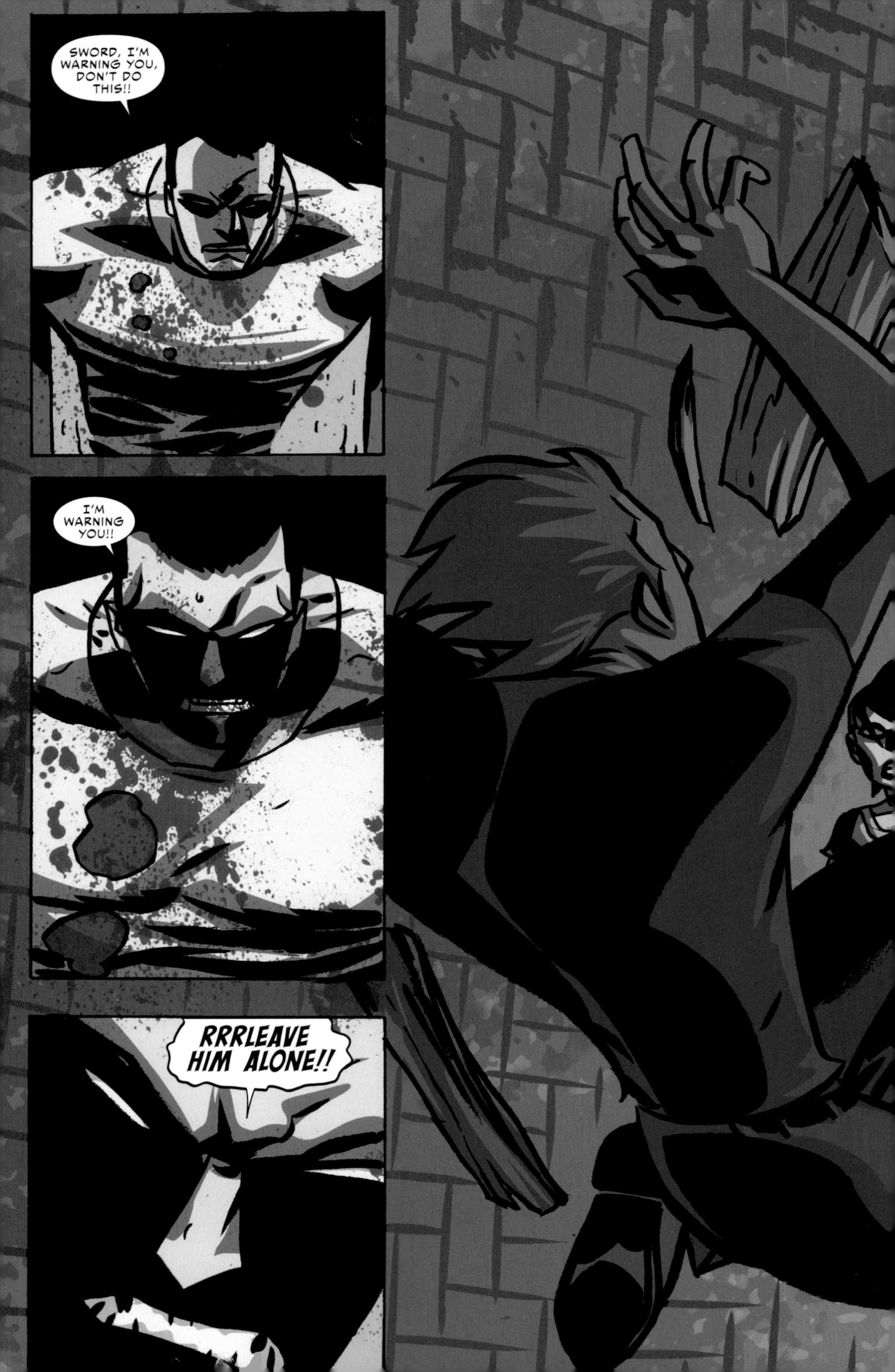
SWORD, I'M WARNING YOU, DON'T DO THIS!!
I'M WARNING YOU!!
RRRLEAVE HIM ALONE!!

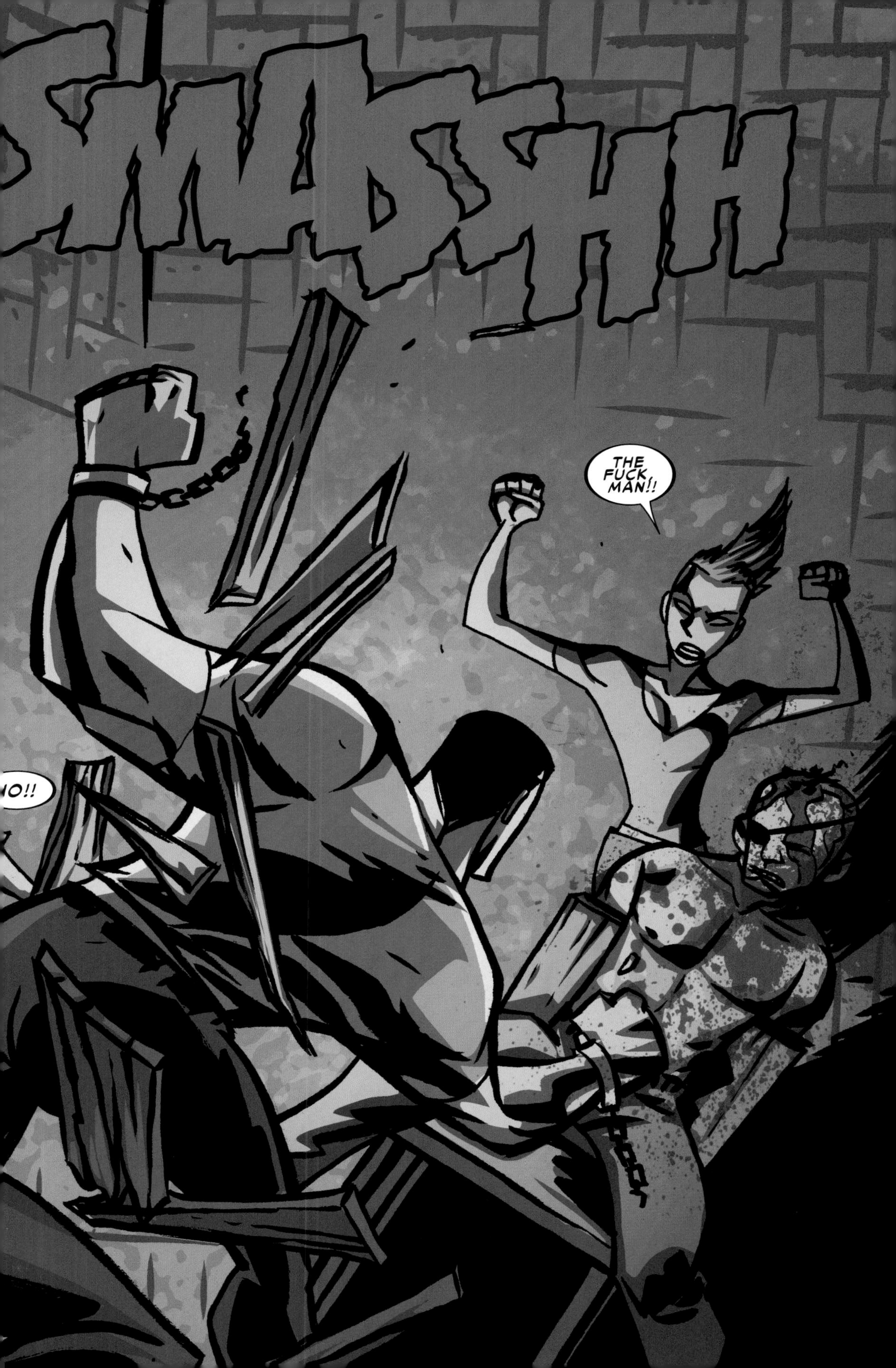

SMASHH
THE FUCK MAN!!

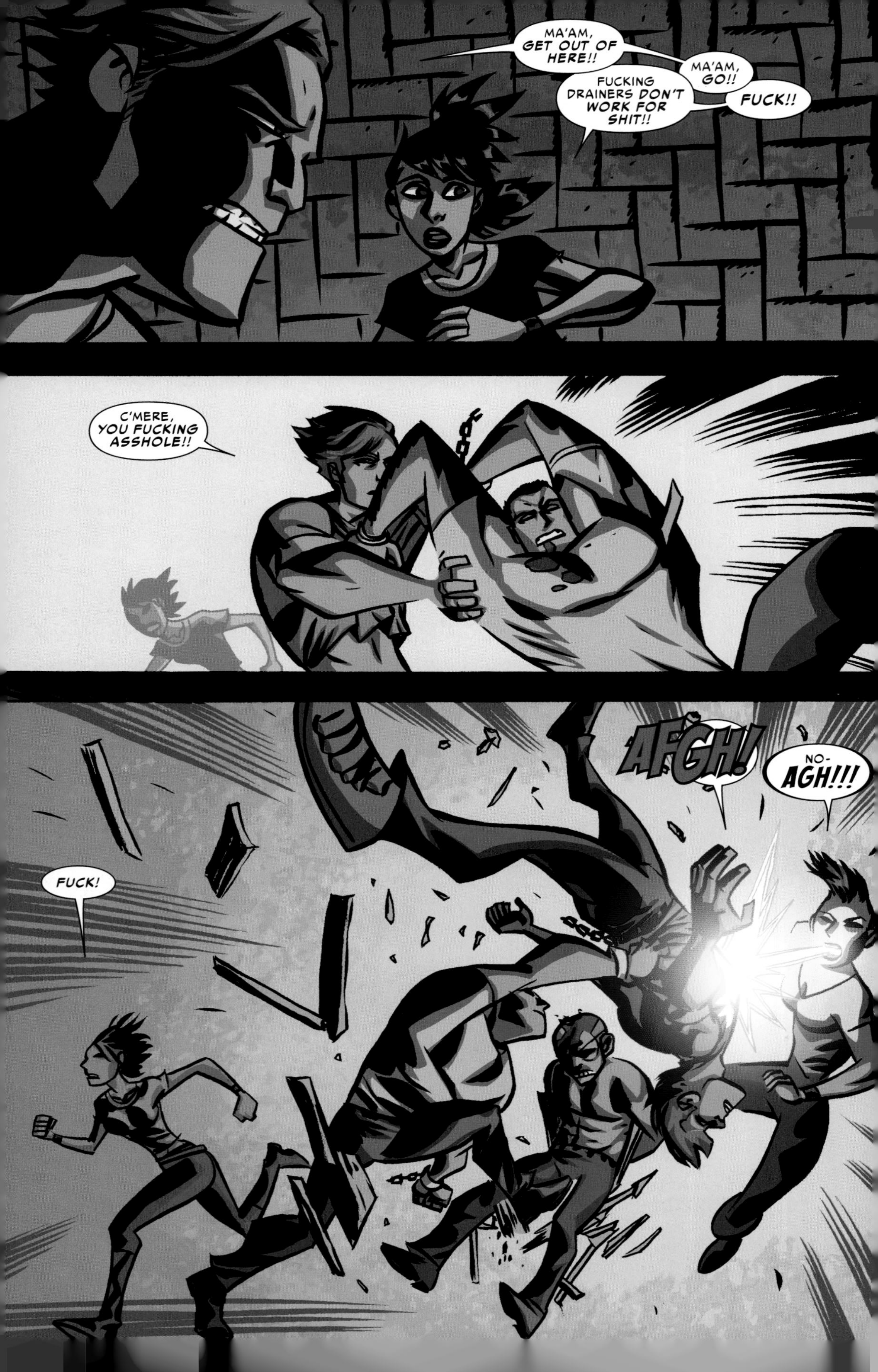
MA'AM, GET OUT OF HERE!!
FUCKING DRAINERS DON'T WORK FOR SHIT!!
MA'AM, GO!!
FUCK!!
C'MERE, YOU FUCKING ASSHOLE!!
AFGH!
NO-AGH!!!
FUCK!

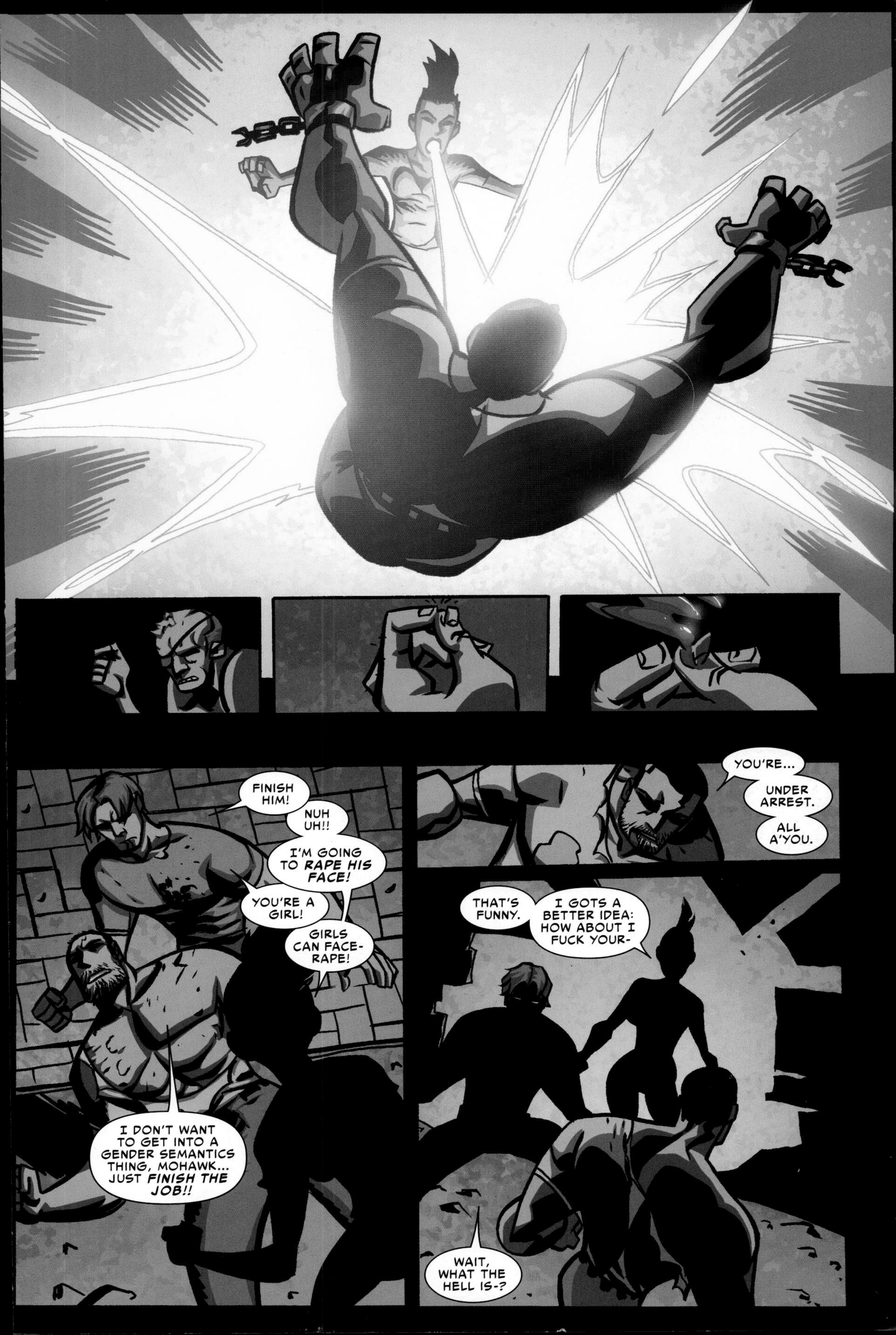
FINISH HIM!
NUH UH!!
I'M GOING TO RAPE HIS FACE!
YOU'RE A GIRL!
GIRLS CAN FACE-RAPE!
I DON'T WANT TO GET INTO A GENDER SEMANTICS THING, MOHAWK... JUST FINISH THE JOB!!
YOU'RE...
UNDER ARREST.
ALL A'YOU.
THAT'S FUNNY.
I GOTS A BETTER IDEA: HOW ABOUT I FUCK YOUR-
WAIT, WHAT THE HELL IS-?

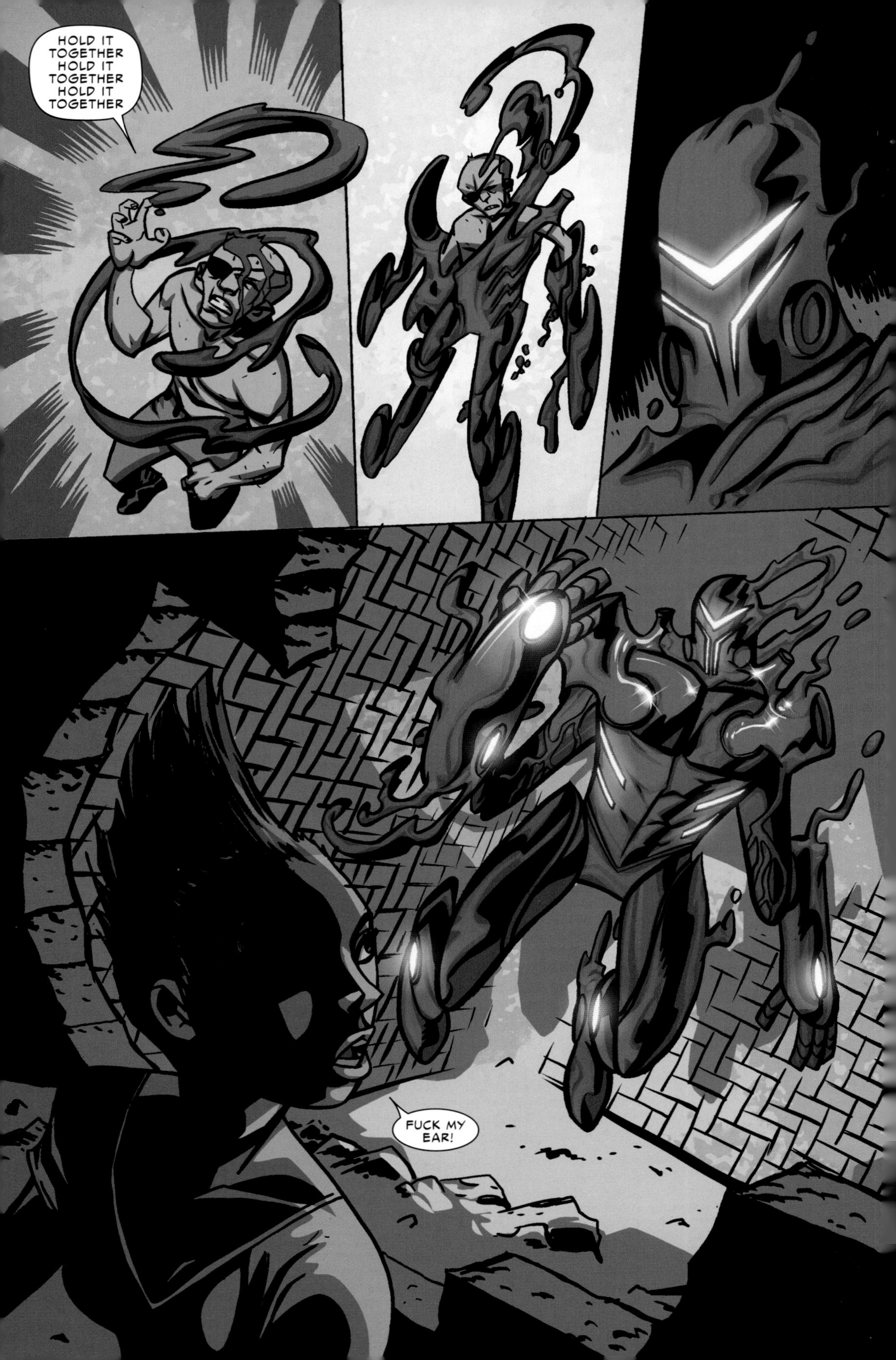
HOLD IT TOGETHER HOLD IT TOGETHER HOLD IT TOGETHER
FUCK MY EAR!

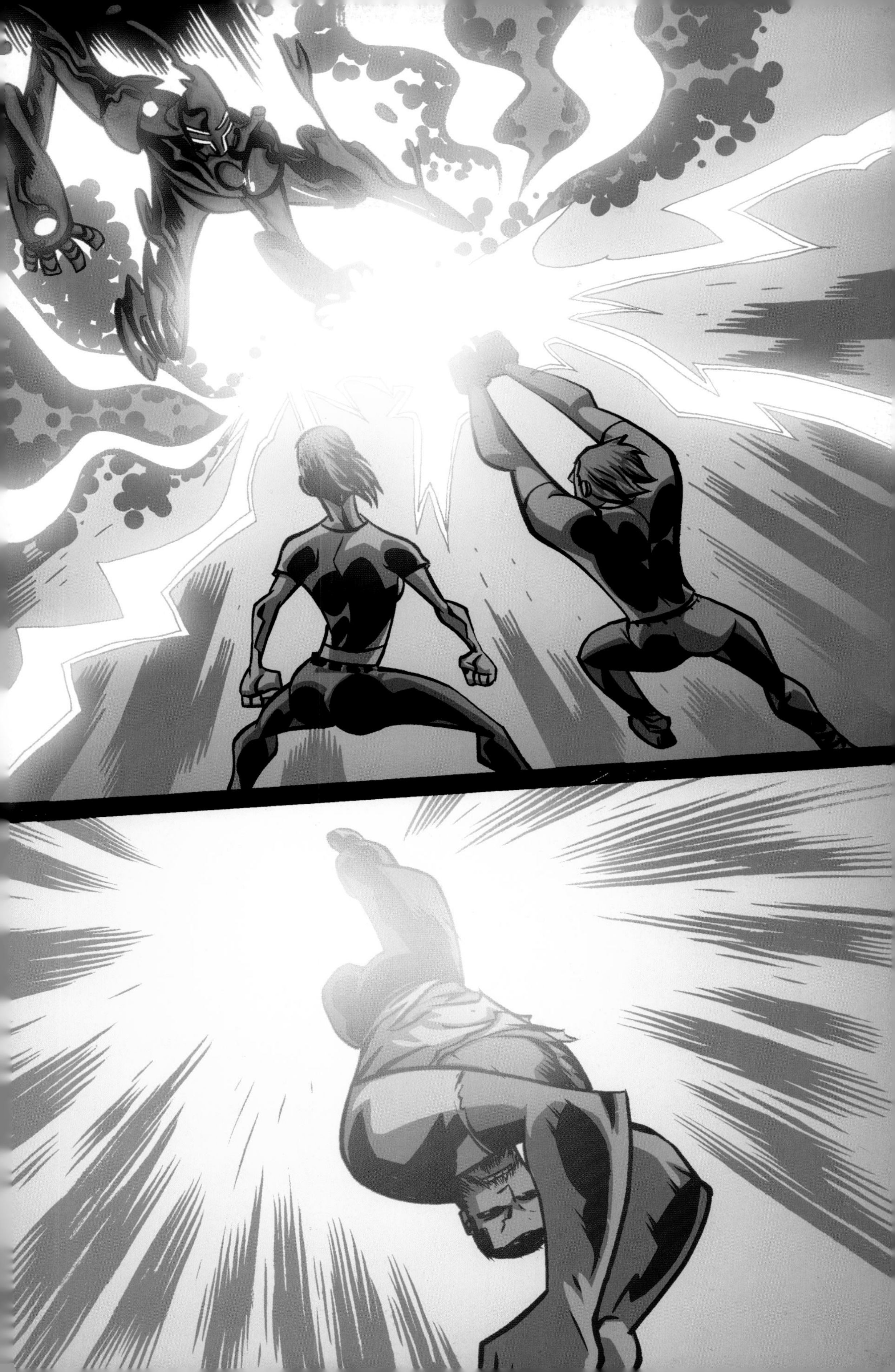

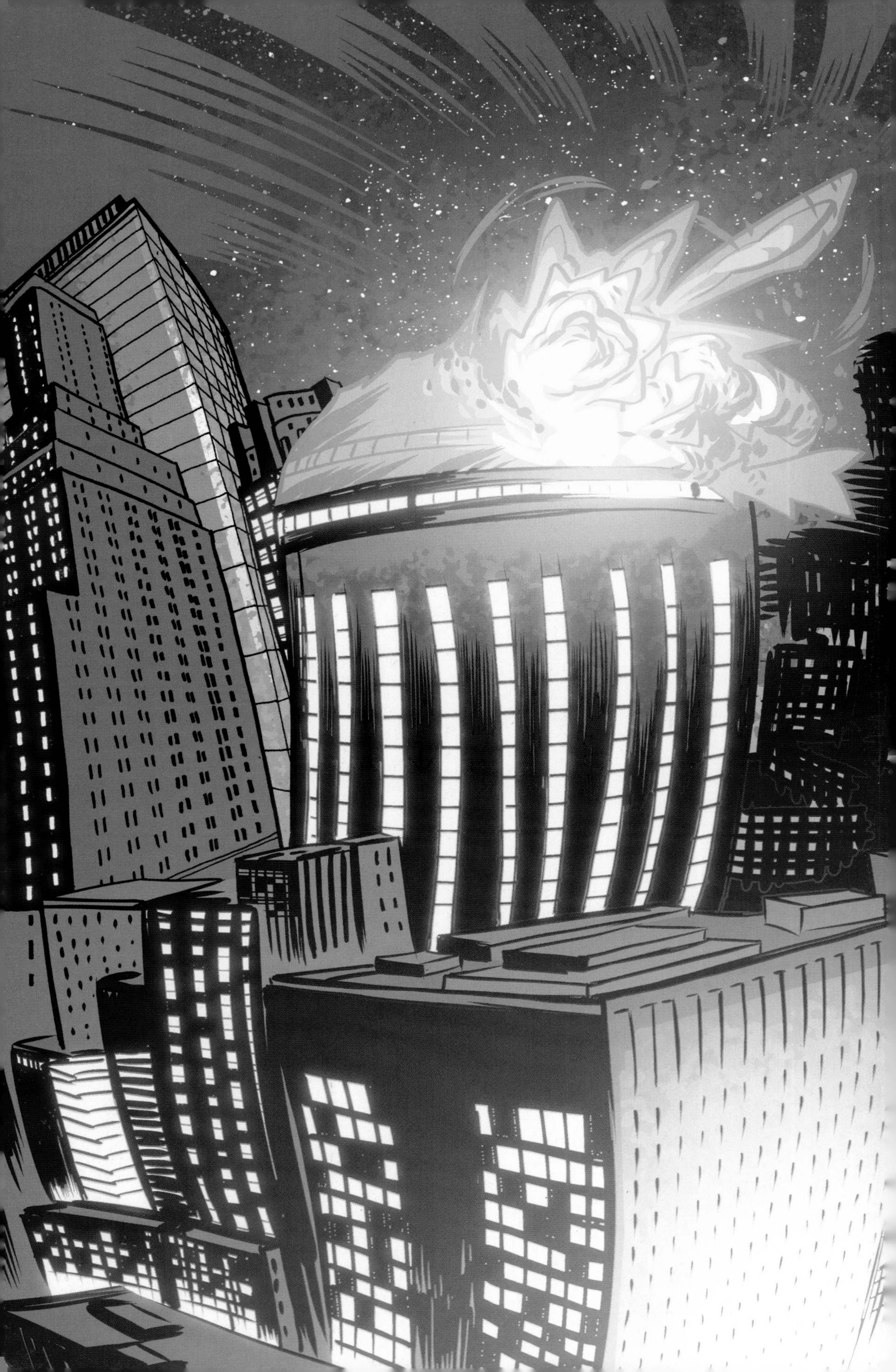

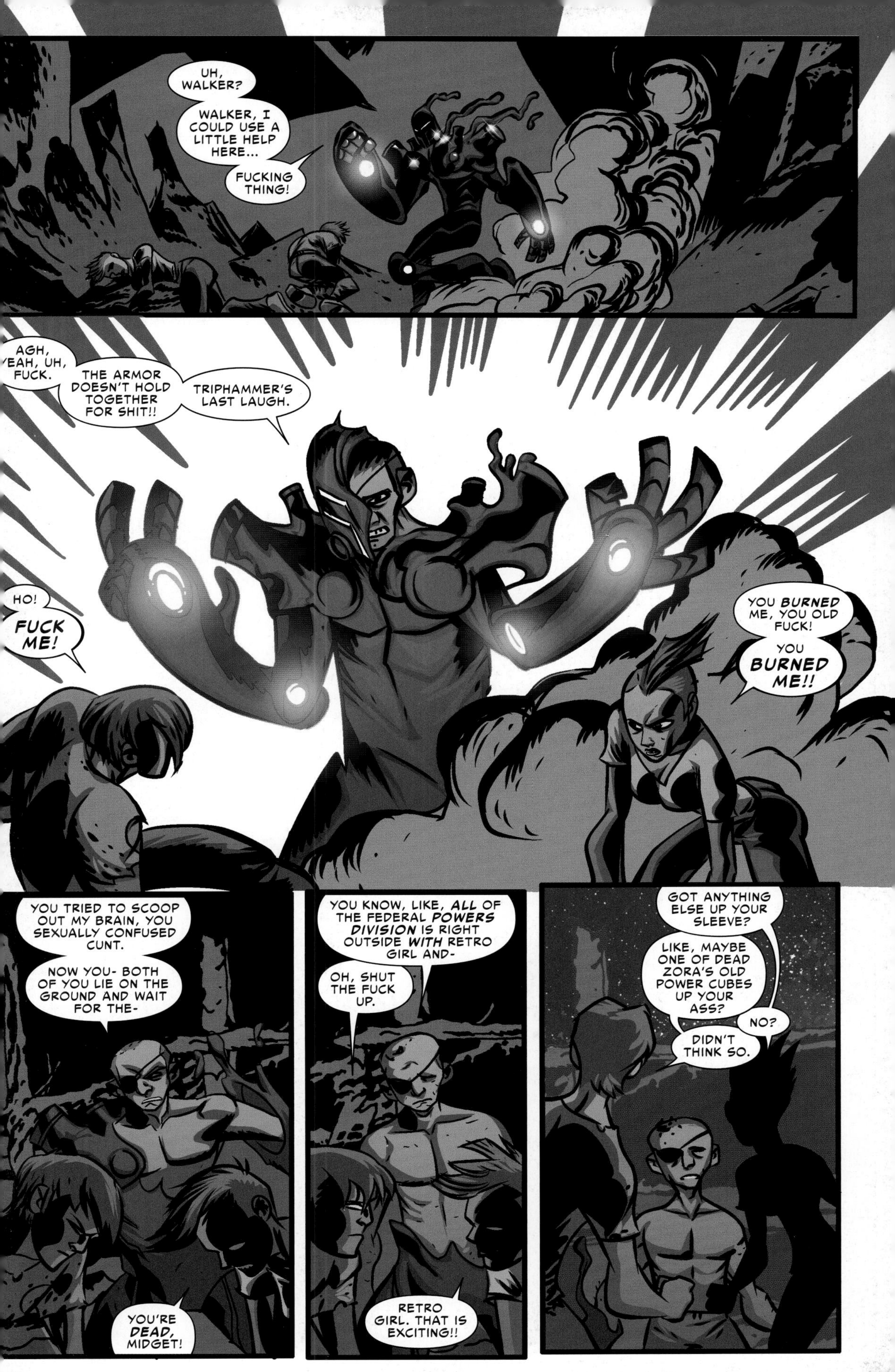
UH, WALKER?
WALKER, I COULD USE A LITTLE HELP HERE...
FUCKING THING!
AGH, YEAH, UH, FUCK.
THE ARMOR DOESN'T HOLD TOGETHER FOR SHIT!!
TRIPHAMMER'S LAST LAUGH.
HO! FUCK ME!
YOU BURNED ME, YOU OLD FUCK!
YOU BURNED ME!!
YOU TRIED TO SCOOP OUT MY BRAIN, YOU SEXUALLY CONFUSED CUNT.
NOW YOU- BOTH OF YOU LIE ON THE GROUND AND WAIT FOR THE-
YOU'RE DEAD, MIDGET!
YOU KNOW, LIKE, ALL OF THE FEDERAL POWERS DIVISION IS RIGHT OUTSIDE WITH RETRO GIRL AND-
OH, SHUT THE FUCK UP.
RETRO GIRL. THAT IS EXCITING!!
GOT ANYTHING ELSE UP YOUR SLEEVE?
LIKE, MAYBE ONE OF DEAD ZORA'S OLD POWER CUBES UP YOUR ASS?
NO?
DIDN'T THINK SO.

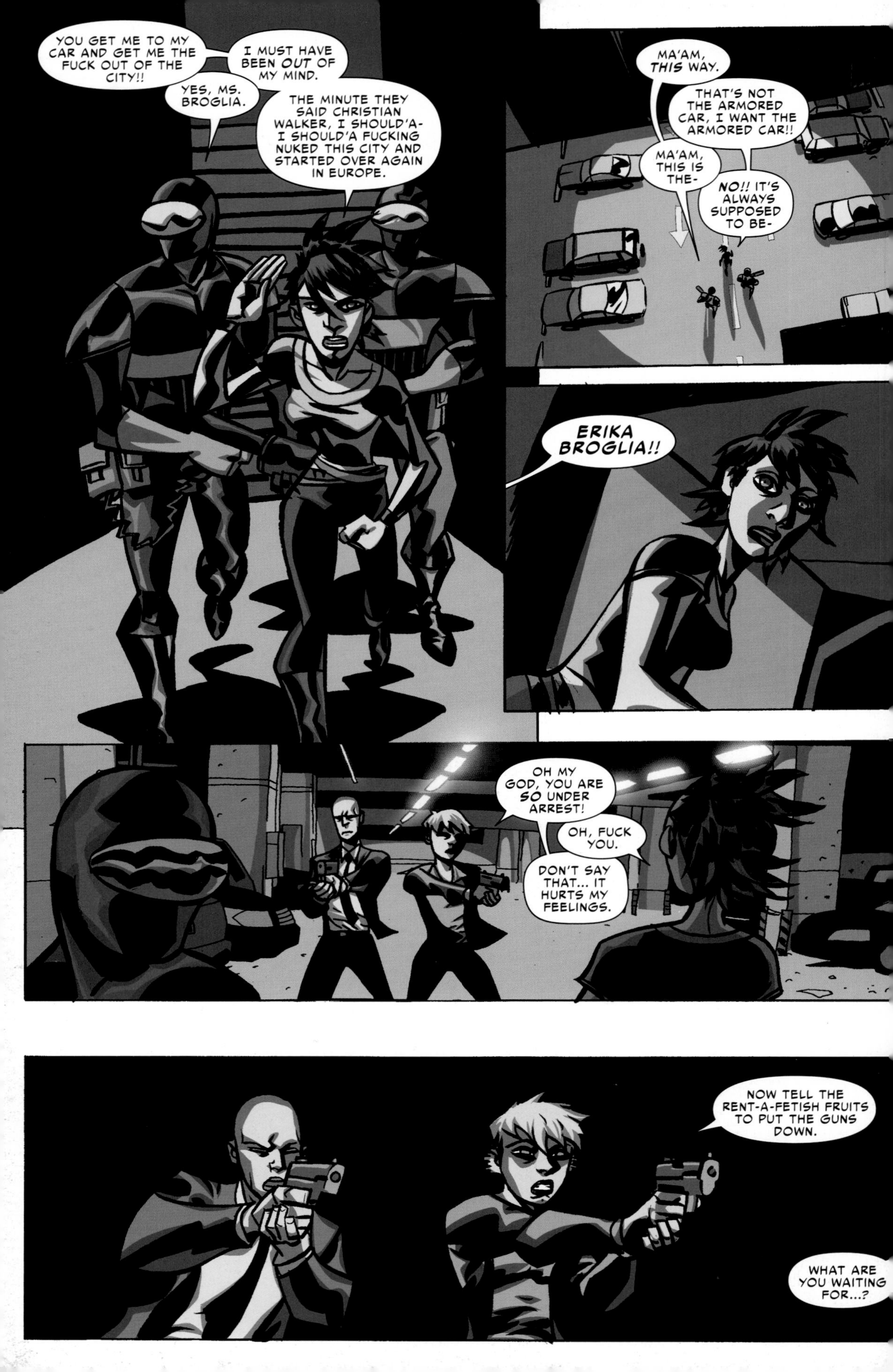
YOU GET ME TO MY CAR AND GET ME THE FUCK OUT OF THE CITY!!
YES, MS. BROGLIA.
I MUST HAVE BEEN OUT OF MY MIND.
THE MINUTE THEY SAID CHRISTIAN WALKER, I SHOULD'A- I SHOULD'A FUCKING NUKED THIS CITY AND STARTED OVER AGAIN IN EUROPE.
MA'AM, THIS WAY.
THAT'S NOT THE ARMORED CAR, I WANT THE ARMORED CAR!!
MA'AM, THIS IS THE-
NO!! IT'S ALWAYS SUPPOSED TO BE-
ERIKA BROGLIA!!
OH MY GOD, YOU ARE SO UNDER ARREST!
OH, FUCK YOU.
DON'T SAY THAT... IT HURTS MY FEELINGS.
NOW TELL THE RENT-A-FETISH FRUITS TO PUT THE GUNS DOWN.
WHAT ARE YOU WAITING FOR...?

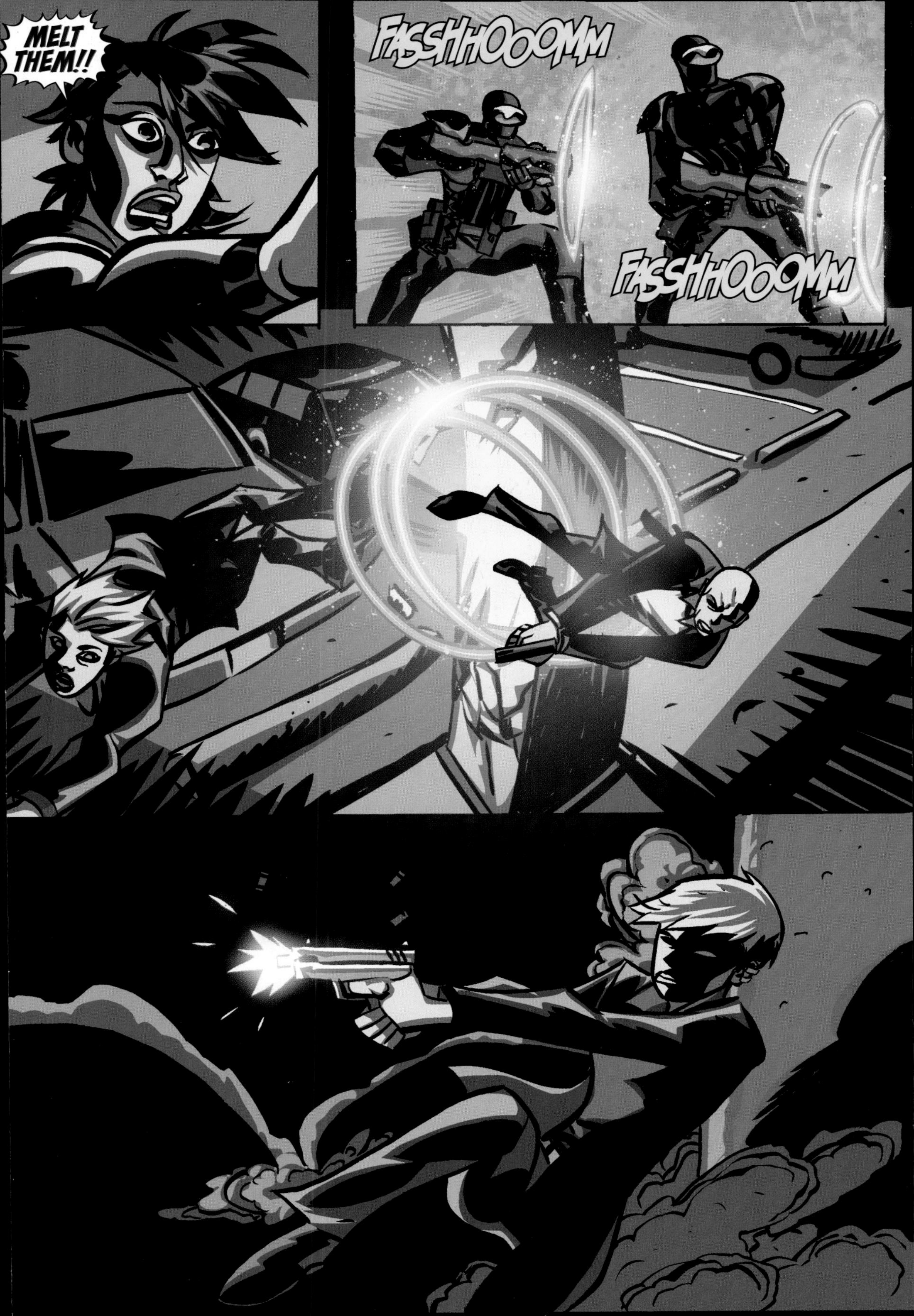
MELT THEM!!
FASSHHOOOOMM
FASSHHOOOOMM

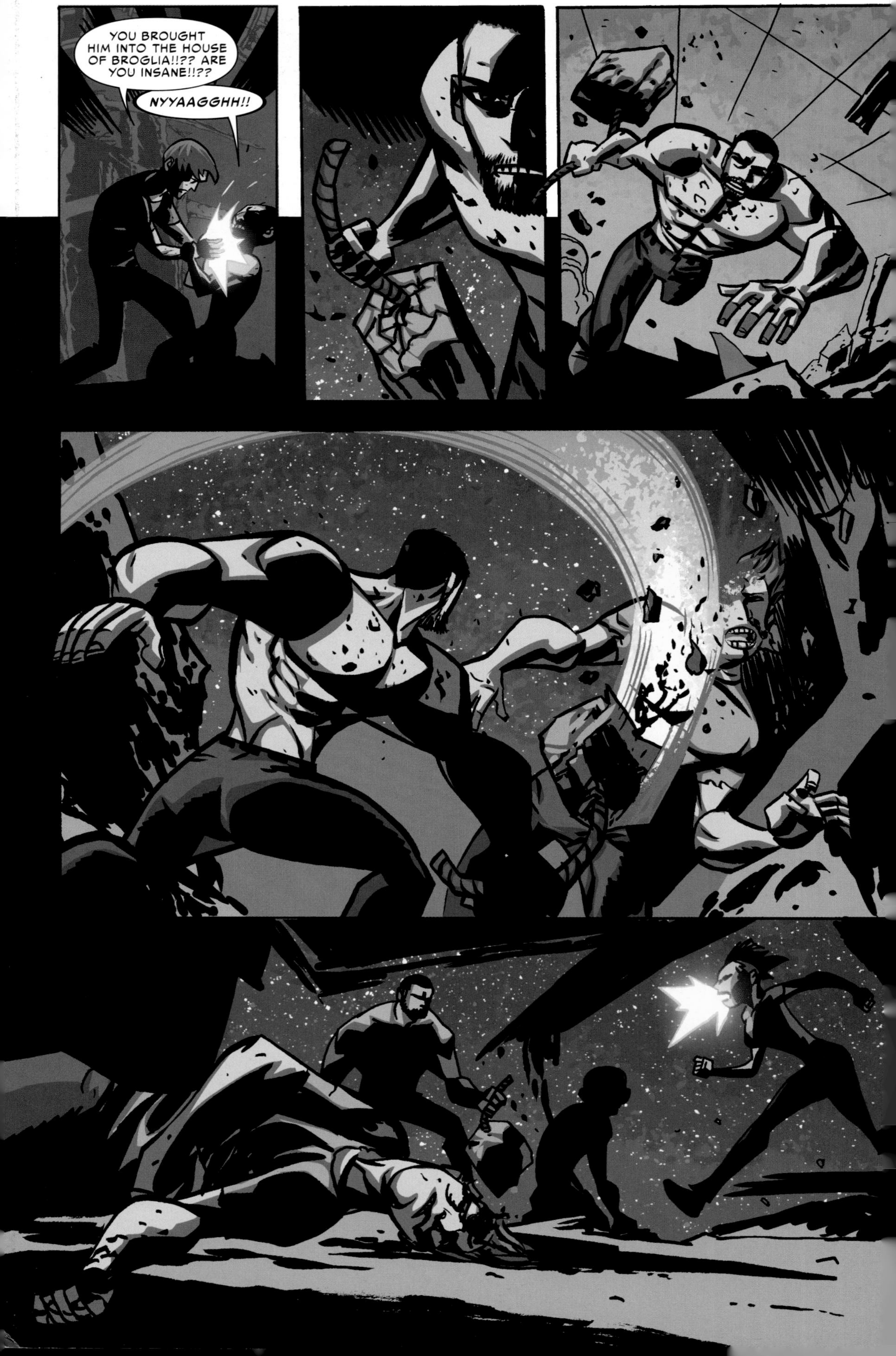
YOU BROUGHT HIM INTO THE HOUSE OF BROGLIA!!?? ARE YOU INSANE!!??
NYYAAGGHH!!

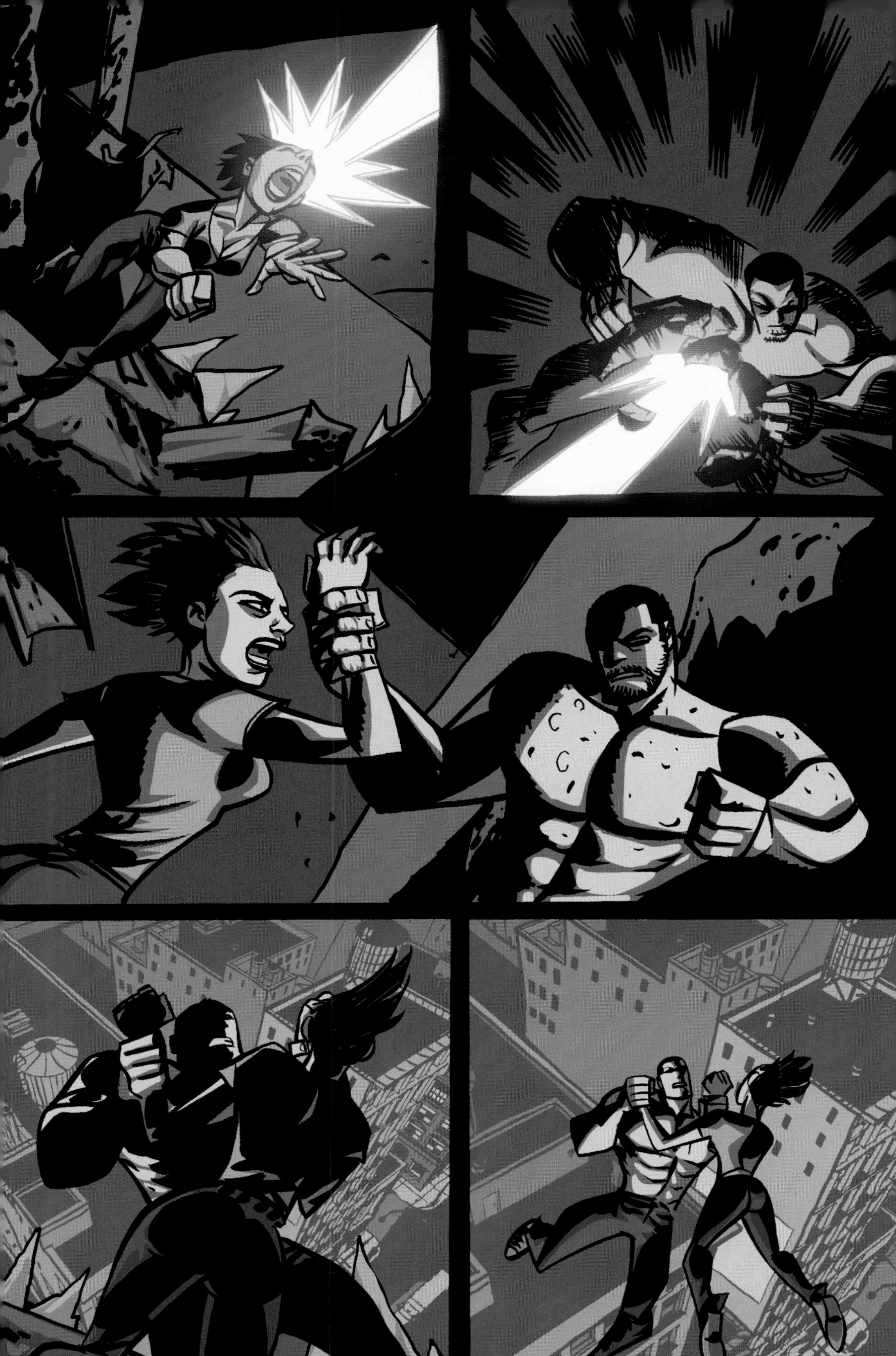

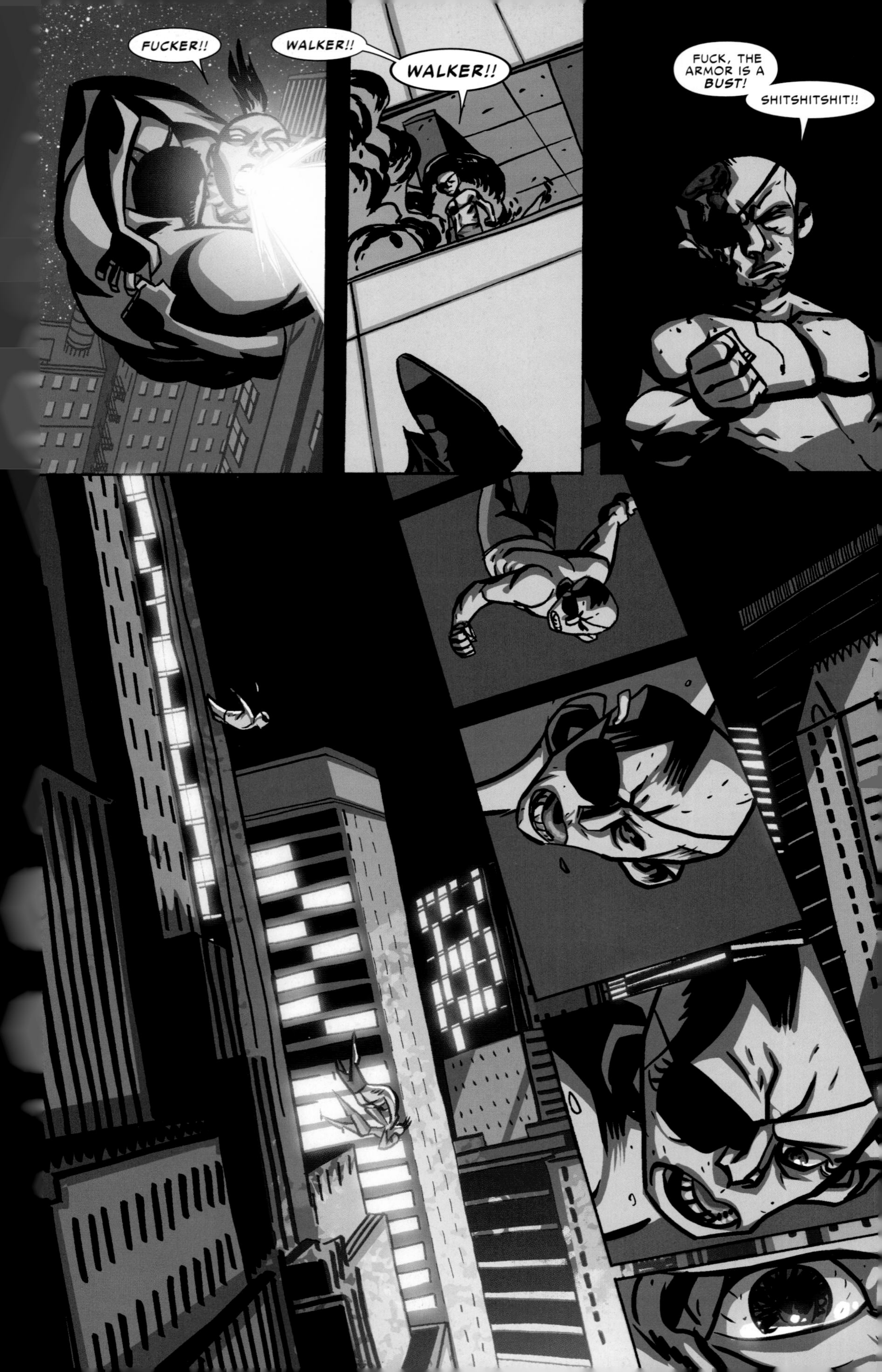
FUCKER!!
WALKER!!
WALKER!!
FUCK, THE ARMOR IS A BUST!
SHITSHITSHIT!!

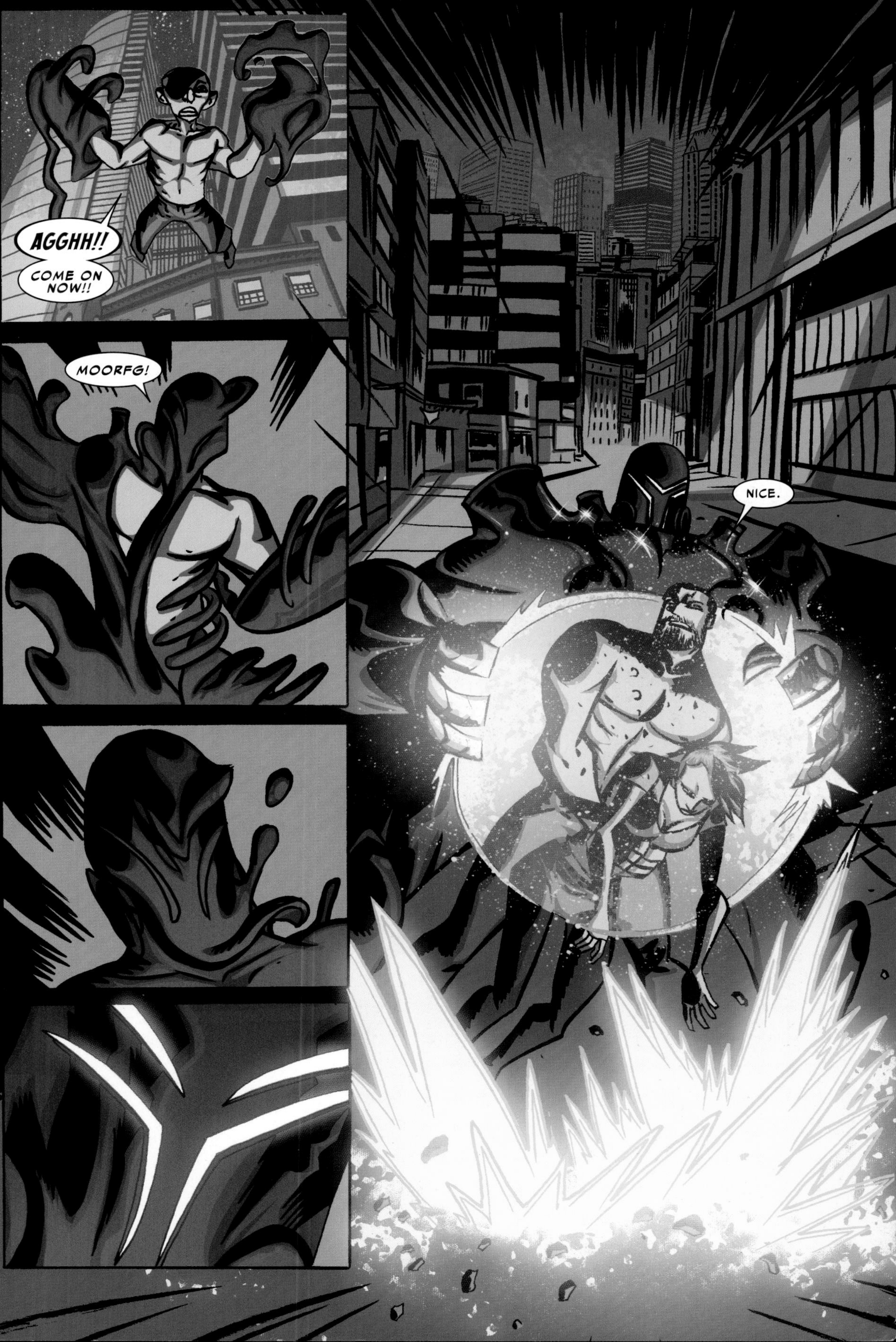
AGGHH!!
COME ON NOW!!
MOORFG!
NICE.

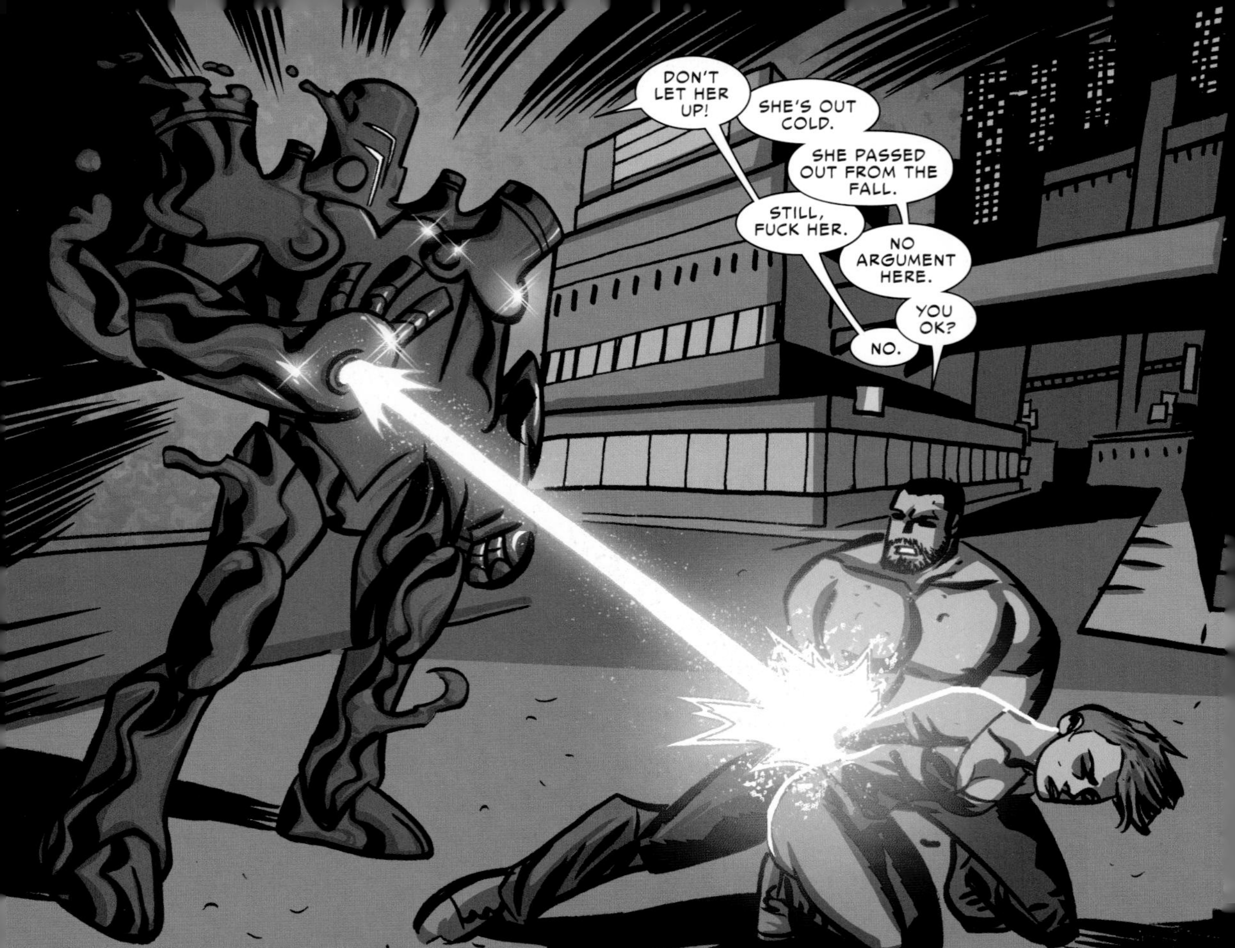
DON'T LET HER UP!
SHE'S OUT COLD.
SHE PASSED OUT FROM THE FALL.
STILL, FUCK HER.
NO ARGUMENT HERE.
YOU OK?
NO.
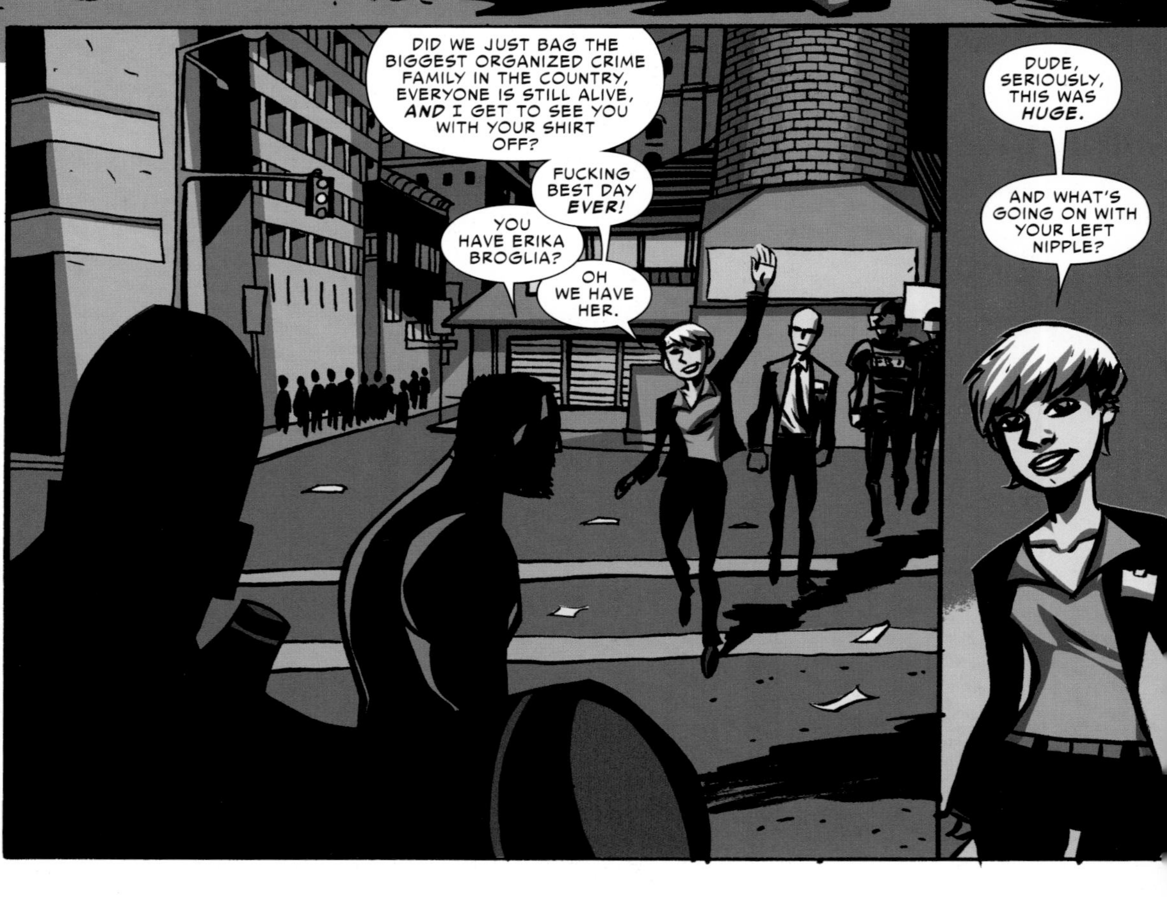
DID WE JUST BAG THE BIGGEST ORGANIZED CRIME FAMILY IN THE COUNTRY, EVERYONE IS STILL ALIVE, AND I GET TO SEE YOU WITH YOUR SHIRT OFF?
FUCKING BEST DAY EVER!
YOU HAVE ERIKA BROGLIA?
OH WE HAVE HER.
DUDE, SERIOUSLY, THIS WAS HUGE.
AND WHAT'S GOING ON WITH YOUR LEFT NIPPLE?

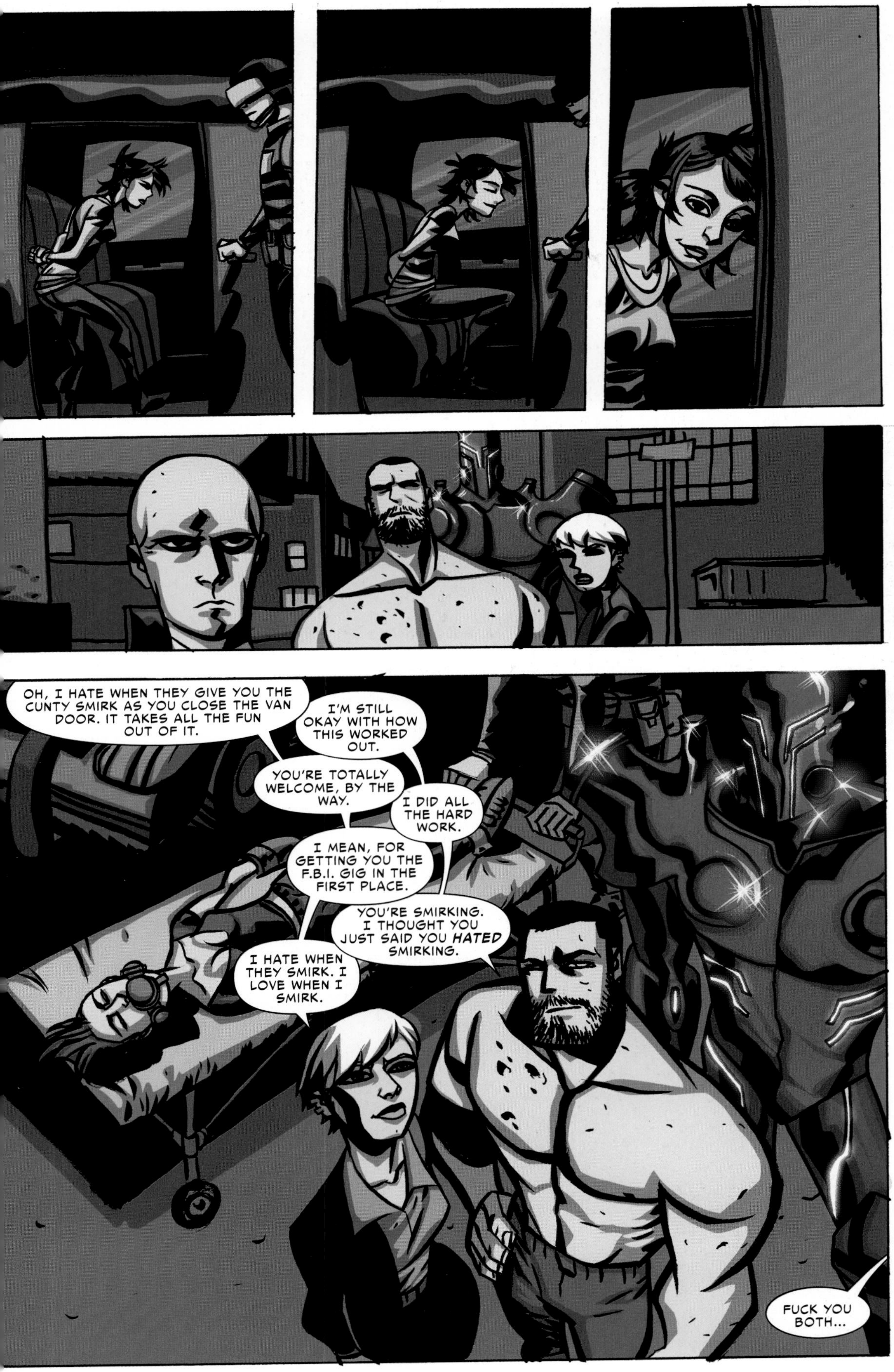
OH, I HATE WHEN THEY GIVE YOU THE CUNTY SMIRK AS YOU CLOSE THE VAN DOOR. IT TAKES ALL THE FUN OUT OF IT.
I'M STILL OKAY WITH HOW THIS WORKED OUT.
YOU'RE TOTALLY WELCOME, BY THE WAY.
I DID ALL THE HARD WORK.
I MEAN, FOR GETTING YOU THE F.B.I. GIG IN THE FIRST PLACE.
YOU'RE SMIRKING. I THOUGHT YOU JUST SAID YOU *HATED* SMIRKING.
I HATE WHEN THEY SMIRK. I LOVE WHEN I SMIRK.
FUCK YOU BOTH...

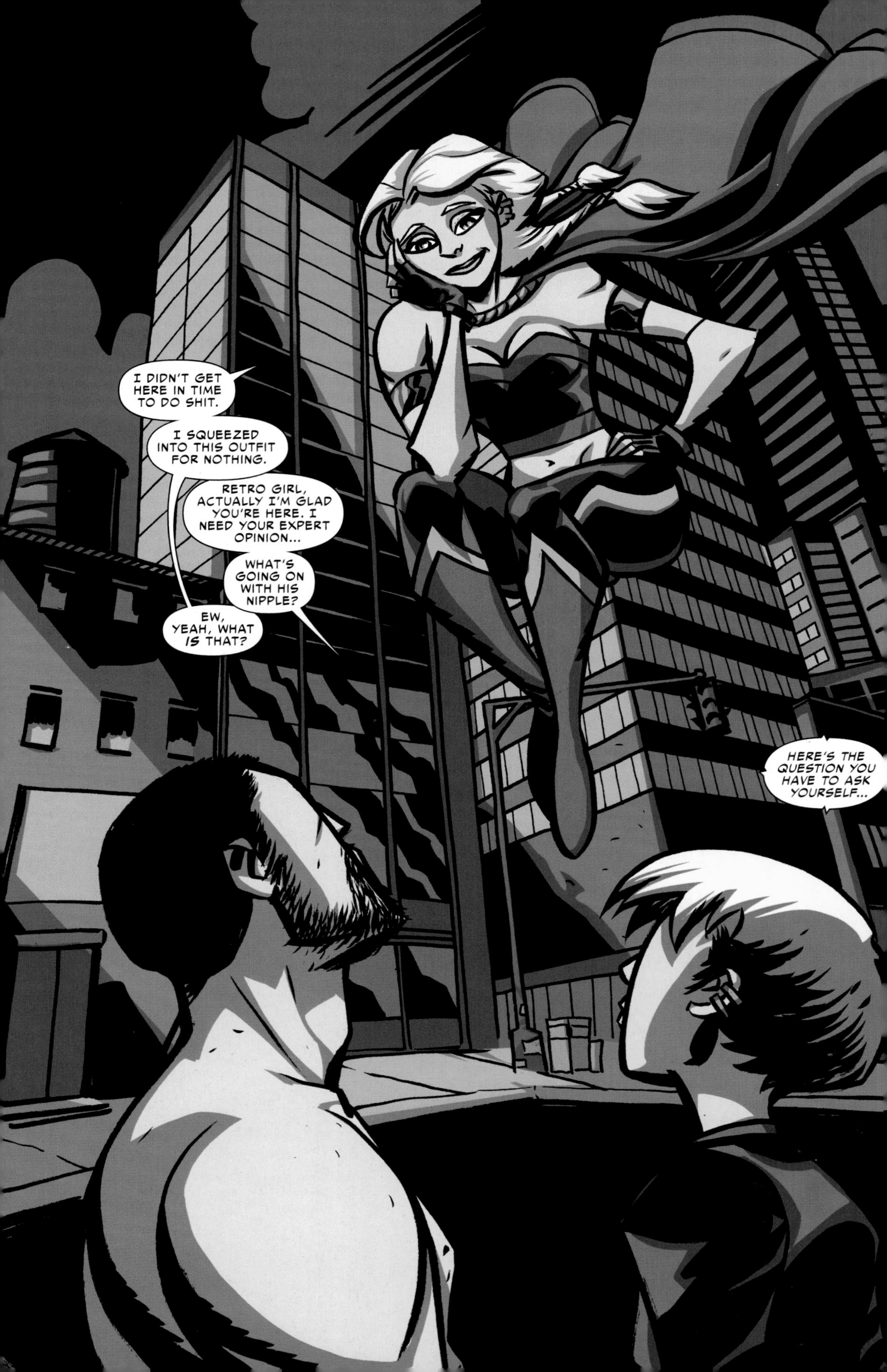
I DIDN'T GET HERE IN TIME TO DO SHIT.
I SQUEEZED INTO THIS OUTFIT FOR NOTHING.
RETRO GIRL, ACTUALLY I'M GLAD YOU'RE HERE. I NEED YOUR EXPERT OPINION...
WHAT'S GOING ON WITH HIS NIPPLE?
EW, YEAH, WHAT *IS* THAT?
HERE'S THE QUESTION YOU HAVE TO ASK YOURSELF...

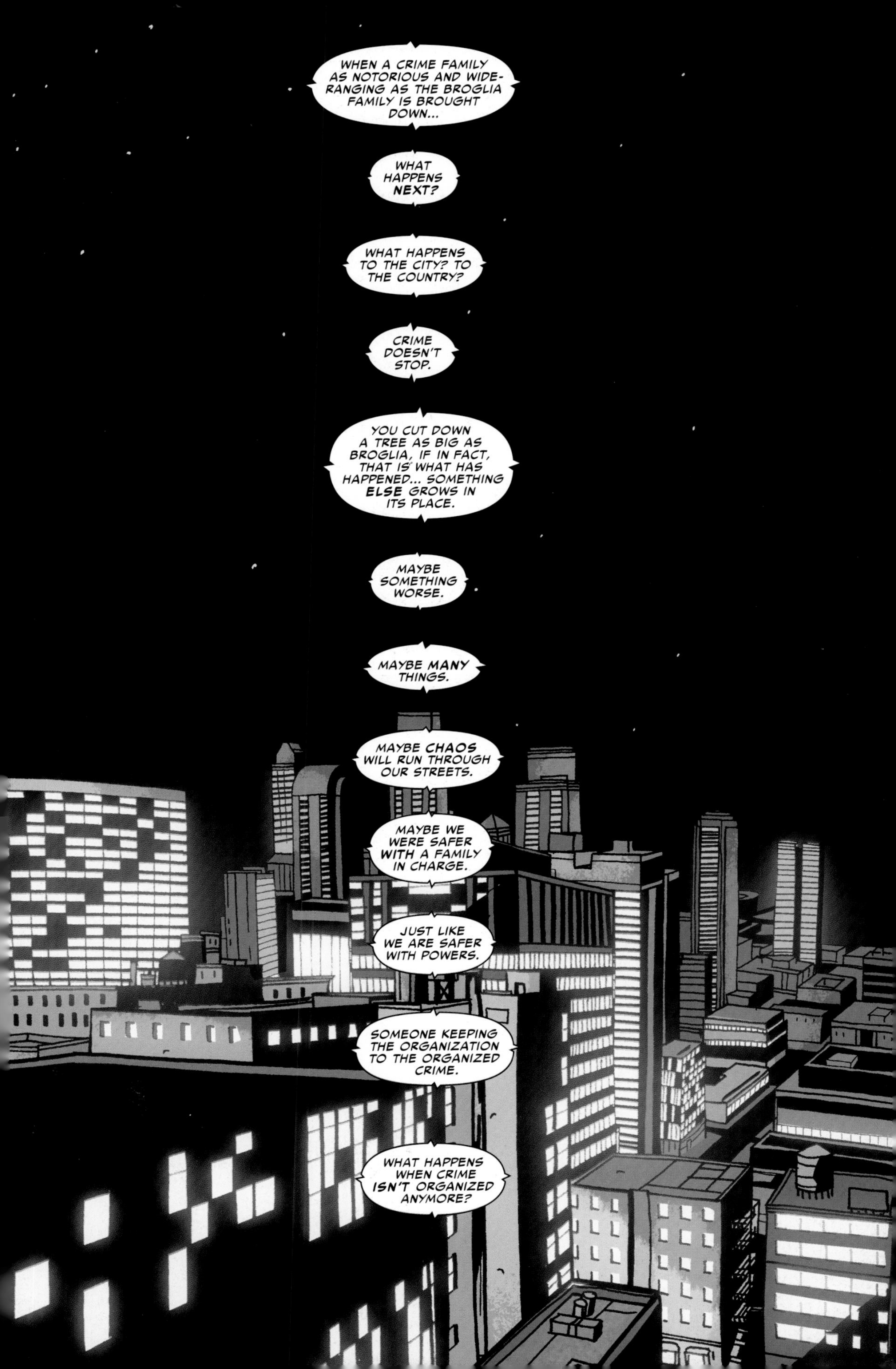
WHEN A CRIME FAMILY AS NOTORIOUS AND WIDE-RANGING AS THE BROGLIA FAMILY IS BROUGHT DOWN...
WHAT HAPPENS NEXT?
WHAT HAPPENS TO THE CITY? TO THE COUNTRY?
CRIME DOESN'T STOP.
YOU CUT DOWN A TREE AS BIG AS BROGLIA, IF IN FACT, THAT IS WHAT HAS HAPPENED... SOMETHING ELSE GROWS IN ITS PLACE.
MAYBE SOMETHING WORSE.
MAYBE MANY THINGS.
MAYBE CHAOS WILL RUN THROUGH OUR STREETS.
MAYBE WE WERE SAFER WITH A FAMILY IN CHARGE.
JUST LIKE WE ARE SAFER WITH POWERS.
SOMEONE KEEPING THE ORGANIZATION TO THE ORGANIZED CRIME.
WHAT HAPPENS WHEN CRIME ISN'T ORGANIZED ANYMORE?

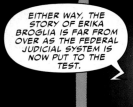

EITHER WAY, THE STORY OF ERIKA BROGLIA IS FAR FROM OVER AS THE FEDERAL JUDICIAL SYSTEM IS NOW PUT TO THE TEST.

WILL SHE STAND TRIAL FOR HER NUMEROUS CRIMES, OR WILL SHE, LIKE HER FAMILY BEFORE HER, FIND A WAY TO DANCE BETWEEN THE RAIN-

GLEE GLEE

I own you, Meltzer. I get out or your daughter dies.

NEXT: ICONS

POWERS
COVER GALLERY

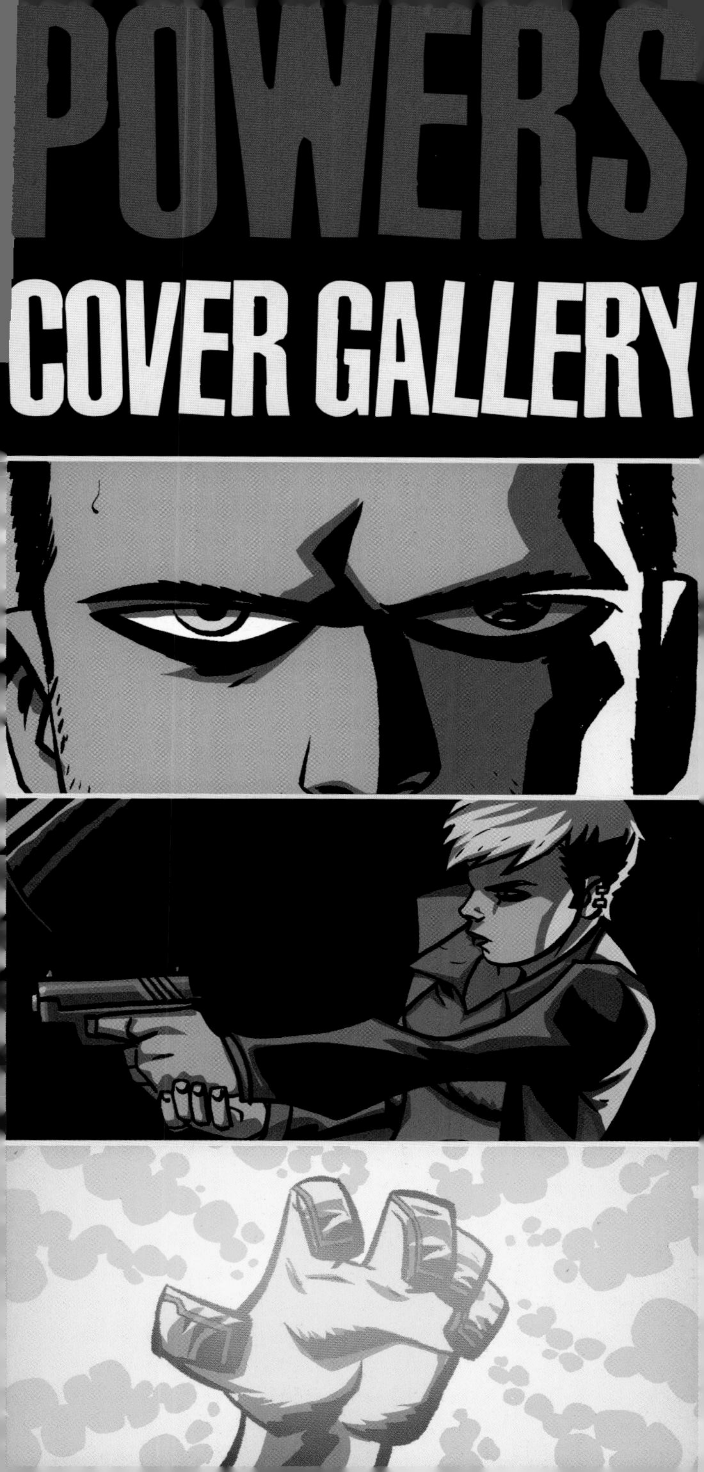

POWERS: BUREAU #1

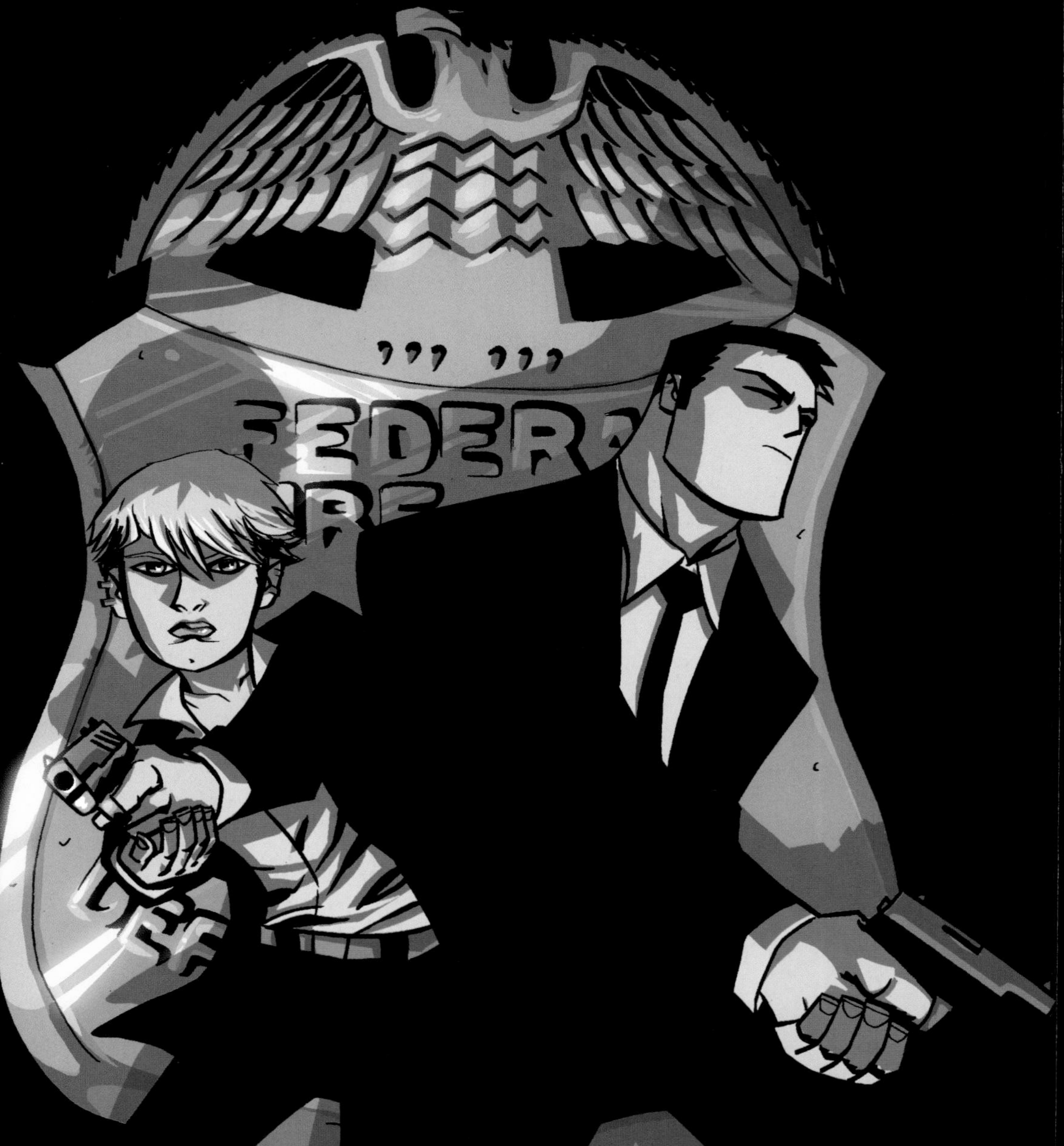
AVON
2012

POWERS: BUREAU #1
Variant Cover by David Mack

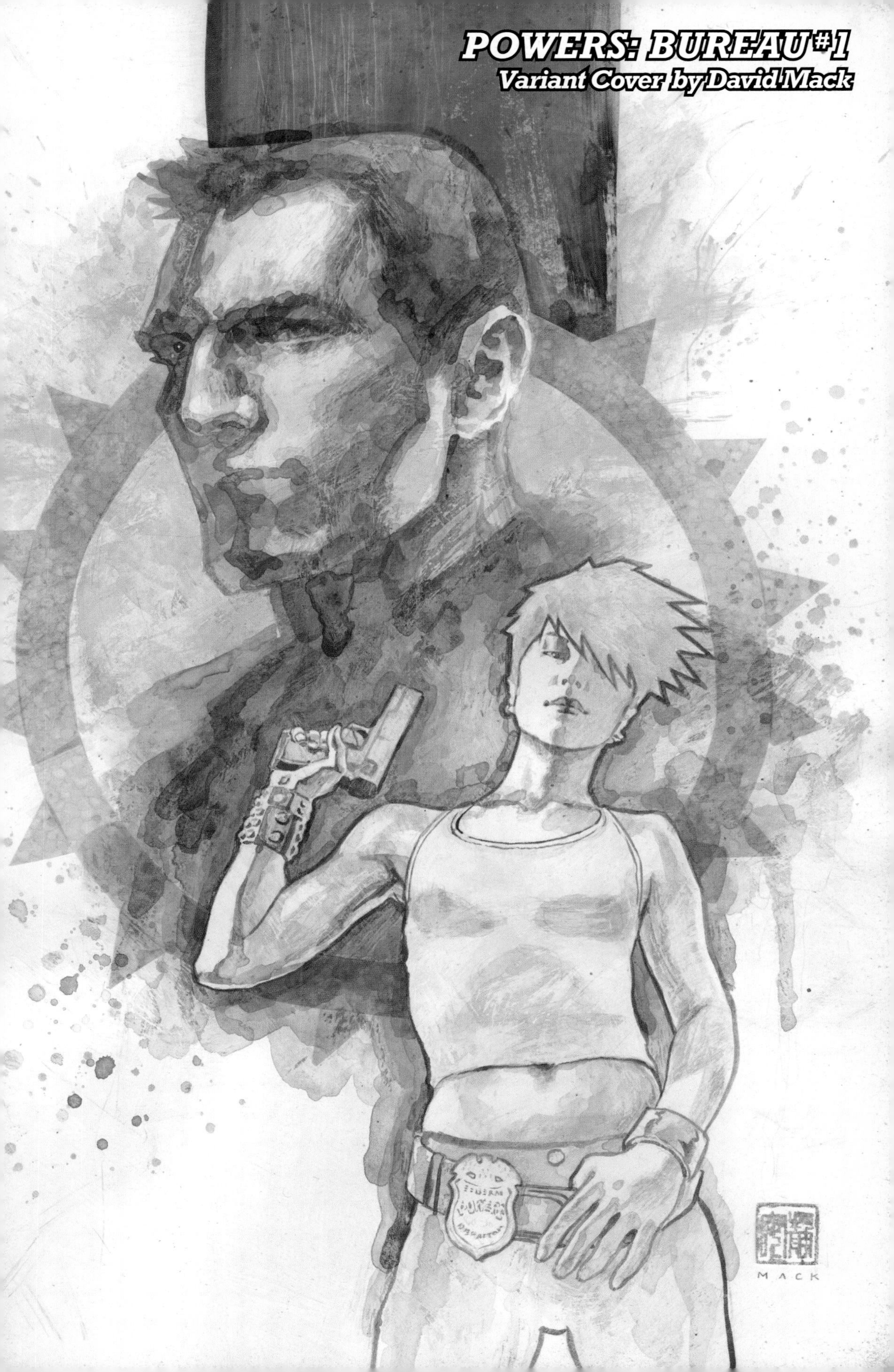
MACK

POWERS: BUREAU #1
Variant Cover by David LaFuente

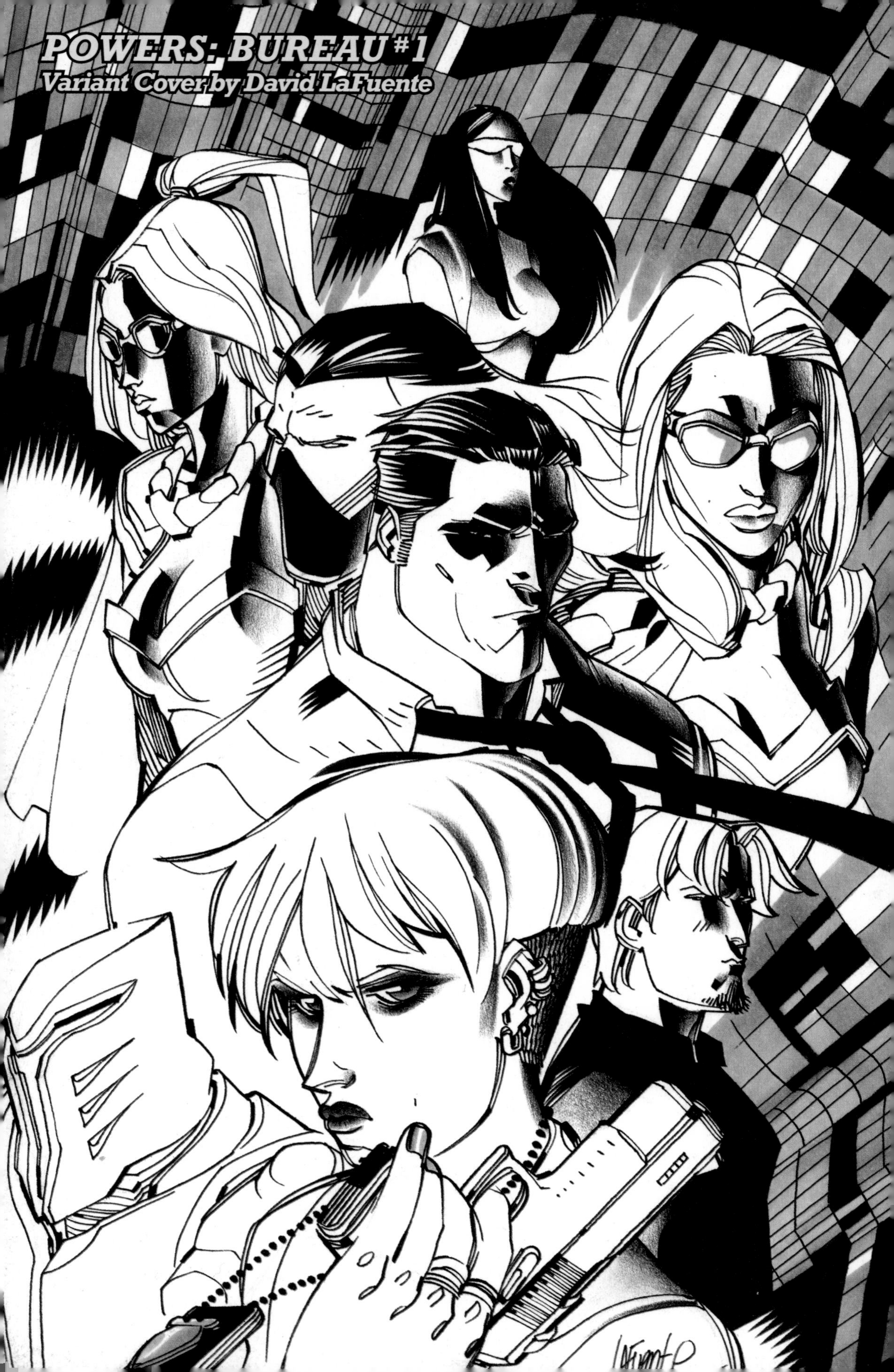

POWERS: BUREAU #2

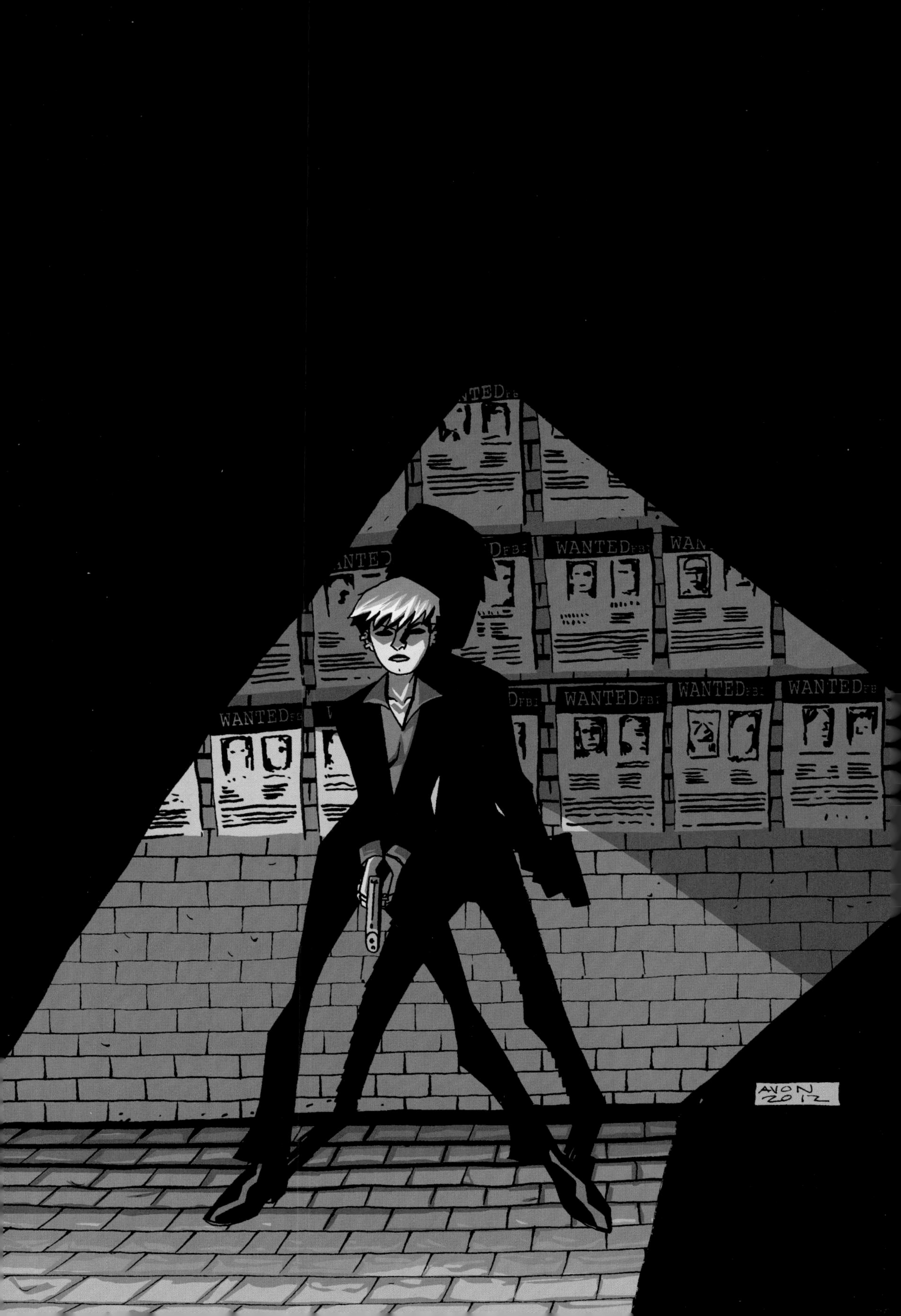
WANTED FBI
WANTED FBI
WANTED FBI
WANTED FBI
WANTED FBI
AVON 2012

POWERS: BUREAU #3

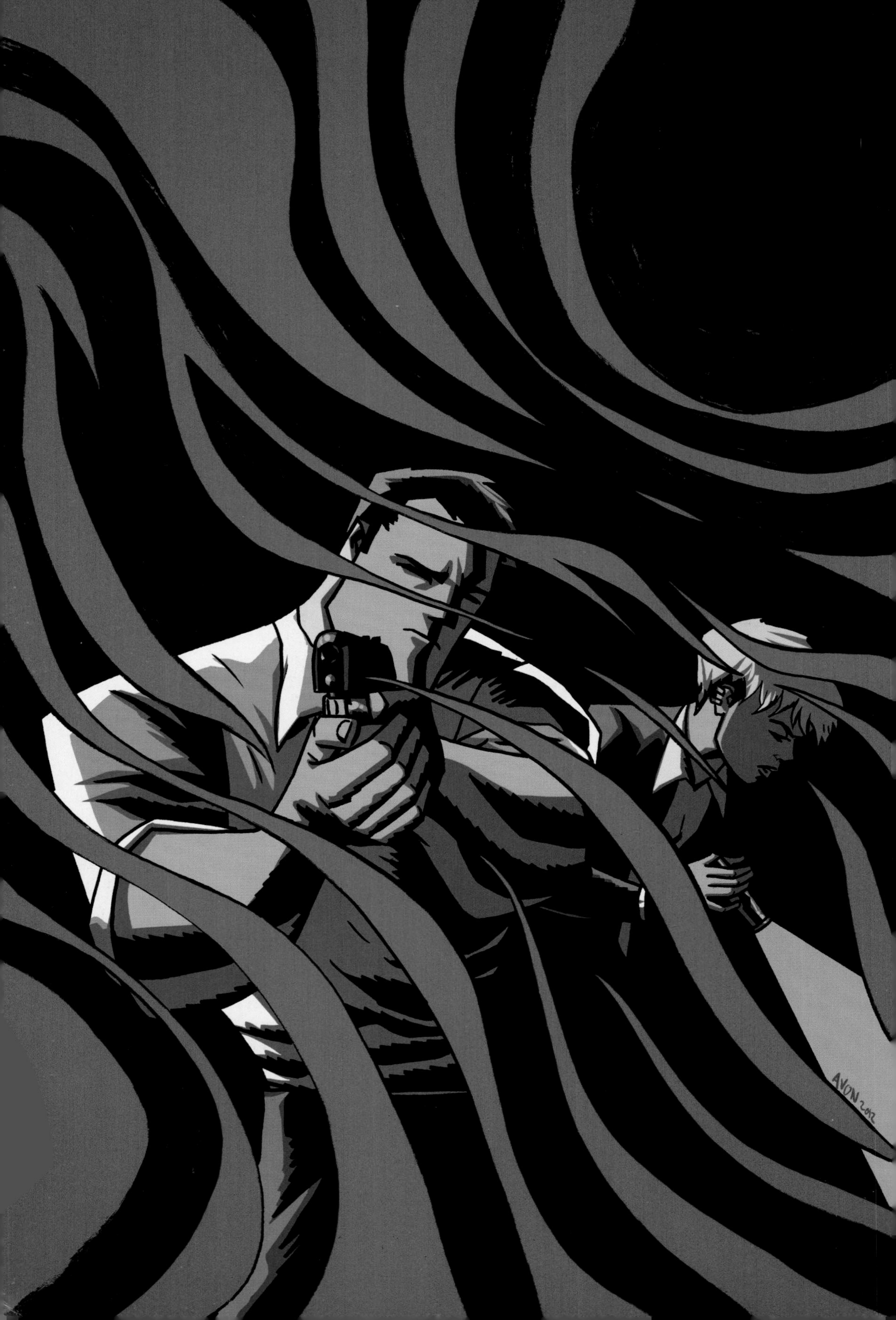
AVON 2012

POWERS: BUREAU #4

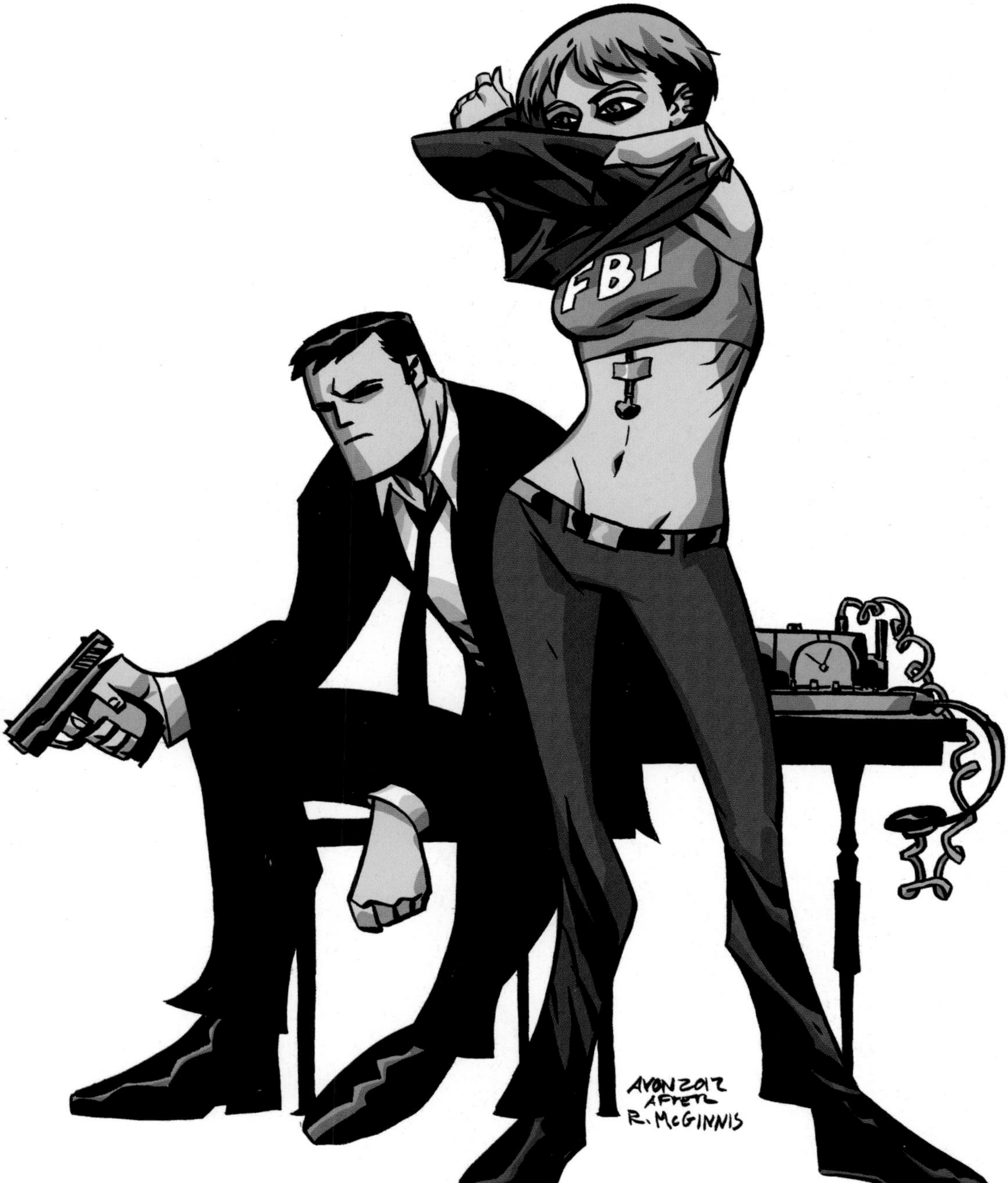
FBI
AVON 2012
AFTER
R. McGINNIS

POWERS: BUREAU #5

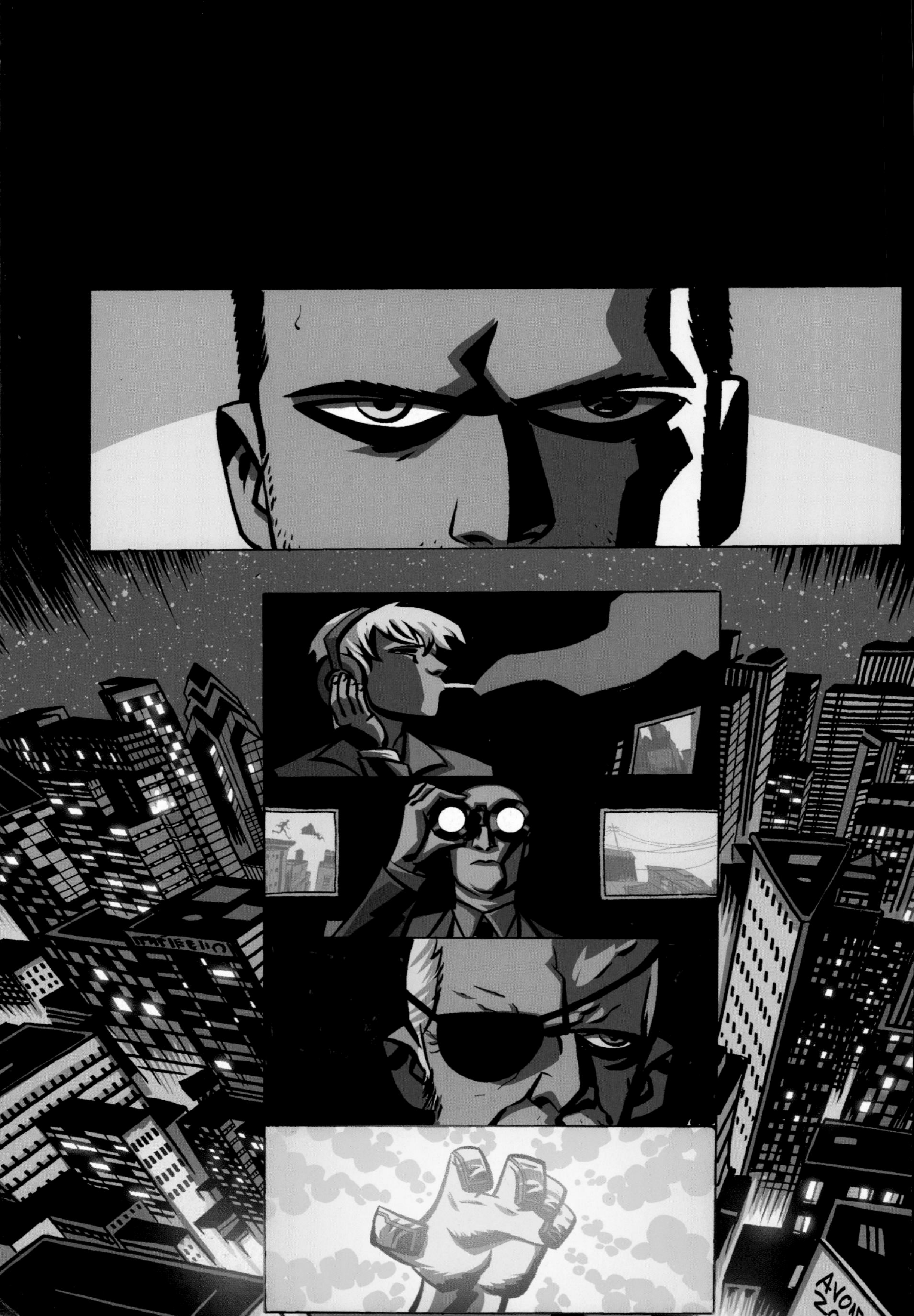

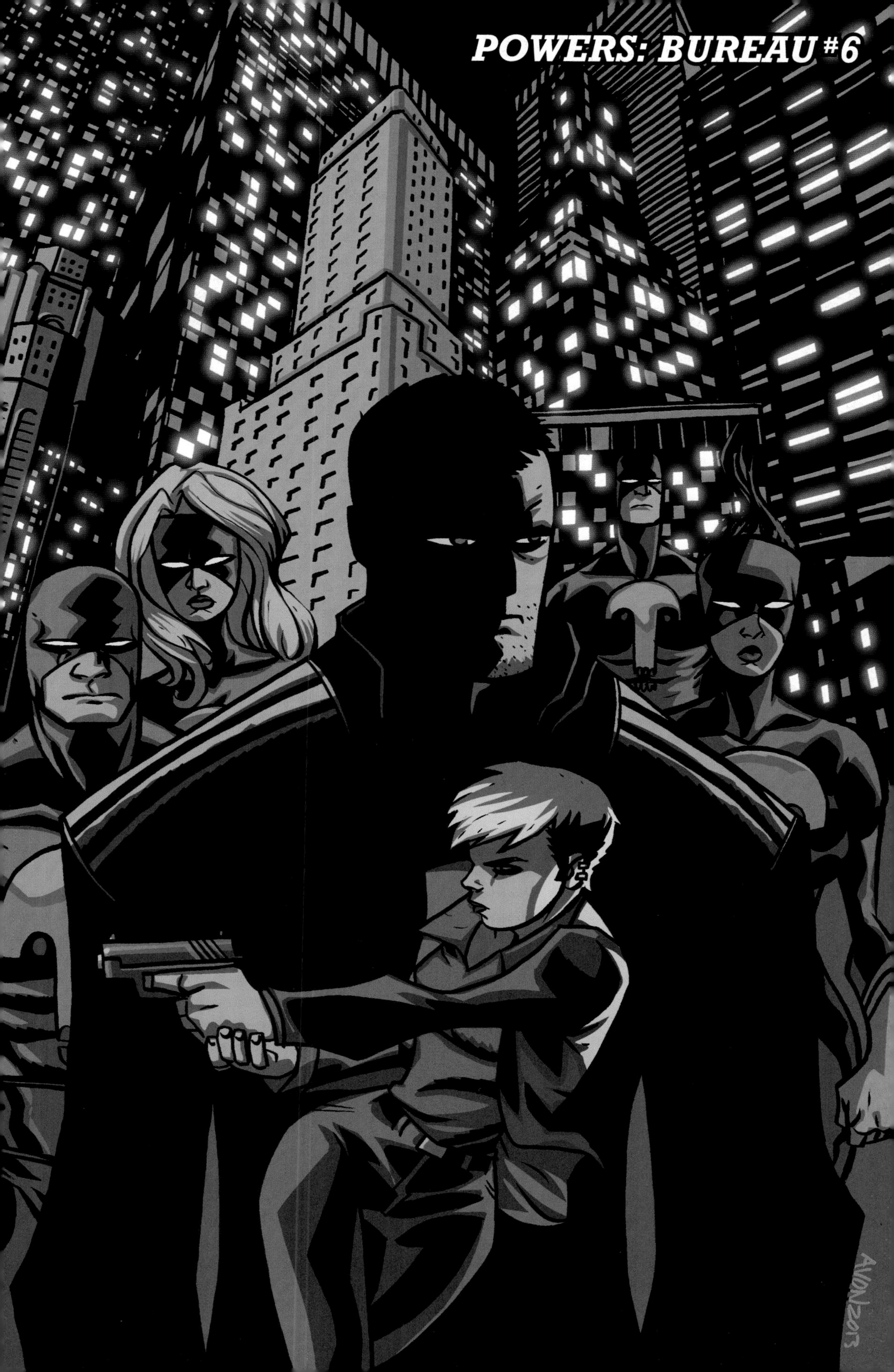
POWERS: BUREAU #6

COVER SKETCHES

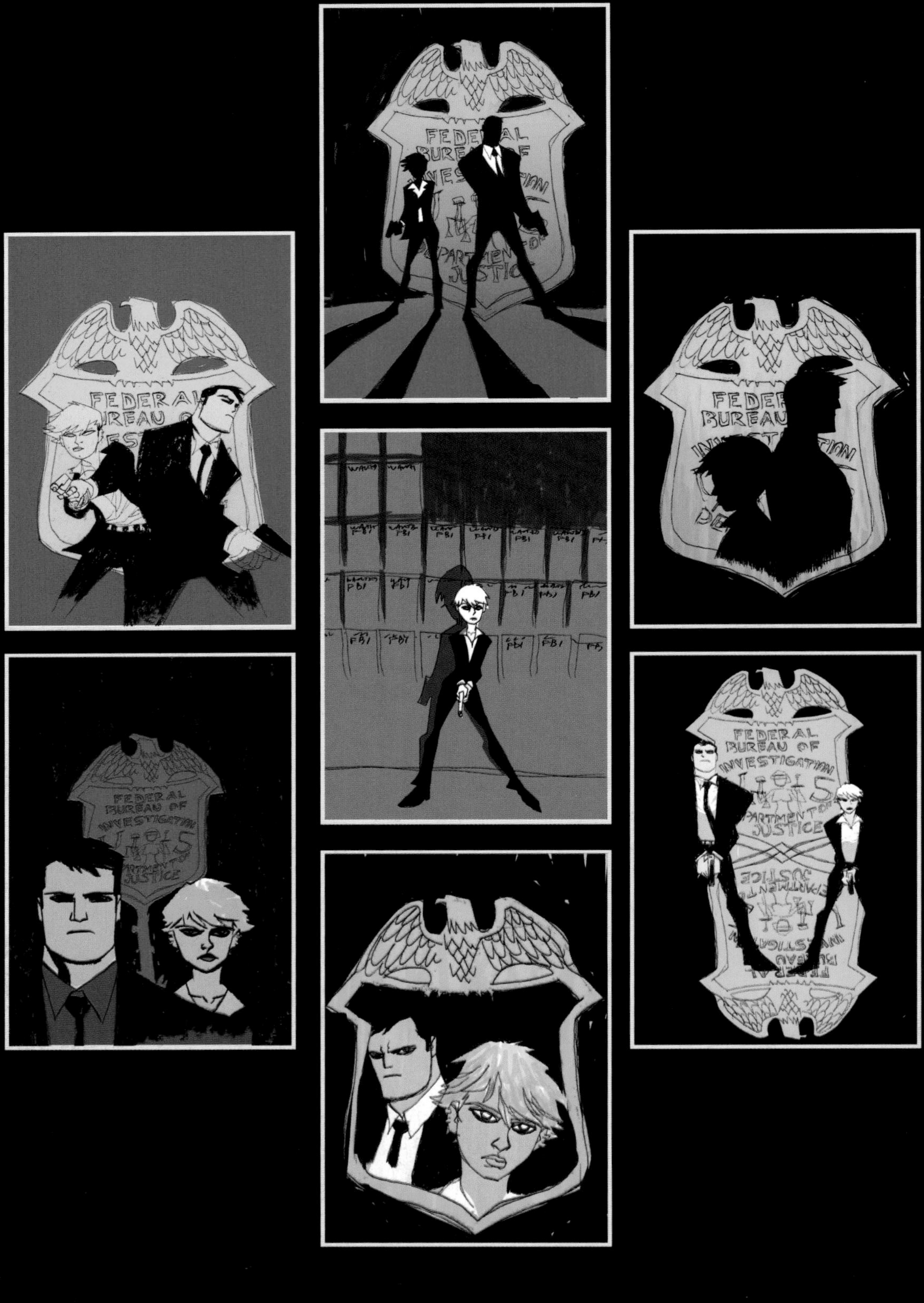
FEDERAL
BUREAU OF
INVESTIGATION
DEPARTMENT OF
JUSTICE
FBI

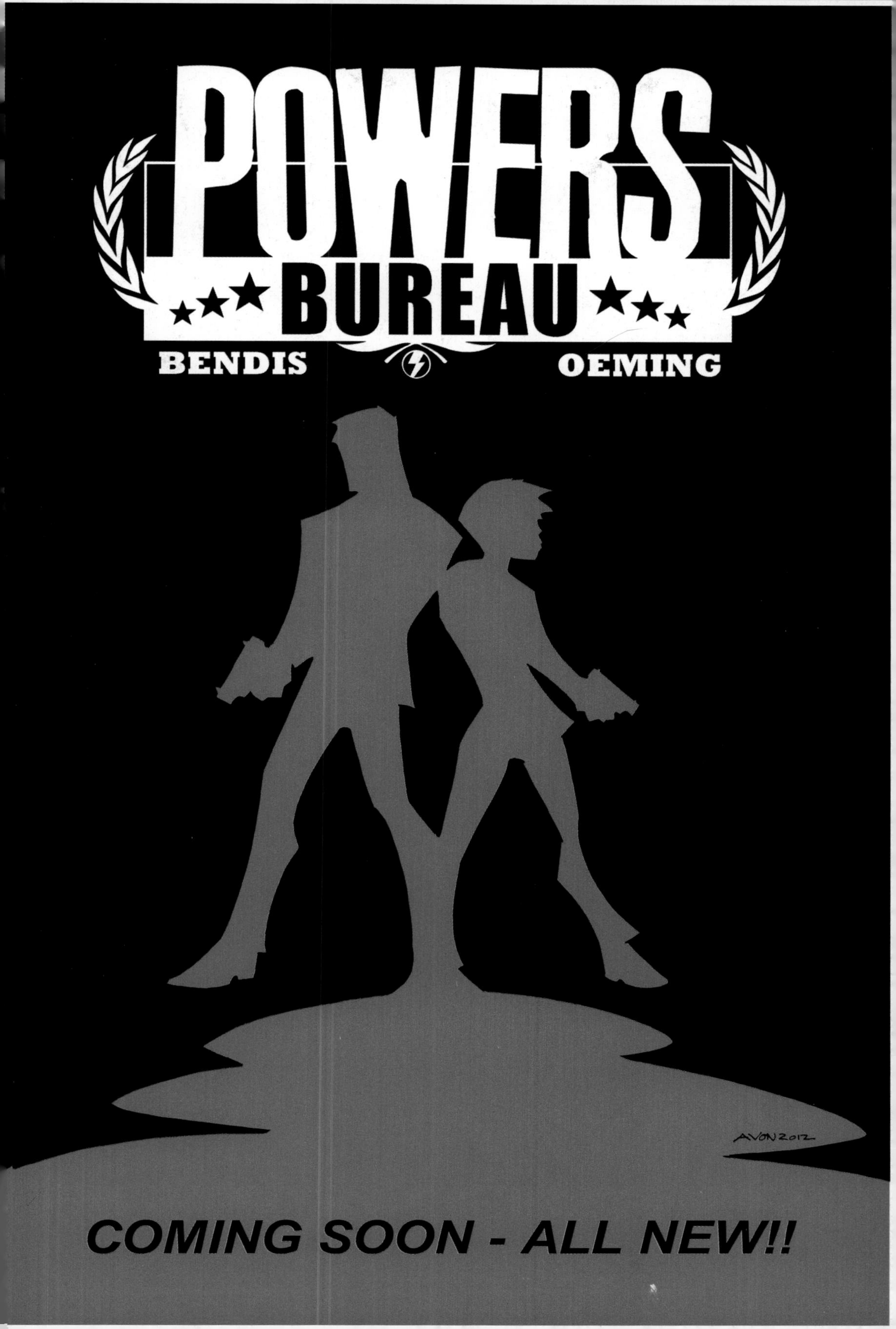
POWERS
BUREAU
BENDIS
OEMING
AVON 2012
COMING SOON - ALL NEW!!

Unused Page From Issue #2

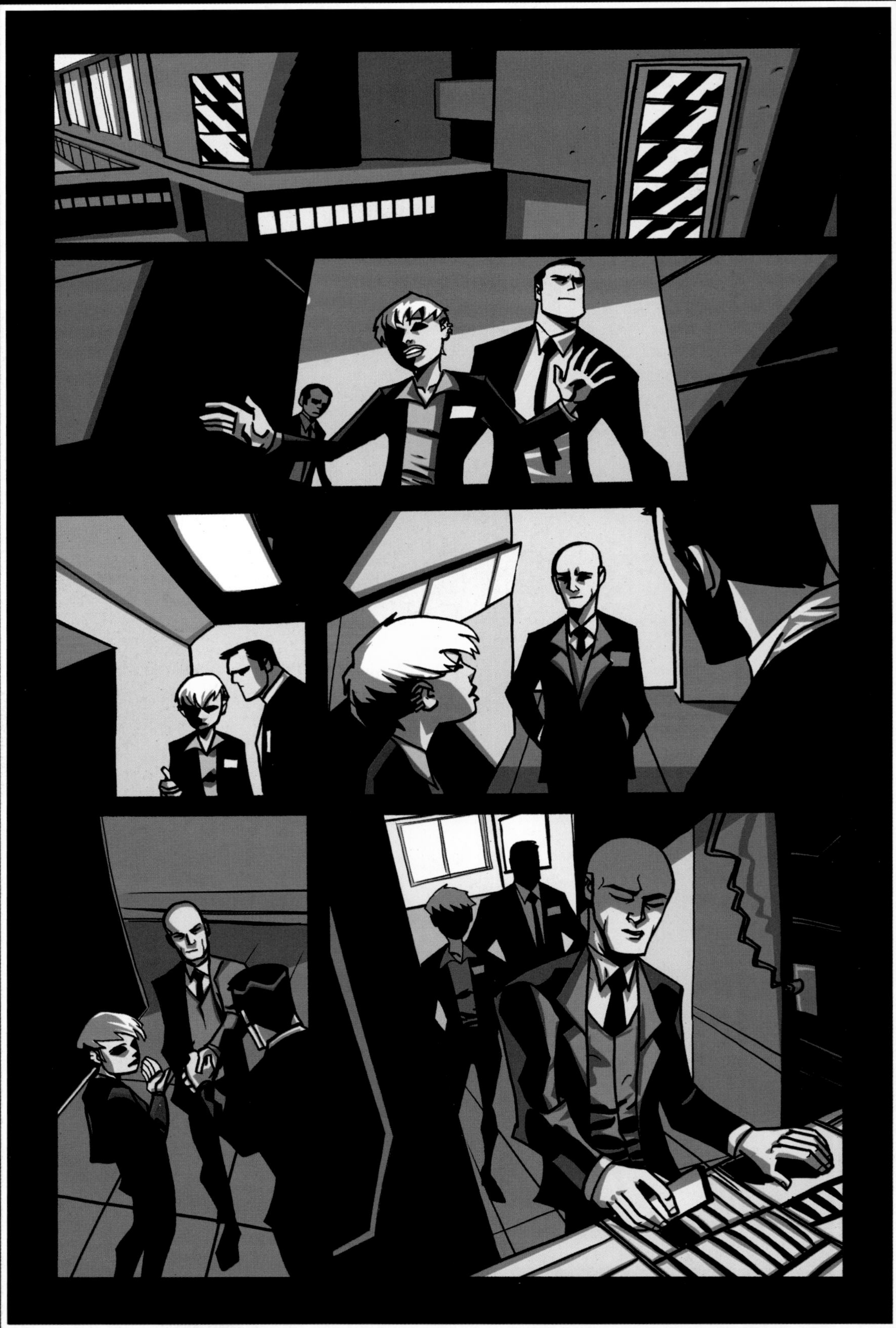

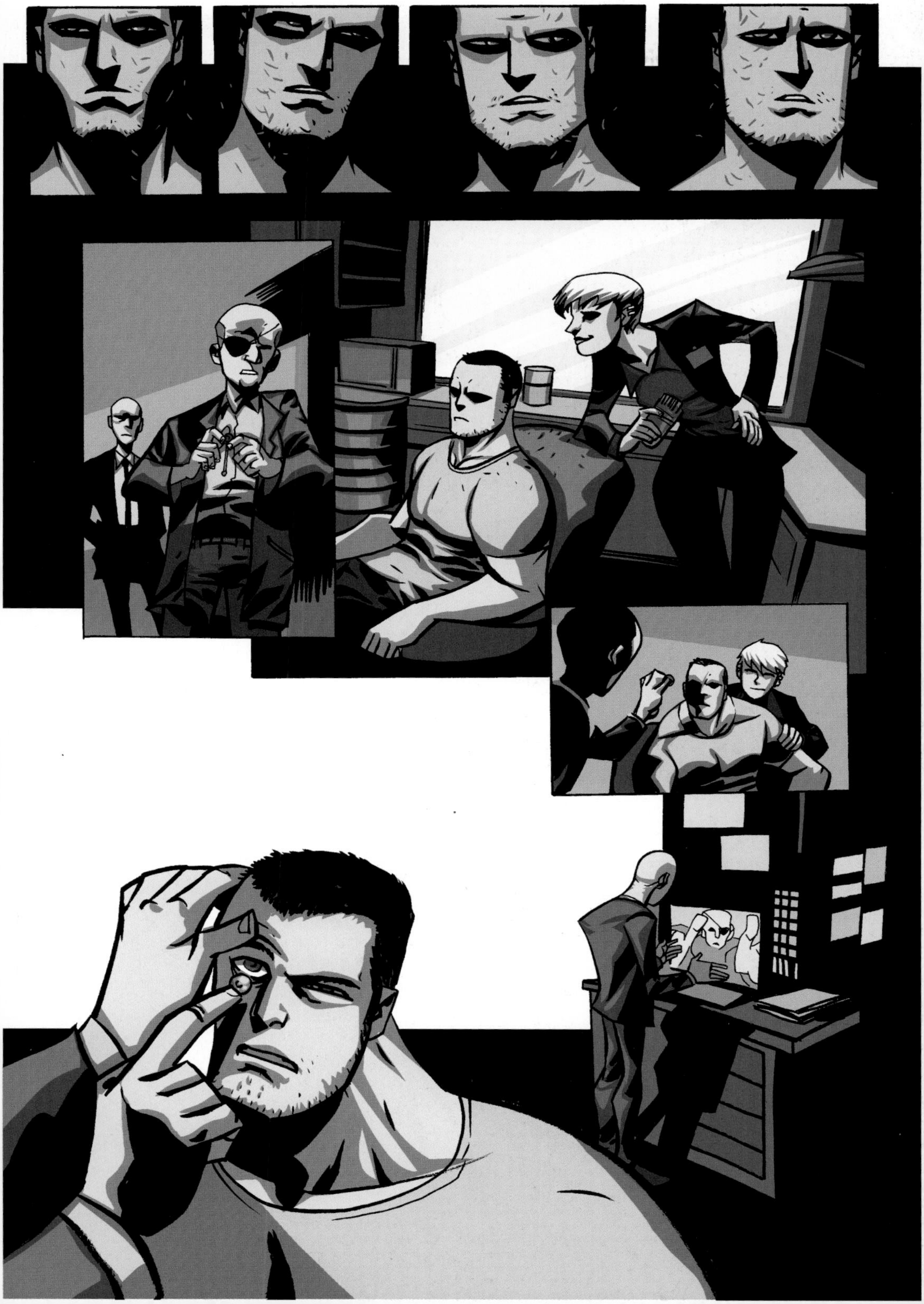

EXCERPT FROM
POWERS: BUREAU
ISSUE #6

BY BRIAN MICHAEL BENDIS
AND MICHAEL AVON OEMING

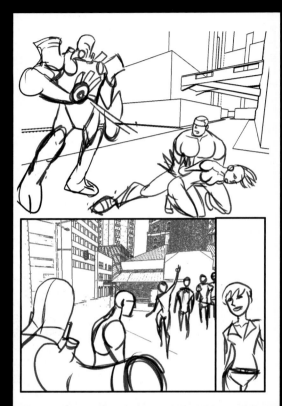

PAGE 20 —

1-

NICK

Don't let her up!

WALKER

She's out cold.

She passed out from the fall.

NICK

Still, fuck her.

WALKER

No argument here.

You ok?

NICK

No.

2- Deena and Meltzer approach, Deena is happy that Walker is alive and teases him for showing off his abs.

DEENA

Did we just bag the biggest organized crime family in the country, everyone is still alive, AND I get to see you with your shirt off?

Fucking best day EVER!

WALKER

You have Erika Broglia?

DEENA

Oh we have her.

3-

DEENA (CONT'D)

Dude, seriously, this was HUGE.

And what's going on with your left nipple?

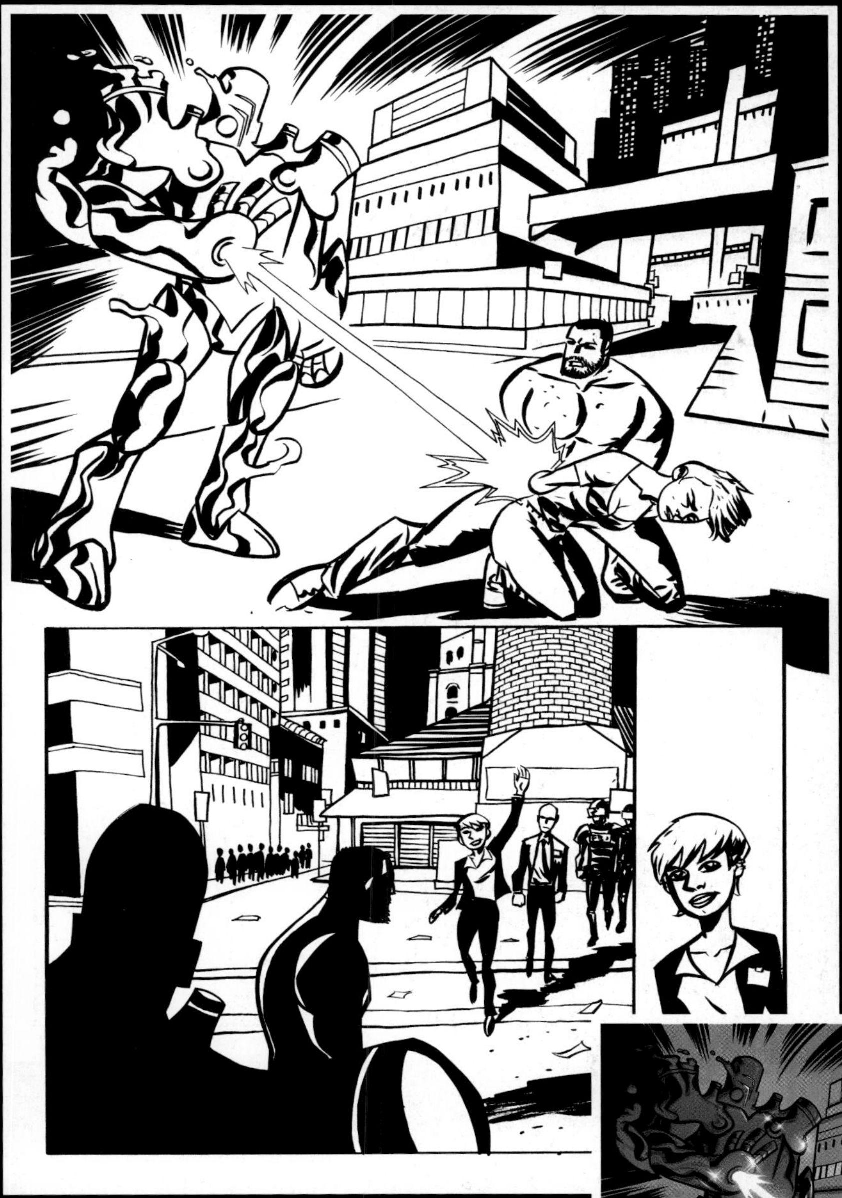

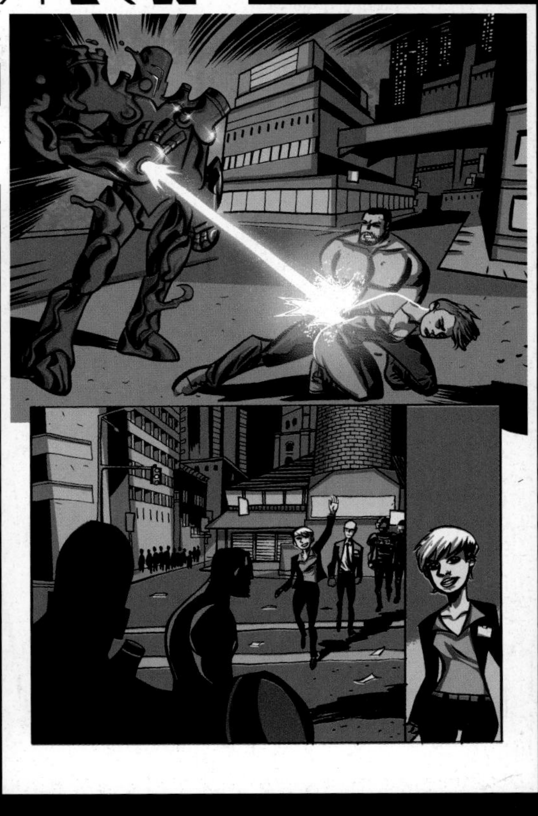

PAGE 21 —

1- 4 Erika is put into the jail van. As the door closes, she looks over at Meltzer with a smile.

5- After they react, they look up as Mohawk is being wheeled away.

DEENA (CONT'D)

Oh, I hate when they give you the cunty smirk as you close the van door. It takes all the fun out of it.

WALKER

I'm still okay with how this worked out.

DEENA

You're totally welcome, by the way.

WALKER

I did all the hard work.

DEENA

I mean, for getting you the FBI gig in the first place.

WALKER

You're smirking. I thought you just said you HATED smirking.

DEENA

I hate when THEY smirk. I love when I smirk.

VOICE OFF PANEL

Fuck you both...

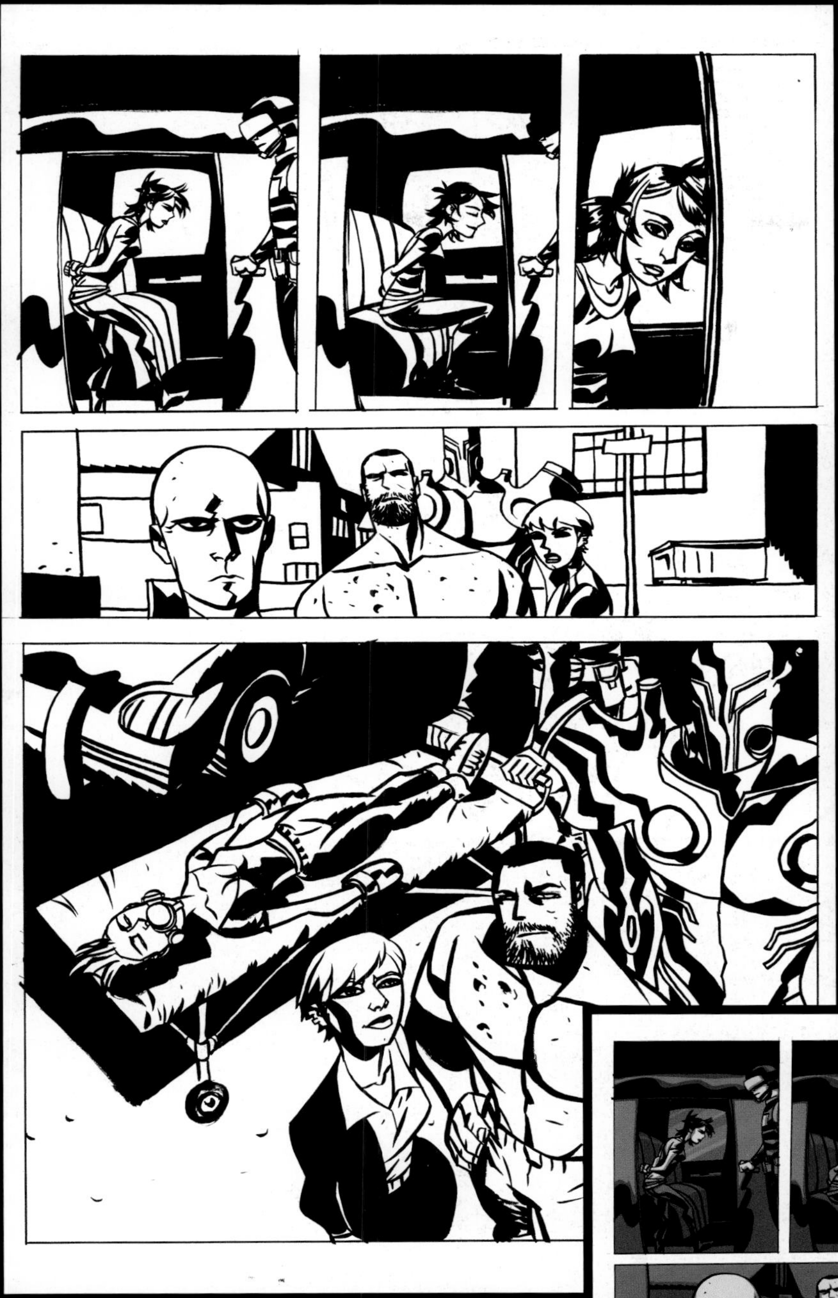

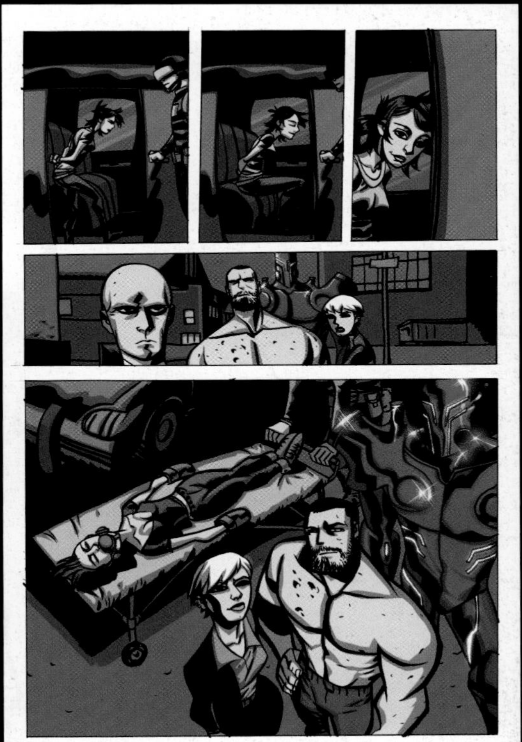

etro Girl who has arrived too late. But she is happy he

e in time to do shit.

this outfit for nothing.

ally I'm glad you're here. I need your expert opinion

n with his nipple?

S that?

tion you have to ask yourself

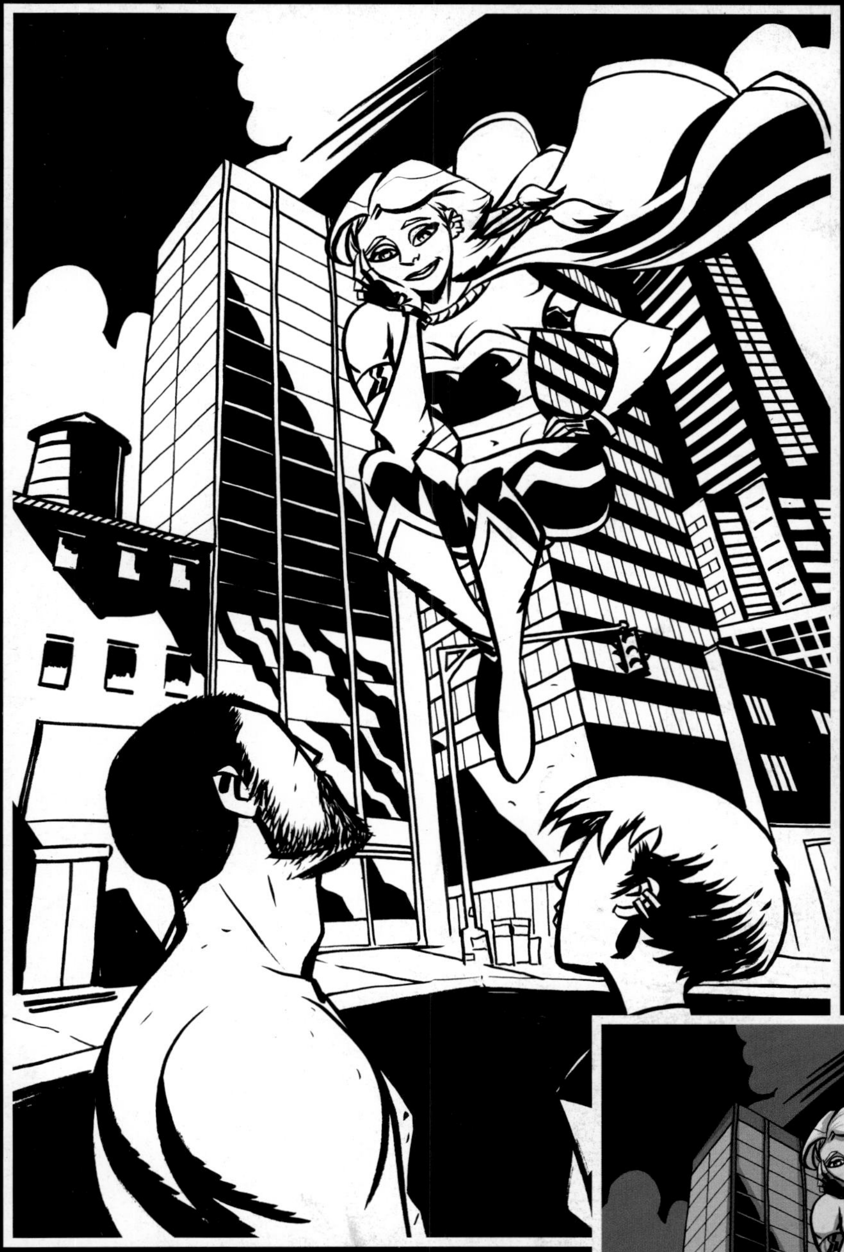
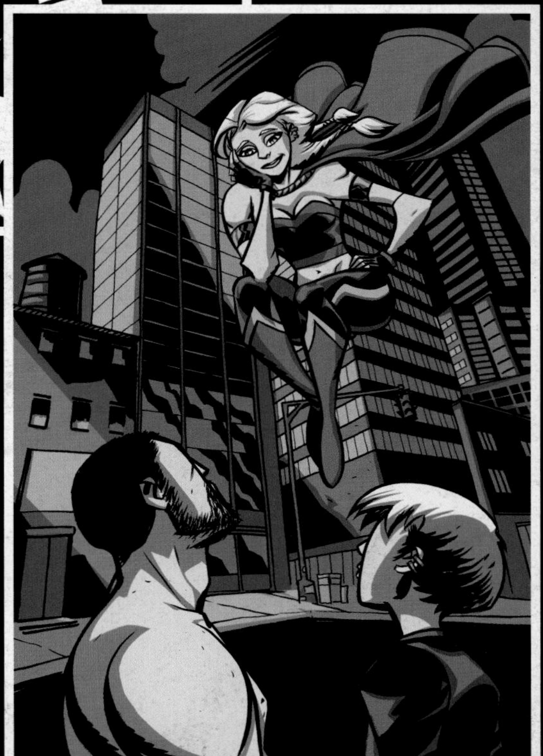

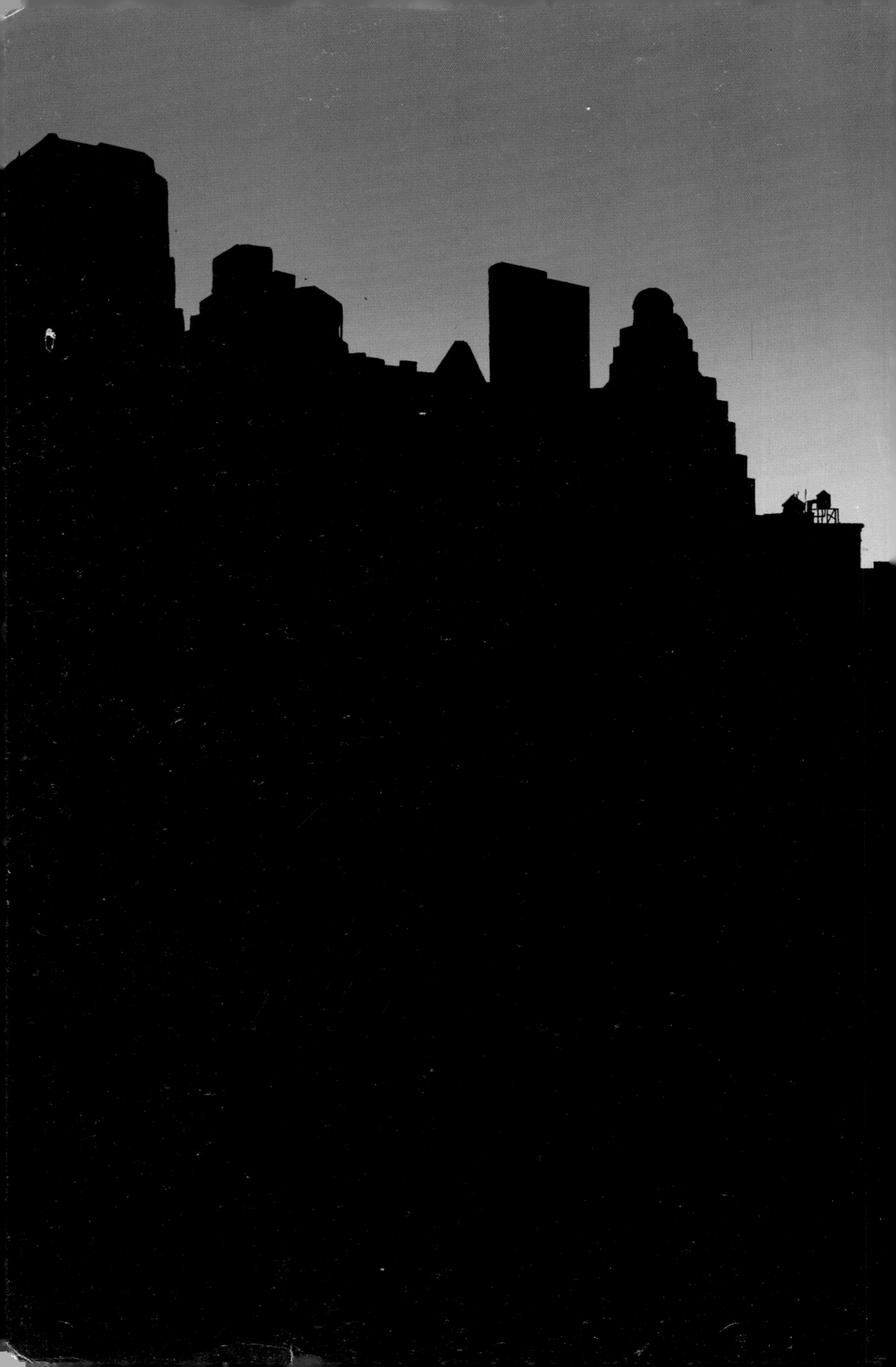